Process and Practice

Process and Practice

A Guide for Developing Writers

FOURTH EDITION

Philip Eggers
Borough of Manhattan Community College
The City University of New York

 LONGMAN

An imprint of Addison Wesley Longman, Inc.

New York • Reading, Massachusetts • Menlo Park, California • Harlow, England
Don Mills, Ontario • Sydney • Mexico City • Madrid • Amsterdam

Acquisitions Editor: Ellen Schatz
Developmental Editor: Megan Galvin
Associate Editor: Lynn M. Huddon
Supplements Editor: Donna Campion
Project Coordination: Electronic Publishing Services Inc.
Cover Designer: Kay Petronio
Art Studio: Electronic Publishing Services Inc.
Photo Researcher: Mira Schachne
Full Service Production Manager: Eric Jorgensen
Manufacturing Manager: Hilda Koparanian
Electronic Page Makeup and Text Design: Electronic Publishing Services Inc.
Printer and Binder: R. R. Donnelley and Sons
Cover Printer: Phoenix Color Corporation

For permission to use copyrighted material, grateful acknowledgment is made to the copyright holders in footnotes throughout the text.

Library of Congress Cataloging-in-Publication Data

Eggers, Phillip
    Process and practice: a guide for developing writers/
  Philip Eggers.—4th ed.
     p. cm.
    Includes Index.
    ISBN 0-321-01215-1
    1. English language—Rhetoric. 2. English language—Grammar.
  3. Report writing. I. Title
  PE1408.E356 1997
  808'.042-cd21   97-14414
                                                                            CIP

ISBN 0-321-01215-1
12345678910—DOC—00999897

CONTENTS

Preface xi

    To the Instructor xi

    To the Student xv

1   Prewriting 1

FREEWRITING 2

    If English Is Not Your First Language 3

FOCUSED WRITING 5

KEEPING A JOURNAL 7

BRAINSTORMING: MAKING LISTS 7

ORGANIZING IDEAS 9

    Grouping 9

    Clustering 11

    Outlining 15

OTHER PREWRITING ACTIVITIES 17

    Ask Yourself Questions 17

    Use the Five Senses 17

    Keep a Learning Log 17

    Write Imaginary Letters 17

READING ALOUD: GETTING FEEDBACK 17

    Types of Feedback to Get from Your Listeners 18

INCLUDING YOUR AUDIENCE 19

    Find the Right Voice 20

    Use Appropriate Vocabulary 20

    Respect Your Readers' Opinions 21

    Recognize Your Readers' Knowledge of the Subject 21

    Write for the Same Audience Throughout 21

MAKING YOUR POINT 22

SUPPORTING YOUR POINT 25

THINKING CRITICALLY 26

    Goals for Paragraph and Essay Writing 27

COMPUTERS AND THE PREWRITING PROCESS 29

    Advantages of Word Processing 29

    Invisible Writing 30

Software Available 30
Getting Started 30
REMINDERS ABOUT PREWRITING ACTIVITIES 31

2   Practicing Paragraphs 33

PARAGRAPH BASICS 34
Recognizing Paragraphs 34
Signaling Paragraphs 34
Determining Paragraph Length 34
USING TOPIC SENTENCES 36
USING KEY WORDS IN TOPIC SENTENCES 40
WHAT MAKES A PARAGRAPH GOOD? 45
Paragraph Unity 45
Paragraph Coherence 48
Paragraph Transitions 55
Paragraph Development 60
TYPES OF PARAGRAPHS 63
NARRATION: TELLING ABOUT AN EVENT 64
Critical Thinking in Narrative Paragraphs 65
DESCRIPTION: TELLING ABOUT PERSONS, PLACES, AND OBJECTS . 66
Critical Thinking in Descriptive Paragraphs 70
EXPOSITION: COMPARING, EXPLAINING, DEFINING, CLASSIFYING,
ANALYZING CAUSE AND EFFECT 72
Comparative Paragraphs 72
Attention to Detail 74
"How To" Paragraphs 76
Definition Paragraphs 78
Classification Paragraphs 81
Cause and Effect Paragraphs 83
Critical Thinking Rules for Cause and Effect Analysis 84
PERSUASION: WRITING TO CONVINCE 87
Critical Thinking Rules for Persuasive Writing 88
REVISING PARAGRAPHS: A REVIEW 92
Revising the Topic Sentence 92
Revising for Unity 93
Revising Paragraphs for Coherence 93
Revising Paragraphs for Better Development 94
COMPUTERS AND PARAGRAPH PRACTICE 95
REMINDERS ABOUT WRITING PARAGRAPHS 96

3   Writing Short Essays 98

RECOGNIZING THE ESSAY 99
BUILDING ESSAYS OUT OF PARAGRAPHS 99
    Essay Diagram 99
    Sample Essay 100
PRACTICING THESIS STATEMENTS 102
    Thesis Statements Must Be Broad 102
    Thesis Statements Must Be Precise 103
INTRODUCTORY PARAGRAPHS 105
    Starting with the Three-Step Design 105
    How *Not* to Begin 106
CONCLUDING PARAGRAPHS 109
    How *Not* to Conclude 109
    Sample Concluding Paragraph 110
MODES OF DEVELOPING SHORT ESSAYS 111
THE NARRATIVE MODE: TELLING ABOUT AN EVENT 111
    First-Person Narration: Telling About Your Own Experience 111
    Exploratory Draft 114
    Revising Narrative Essays 115
    Critical Thinking in Narrative Essays: Finding Your Main Idea 116
    Sample Essay: Narrative Mode 116
    Third-Person Narration: Telling About a Public Event 120
    Sample Narrative: Writing About the Oklahoma Bombing 120
THE DESCRIPTIVE MODE: TELLING ABOUT
A PLACE OR PERSON 129
    Telling About a Place 129
    Critical Thinking About Descriptive Essays 129
    Sample Essay: Descriptive Mode 131
    Portraying a Person 134
    Sample Essay: Portraying a Person 134
THE EXPOSITORY MODE: DISCUSSING AN ISSUE 139
    Essays Based on Examples 140
    Sample Expository Essay: Multiple Examples 141
    Problem/Solution Essays 143
    Critical Thinking Analysis 144
    Sample Essay: Solving a Problem 145
    Solutions to Social Problems 147
    Critical Thinking Guidelines 148
    Outlining Essays on Social Issues 150
    Sample Essay: Solving a Social Problem 150
    Essays Based on an Autobiographical Example 153
    Sample Essay 1: Autobiographical Example 154

Sample Essay 2: Autobiographical Example 156
THE PERSUASIVE MODE: ENUMERATING REASONS 160
Sample Essay: Enumerating Reasons 160
THE PERSUASIVE MODE: THE DIALOGUE PATTERN 163
Critical Thinking on Controversial Issues: The Dialogue Pattern 163
Sample Persuasive Essay: The Dialogue Method 164
Brainstorming the Opposite Side: Talking Points
Against the Death Penalty. 169
REVISING ESSAYS: A REVIEW 175
Essay 1: English Spoken Here 176
Essay 2: When Is the Right Time to Start a Family? 177
COMPUTERS AND ESSAY WRITING 179
REMINDERS ABOUT WRITING ESSAYS 180

4   Improving Your Writing Style **183**
IMPROVING YOUR REVISED DRAFTS 184
Sample Draft: Music and Art Courses in College 185
Revised Version: Why Paint and Fiddle? 186
IMPROVING YOUR CHOICE OF WORDS 190
Being Precise 190
Using Correct Connotation 191
Using Your Dictionary and Thesaurus 192
Using Specific Language. 194
Reducing Wordiness. 197
Using the Active Voice for Strength 202
Using Strong, Vivid Verbs 204
Using Idioms Correctly 206
If English Is Not Your First Language 208
IMPROVING SENTENCE EFFECTIVENESS 208
Avoiding Repetition 209
Varying Sentence Beginnings 210
Varying Sentence Length and Type 213
COMBINING SENTENCES TO IMPROVE YOUR STYLE 216
Free and Embedded Modifiers 220
Who, Which, and *That* Clauses 223
How, When, Where, and *Why* Combinations 225
IMPROVING YOUR STYLE WITH A WORD PROCESSOR 229
REMINDERS ABOUT IMPROVING YOUR STYLE 230

**5   Proofreading Your Writing
and Reviewing Grammar** **232**
PROOFREADING AND CORRECTING THE REVISED ESSAY 233
Proofreading Hints. 233

REVIEWING BASICS 235
DIAGNOSTIC TEST. 235
HOW WORDS WORK: RECOGNIZING PARTS OF SPEECH. 239
SUBJECTS AND VERBS. 241
    Identifying Subjects 242
    If English Is Not Your First Language 243
    Multiple Subjects. 244
    Hard-to-Find Subjects 245
    Identifying Verbs 247
    Multiple Verbs 248
    Helping Verbs. 249
    Verbals: The Fake Verbs 250
FRAGMENTS. 252
    Telling the Difference Between Fragments and Sentences. 252
    Subordinate Clauses and Subordinating Conjunctions 252
    Subordinate-Clause Fragments 253
    Added-Clause Fragments 255
    Added-Phrase Fragments 256
    Added-Verb Fragments. 260
    Three Ways to Correct Fragments 262
SIMPLE, COMPOUND, AND COMPLEX SENTENCES. 264
RUN-TOGETHER SENTENCES 265
COMMA SPLICES 268
    Correcting Comma Splices. 268
CORRECTING BY SUBORDINATING. 272
SUBJECT-VERB AGREEMENT. 275
    Singular and Plural Subjects 275
    If English Is Not Your First Language 278
    Finding and Correcting Errors in Agreement. 278
    Special Problems with Agreement 280
    S Endings: A Review 292
SPECIAL PROBLEMS WITH VERB TENSES 294
    Recognizing Tenses 294
    D Endings in the Past Tense 295
    When *Not* to Use *D* Endings 296
    The Past Tense of Irregular Verbs 298
    Past Participles 300
    Avoiding Shifts in Verb Tense. 305
    Verb Tenses in Writing: Some Guidelines. 306
    If English Is Not Your First Language (Progressive Tenses) . . . 308
ADJECTIVES AND ADVERBS. 310
    Telling the Difference Between Adjectives and Adverbs 310

Adjectives in Comparisons 313
Adverbs in Comparisons. 314
Misplaced and Dangling Modifiers 317
If English Is Not Your First Language 322
PRONOUNS 324
Types of Pronouns 324
Pronoun Case 324
Pronoun Case: Using *Who* and *Whom* 327
Pronouns and Antecedents 329
SHIFTS OF PERSON 332
PARALLELISM 336
Examples of Parallel Combination. 336
Examples of Combinations That Are Not Parallel. 336
Parallel and Nonparallel Sentences Compared 337
MIXED SENTENCES. 340
If English Is Not Your First Language 343
PUNCTUATION 344
Commas 344
Apostrophes. 359
End Punctuation: Periods, Question Marks, and Exclamation Points 361
Semicolons 362
Colons 364
CAPITALIZATION. 367
What You Should Capitalize 367
SPELLING. 369
Spelling Rules 370
Common Mix-ups. 374
Pronoun Mix-ups 377
Look-alikes/Sound-alikes 380
REVIEW TEST 387
REMINDERS ABOUT PROOFREADING YOUR WRITING 391

PREFACE

TO THE INSTRUCTOR

I have been gratified to hear from teachers and students who have used the first three editions of *Process and Practice* that its balance of compactness and substantial coverage has worked well for them. The book seems to be effective in providing college writers the twin keys to improvement: mastering the whole writing process and practicing the basics of grammar, usage, and style within that process. In this fourth edition, *Process and Practice* retains its original purpose: to provide instructors with a means to help students improve their writing in these two areas where they most often need instruction. The organization of the book also remains the same: *Process and Practice* is built around the easily recognizable stages of the writing process, placing each activity or drill in its proper context as part of an organic whole. Once students become familiar with the whole process, they can see a reason for improving their grasp of sentences or paragraphs without feeling that they are being put through isolated verbal gymnastics.

Every decade brings changes in student populations, institutional structures, and technology that force us to modify and refine our teaching methods. In the short period since the publication of the third edition of *Process and Practice,* several trends in particular have made it advisable to widen the scope of the book. The first is the growing need for instruction in critical thinking. Today's students, conditioned by the split-second cross-cutting of videos and films, the erotic allure of commercials, the visceral pandemonium of popular music, and the touch and click interaction of computer technology, demonstrate a quickness and savvy unmatched by previous generations. Many of them, however, have devoted less time than their predecessors to careful reading and reflective discourse, despite the fact that the career market offers its greatest opportunities to graduates who possess high-level analytical skills. As a result, writing teachers have been recognizing a growing need for critical thinking instruction at all stages of the writing process.

Along with critical thinking, two other elements have come to be stressed more than ever in writing classrooms. Peer critique and multi-draft revision, which only innovative teachers employed a few decades ago, are now regarded as indispensable components of writing pedagogy by almost all teachers of composition. Even in courses where the chief goal is helping students pass a one-draft timed essay examination, most instructors use at least some group work and supervise the revision of several drafts on some writing assignments. Although they may vary widely in the frequency with which they employ small group work and the number of drafts they request from students for each essay, nearly all teachers now consider peer feedback and revision for content and organization integral to the writing process.

Another trend that is redefining educational needs in some areas of the country is the mushrooming population of non-native speakers of English, many of whom possess strong academic motivation and extensive training. English teachers face a new challenge with such students, whose writing proficiency ranges from the most elementary smatterings of English as a second language to the highest levels of literacy and fluency. Such students typically have more difficulties with idiom and syntax than native speakers but may understand formal grammar better. Hence writing teachers working with ESL students may sometimes have to add new methods to the ones they employ with native speakers.

Responding to these developments, I have broadened the coverage of *Process and Practice* in the fourth edition to include, among other improvements, critical thinking activities, group projects, additional exercises on revision in Units 2 and 3, and exercises for ESL students. Such additions do not, however, reduce the emphasis on the writing process itself, which remains, if anything, more important than ever. Writing teachers still have to guide students, native speakers, and second-language students alike, through the entire cycle, from prewriting to final proofreading. This process, of course, is recursive and irregular, more nearly a spiral than a straight line. Each writing assignment repeats the cycle at a slightly more advanced level. Therefore the organization of any writing textbook can only approximate the actual process of an individual writer, and no sequence of topics can perfectly match the work of a semester's writing course, since much retracing and foreshadowing is necessary and every element bears some relation to other elements. Grammar especially, although most crucial in the final proofreading stage, is an aspect of verbal communication at any stage, always looming as a source of anxiety for students with conspicuous deficiencies in writing or with limited knowledge of English as a second language.

Despite all these complications, the sequence of the five units of *Process and Practice* seems to have served the needs of the teachers and students who have used the previous three editions. The progression of topics follows the simplest possible logic: moving from the first stages of prewriting in Unit 1 through the project of developing, organizing, and revising paragraphs and short essays in Unit 2 and Unit 3, respectively, to the later stages of stylistic improvement in Unit 4 and final proofreading for errors in Unit 5.

This arrangement, of course, does not mean that your assignments for a semester's course must rigidly follow the progression of units. Obviously, it does not mean, for example, that because proofreading is most important in the later stages of the writing process and appears in the last unit that students should work on grammar only at the end of the semester. Grammar is a different issue for each student and each class. For that reason, Unit 5 can be used as a stand-alone handbook for individual students, as a guide for targeted work by the whole class on topics needing special attention, or as a workbook assigned sequentially throughout the course. You will inevitably make reference to material in units other than the one you are working on at any given time; in fact, footnoted cross-references in earlier units encourage students to use Unit 5 concurrently with Units 2 and 3. Following the general sequence of Units 1 through 4 does make sense, however. You will no doubt want to introduce students to prewriting activities first and move on to creating paragraphs and essays later. Students will do revision and proofreading throughout the semester, but you will probably want to emphasize stylistic features of the kind covered in Unit 4 after they have developed fluency and practiced composing essays.

As a point of controversy among writing instructors, teaching the paragraph is probably second only to teaching grammar. At some colleges, whole courses focus primarily on paragraph writing, while at others the paragraph is never discussed outside the context of the whole essay. The organization of units in *Process and Practice* is intended to allow for differing teaching methods: In Unit 2 you can either teach paragraph writing as a separate skill, like the backhand in tennis, or simply call attention to the paragraph as an important feature of the essay and move more quickly to Unit 3, returning to Unit 2 if students appear to need review of certain features of the paragraph. Within this flexible range, however, the sequence of units rests on certain assumptions: That developing writers should acquire fluency through prolific prewriting activities before working on anything else, but that once they reach the point of formal composition, they need clear, simple models to help them organize material. Paying attention to paragraph strategies, rhetorical modes, and the structure of essays will not inhibit fluency if such work is done in conjunction with plenty of freewriting, focused writing, and other spontaneous activities.

Each student has individual strengths and deficiencies that present a unique challenge to the instructor, who must be flexible enough to adopt differing approaches but consistent enough to impress upon all students the importance of critical thinking, development, revision, and correct usage. In the midst of technological transformation and changing student populations, *the teacher remains the most important factor in the learning cycle.* A textbook can be no more than a tool in the hands of the expert. Designed properly, however, it can be a valuable tool indeed. I hope that the fourth edition of *Process and Practice* will serve your needs and the needs of your students effectively.

FEATURES NEW TO THE FOURTH EDITION

- **CRITICAL THINKING INSTRUCTION AND EXERCISES** in the first three units, emphasizing the importance of critical thinking in all stages of the writing process and in all rhetorical modes

- **GROUP PROJECTS** throughout the text encourage collaborative work and expedite the learning process through activities such as group brainstorming, planning, revising, giving feedback, and editing

- **SECTIONS FOR ESL STUDENTS** in all units along with exercises designed to highlight the issues and problems most frequently faced by writers of English as a second language

- **INCREASED EMPHASIS ON REVISION** in Units 2 and 3 to focus more effectively on revision of structure and content before students concentrate on style in Unit 4

- **END-OF-UNIT REMINDERS** to assist students in reviewing the material just studied and provide a checklist of major topics

- **STREAMLINED SECTIONS ON NARRATIVE AND DESCRIPTIVE MODES AND EXPANDED COVERAGE OF PERSUASIVE WRITING** in Units 2 and 3 in response to the increasing demand for critical thinking and preparation for writing in the disciplines

- **UPDATED SAMPLE PARAGRAPHS AND ESSAYS** throughout text with new topics that will keep students engaged with recent events and issues (60 percent new)

- **REVISED UNIT 4** stressing stylistic improvement as a stage of the writing process distinct from organizational revision covered in Units 2 and 3

- **STREAMLINED AND UPDATED SECTIONS ON COMPUTERS** following each unit, which include computer exercises and discuss ways that word processing can be used to improve writing at each stage of the process

- **NEW AND STREAMLINED DIAGNOSTIC TEST AND REVIEW TEST** in Unit 5 help students to determine their level of grammatical proficiency before and after studying the topics

FEATURES CONTINUED FROM THE THIRD EDITION

- **COVERAGE OF THE ENTIRE WRITING PROCESS** from prewriting activities through composition of paragraphs and essays to revision and proofreading

- **EXERCISES** that reinforce lessons by using current topics of interest to which students can relate

- **WRITING ACTIVITIES** that place lessons within the context of the students' own writing

- **CLEAR, LIVELY, AND READABLE EXPLANATIONS** that appeal to students as adults of various ages, with diverse interests and backgrounds

- **BALANCED EMPHASIS ON PROCESS AND PRODUCT** that validates the efforts students make in brainstorming, drafting, and revising, as well as the importance of presenting a correct, well-written final copy

- **SAMPLE ESSAYS AND PARAGRAPHS** that illustrate varied kinds of good writing, work done by both students and professional writers

- **SENTENCE COMBINING EXERCISES** in Unit 4 to help students develop syntactic maturity

- **CROSS-REFERENCES TO GRAMMATICAL TOPICS** in the form of footnotes in Units 2 and 3 that connect features of the writing process with grammatical problems that often occur at the stages being covered

An instructor's manual is also available to qualified adopters.

ACKNOWLEDGMENTS

I am first of all grateful for the close editorial guidance and assistance of the editorial staff at Addison Wesley Longman: Ellen Schatz, Lynn Huddon, Megan Galvin, and Mira Schachne. Their contributions have enabled me to make many improvements in the fourth edition that would not otherwise have been possible.

I also want to thank the following reviewers of this fourth edition for their critical remarks and helpful recommendations: Judy H. Boles, Chattanooga State Technical Community College; Arlene G. Clarke, American River College; Martha French, Fairmont State College; Clifford Gardiner, Augusta College; Catherine B. Gifford, Pensacola Junior College; Dianne Gregory, Cape Cod Community College; Olivia Ann B. Gresham, Nicholls State University; Marsha Groff, Texas A & M at Corpus Christi; Lee Brewer Jones, DeKalb College; Mary Likely, Nassau Community College; Martha Martin, Old Dominion University; Peggy R. Porter, Houston Community College Northwest; Jack Scanlon, Trinton College; Donald R. Stoddard, Anne Arundel Community College; and Betty Jeane Wallace, Sinclair Community College.

My colleagues and students at Borough of Manhattan Community College continue to be the main source of what I know and learn about the writing process. Their suggestions and responses to the first three editions of *Process and Practice* have been indispensable to me in gauging the effectiveness of many aspects of the book. Finally, to Jane, Victoria, David, Wendy, and Michael, I am boundlessly grateful for giving special meaning to the process and practice of living.

TO THE STUDENT

Perhaps you are one of the lucky students who can devour whole books in a few hours or who love to write poems, diaries, and term papers. Or you may be one of those who "hate English," or believe they do, and who would rather suffer through root canal therapy without anesthesia than write another 500-word theme. Or possibly you like to write and love books but are hesitant to speak in class and feel self-conscious about your writing because English is not your first language. Like most people, you probably enjoy reading and writing at least once in a while, but even the best writers report a certain amount of struggle in their attempts to make the words come out right. Every writer is different, but whatever your experience has been, I hope this book will help you grow as a writer.

Process and Practice is not intended to make your writing like a product on an assembly line, the same as everyone else's and following the same formulas. Rather, this book will draw you into the *process* of mental discovery that writing almost magically entails. As you become a better writer, you will gain a keener sense of yourself as an individual. Nothing is more human and more individualistic than writing, yet writing flourishes best as a social activity. By writing as part of a group, you will discover your powers as well as your weaknesses, and your talents as well as the areas where you repeatedly make mistakes. As you share your writing with others, you will develop a distinctive style and voice. Your writing will become as individual as your personal experiences because it is from these experiences that most of your ideas will come. The activities in Unit 1 will help you explore your experiences and start to write about them without becoming distracted by anxieties over errors. In Unit 2 and in Unit 3 you will explore paragraph writing and essay writing. The exercises and writing assignments in these units will teach you to develop and organize material, to connect specific experiences to general ideas, and to support topic sentences and thesis statements with interesting, convincing examples. Unit 4 will give you practice in sharpening your sense of style, helping you notice *how* you write as well as *what* you write.

Although the *process* of discovery and expression is the goal, frequent *practice* is also important. Gaining control over the basics of grammar, spelling, and punctuation by means of the exercises in Unit 5 will free you to achieve the larger goals of the writing process. Mastering the basics will not turn you into a conformist, even though the rules of grammar and spelling are the same for everybody. In fact, errors themselves tend to be repetitious and uncreative; only by freeing yourself from errors can you reach your full potential as a writer. Use Unit 5 as you need it. Find out through the diagnostic test and your teacher's advice how much intensive work you need and in what areas. If you need intensive work in several areas, adopt the no-pain/no-gain attitude of physical fitness trainers. The results are worth it. Mastering the basics is satisfying in itself, and even more important is the pleasure of writing with feeling, precision, insight, and originality.

Philip Eggers

U N I T

1

Prewriting

The first stage in the writing process includes prewriting activities. Some of these will limber up your mental muscles and get the ink flowing. Others will allow you to explore topics without pausing to worry about organization or corrections. Remember that your prewriting activities are for practice and exploration; in doing them you should concentrate on facts, ideas, and feelings more than on the language itself. You should be trying to discover as much as you can, not trying to avoid red marks on your paper. In prewriting activities, unlike the later stages of the writing process, more is always better, so keep your pen moving.

Freewriting

First of all, write. Write about anything on your mind, and let your mind wander. Write for five or ten minutes without letting your pen stop. If you can't think of anything, write the same word several times until you get moving again. There is no such thing as right or wrong in this activity, except for stopping before the time is up.

This kind of writing is called **freewriting** or automatic writing. Freewriting means writing, without pausing, for a given length of time or until you have written a certain amount, such as a full page. You can develop fluency in freewriting by doing it regularly. If you sometimes find yourself saying, "I can't get started," freewriting will make it easier for you to become unstuck. If your teacher does not require you to do it, practice freewriting on your own, especially in the first weeks of your writing course. If you become anxious about being timed when you write, you may want to aim for filling up a page when you freewrite. Writing at least a page at a time makes you better able to reach for the full paragraph and complete essay later, even though your freewriting sample may be very different from actual paragraphs and essays. For one thing, your sample may contain repetitions and mistakes, and may wander from one topic to another. Some of what you say may be nonsense; some of it may seem to come from left field. The main purpose of freewriting is to let your writing flow rhythmically and endlessly, like the current of a river. Sometimes it won't: There may be a few rocks in the river, and you may get stuck. With practice, however, your pauses will become brief, and the river will flow again.

Here are two examples of freewriting done by students:

A. *It's time to do some freewriting again, the way we usually do at the beginning of the period. I don't have anything in my head to write about today. Yesterday I was upset because of the quiz in biology that I got a C- on, and I didn't think the last set of questions was fair because it covered some material that wasn't in the assigned section. Today at least I don't have any tests to worry about, but I am thinking about not having enough money every week, especially when I want to buy new clothes. Maybe I can get a job on campus for part of the term, they say that temporary jobs are posted in the placement office and if you look early on Monday morning you might get there before the good ones are taken. I don't really know weather I can handle a job right now though, it takes a lot of time to keep up with the homework and I have a right to <u>some</u> kind of social life. Not to mention getting to know Kent better, since he seems to be interested in me, and I think I'm* *beginning to get interested in him since he stopped hanging around Sally so much. I don't know if I really trust him though, and some of his friends are real dorks.*

B. *If I keep writing everyday like this maybe I will turn out to be a short story writer or a novelist, or better yet a screen writer. I bet I could write scripts better than some of the ones I've seen in the films that came out this year. Maybe it would be better to write articles about things like travel, or having your own business, or marriage and divorce. I wonder if famous writers wrote like this without stopping, and did they make alot of mistakes when they didn't stop to look at what they wrote? How did people used to write when they didn't have any computers to check their spelling or let them change anything with a click of a mouse? I'm not sure why we write like this every day, but I think I may be getting better at it, because I don't have to stop and get all worried because I can't think of anything to say. Now when we freewrite, I just pretend I'm talking on the phone with Amy and writing is as easy as talking, and I never had any trouble knowing how to talk. Not since I was ten months old, at least that's what my mom says: I started talking when I wasn't even a year old, and I'm still talking.*

These students were not trying to write essays on assigned subjects; instead, topics came to them as they wrote. Try to develop a conversational ease in your freewriting: Pick up a topic and stay with it as long as it interests you, the way people do in conversation. You learn to focus on an idea, develop it and move from one idea to a related one. By doing freewriting every day in a journal you may find that you begin to sharpen your statements of ideas. Instead of having vague, muddy impressions of your experiences, you will begin stating clear opinions about them. Don't try to do anything more than keep the words coming. The improvement comes unconsciously.

If English Is Not Your First Language

Students who are learning to speak and write English as a second language often like to use their native language in the early stages of composing. Using your native language to do freewriting or some of the other prewriting activities described in this unit can help you express yourself fluently, explore and organize ideas, and see relationships. However, it is extremely important that you do plenty of free and focused writing in English as well. To write correctly and fluently in English, you must learn to think in English and not always translate from your first language.

EXERCISE I
Freewriting

Practice freewriting by writing without stopping for five minutes. Don't hurry; just keep the pen moving. Begin with a key word so that your mind is focused, but don't try to compose a formal essay. Here are some possible key words: *college, weekends, teachers, shopping, jobs, cars, sports, parents.* After five minutes of writing, stop. How much have you written? You will probably find that when you do not have to worry about grammar, spelling, organization, or your teacher's criticisms, you are able to write a whole page in a very short time.

Do a five-minute exercise like this every day for a week. When this routine becomes easy, try ten-minute writing sessions. Begin with some key word or idea in mind, but don't try to "stay on the topic"; just write the way you talk. If you discover yourself writing so well that you actually want to read your freewriting sample to someone, go right ahead. But do not write with the intent of satisfying a critic. You may feel more confident and expressive writing just for yourself.

EXERCISE II
Freewriting

Without timing yourself, write continuously until you have filled an 8½-by-11-inch page. If you feel comfortable doing this activity, try it once noting the time you start and the time you stop, but don't worry about the time as you write. You will probably be surprised at how quickly you can write a full page. If you worry about completing timed essay examinations, which usually have one-hour or two-hour time limits, you may find that while freewriting you can do essay-length writing in far less than these time limits. If you have more success with page limits than with time limits, try freewriting up to two pages until you become comfortable with that length. Keep freewriting daily until you notice a real improvement in fluency—at least three to four weeks.

EXERCISE III
Freewriting

Collect all of your informal writing in one journal or notebook. Don't worry about how unimportant some of the entries may seem. Your informal writing is your best source of ideas for essay topics later because it expresses your opinions and interests. Since all formal essays should begin with prewriting activities, your journal will provide some ready-made prewriting that will get you started on formal assignments.

Focused Writing

After you have been freewriting for several weeks, you will develop a new attitude toward writing. Writing will become an everyday activity, like walking, conversing, and reading. You will stop regarding writing as a formal, specialized job that you can do only when wearing a suit. You will stop worrying about a teacher looking over your shoulder with a red pencil, poised to find your mistakes. You will write for yourself because you like to write—anywhere it is convenient, any time you feel like it, and about any subject on which you want to state your opinions.

This new positive attitude will make your writing easier, but it will not produce finished, organized essays. The next step is **focused writing,** which will bring you a little closer to the process of composing organized paragraphs and essays. Focused writing is a not-quite-so-free exercise in which you write on a single topic during a chosen period of time. As in freewriting, you maintain a steady rhythm, concentrating on letting the words flow without being distracted by problems of grammar, spelling, and organization. In focused writing, however, you steer in one direction. In freewriting there is only one don't: Don't stop. In focused writing there are two: Don't stop, and don't wander off the subject. Naturally, you will do this better if you have become comfortable doing freewriting. And, of course, you should phase in your focused writing by choosing subjects familiar to you. Here is one student's focused writing about subways:

> *The subway is a pain in the neck. It smells terrible down there. Bag ladies with infected feet and bums always begging, then the train takes so long to come. Sometimes I lean over the track and I wanna go down the track to meet it. When I get on the train sometimes I have to stand up usually when my feet are hurting and the train is shaking and its all hot and stuffy. You think you're just going to die! On the subway tracks sometimes you can see the rats walking around looking for food and they look real nasty. Some of them are big and fat like cats. During the summer the subway is hot and during the winter it's cold. It is like going down into hell. Boxes crushed from trampling feet, newspapers flying here and there. Coffee cups are placed on any convenient spots and cigarette butts are everywhere. Trains pulling in and out of the station sound like a volcano. If you try to speak to the person next to you, they can't hear a word you are saying.*

This student stayed on the topic very well and expressed some strong feeling about her experience with the subway. She did not plan to express a particular emotion; she simply explored the thoughts and feelings she already had. You may find yourself jumping from one thought to another and making some writing errors. The important thing, however, is to discover how much you can say about the subject.

EXERCISE I

Focused Writing

Do focused writing for five minutes beginning with the statement, "I have always liked (or disliked) my _____ ." (Fill in some feature of your appearance, such as your hair, weight, height, nose, face, eyes, etc.) Write about how this feature has brought you satisfaction or dissatisfaction.

EXERCISE II

Focused Writing

Do focused writing for five minutes beginning with the statement, "There are many things I like about being _____ years old." Tell about the advantages of being your age and how you feel about it.

GROUP PROJECT

Focused Writing

Working with two or three other students as a writing group, look over the list of topics below and choose one the group likes best. Discuss what you find interesting about the topic and how each member identifies it with his or her own experience. Every member of the group should then do focused writing for ten minutes or two pages (whichever you find easier) on the topic. Read your writing aloud to one another and discuss what new ideas and facts came out in the process of writing.

1. Current fashions among college students
2. How computers make life easier or harder
3. Career opportunities for college graduates
4. Different attitudes toward money
5. Different attitudes toward marriage
6. Television talk shows
7. Kinds of music

Keeping A Journal

In some college courses, not just English courses but also content courses in other subjects, you may be asked to keep a journal in which you write down your responses to assigned readings or class discussions. Journal writing will enhance your understanding of the course material by making you a more active participant. Your instructor may also use these journals as idea banks from which to draw topics for essays and research paper topics. Even if you are not required to keep journals in all courses, a learning journal will help you focus your ideas better and provide material to review before examinations.

What should you enter in a journal? Your instructor may give you guidance on what she or he wants; otherwise, you will probably gain more from expressing your own thoughts about the course material than from trying to aim for the "right" ideas. Journals can help you develop critical thinking skills, express your preferences and dislikes, and relate course assignments to your personal experience. Not having to worry about making mistakes, displeasing a grader, or leaving something out will allow you to pursue your insights more fully than you can in formal term papers. A journal can make the difference between success and failure in a course, or between enjoying a course and being bored with it.

Brainstorming: Making Lists

Another prewriting activity is **brainstorming**—spilling all the facts, ideas, examples, and feelings you have on a particular subject. Brainstorming is much like focused writing except that you do not write continuously. You simply jot down everything you can in the form of a big list. Making lists gives you practice in exploring the full range of a subject. The list can be a jumble of words, phrases, and statements. Don't censor yourself; selecting and organizing come later. You have made plenty of lists before in your life—shopping lists, lists of things to do, lists of books to read, and lists of people to invite. When you made such lists, you didn't worry about spelling or grammar; you just didn't want to miss anything or anyone important. Do that when you make lists as a prewriting activity.

Remember: The biggest problem for most beginning writers is not what they do wrong but what they do incompletely or never do at all. They often do not include enough concrete details, varied ideas, and specific words to make their essays really interesting and informative. Brainstorming a subject helps you find those facts and ideas that will keep your reader interested. Notice the specific perceptions and details this student included in the list she made about the classroom in which she was sitting:

large trapezoid shape	tan carpet, needs cleaning
It's too hot in here.	coat hangers, no coats
Venetian blinds, one broken	I had French here last term.

movie screen
chalkboard, algebra equations
37 chairs, bright colors
sound proof ceiling
clock over door, one hour behind
Why do I dislike this room?
one wall solid windows

view of the new student center
room number M33
map of Caribbean on back wall
no wastebasket, cups on floor
chairs arranged in irregular rows,
    four and a half rows

Making lists on larger topics will challenge your mind still more; you won't be able to just write down what you see. Instead, you may have to find the ideas inside your head. If your list seems jumbled, you can select and organize your material later when you begin composing drafts of your essay. Here is a list containing everything one student could think of about jobs:

pay scales
jobs in health care
private industry
I have had three jobs.
computers changing many jobs
discrimination against senior citizens
changes in future job market
husband and wife both working
jobs in socialist countries
women in "men's" jobs
unions
commuting to work
health hazards on some jobs
unemployment
pensions
jobs overseas
owning small businesses
blue collar jobs

military, government jobs
college training for jobs
changing jobs and careers
interviewing for jobs
jobs for immigrants
why people choose jobs
temporary jobs
working while going to college
boring jobs
jobs in entertainment
forty hour week
vacations
fringe benefits
counseling for jobs at college
jobs for handicapped people
jobs that change locations often
dangerous jobs
minimum wage

EXERCISE

Brainstorming

Make a list of everything you notice about a room you are in—a classroom, a room at home, or an office where you work. See how many details you can mention, and include some thoughts about the room. Compete with another student to see whose list has more entries. Train yourself to be a sharp observer.

> ### GROUP PROJECT

Brainstorming

Brainstorming will help you most effectively if you do it with your writing group. To begin, have your group select one of the subjects below. Elect a recorder for the group who will make a list of every fact and idea the group can mention in a brainstorming session. Second, choose another topic and have each member brainstorm in writing alone; then, the recorder should combine the lists into one composite list. Save both group lists for later work in organizing.

1. Substance abuse in high school and college
2. Divorce in today's society
3. Technology and changes in education
4. Forms of sexism in today's society

Organizing Ideas

GROUPING

Before you do any serious composing of paragraphs or essays, practice grouping ideas. Learn to see large patterns before you fill in details; make rough sketches of your subjects before you work out the fine points. After you compile lists, look them over to identify the large groups of ideas into which they can be divided. Some items may not fit and will have to be dropped. Look back at the student's list concerning jobs and divide the items into the categories below.

Types of jobs: **Problems with jobs:**

Rewards of jobs: **Preparing for jobs:**

Other (items that do not fit the previous categories):

EXERCISE I

Grouping

All of the items in the following list have to do with college, but they belong in different categories or subgroups. Identify three main categories. Three items in the list do not fit any of the three main categories. List these three separately.

accounting	activities fee	karate club
debating team	college deans	cost of books
tuition	glee club	astronomy
clothing expenses	drama society	cost of equipment
foreign films	American history	insurance cost
student government	grade point average	French club
chess team	sociology	wrestling team
room and board	travel expenses	Spanish
psychology	anthropology	telephone bills
mathematics	chemistry	

Name the three categories: 1. _Subjects_

2. _Mathematic_ 3. _Expenses_

Name the three items that do not fit: 1. _College deans_

2. _clothing expense_ 3. _insurance cost_
_G.P.A_

EXERCISE II

Grouping

Identify the three main categories of items in the following list. The general subject is teenage problems. Two of the items do not belong in any of the three subgroups. List these two separately.

peer group's use of drugs	sharing secrets with brothers and sisters
parents too strict about curfews	having to share a room at home
absenteeism from school	fads in clothing and hair styles among peers
choosing courses in school	
sharing family chores	boredom with classes
talking to parents about sex	dropping out of school
alcoholism among peers	showing respect for parents
competition with brothers and sisters	teenage gangs
changing schools	

organized crime
school counselors not helpful
parents don't understand
not popular with peer group
jealousy among friends
foreign cars
too much academic pressure
getting respect from parents
danger from sexually transmitted
   diseases

ethnic differences among friends
younger brothers and sisters invading
   one's privacy
girls being interested in older boys
snobbishness among friends
too much emphasis on grades
athletes get all the attention in school
teenage pregnancy

Name the three categories: 1. _____ *Nobody likes school* _____
2. _____ *foreign cars* _____ 3. _____ *too much reading's pressure*
Name the two items that do not fit: 1. _____ *boredom with chores*
2. _____ *Peer group's use of drugs*

EXERCISE III

Grouping

Choose one of your lists from the brainstorming exercises. Divide the items into categories as in the exercise above, eliminating any items that do not fit into your three or four main groups.

CLUSTERING

Another prewriting activity that many students and teachers find valuable is **clustering** (also called mapping): A way of making an informal diagram of your thoughts on a subject and showing connections between ideas. Whereas brainstorming helps you find facts and ideas on a subject, clustering helps you see links between subtopics. Begin clustering by writing your main topic in the middle of the page and circling it:

Careers for Women

Next, develop a diagram spreading out like a spider in all directions, showing some of the related ideas:

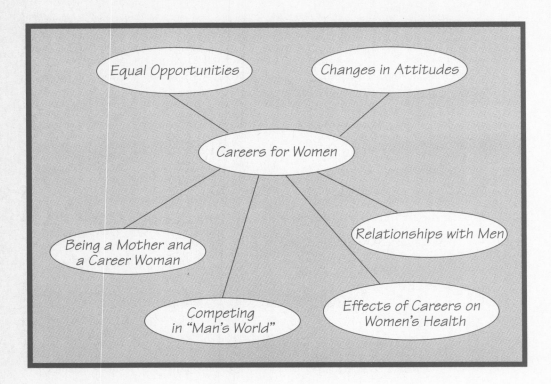

Each of these related ideas has many facts, thoughts, and examples connected to it. The diagram on the facing page shows how you fill in the map as much as you can.

Don't worry if your cluster begins to spread out all over the page. The more ideas the better. What can you do with a cluster?

1. Discover new ideas on the topic.
2. See links between subtopics.
3. Narrow your topic if it is too broad.

"Careers for Women" is obviously too broad for an effective essay. Looking at the cluster, you might decide that only one part of it would give you a better

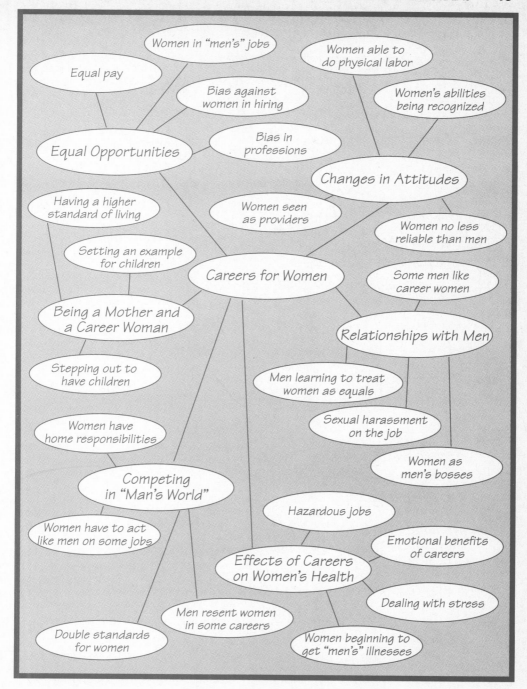

thesis. How about "Women Are Beginning to Feel the Effect of Careers on Their Health"? Now make a more detailed cluster on that topic:

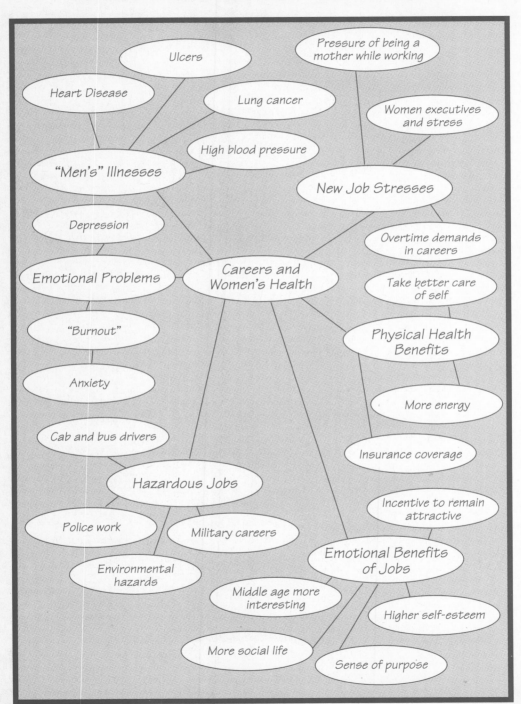

EXERCISE

Clustering

The following cluster has been partially filled in. On a separate sheet, complete the cluster with items that relate to each of the subtopics in the cluster.

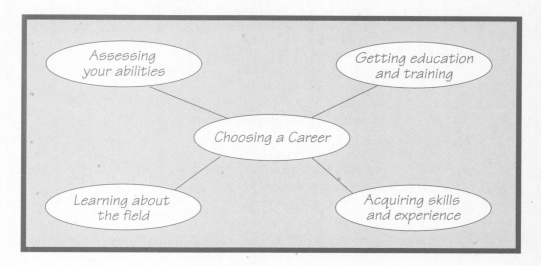

OUTLINING

Making an outline can be useful after you have explored the range of your topic through activities such as focused writing, brainstorming, and clustering. At this point you should have a sense of your main point, the subtopics, and the supporting material under each subtopic. In making an outline, you will be choosing an effective sequence for the subtopics and supporting material. Although an outline provides a detailed skeleton for an essay, do not attempt to use it like a sewing pattern or blueprint that must be followed at all costs. *In the process of composing and revising, you will often discover new thoughts, facts, and strategies that necessitate a rearrangement of your material.* An outline will help you keep your ideas clear, but it should not prevent you from exploring new ideas or revising your work. Be ready to make a revised outline at a later stage of the composing process so that you can visualize the changes you want to make.

The classic form for an outline includes large Roman numerals for the main headings, capital letters for subtopics, and Arabic numerals for sub-subtopics, like this:

Main Subject: Health Issues for Professional Women

    I. Health Benefits for Professional Women
       A. Physical health benefits of careers
          1. Insurance coverage

2. Incentives to maintain health
3. Physical energy from sense of purpose
4. Better health from higher standard of living
B. Emotional benefits of careers
1. Greater self-esteem
2. More active social life
3. Stronger sense of purpose
4. More vitality with aging
II. Health Problems of Professional Women
A. New job stresses
1. Women executives and stress
2. Overtime demands in careers
3. Pressures of parenting and careers
B. Hazardous jobs
1. Military careers
2. Environmental hazards
3. Police and security work
4. Cab and bus drivers
C. "Men's" illnesses
1. High blood pressure
2. Heart disease
3. Lung cancer
4. Ulcers
III. Changes Needed in the Workplace
A. Better family insurance
1. Employee plans
2. Private managed care
B. Sensitivity to women's health needs
1. Preventive care
2. Nutritional information
3. Counseling for substance abuse
4. Domestic abuse counseling
5. Parental leave
C. Awareness of health hazards
1. Environmental work hazards
2. Accident prevention

EXERCISE

Outlining

Using the cluster you created for "Choosing a Career," make an outline similar to the one above. Arrange the subtopics in a sequence that might be effective in an essay, and supply as many supporting points as possible. You may want to add material not included in your cluster and eliminate material that does not fit your outline.

Other Prewriting Activities

No single prewriting technique is best for everybody. All writers have to find techniques that work best for them in exploring topics and arranging material. Here are a few other methods that may work for you.

ASK YOURSELF QUESTIONS

Journalists use the *five Ws*—**who, what, when, where, and why**—to develop their material. Ask yourself these questions about your subject. Imagine that you are being interviewed about your topic. What questions would an interviewer ask you? What specific answers would you give?

USE THE FIVE SENSES

Good writing makes imaginative use of all five senses, not just sight. Make a list of facts about a familiar object, such as a coin, a hat, a piece of jewelry, or a pear. Underline all facts that are not visual. Have you mentioned impressions of **taste, touch, hearing,** or **smell?**

KEEP A LEARNING LOG

In classes that you find difficult, write for five minutes after every class session summing up what you have learned that day. This exercise will give you a record to use for review before tests, and it will reinforce your memory of what you learned. It will sometimes highlight areas you failed to understand and need to ask the instructor or tutor about. If the class requires term papers, you may find the topics for papers in entries you made in your learning log.

WRITE IMAGINARY LETTERS

In addition to writing actual letters to real friends and family members, you may find it stimulating to write letters to people in the news whose actions or opinions arouse your anger or enthusiasm. You need not send such letters; simply writing them serves a creative purpose. Once in a while, you may even decide to mail one—and you may receive an answer!

Reading Aloud: Getting Feedback

At all stages of the writing process, you can benefit by reading your writing aloud to other people. Don't cringe! Once you become used to reading your writing aloud, you will enjoy it. Many people are a little self-conscious at first; if you are, try reading to just one person with whom you feel comfortable, and have that person read his or her work to you. The other person does not have to be an expert on grammar or even highly educated. The purpose of reading aloud is not chiefly to catch mistakes; it is to help you explore the subject further and discover whether your writing comes across the way you expect it to.

Your instructor may have you read aloud in class, either in a small group or with the whole class listening. This is a big opportunity; take advantage of it as much as you can. Listen to what others say about your writing. They may often say what you expect, and your meaning and feelings may come across exactly as you intended. Sometimes, however, other people will respond differently than you thought they would. They may ask for more information on something that was not clear to them; they may share their excitement over what aroused them; they may suggest related ideas or facts that you should include; and they may disagree with your opinions. Listen to all of it. You don't have to agree with everything said, but you should consider it.

In the prewriting stage, getting feedback will chiefly help you discover the possibilities of your subject and clarify your attitude toward it. When other people tell you in their own words exactly what they think you have said, meant, or felt, they help you form a clear picture of your own purpose. Sometimes what they think you meant is not what you really meant. In that case, you may have to state your ideas differently. Sometimes, too, other people detect your hidden feelings and intentions; if so, you'll need to decide if you should bring them out more clearly. Reading your material to others gives you the opportunity to consider their discoveries for your rewrite.

TYPES OF FEEDBACK TO GET FROM YOUR LISTENERS

Here are some guidelines on getting feedback. When you have another person or group of persons listen to you read your writing aloud, ask for responses that focus on:

What You Said

At first it may seem silly to have them merely repeat your ideas, but by doing this they help you to clarify your own thoughts and feelings and to discover whether you really communicated them.

What You Felt About the Subject

When you do focused writing, you are not thinking much about your feelings—you are just expressing them. A listener can often recognize your feelings better than you can.

What Interested the Listener Most

You may be surprised to find that some of your minor details excited the listener more than the ideas you considered important. Be open to your listener's reactions; these reactions often give you hints on what to expand and emphasize.

What the Listener Wanted to Hear More or Less About

While doing focused writing, you don't think much about the reader. Feedback from a listener afterward, however, can help you determine what will interest readers and what will bore them. One listener may not give you a completely reliable indication; however, if you get the same response from many people in a group, consider it carefully!

What the Listener Did Not Understand

One lesson all beginning writers need to learn (and advanced writers should never forget) is that readers cannot read your mind; they can only read what you put on the page. There is no guarantee that they will know what you mean just because your meaning is clear in your head. Only the listeners can tell you what they do not understand. Of course, some listeners may not be paying attention, so a single person's reaction is not always enough. Write so that no *careful* listener can misunderstand you.

GROUP PROJECT

Getting Feedback

Join two or three other students to form a writing group. Choose one person to record the spoken feedback given by the members of the group. Each writer should select his or her most interesting piece of focused writing done so far and read it aloud to the group. The recorder should ask for feedback on each piece in all of the categories listed above and note the group's responses. After the group discussion session, the recorder should give each writer the recorded notes about his or her writing.

Including Your Audience

Once you have become comfortable reading your writing aloud, especially if you have done it with a group, begin considering your audience as you write. Freewriting and focused writing are not intended for an audience; they are just practice in achieving fluency. Finished, organized writing, however, such as college term papers, business reports, letters, and magazine articles, always aims at a particular reader or group of readers. In such writing, you will want to inform, entertain, persuade, or share experiences and emotions. The way you express yourself on paper is influenced by the person or group for whom you are writing. Although your style should always be your own, your audience determines in part what facts you include, the level of your vocabulary, the tone you adopt (serious, funny, casual, formal, etc.), and how much explaining you do.

Here are some guidelines to follow in writing for your audience.

FIND THE RIGHT VOICE

Your writing should sound authentic and should be appropriate for the subject, situation, and reader. Since most of your college writing will be read by the teacher and other members of the class, your tone should be natural and direct but not as personal as if you were writing to a close friend or family member. Don't strain to sound "intellectual" or "businesslike" either, or you may adopt a voice that sounds artificial. Here is a sample of writing that shows this kind of straining:

> Accounting has often been considered by myself to provide the required remuneration and advancement potential necessary for me to further my goals in a professional career of my choice. Additionally, such a career possibility will enable me to enhance myself in my pursuit of fulfillment of my personal satisfaction.

What's wrong with this? The writer is so busy trying to sound impressive that he or she winds up not saying much of anything. It's better not to be pompous. Write the way you would talk to other adults in a semiformal situation such as a job interview:

> I have chosen to become an accountant for several reasons. Having above average ability in mathematics and a quick memory, I should be able to do the work well. I also enjoy being efficient and helping others improve the efficiency of their work. The high salaries earned by successful accountants appeal to me as well, and my parents will be pleased if I become the first C.P.A. in the family.

This passage may be less "impressive" because it doesn't use many big words, but it has something to say and sounds like an actual person talking to someone else. Finding the right voice means using a tone somewhere between stilted, artificial language and the casual language of private conversation.

USE APPROPRIATE VOCABULARY

For most college writing, use adult vocabulary. Explore the range of word choices available, always trying to use the most precise words, not just the biggest ones. If you are studying a technical field like nursing, remember that nonspecialists may not know technical terms, so define these terms if you use them. Use slang and street talk, at the other extreme, only for special effects such as humor or surprise. Slang tends to make writers lazy, leading them to rely on the first word that comes to mind instead of considering more precise options. For example, a slang term that has been around for a long time is *knock*—to "knock" something you don't like. Consider some alternatives—*put down, belittle, disparage, minimize, denigrate,* and *ridicule.* Most slang terms, which began as colorful and imaginative inventions, quickly become stale; they are the mark of a careless writer or speaker. Using frequent slang will cause the reader to doubt your grasp of the subject and the seriousness of your intentions. Select the best words for your purpose: simple language if you write for children, adult language for adults, and technical language for specialists. And don't forget to look for **synonyms** (words that have similar meanings) in a thesaurus.

RESPECT YOUR READERS' OPINIONS

Readers will be annoyed if you talk down to them and leave them no room to disagree. Give them the right to have their own opinions and feelings. Some writers prefer to antagonize their readers in order to provoke an angry exchange of opinion; in most college writing, however, your purpose is to weigh evidence and present ideas, not to propagandize or incite anger. If you wish to explain facts or persuade the reader to agree with your opinion, being dogmatic may cause readers to stop reading entirely or to ignore your points. Showing that you are open-minded enough to accept differences of opinion, on the other hand, may win readers to your side.

RECOGNIZE YOUR READERS' KNOWLEDGE OF THE SUBJECT

If you are writing informatively for people who know very little about your subject, explain everything they need to know. If you are writing about basketball and your readers are all coaches, however, don't explain what a free throw is.

WRITE FOR THE SAME AUDIENCE THROUGHOUT

Sometimes students begin term papers with a general introduction that tells the reader facts any nine-year-old would know, then suddenly jump to a specialized, technical discussion. Decide whom you're writing for, experts or beginners.

GROUP PROJECT I

Including Your Audience

Your writing group should select <u>one</u> of the following assignments. Each member should bring to class a contrasting sample of writings in the assigned category and read the samples aloud to the group. The group should discuss the ways in which the two samples have been influenced by the audience for whom they were written. Consider the differences in (a) facts selected or omitted, (b) use of language, and (c) attitudes or biases.

1. Choose a passage from a standard local newspaper intended to inform and a passage from a tabloid such as *The National Enquirer* intended to entertain.
2. Choose a passage from a magazine intended mostly for women and a passage from a magazine intended mostly for men.
3. Choose a passage from an elementary or junior high school textbook and a passage from a college textbook.

> **EXERCISE**

Including Your Audience

Write about the same subject for two widely different groups of readers. Do this as focused writing. Choose a subject that both groups would be interested in but would have different attitudes about. Don't plan to write differently in the two samples—just write for the particular audience, and notice afterward how your audience unconsciously affected what you said. Here are some suggestions; write about:

1. College—for a group of high school students and a group of professors
2. Marriage—for a group of divorced people and a group of children
3. Jobs—for a group of political leaders and a group of unemployed people
4. Crime—for a group of prison inmates and a group of police officers
5. Your home town—for people who live there and people who have never been there
6. Your area of study—for a group of experts and people who are beginning to study it

Making Your Point

While practicing freewriting and focused writing, you thought only about putting plenty of words on the page without stopping. You probably discovered, however, that as you explored some subjects, you had strong opinions and feelings about them. You discovered purposes that you had not planned, such as "I want to complain about the subways" or "I want to tell you how exciting it is to be nineteen years old." Perhaps when you read your work aloud, some of your listeners helped you to identify some of these unstated purposes by saying things like "You certainly are angry about the way they treated you on the job" or "You described your sister so well that I feel I've already met her."

Prewriting is a form of exploring what you think and feel. As you move into actual composing, however, you will begin writing with a stated main point. You will learn to tell the reader what you are going to say—not just what your topic is, but how you are going to write about it: defend it, attack it, describe it, compare it with something else, analyze its parts, define it, or persuade the reader to accept your opinion of it. Knowing your purpose is all-important. Many essays succeed or fail because the writer either did or did not have a strong point that was clear throughout the essay. Learn to recognize the difference between merely choosing a topic and knowing how you want to discuss it. "Women's Health Problems" is a topic; "Career Women Face Special Health Problems" is a main point.

EXERCISE 1

Making Your Point

Make a point about each of the following topics. First write nonstop for a few minutes on each topic. Then find a point you have made about the topic and write it in the blank.

Example:

Topic: Professional basketball

Point: *Stars from foreign countries playing in the NBA have made basketball a global sport.*

1. Topic: Marriage

   Your point: _I went to be my sister marrien._

2. Topic: Drug use on campus

   Your point: _Drug use on campus was not good idea_

3. Topic: Diets

   Your point: _most people ar diety now_

4. Topic: Educational television

   Your point: _That was h good point for study_

5. Topic: Pornography

   Your point: _____

> ## EXERCISE II

Making Your Point

Read both of the following passages and tell which one starts with a clearly stat-ed point and supports that point all the way through. Which one wanders in different directions and keeps bringing up new points instead of developing one main point?

A. College athletes deserve to be paid because they bring money and prestige to their colleges. The benefits that top athletes bring to their schools are enormous. Many colleges like UNLV, Duke, and Notre Dame attract good students because athletes have made these colleges prestigious, yet these same athletes are not paid for their work. Furthermore, sports bring large amounts of money to the schools, but none of this income goes to the athletes in the form of salaries. Athletic coaches, faculty members, and administrators at these colleges are paid high salaries, while the athletes work just as hard for nothing. In the age of television, the financial benefits gained by colleges, com-mercial sponsors, and vendors from basketball tournaments and football bowl games add up to millions. If talk show hosts and newscasters can earn millions of dollars a year, the talents of college athletes also deserve high salaries.

B. Sports in college are exciting, but there is some controversy surround-ing them. Some colleges give a lot of scholarships to athletes but they don't have enough sports facilities for ordinary students. Some athletes have a hard time keeping up with the academic work because they have to practice all the time. Most colleges in our conference give athletic scholarships, but they usually aren't enough to cover all your expenses. Our team came in second in the conference last year, but we have a chance to win first place this season. Another issue is the question of whether top athletes should leave college and turn professional before graduating. Our quarterback is thinking of signing a professional con-tract. If he does, our team will be lucky to come in third or fourth in the conference. The women's teams are much better since the school hired a new athletic supervisor two years ago. Some people like to watch pro football, but I think college sports are the best because the fans have more loyalty to their teams. Sometimes there are too many injuries in some sports; some people think that boxing is too dangerous and ought to be changed or eliminated.

Passage A starts with a clear purpose—to convince us that college athletes ought to be paid. Then it goes on to give reasons why this is true. Passage B, however, reads more like focused writing: It stays on the broad subject of sports, but it brings in many disconnected ideas, such as athletic scholarships, the local college's chances of winning, women's teams, and athletic injuries. Passage B would be useful as a warm-up exercise for exploring ideas, but Passage A is a fully developed paragraph of the kind we will study in Unit 2.

Supporting Your Point

There are many ways to support a point, as you will learn in Units 2 and 3. Whatever method you are using, you should always follow one rule: Include enough details to support the point. When you make a point, the reader expects you to explain what you mean and illustrate it with facts and examples. This part of writing means work for you, but it makes your writing much more enjoyable, interesting, and informative. Supporting your point does not mean repeating it in slightly different words. Remember to <u>show</u> rather than <u>tell</u> the reader what you mean. If your sister tells you, "I just met a terrific guy last night," you expect her to fill you in with facts about what he looks like, where he's from, and how he acts. Do the same thing when you write: Lead off with an interesting statement, then follow up with specific evidence to support it.

▶ EXERCISE

Supporting Your Point

Read the passage below. In the first blank, write, in your own words, what the point of the passage is. Next list five supporting facts in the passage that illustrate the point.

> Anyone watching television and reading the newspapers can see that relations between the police and urban teenagers are in trouble. One could mention the rap artists who have expressed hostility to police for using excessive force, or one could cite the growth of gangs that seem to consider the police as a bigger enemy than other gangs. Articles appear frequently about the need for civilian review boards to study cases of alleged police brutality, and everyone knows that the Los Angeles riots in 1992 were touched off by the acquittal of police officers who were videotaped beating Rodney King. The acquittal of O.J. Simpson in 1995 also resulted partly from a climate of distrust toward police officers' statements and behavior. Talk shows have featured police

officers and commissioners explaining how difficult and dangerous their work is, and gang members have been interviewed expressing their frustration. Television shows portraying real police officers in action have been created to improve the public's perceptions of police departments throughout the country. Police officers face greater danger than ever because there are so many handguns in the possession of adolescents and even children, and inner city teenagers and young men face greater difficulty than ever finding good jobs and career opportunities.

Main Idea: _____

_____

Five Supporting Facts: 1. _____

                           2. _____

                           3. _____

                           4. _____

                           5. _____

▶ WRITING ASSIGNMENT

Supporting Your Point

Begin with the statement, "A college education will make my life better." Then write a passage in which you include at least five specific ways you expect your life to improve because of your college education.

Thinking Critically

Once you have learned to identify your main point in prewriting exercises, you are well on the way toward composing more formally developed paragraphs and essays. A further skill that is necessary to effective paragraph and essay writing is **critical thinking.** Critical thinking is involved in almost all stages of the writing process; even in the earliest stages you should pay attention to the principles of critical thinking. Although it is possible to start with a first draft that lacks clear, careful thought and improve the line of argument later, it is far easier and more effective to **do some critical thinking about your topic before you compose paragraphs and essays.** To check your paragraphs and essays for critical thinking after you have composed them, *see the sections on critical thinking* *in Unit 2, pp. 65, 70, 84–5, 88–90 and in Unit 3, pp. 116, 129, 144, 147–150, 163–4.*

Goals for Paragraph and Essay Writing

- Read your work a day or two after you have written it. Pretend that it was written by someone else and that you disagree with what the writer is saying. Does it still make sense? Does it read thoughtfully and persuasively? Does it seem reasonable and open-minded? Are the opinions based on evidence and careful analysis?

- Identify the main idea you want to express. Underline a sentence that best conveys that idea. Find the arguments and evidence supporting that idea; circle them in your text. Are there enough facts and arguments to support your main idea? Do any of your supporting points or facts now seem irrelevant or illogical?

- Read your work aloud to another writer, or to your writing group. Explain to the other person what you think your main idea is and what arguments and facts you have used to support it. Listen to that person's opinions about the strengths and weaknesses of your work. Does that person disagree with any of your arguments or dispute any of the facts you have presented? Does he or she think you have exaggerated or oversimplified anything, or that you show bias?

- Before composing an organized paragraph or essay, participate in a discussion of your topic with others, in either a whole class discussion or a small group exchange. Listen especially to differing views and have them in your head when you compose paragraphs and essays. Taking others views into consideration in your writing will show a more informed, open-minded grasp of the subject and will interest the reader more.

GROUP PROJECT

Critical Thinking

Working with your writing group, analyze one of the passages below as follows: One member should first read each paragraph aloud while the entire group listens carefully. Next, list the weaknesses of each passage. Finally, choose one passage and have each member do some focused writing of about a half a page explaining what he or she thinks about the subject. Read all of these passages aloud to the group, and identify points that the original writer overlooked. Show how the writer could have given better support for the point.

A. *Students ought to be allowed to take any courses they want in college. College is like a store where you go in and buy whatever you want. Nobody tells you what groceries you have to buy or what style of clothes you have to try on in a store, so colleges should not tell students what courses they have to pay for. I had to take advanced mathematics in college, even though I had four years of math in high school and I want to major in business. I shouldn't have to take a foreign language either unless I decide it will fit into my career plans. If colleges let students take any courses they want, the boring and useless courses wouldn't attract any students, and only the interesting and valuable ones would continue to be taught. Students would get a better education that way, and they wouldn't mind paying so much tuition.*

B. *Reading books isn't very important any more. Nowadays you can learn more on videotapes, CD-Rom, and the Internet than from any books. People tell you that you have to read books because their minds are stuck in the past. Actually you can learn more about current events from television news than from newspapers, and if you watch television films about history, you remember it better than from reading dull text-books. Novels and plays are all available as films, and you can learn a language by means of videotapes or CD-Rom disks. When you read a book, you wear out your eyesight trying to figure out what the author is saying, but now you can see and hear the actual events right in front of you. People claim that reading is important just because it is harder to do, but I say, if you can learn something easier and faster another way, then do it.*

C. *Teenagers today are no good. They don't have any respect for their elders, the way my generation did, and they think they are entitled to anything they want but don't want to work for it. They drop out of school and get pregnant when they are only sixteen, and then they blame their parents for not giving them enough. Instead of working for the future, they spend all their time hanging out and getting into trouble. They care more about designer clothes and expensive sneakers than knowing right from wrong. Their heroes and role models are mostly overpaid entertainers with messed up lives. In my time, we had to work hard to graduate from high school, and we considered it a privilege to go to college at all.*

Now they think somebody should give them a college degree even though they don't want to do any homework to earn it. It's society's fault for not having any standards.

Computers and the Prewriting Process

More and more students today compose and edit their essays on computers. You probably have access to a word processing program at school or at home, at least for occasional use. If you are lucky enough to have one available frequently, don't wait to use it until you think of yourself as an advanced writer. Many students practice prewriting activities like brainstorming, arranging, and outlining on computers.

ADVANTAGES OF WORD PROCESSING

As a beginning writer, you can benefit greatly from word processing technology. With a word processor you can create a document and change it easily in all sorts of ways before considering it completed. Later units of this book take up the kind of composing, revising, editing, and proofreading that you will do in writing formal compositions. Many of the advantages of word processing involve these later stages of writing. However, word processing also offers advantages for prewriting activities. You may feel freer to explore your ideas and feelings on a computer, because you will worry less about making mistakes. Part of the trouble many beginning writers have with writer's block comes from their fear of messing up the neat page they are producing.

If you have not worked on a computer before, you may think of it as a machine to be used only after you have done much scribbling and scratching beforehand. Wrong: Don't save the computer for the later stages. The chief advantage of word processing is that you can "scribble" and make as many changes as you like until you are ready to consider your work completed. Even if you find the keyboard uncomfortable at first, try freewriting and focused writing on a computer anyway. And don't give up too soon; nearly all problems with computers are minor and can be overcome with the right instructions.

Opponents of computers in the writing classroom sometimes object that spell check and style analysis programs make students lazy—that they depend too much on the machine to do their work for them. You will probably find instead that spell checks, in addition to catching your typos, will teach you to be more conscious of your areas of weakness. Be warned, however: A spell check will not catch the look alike/sound alike words like *there, their,* and *they're.* These you must know. Furthermore, at this stage of technology, grammar checks will not help you much. They are reliable enough only to raise questions for writers who already know grammar. They will certainly not relieve you of the responsibility to master grammatical terms, patterns, and concepts.

One thing a computer <u>can</u> do for you in the earliest stages of your writing is to help free you of the inhibitions that come from worrying too much about mistakes. On a computer, with its limitless resources for revision and correction before you print the document, you have the opportunity to write more freely than ever before. *You* are still the one in charge of exploring your ideas, putting down and arranging the words, composing, editing, and correcting.

INVISIBLE WRITING

You may find that freewriting and focused writing are more fun to do on a computer than on paper. Even if you cannot touch-type, you will be able to write an impressive amount in a short time using a word processor. One kind of prewriting activity that you can do on a computer but not on paper is called **invisible writing.** Some students find this even better than freewriting on paper for developing an uninhibited flow of words. To do invisible writing, turn the screen light down so you cannot see what you write, then write without stopping for a designated number of minutes. When you have finished, turn up the screen light and read your writing. Students who become blocked by their fear of errors sometimes write more freely this way—they seem to be carrying on a conversation with the machine rather than producing a text full of errors. You may find that invisible writing loosens you up. Like other prewriting activities, it is a skill-builder that works better for some writers than for others.

SOFTWARE AVAILABLE

An enormous amount of software is available for writers. Most new computers nowadays come with word processing software included. With any Windows program, for example, an adequate word processing application called *Write* is included. Many personal computers even include more complicated programs, such as the two most popular, Microsoft *Word* and *WordPerfect,* which come in both Windows and DOS format. You can, of course, purchase such advanced programs separately, though for almost all college writing the simplest programs are quite adequate. The advanced features that appeal to scholars, professional writers, and corporations are not really necessary at this stage.

GETTING STARTED

Nearly all advanced college students now use word processing. Typewriters are not used much anymore, and you cannot expect to turn in all of your college compositions and term papers hand written in advanced courses. Whether or not you are required to include it in your work as a beginning writer, take advantage of any opportunities you have to phase it into your college work. It may help you now and will certainly prove necessary later. (If you are just beginning to learn about word processing, you may want to read a well-known author's account of his first attempts to use it: William Zinsser, *Writing with a Word Processor,* New York, Harper & Row, 1983.) If you do not touch type, it is not difficult to learn using typing lessons now available in the form of computer software.

Reminders About Prewriting Activities

◆ Do **freewriting** and **focused writing** to achieve fluency and overcome writer's block. Practice writing without stopping for an entire page or for five minutes so that writing becomes as comfortable as conversing.

◆ Keep a **journal** to record your thoughts, explore ideas, and create an idea bank for paragraph and essay writing. Use your journal as a way of making thoughtful writing a daily activity and as a means of reinforcing your learning in college courses.

◆ **Brainstorm** and make lists to gather the information on a topic. Be aware that you know much more about any topic than you can recall at first. Before composing, take some time exploring the full range of facts and ideas on the topic. This activity works even better with a group.

◆ Organize material by **grouping, clustering** and **outlining.** Facts and ideas are useful only if you can relate them to each other and to a main idea. Clustering will help you identify these relationships, separating main parts of the topic from subordinate parts.

◆ Try **other prewriting activities** such as asking yourself questions, using the five senses, keeping a learning log, and writing imaginary letters. Each writer is different. Experiment to find out what activities help you most in gathering and organizing facts and ideas before you actually compose paragraphs and essays.

◆ **Read your writing aloud** and get feedback to clarify and develop ideas. You probably have confidence in your abilities as a writer, but don't forget the valuable support you get from the responses of other writers. Even the best writers gain from listening to their readers' responses and suggestions. The better you are, the more others can help you.

◆ **Make a clear main point and support it.** All effective writing depends on this two-part principle. As you compose paragraphs and essays in Units Two and Three, be sure that the main point of every writing assignment is clear to you and to your readers.

◆ Practice **critical thinking** throughout the writing process. Good writing and good thinking go together. Avoid the faults of careless thinkers and develop the habit of looking at evidence with an open mind.

◆ **Use computers** to enhance your prewriting activities. Learn to use a familiar word processing program such as *WordPerfect* or Microsoft *Word*. Although word processing is designed to facilitate composing and revising, some prewriting activities are fun to do on computers as well.

U N I T

2

Practicing Paragraphs

In the first unit you practiced many kinds of prewriting activities. Usually you wrote a page or more at a time without thinking about organization or grammar. Continue to do prewriting, especially the kind that seems to work best for you—focused writing, brainstorming, clustering, or writing journals. Think of prewriting exercises as warm-ups. An athlete, even a top professional, does warmup exercises both during the off-season and before a game. In the same way, professional authors often write journals and use other prewriting techniques before they compose an article, chapter, or book. Prewriting activities, however, are only warm-ups. To create a finished essay, you must learn to organize and develop your material so that it supports a main point. To acquire this skill, practice writing paragraphs. It is possible to start right out with whole essays, but most writers do better if they first master the chief building block of the essay: the paragraph.

Paragraph Basics

This section covers key aspects of paragraphs—recognizing them, signaling where they begin, determining their length, creating topic sentences, and using key words in topic sentences. Bear in mind that what you are learning here and in the rest of this unit is intended only to help you write better essays, not to focus on paragraphs as finished products separate from essays. The skills you work on in creating paragraphs are the same skills you will use in a more extended way to create essays in Unit 3.

RECOGNIZING PARAGRAPHS

A paragraph is a medium-sized block of writing that discusses one topic, or idea, which is often stated in the first sentence. Although you will be creating paragraphs by themselves in this unit, think of the paragraph as part of a larger piece of writing—an essay, story, article, chapter, report, or business letter. You will be practicing paragraphs separately in order to create better developed and organized essays.

SIGNALING PARAGRAPHS

Show your reader where your paragraphs begin by indenting—that is, by starting the first sentence about half an inch from the left margin, or five spaces when you type. (Exception: In some business letters you may skip a line before every paragraph instead of indenting.) The last sentence in your paragraph may end anywhere on the line from left to right; leave the rest of the line blank, like this one.

In most ordinary writing, you will see about two or three paragraphs on every page. See the example on the following page.

DETERMINING PARAGRAPH LENGTH

In this unit you will practice writing full paragraphs, the kind that make up the body of an essay. Such paragraphs usually contain one hundred to two hundred words, or about seven to twelve sentences. Introductory and concluding paragraphs are usually shorter, as are paragraphs used for making transitions and paragraphs in dialogue. In published writing, paragraphs may be very short, as in newspaper reports with narrow columns, or very long, as in dense technical articles. What makes a paragraph the right length is not merely the number of words but the way the words fulfill the writer's purpose.

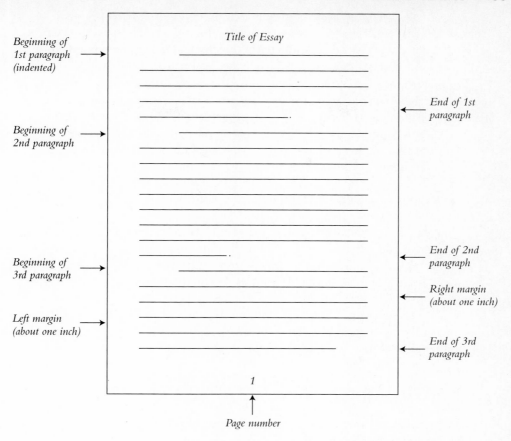

Beginning of
1st paragraph
(indented)

Title of Essay

End of 1st
paragraph

Beginning of
2nd paragraph

End of 2nd
paragraph

Beginning of
3rd paragraph

Right margin
(about one inch)

Left margin
(about one inch)

End of 3rd
paragraph

1

Page number

Read the following sample paragraph, noticing its length and overall plan along with the structural details pointed out in the margin. This paragraph was written by a student who was experienced at developing ideas and tying them together.

Sample Paragraph

Topic sentence states opinion

Key words limit topic

Body of paragraph discusses topic

Mandatory drug testing on the job is *unfair* to individual workers. Many employers are considering the possibility of forcing their workers to take random drug tests. *These* employers understandably worry about the harm drugs can do in the workplace. Certainly drug testing is proper in jobs where the safety of the public is at stake, like piloting planes, but making all workers take drug tests is an invasion of their privacy. Employers never take drug tests themselves, and no one has proved that the tests are foolproof. *Therefore* it is *not fair* to make workers risk losing their jobs by taking *such* tests. If companies are worried about workers being unproductive because of drug use, they can check productivity directly and penalize anyone who isn't doing a good job, whether the reason is laziness, alcoholism, emotional problems, or drug abuse. As bad as drug abuse is, workers can be hooked on other problems just as much, and none of *these* are tested. It is *no fairer* to impose frequent drug testing on workers than to make them take weekly psychological examinations or marriage therapy or check their gambling debts. Invading individuals' privacy by *such* mandated tests is *unfair.*

Transitional words link statements

Length of this paragraph: 199 words, 10 sentences

This paragraph contains a topic: mandatory drug testing. The first sentence builds this topic into a topic sentence by adding a verb, *is,* and a descriptive phrase, *unfair to individual workers.* The rest of the paragraph discusses the idea stated in this topic sentence. To hold the paragraph together, the writer repeats key words like *unfair* and includes connecting words and reference words like *such, these,* and *therefore* to show links between statements. Finally, to avoid boring the reader, the writer varies her sentences, making some short and simple, others longer and more complicated. Above all, she never wanders off the point.

Using Topic Sentences*

Every effective paragraph has a main purpose. Usually this purpose is to express a single idea. In the preceding sample paragraph the idea was that mandatory drug testing on the job is unfair. Your topics should be as clear and specific as this one. One way to be sure they are is to use precise **topic sentences.**

A topic sentence is the sentence, usually the first one in the paragraph, that states the main point of the paragraph. Experienced writers sometimes put topic sentences in the middle or at the end of a paragraph. Occasionally the topic may be so obvious throughout the paragraph that the writer does not need a topic sentence. Despite these exceptions, you should practice beginning your paragraphs with topic sentences, which will help you to identify your main points and stick to them. A topic sentence makes a promise to the reader. It says, "This is what this paragraph is going to discuss." It charts the direction and boundaries of the paragraph. *It should be broader than any other sentence in the paragraph— broad enough to include all the other sentences—but no broader.* If the topic sentence is too general, it will draw boundaries too wide for a paragraph to fill. If the

*Review fragments, run-together sentences, and comma splices in Unit 5.

topic sentence is too narrow and factual, it will fail to draw any boundaries for the rest of the paragraph. Can you tell the difference between a broad statement and a limited statement? Which of the following three statements is broadest? Which is most limited?

1. Several of my courses this term require a large amount of homework.
2. My sociology professor assigned a twenty-five-page report and five hundred pages of reading.
3. College is very difficult.

Only one of these would make an effective topic sentence for a paragraph:

Statement 3 is too broad for a single paragraph: Discussing all the features of college work and college life that are difficult would take up many pages.

Statement 2 is merely a factual statement; it leads nowhere. Sentence 2 is the kind of statement that is useful to support a topic statement.

Statement 1 might make a good topic sentence because it is broad enough to include a number of supporting examples (individual courses) but limited enough to be discussed in a paragraph. Furthermore, it serves as a guide, leading the reader to expect a discussion of how much homework each course demands.

Exercise I

Topic Sentences

If the following sentences were in the same paragraph, which one would make a good topic sentence that includes all the others? Which sentence is not on the topic and would not belong in the same paragraph with the others?

1. Violinists, singers, and steel pan players often perform on the sidewalk.
2. Television interviewers sometimes ask passers-by for their opinions on current events.
3. The street life in Manhattan offers visitors a variety of distractions.
4. Dancers on roller blades display uncanny grace and virtuosity.
5. Most of the large stores are not open on Sunday.
6. Vendors hawk scarves, wallets, jewelry, handbags, and toys on many street corners.
7. Con artists lure passers-by into card games.
8. Political volunteers stop pedestrians to gather signatures on their petitions.
9. Young men and women hand out free passes to live television shows, advertisements for new clothing stores, and samples of new products.

Which sentence makes a guiding statement about a whole paragraph topic? _____

Which sentence is not on the topic at all? _____

How many sentences give factual support for the topic sentence? _____

Exercise II

Topic Sentences

Do a prewriting exercise of your own choosing (focused writing, clustering, brainstorming, and so on) about your own neighborhood. Then look over your material and find a key idea. Write this idea in the form of a topic sentence. List as many supporting details as you can. Write a paragraph of about 150 words beginning with the topic sentence you composed. Be sure to stay on the topic!

Exercise III

Topic Sentences

Read the paragraphs below, noticing all the supporting points. Then write a topic sentence for each paragraph.

A. _____

_____. Swimming exercises not only the shoulders, arms, and legs but also the large muscles of the back and torso better than other sports do. It is one of the most aerobic sports as well, stimulating both the circulatory and respiratory systems. Few other forms of exercise can equal swimming for producing suppleness through stretching of arm, leg, and torso muscles. Whereas other sports build up separate muscles through short bursts of energy, swimming develops all muscles together in a perfect balance. Furthermore, it enhances the athlete's coordination and rhythm better than most other sports.

B. _____

_____. Despite the claims made for IQ tests, such tests often produce widely different results for the same person. Not only are these tests open to cultural biases, they do not take into account the many kinds of functioning the mind is capable of, from understanding social relationships to identifying musical tones. IQ tests do not account for the way a person reacts to the pressure of a test-taking situation. They do not allow for differences in motivation; is it possible, for instance, that a person who doesn't care about getting a high score will not score as high as someone who does? IQ tests measure a kind of analytical thinking, but they do not give a picture of the person's learning styles, and they do not say much about the person's learning development over a period of years. Finally, they do not tell how the person applies his or her intelligence in everyday life.

C. _____

_____. Although he had a large wardrobe, Ted always wore ties that clashed with his shirts, socks that didn't match, shirts with cuff buttons missing, and pants that hadn't been pressed for months. His room showed similar signs of carelessness, with clothes and books piled three feet deep on the floor, the bed unmade, and papers heaped in a chaotic mess on his desk and bureau. In his relations with his friends, he remained true to form, often forgetting to pay back money they lent to him, showing up an hour late for films and parties, and neglecting to mention messages or requests that friends told him to pass on to others.

Exercise IV
Topic Sentences

As you could tell from the preceding exercise, it takes concentration to match a good topic sentence with a fully developed paragraph. In the next two paragraphs, something is wrong with the italicized topic sentences. Explain the fault of each one—not on the topic of the paragraph, too broad, too narrow, or not clear. Then supply a better topic sentence for each one. Remember that a good topic sentence should have one idea, not two or three.

A. *Being the oldest child in the family has both advantages and disadvantages.* Whether a boy or girl, the oldest child tends to mature quickly by copying adults' behavior and being called on to be a substitute parent for the younger children. As a result, he or she tends to have strong leadership potential and a firm sense of identity. Unlike younger siblings, the oldest child never has to accept clothes or toys passed down used and half broken from older brothers and sisters. For a few years, too, sometimes for quite a few, the oldest child basks in the undivided attention and love of both parents, developing self-confidence and self-esteem as an only child. Later, by serving as a model held up to the younger children for imitation, the oldest child usually gains the habit of influencing and motivating others.

The problem with the topic sentence in paragraph A is: _____

_____.

A better topic sentence for this paragraph would be: _____

_____.

B. *Television commercials are very entertaining.* Last year I saw a commercial for a large discount store that sold appliances. The advertisement claimed that the store's prices were the lowest in the state and that the company stood behind the products it sold. Enticed by the commercial, I ordered a washing machine. Although the price seemed reasonable, I learned afterward that a local appliance store sold it at a lower price. Not only that, but the discount outlet demanded a delivery charge, and the delivery men wanted an additional ten dollars to carry the machine into the house and cart the old one away. Then I learned that, unlike other retail stores, the discount outlet would not install the washer. So, after making several telephone calls to the manufacturer and struggling with hoses, fittings, nuts, and bolts, I hooked up the machine myself. I decided not to believe any more commercials without investigating the facts.

The problem with the topic sentence in paragraph B is: _____

_____.

A better topic sentence for this paragraph would be: _____

_____.

Using Key Words in Topic Sentences

Remember that a topic sentence does more than just name a subject. It expresses an opinion about the subject; it points a direction, opens a discussion, and creates an impression of the subject. A simple statement of fact, such as "It was cold yesterday," does not make a useful topic sentence. Which of these two might make a good topic sentence?

  A. I have a friend named Evelyn.
  B. My friend Evelyn is very competitive.

Suppose you were going to write a paragraph beginning with sentence A. What would the paragraph say about Evelyn? Almost anything is possible, since the topic sentence gives no specific idea. Sentence B would make a better topic statement because it tells what the paragraph should say about Evelyn. What examples of behavior would show how competitive Evelyn is? *Competitive* is the key word in sentence B; it introduces a controlling idea. Most good topic sentences contain such a key word or phrase.

Compare these statements:

> Mertz Rent–a–Car offers *rapid advancement* for ambitious employees.
> Mertz Rent–a–Car is a *nice place to work*.

Nice is one of those catchall terms, like *good, bad, interesting, great,* and *unique,* that lead nowhere in particular. The first statement makes a sharp, clear point that the paragraph could support with specific facts.

Exercise I

Key Words

In the following five sentences, find and underline the key words or phrases that create specific impressions. Explain what ideas or details the key word or phrase leads you to expect the paragraph to include. Think of some examples or explanations of each topic statement.

Example: For a twelve-year-old, running away from home is a *frightening* experience.

Frightening makes you expect to hear about scary personal experiences such as being lost in a dangerous neighborhood and not knowing how to get home.

1. My first driving lesson was a hilarious experience.
2. Professional wrestling usually looks faked.
3. An effective job interview requires a manner that is appropriate for the job.
4. Robin Williams has usually played unconventional film roles.
5. Adjusting to a new roommate requires a cooperative approach.

Exercise II

Key Words

Underline the key word or phrase in each of the following sentences and decide whether the statement would make an effective topic sentence. If it would, write OK in the blank. If the key word or phrase is too vague, write a more precise one in the blank.

Example:

The first year of college is <u>different.</u>   *more demanding than high school*

Living in a dormitory is very <u>convenient</u>
for first year students.   *OK*

1. *Sixty Minutes* is a good program to watch.   _gooder than other Progrm_
2. The layout of the campus is awkward for drivers.   _ok_
3. Studying religion made Felix more tolerant of others.   _ok_
4. Meditation is good for some people.   _not every body_
5. A liberal arts major is better than a vocational major.   _ok_
6. Living in a foreign country teaches you a lot of things.   _better subject_
7. Arranging a wedding requires a careful plan.   _that true_

Group Project

Key Words

Working with your writing group, have each student compose a paragraph using a topic sentence from the preceding exercise (with the improved key word if there is one). Read each paragraph aloud, and compare key words and supporting details for effectiveness. The recorder should take notes and give each writer the feedback on his or her paragraph.

Exercise III

Key Words

Read the following two paragraphs, noticing the topic sentences and supporting examples. Then answer the questions.

A. My aunt is the friendliest person in her neighborhood. She is always there when somebody needs her, and she is busy doing all kinds of things all the time. She has many talents, such as photography, singing, and designing greeting cards for the small company she runs. She likes to travel, especially in South America and the Caribbean. She sets high standards for herself and others, and her favorite saying is, "Good luck doesn't just come to you; you have to find it." She used to work in a day care center, but when it closed, she decided to look for *work in other fields. She is very careful about her appearance and chooses beautiful clothes that match her hair and features. Some people think she is too impatient when others disagree with her, but she always knows how to deal with difficult personal situations. She will probably go on living in her neighborhood for a long time, but some day she wants to go back to her country because her dream is to run her own travel business.*

B.   *My uncle is the most generous person I know. He gives to others of his time, his money, and his efforts. Although not a wealthy man, he has helped five nephews and nieces immigrate to the United States by paying for their airline tickets, giving them advice about immigration rules, and getting them jobs. Other relatives and friends always borrow money from him and sometimes forget to pay it back. When anyone is sick or in trouble, he is the first person to visit them and help them buy groceries, get medicine at the pharmacy, call a lawyer, or fix their sink. Sometimes he brings his car over to help people move their belongings to another apartment, and he often lets people from out of town stay at his home for nothing. He is famous in the family for being an altruistic person, and he will never let anybody pay him back for the help he gives them. He always says, "What goes around, comes around," and if he ever does need anything, there will be a lot of people ready to help him.*

1. What is the key word or phrase in the topic sentence of paragraph A?
   _____ Paragraph B? _____
2. Which of the two key words more clearly identifies the paragraph topic?
3. Which paragraph stays on one specific topic more closely? _____
4. Which paragraph is arranged more logically? _____
5. What could be done to improve the faulty paragraph? _____
   _____

Exercise IV

Key Words

Create a topic sentence based on each of the topics below. Be sure to include a specific key word or phrase and circle it.

Example:

Topic: my hometown

Topic Sentence: *My hometown is very old-fashioned.*

1. Topic: my family

    Topic sentence: _____

2. Topic: my job

    Topic sentence: _____

3. Topic: traveling by airplane

    Topic sentence: _____

4. Topic: current hair styles

    Topic sentence: _____

5. Topic: credit cards

    Topic sentence: _____

▶ Writing Assignment

Key Words

Think about someone you know who has an unusual way of behaving. Brainstorm for ten minutes, listing everything you can think of about how this person behaves. Then look over the list and find one main point that you can make about this person—a point that will include most of the details you have listed. Eliminate the details that do not fit this point. Write a topic sentence using a key word or phrase to describe this person's behavior, and compose an exploratory draft of a paragraph on this subject. Look over your draft to be sure that all sentences belong on the topic and that the whole paragraph reads smoothly. Make revisions and write a final draft.

   Read this paragraph after you have brainstormed your topic. Notice how the student who wrote this paragraph succeeded in stating a clear topic sentence and developing it in an interesting way. Try to make your final draft equally unified and interesting.

Sample Paragraph:

A Person with an Unusual Way of Behaving

Larry has an annoying way of antagonizing his classmates. Whenever he comes to class, he arrives late and tries to disrupt what- ever is going on, sometimes bringing along a friend who isn't a member of the class. If the other students are working in small groups, he stomps over to a group on the far side of the room and stands over some women in the group and starts harassing them. If the teacher tries to make him join a group and do some serious work, he starts claiming loudly that the teacher always gives him low grades he doesn't deserve. Sometimes in the middle of a class discussion, he starts a quarrel with another student, saying he made stupid statements. When other members of the class are giving oral reports, he winks at them and tries to make them laugh, and when the teacher is trying to help another student with her writing, he waves his hand in the air and tries to call attention to himself. After class, when other students want to ask the teacher questions, he pushes ahead of them and demands that the teacher explain why he didn't get an A on his last paper. He thinks he is funny and smart, but nobody else does.

What Makes a Paragraph Good?

In learning to compose good paragraphs, you will also learn most of what it takes to compose good essays. Although you do not have to pay special atten- tion to your paragraphs when you create exploratory drafts, your final drafts will need well-constructed paragraphs to be effective. In this section you will learn the qualities of good paragraphs so that you can create them yourself. The four main elements that combine to make effective, purposeful paragraphs are **unity, coherence, transitions,** and **development.**

PARAGRAPH UNITY

The prefix *uni* means *one.* A unified paragraph has *one* clear purpose. The topic statement, as we have already discussed, is limited enough so that the rest of the paragraph can support it well; no statements wander off the topic. In your focused writing, you tried to stay on one topic, but a short piece of focused writing is still not a unified paragraph. In your focused writing you did not compose a topic sentence with a key word or phrase that would fit exactly the amount of writing you were planning to do. At times you may even have had a brilliant new idea and wandered off the topic like a shopper after an unexpected bargain. You did not worry about the structure or organization of your writing.

Now you will concentrate on the paragraph as a finished product made from the raw materials of your ideas and statements in your focused writing. Above all you must identify your topic and stay on it. Every sentence in your paragraph should follow logically from the one before, and all sentences should give facts, ideas, or examples that support the topic statement.

Exercise 1

Paragraph Unity

This exercise gives you practice in recognizing sentences that support a topic. First read the topic sentence; then read each of the ten sentences that follow. If the sentence supports the topic statement, put a check mark in the blank next to it. If it does not, leave the space blank.

Example:

Topic Statement: *Letter grades (A, B, C, D, F) sometimes harm a college student's learning process.*

_____ 1. Students who concentrate too much on grades tend to avoid difficult courses in which they might learn much.

_____ 2. Grades are usually given out twice a semester.

_____ 3. The fear of low grades makes some students hesitant about expressing opinions that disagree with those of the teacher.

_____ 4. Competition for grades gives students a big incentive to learn.

_____ 5. Average students know they cannot earn top grades, and they often become discouraged about learning.

_____ 6. Colleges that give grades have a higher percentage of graduates continuing on to graduate school than those that do not give grades.

_____ 7. Grades increase stress, causing some students to lose concentration.

_____ 8. Grades do not reward work done creatively beyond the scope of a course.

_____ 9. Students with high grades are not always "nerds"; some of them are very popular.

_____ 10. The threat of low grades damages the relationship between teachers and students that is necessary for optimal learning.

Exercise II

Paragraph Unity

The following paragraph is unified except for two sentences that wander off the topic stated in the first sentence. Underline these two irrelevant sentences.

> Physician assistants have high-level professional careers. They must have enough clinical training, academic preparation, and communication skills to provide health care under the supervision of a doctor. The cost of medical care is making it hard for most people to find insurance coverage nowadays. Physician assistants work in hospitals, clinics, nursing homes, college health services, and government agencies. They perform such tasks as giving physical examinations, taking patients' medical histories, doing certain therapeutic and diagnostic procedures, and providing follow-up care and counseling for patients. Physician assistant programs are offered in colleges, schools of public health, and medical schools. Applicants must have experience working in health care. Technology is changing the practice of medicine rapidly. Programs are generally for two years and include both medical education and clinical experience. In most states graduates must then pass the Physician Assistant National Certifying Examination before being licensed to practice. Later they must continue to receive updated medical training, acquiring Continuing Medical Education (CME) credits every few years, and must pass recertifying examinations to maintain their professional status.

Now read the paragraph aloud with the two irrelevant sentences omitted. It reads more smoothly, doesn't it? Unrelated sentences interrupt the flow of thought and lead the reader off the path, destroying the unity of the paragraph.

Exercise III

Paragraph Unity

The following paragraph also contains two sentences that are not on the topic. Underline the two sentences and read the paragraph aloud with the two sentences omitted.

> The career outlook for young people in the twenty-first century will be dramatically different from that of their parents' generation. As the country shifts from an economy based on industrial production to one of providing services, new kinds of jobs with new requirements will replace the secure jobs of the past. College education, communication skills, and technological training will be at a premium. Going to college is often emotionally difficult for students who have never lived away from home. Workers with

the greatest flexibility, who can update their skills, acquire new training, and change jobs, will be most likely to succeed. Since the workforce will include far more women and people of varied cultural backgrounds than in the past, workers who adapt well to a diverse workplace will have a definite advantage. Since fringe benefits are likely to be less available than in the past, workers will have to learn how to manage their own insurance policies, retirement plans, and investments to attain the kind of security employers once provided. Americans spend more money on entertainment than ever before. More employees than in the past will do work at home through computers, and the number of free-lance consultants will increase. Husbands and wives will have to work together as never before on dual career planning to allow time for child rearing and family activities. The economy of the future will require self-reliance, lifetime learning, and adaptability of those who want to succeed.

PARAGRAPH COHERENCE

Not only should all sentences in a paragraph support the topic statement, but they should be *arranged in a clear, recognizable order.* **Coherence** means that all the parts of something *cohere,* or hang together. To produce a car engine, you have to have all the right pieces, but you also have to fit the pieces together correctly so the engine can run. To write a coherent paragraph, *make every sentence follow logically from the one before.* The sentences should read in a natural sequence, like numbers in a row—1, 2, 3, 4, 5—not jump around unpredictably like random numbers—1, 7, 3, 8, 4, 9.

A paragraph with a natural sequence is easier to read than one without shape and will serve its purpose more effectively, whether the purpose is to express a feeling, state an opinion, convey an experience, or persuade the reader to agree.

Here is a paragraph that lacks coherence:

> My first attempt to register for courses in my freshman year was one of the worst experiences of my life. I'll never go through that again! Most of the courses I wanted to take were already closed, so I had to settle for whatever I could get. The first frustration came when I entered the gymnasium and was told that freshmen had to register in the student union. I discovered that I had to stand in not one line but six lines—one for each course I wanted. As I was heading back to my dorm room about ready to explode, I met a friend who told me that I was right in the first place, but now I was late and would have to wait in line because everyone was ahead of me. When I got to the student union, someone told me that freshmen couldn't register until the next day. After I finished five hours later, I found out that I could have done all my registering a week earlier just by seeing my adviser. Nobody had

told me it would be difficult, so I was not prepared for five hours of waiting in six long lines, not being able to get the courses I wanted, and constantly receiving misinformation.

Revision for Coherence

The first sentence in the preceding paragraph is a fairly clear and specific topic sentence and all of the following statements support it, but the paragraph is confusing because the order of sentences has been jumbled. Here is the paragraph arranged in a coherent order:

My first attempt to register for courses my freshman year was one of the worst experiences of my life. Nobody had told me it would be difficult, so I was not prepared for five hours of waiting in six long lines, not being able to get the courses I wanted, and constantly receiving misinformation. The first frustration came when I entered the gymnasium and was told that freshmen had to register in the student union. When I got to the student union, someone told me that freshmen couldn't register until the next day. As I was heading back to my dorm room about ready to explode, I met a friend who told me that I was right in the first place, but now I was late and would have to wait in line because everyone was ahead of me. I discovered that I had to stand in not one line but six lines—one for each course I wanted. Most of the courses I wanted to take were already closed, so I had to settle for whatever I could get. After I finished five hours later, I found out that I could have done all my registering a week earlier just by seeing my adviser. I'll never go through that again!

Coherence can be achieved in paragraphs by arranging the material according to **time sequence, spatial sequence,** or **climactic sequence.**

1. TIME SEQUENCE

The sample paragraph you just read is arranged in **time sequence.** It describes a series of actions taking place one after the other: the attempt to register at the gym, the wild-goose chase to the student union, the return to the gym, the five hours of waiting in line, and the discovery that all this could have been avoided. Time sequence is the easiest way to arrange material in a paragraph. You have undoubtedly used it in writing you have done about personal experiences. The main thing to keep in mind is to make the sequence of actions clear; don't leave out any steps that the reader needs.

In the next paragraph several gaps occur in the sequence of statements. As a result, the action is difficult to follow. Find the places where something is left out. What belongs in these spaces?

> *When Alex has to study for a test, he uses a system that never fails to earn him a high grade. First he makes sure that he understands what the instructor wants students to know for the test. As the date of the exam approaches, he makes a list of all the topics he is supposed to know for the exam and checks off the ones he already knows. Then he studies each remaining topic until he is sure he has mastered it. His next step is to ask a classmate to quiz him on each of the topics he has just reviewed. One week before the exam, he makes up an exam for himself, trying to guess what the actual questions will be. He spends an hour or two writing answers to the questions. When he takes the exam, he is always relaxed and ready, and he claims that his system is so successful that he is going to get a patent on it.*

Revision for Coherence: Time Sequence

This student's paragraph came out easier to read when he revised it to include information missing from the first draft:

> *When Alex has to study for a test, he uses a system that never fails to earn him a high grade. First he makes sure that he understands what the instructor wants students to know for the test. He does this by taking careful notes when the teacher explains what she wants; then he reads over the notes and asks questions in the next class session about anything that is unclear to him. As the date of the exam approaches, he makes a list of all the topics he is supposed to know for the exam and checks off the ones he already knows. Then he studies each remaining topic until he is sure he has mastered it. His next step is to ask a classmate to quiz him on each of the topics he has just reviewed. One week before the exam, he makes up an exam for himself, trying to guess what the actual questions will be. He spends an hour or two writing answers to the questions. The day before the exam, he exercises in the afternoon and watches his favorite sitcoms on television in the evening and goes to bed early. When he takes the exam, he is always relaxed and ready, and he claims that his system is so successful that he is going to get a patent on it.*

Group Project

Time Sequence

Working with your writing group, compose a paragraph telling about what some imaginary person does in his or her job. Give the person a name, and take turns having each writer add one sentence after another until the paragraph is complete. Be sure that every sentence reads smoothly after the one before it; use words like *first, next, after,* and *finally* to signal time. The group recorder should then read the paragraph aloud for possible revisions.

Writing Assignment

Time Sequence

Look through your prewriting exercises and find one that includes an experience that took place in time sequence. This can be either something that happened to you or some other event you wrote about. You will need about half a page of writing to make a normal-sized paragraph. Revise your writing to make a unified paragraph written in time sequence. Since you were not trying to compose neat paragraphs in your prewriting exercises, you may have to add steps that were left out, remove irrelevant sentences, and make other corrections.

2. SPATIAL SEQUENCE

Another way of achieving coherence in your paragraphs is by arranging statements in **spatial sequence.** This means that your description follows the placement of items in space, for example, inside to outside, front to back, side to side, up to down, near to far. As with time sequence, be sure not to leave any confusing gaps, and use enough details so that the reader has a clear picture of what you are describing. The paragraph should move like a camera panning (as filmmakers call it) slowly over a scene. If you have ever tried making home videos, you know that if you move the camera too fast, the film will be hard to follow. In filmmaking and writing alike, the viewer or reader must spend enough time on a few important details to recognize the arrangement, and the focus has to move gradually enough so the picture does not become a confusing blur.

The paragraph that follows is arranged in spatial sequence. What direction of movement does it use to achieve coherence?

As he approached the town, Fred began to sense familiarity. The shopping mall he passed just inside the city limits seemed new to him, because all the buildings were fairly new. Just beyond it, however, he passed a used-car lot that he seemed to know, even though he didn't recognize the name. Soon he crossed some old railroad tracks, and now he knew he had driven this way before. He slowed down as he spotted Dom's service station on his left, and realized he had known it would be there. His memory told him there would be a high school just over the hill on his right as he entered the business section of town. There it was. As he drove past the high school from which he had graduated and nosed his car in anticipation toward the remodeled courthouse in the center of town, he knew he had accidentally returned to his hometown, modernized beyond recognition in the suburbs but still the same at its heart.

In describing a place, such as a building, a neighborhood, or a room, use spatial sequence to give coherence to the picture. Otherwise the details will add up to a jumbled mess. Here is a paragraph that lacks coherence because the descriptive details are not arranged in a recognizable order:

There was a huge pile of dirty laundry left near the door two weeks ago. One desk was barely visible under a mound of loose term papers, audio cassettes, books and magazines lying open, and camera equipment. One bed was made drum-tight like a marine recruit's bunk. Another desk lined up straight against the wall had every item in place, with pens and pencils positioned in parallel rows, books matched on the shelves above according to height, and papers stacked evenly on one corner. A broken stationary bicycle was lying on its side with a set of free weights scattered under and around it. The other bed looked as if a barroom fight had taken place on it—the torn and stained wool blanket was littered with cigarettes, crumpled soda cans, socks, and underwear. There was also a computer table with a monitor and printer polished to look like new, and a desk chair carefully placed one foot behind the table.

Revision for Coherence: Spatial Sequence

The above paragraph has plenty of descriptive details, but it is hard to follow because the details are not arranged in any pattern. Arranged in spatial order, however, the details make a coherent paragraph with the addition of a clear topic sentence and some "spatial orientation" words:

Michael and Sean's dormitory room looked like an apartment for the odd couple. Everything on the left side showed Sean's incredible sloppiness; everything on the right showed Michael's obsessive tidiness. As you entered the room and looked to the left, you saw first a huge pile of dirty laundry dumped near the door two weeks ago. Behind it was a broken stationary bicycle lying on its side with a set of free weights scattered under and around it. Beyond that was a bed that looked as if a barroom fight had taken place on it—the torn and stained wool blanket was littered with cigarettes, crumpled soda cans, socks, and underwear. The desk in the far corner was barely visible under a mound of loose term papers, audio cassettes, books and magazines lying open, and camera equipment. By contrast, the right side of the room was geometrically perfect. The front was taken up by a bed made drum-tight like a marine recruit's bunk. The desk, lined up straight behind it against the wall, had every item in place, with pens and pencils positioned in parallel rows, books matched on the shelves above according to height, and papers stacked evenly on one corner. Standing in the far right corner was a computer table with a monitor and printer polished to look like new and a desk chair carefully placed one foot behind the table.

Writing Assignment I

Spatial Sequence

Imagine you are driving in a place that is familiar to you. Compose a paragraph describing your impressions as you draw nearer and nearer to a particular spot. Remember to include enough details to communicate the overall movement from far to near.

Writing Assignment II

Spatial Sequence

Brainstorm to collect facts about your room. Do not think about composing or arranging. Once you have your list of facts, look it over and try to think of a topic statement that will make your description interesting. Find a key word— *mysterious, boring, messy, casual, neat, colorful*—to describe the overall impression of your room. Then write an exploratory draft in which you describe the room spatially, for example from front to back or left to right. Look over your draft to see if you left anything out or need to add details or make corrections. Write a final draft.

3. CLIMACTIC SEQUENCE

A third kind of paragraph arrangement is called **climactic sequence.** In this arrangement, sentences build to a climax. They start with less important or less emphatic statements and end with the most important or most emphatic statements. Climactic sequence is effective in paragraphs that discuss ideas rather than tell stories or describe places. A paragraph in climactic sequence may give a series of facts, reasons, or examples to support a point. When you write such paragraphs, be sure to include enough facts and ideas to support your point, and make each sentence follow from the one before and build to a climax.

Here is a paragraph that follows a climactic sequence:

Learning a second language takes time and effort, but it brings many benefits. First, it provides a kind of mental exercise that makes your memory sharper and your thinking more flexible. It also teaches you a grammatical structure that helps you understand the parts of speech and how they work in your own language. In addition, it can make traveling more interesting because you can understand a country better when you speak the lan-

© 1998 by Addison-Wesley Educational Publishers Inc.

*guage. In today's global economy, where business is conducted in many lan-
guages, being able to speak a second language can make you more employ-
able as well. Even more important, knowing a second language allows you to
appreciate great works of literature and films in that language in a way
that people who have to rely on translations cannot. Above all, learning a
second language means acquiring another culture, which makes you a richer, more interesting, more open-minded and wiser human being.*

This paragraph lists some of the benefits of learning a second language. The
writer puts them in a sequence that she believes builds from the somewhat less
important advantages to the most important ones. Do you agree with her priorities? Would you arrange them in the same order?

Climactic sequence can also be useful in discussing personal topics. In the
following paragraph a student discusses the advantages of renting films and
watching them on a VCR. Again, the order of sentences moves from the less
important to the more important.

*Renting films and watching them on my VCR has quite a few advantages.
I don't have to wait until a particular time for a film to begin at a local
theater and maybe even wait in line, taking the chance of not getting a
ticket. I can also watch the film several times if I want to, or stop it in
the middle and rerun part of it if I missed something. Instead of having
to pay $7.00 or $8.00 to watch a film at a theater—twice as much if
I take my girlfriend—I can rent a film for $2.71 at the video store where
I am a member. The biggest advantage of all is that I can choose a film
from hundreds of movies available at the video store instead of having
to see one of the four showing at the theater near my home.*

Exercise

Climactic Sequence

Number the following statements in the order you would arrange them in climactic
sequence, putting 1 first as the least important and 5 last as the most important.

Example:

Topic Statement: *Attending a large state university has many benefits.*

Supporting statements:

_____ 1. Large state universities offer a wide range of courses and majors.
_____ 2. Sports programs are often outstanding at large state universities.
_____ 3. Tuition costs, at least for state residents, are usually moderate at
state universities.

_____   4. Many clubs and social activities are available at large state universities.

_____   5. Large enrollments at state universities provide many opportunities for making friends.

Writing Assignment

Climactic Sequence

Choose one of the topics below for a paragraph to be written in climactic sequence. First brainstorm or do focused writing on the topic. List as many supporting statements as you can, being sure to include only those that specifically support the topic. Using your list of supporting statements, write a first draft beginning with the topic sentence and including your supporting statements in order of increasing importance. You may want to number your statements as in the preceding exercise before writing the rough draft. Write a final draft, being sure that your sentences read smoothly.

Suggested topic sentences:

1. Waiting until about age 30 to have a baby is a practical idea.
2. Current fashions are convenient.
3. State lotteries have a number of benefits for society.
4. Single-sex schools have several drawbacks for college students.
5. I read personal advice columns for a number of reasons.

PARAGRAPH TRANSITIONS*

Successful paragraphs move the reader along smoothly from beginning to end. Remember the main rule: *Every sentence should follow logically from the one before.* Having a logical arrangement based on a recognizable order—time sequence, spatial sequence, or climactic sequence—is the most effective way to achieve continuity. In addition, you should use **transitional expressions** to signal connections to the reader. Your overall plan is like an itinerary you have worked out for a trip. Transitional expressions are like the road signs you will need occasionally to be sure you are going in the right direction.

Transitional Words and Phrases

For Adding Information	also, and, besides, first (second, third), furthermore, in addition, likewise, moreover, too
For Showing Opposites and Contrast; for Showing Time	although, after, afterward, at last, at that time, before, beforehand, but, earlier, even though, however, later, meanwhile, nevertheless, on the other hand, soon, then, while

*See correcting by subordinating and punctuation (semicolons, commas) in Unit 5.

For Showing Place	above, adjacent to, behind, below, beyond, farther, here, nearby, next to, opposite to, to the left, to the right
For Showing Results or Conclusions	as a result, consequently, finally, hence, in conclusion, so, then, therefore, thus
For Showing Examples	chiefly, especially, first of all, for example, for instance, for one thing, in general, mainly, namely, particularly, specifically

Tie your sentences together by repeating key words. Learn to use transitional words and phrases like those listed here to show connections between statements. Use **pronouns** (*he, she, it, you, they, we*) to refer to persons, places, and things already mentioned, always making sure the person or thing to which any pronoun refers is absolutely clear. Look over your previous writing to see which transition words you have never used. Practice using these and develop the habit of guiding the reader by using transition words.

<u>Caution:</u> Some writers who discover they have not been using enough transitional expressions to show connections at first use too many. They may put a transitional word or phrase at the beginning of every sentence. As a result, their writing suddenly becomes mechanical and self-conscious. Remember that these transitional expressions are like road signs: You don't need them at every point along the way, but you do need them at key points where the reader might otherwise lose the train of thought.

What is missing from the following paragraph?

A term paper in physics submitted at Princeton University in the 1970s brought its author nationwide publicity. There was nothing extraordinary about the methods or sources John Aristotle Phillips used. He startled the public by proving that he could design his own atomic bomb. He had access to some books on physics and nuclear technology. He could not use any secret government material. His project showed that an ordinary undergraduate could design a nuclear bomb by using only information available to the public. He had to spend many hours studying these books. His project did not require special expertise or original discoveries. The extra information he needed was also available to the public. He bought some copies of documents in Washington, D.C. He telephoned the DuPont Company about explosives. He had no secret information. He worked on the project several months. He finished his research. He submitted a workable plan for an atomic bomb. He earned an A for the project. The government kept the paper as a classified document.

Revision for Effective Transitions

The paragraph does not read smoothly because transitional words have been omitted. Sometimes you have to pause and figure out the connection between one sentence and the next. Now read the same paragraph with transitional words included:

A term paper in physics submitted at Princeton University in the 1970s brought its author nationwide publicity. <u>Although</u> there was nothing extraordinary about the methods or sources John Aristotle Phillips used, he startled the public by proving that he could design his own atomic bomb. He had access to some books on physics and nuclear technology, <u>but</u> he could not use any secret government material. <u>Therefore</u>, his project showed that an ordinary undergraduate could design a nuclear bomb by using only information available to the public. <u>Even though</u> he had to spend many hours studying these books, his project did not require special expertise or original discoveries. <u>Furthermore</u>, the extra information he needed was also available to the public. <u>For instance</u>, he bought some copies of documents in Washington, D.C., <u>and</u> he telephoned the DuPont Company about explosives, <u>but</u> he had no secret information. <u>After</u> working on the project several months, he finished his research <u>and</u> submitted a workable plan for an atomic bomb. He earned an A for the project, <u>but</u> the government <u>later</u> kept the paper as a classified document.*

Exercise I

Transitional Expressions

Circle the transitional words in the following paragraph. First look back at the list to remind yourself what they are.

Fiction in the media can occasionally be too realistic. For example, a radio drama called The War of the Worlds produced by Orson Welles in 1938 scared thousands of listeners into believing the world was coming to an end. In fact, some started to evacuate the cities and even planned suicide. The first thing that made the show realistic was that many people tuned in late and assumed it was a news report. What

---

*Information from John A. Phillips and David Michaels, *MUSHROOM: The Story of the A Bomb Kid*. Used by permission of William Morrow & Co., Inc. Copyright 1978 by John Aristotle Phillips.

further added to the effect was that most of the drama was presented in unusually effective broadcast style. In addition, Orson Welles gave it unique realistic touches; for instance, he copied the fumbling and vomiting of the announcer who witnessed the explosion of the Hindenberg blimp. As a result, many listeners believed that the Martians were actually landing in New Jersey. Furthermore, many were carried away by the emotional excitement of the battles and disasters that followed. Although many listeners knew it was just a radio play, so many people across the continent were taken in by its realism that reports of suicides, traffic accidents, and stampeding crowds began occurring everywhere. Consequently, the program brought many threats of law-suits; in fact, nearly a million dollars in damages was sought in actions against the network. None of the claims, however, could be backed up, so the network did not have to pay anything. Still they did settle one claim: a man who had spent his shoe money trying to escape the disaster received a new pair of shoes from the radio station.★

Exercise II

Transitional Expressions

In the paragraph below, supply missing transitional words from the following list. Be sure to select words that make sense.

although	but	in addition
also	for instance	in fact
as well as	however	nevertheless
		while

Most students have heard the name of Frederick Douglass. Some,

(1) _____ , have not actually read his autobiography entitled *Narra-*

tive of the Life of Frederick Douglass, an American Slave. They (2) _____

may not have learned about his later life as an abolitionist. (3) _____

his story makes exciting reading for its own sake, it offers (4) _____

_____

★Information from John Houseman, *Run-Through.* New York: Simon & Schuster, 1971.

many glimpses into the lives of both black and white people during the peri-

od of slavery. (5) _____ , it shows much about the family loyalties

of slaves and their longing for freedom and upward mobility. The book

(6) _____ describes vividly some of the atrocities Douglass witnessed.

(7) _____ it is not a work of simple propaganda (8) _____

a creative portrait of a people maintaining their humanity (9) _____

suffering hardship and cruelty. Douglass includes an account of his escape,

(10) _____ his impressions of life in the North. (11) _____

the whole plot reads almost like a nonfiction novel. It does, (12) _____

leave out his later life as a famous orator, journalist, and diplomat.

Writing Assignment
Transitional Expressions

Do some focused writing about a time when you either succeeded or failed in
the effort to achieve some important goal. Read over your writing and make
a list in chronological order of all the steps in this experience. Compose a paragraph in which you use transition words referring to time, such as *first, after, then,
next, later,* and *finally.* Read your paragraph carefully, paying special attention to
transitions. Revise it and write a final draft.

Group Project
Transitional Expressions

Working with your writing group, compose a paragraph on one of the two
well-known people below. Using the biographical facts provided, create sentences that follow in a chronological sequence. Use transitional words referring to time, such as *first, after, next, then, later, while, when,* and *finally* to make the
sequence of events easy to follow. Have your group recorder read your paragraph
aloud; then discuss possible revisions and compose a final draft to read aloud to
the whole class.

Maya Angelou

Born in St. Louis in 1928

Raised by her grandmother,
who ran a small store in Stamps,
Arkansas

Excelled in elementary and junior
high school

Was raped at the age of eight

Became unwed mother at sixteen

Became actress, dancer, and poet as
young adult

Worked for Martin Luther King's
Southern Christian Leadership
Conference in 1960s

Published her best-selling memoir,
I Know Why the Caged Bird Sings,
in 1970

Wrote more memoirs, plays, poems,
and songs in the 1970s and 1980s

Read poem, "On the Pulse of
Morning," at President Clinton's
inauguration in 1993

Read poem at Million Man March
in 1996

Cal Ripken, Jr.

Born in a Baltimore suburb in 1960

Raised Aberdeen, Maryland, in family that traveled often while his
father played in minor leagues
and worked for Orioles

Entered minor leagues in 1978, playing for Miami, Charlottesville,
and Rochester

Entered major leagues in 1981, joining Baltimore Orioles

Played third base and shortstop in
1981 & 1982

Stayed at shortstop from 1983 on

American League Most Valuable
Player in 1983

Best year in 1991, with .323 batting
average, 34 home runs and 114
RBI's; again voted MVP

Played in over 160 games in every
season from 1982 to 1993

On Sept. 6, 1995 broke Lou Gehrig's
record for most consecutive
games (2130)

PARAGRAPH DEVELOPMENT

Although well-developed paragraphs are usually longer than poorly developed ones, **paragraph development** does not depend on length. A long paragraph that wanders off the topic or is repetitious, for instance, is not well developed. Development means supporting the main point with examples, quotations, explanations, facts, statistics, descriptive details, and ideas. There are many kinds of paragraph development, as you will see in the next section of this unit. Some of them may come easily to you; others may require more practice. Some writers, for example, find it easy to write about personal experiences but difficult to write about ideas and social issues. Others are just the opposite: They analyze issues eas-ily but have trouble putting in interesting details when they write about personal experience. Becoming an effective writer means building on your strengths and working on your weaknesses. While you may enjoy one kind of writing because it comes easily to you, don't neglect the kinds that are harder for you. Most kinds of writing prove interesting once you get a little practice.

The first step is to develop the habit of supporting all topic sentences ade-quately and with interesting details and ideas. Some inexperienced writers give

one specific event and stick to it. The sample paragraph that follows is written in the third person and concentrates on one man's specific goal in 1948:

> *Preston Tucker tried to manufacture a dream car in the late 1940s but failed because he was ahead of his time. He hoped to see a low, modern-looking automobile with a one-piece windshield, an aluminum air-cooled engine, and safety features such as a collapsing steering column and a third headlight that turned with the wheels. He collected $25 million by selling stock and franchises, and he bought a huge war plant in Chicago to use as his factory. He worked hard to gain support and publicity, but he ran into difficulties with government agencies as well as newspaper columnists who claimed he was a fake. Furthermore, some of his new ideas could not be carried out with the technology of those days. After building only about fifty Tucker cars, he had to close his plant. Today, the Tucker cars still in existence are rare collectors' items.★*

Critical Thinking in Narrative Paragraphs

In a narrative paragraph you are telling a story. However, that does not mean that you don't have to think. Every story has a purpose, and it takes a lot of critical thinking not only to identify that purpose but also to decide which details support that purpose and which do not. In the paragraph about Preston Tucker you may have noticed there are no details about his personal life, family, training, or experiences after 1948. Why would such details detract from the purpose of the paragraph?

Critical thinking is needed at several stages of composition. <u>Before</u> you compose your first organized paragraph, think about what you want the paragraph to say and what details might support that idea. <u>While</u> you are composing the paragraph, ideas will come to you about your topic and the supporting details. <u>After</u> you have done your first draft, critical thinking will help you in revising your work and deciding what comments from your readers will guide your revision.

Writing Assignment I

Narrative Paragraph, First Person

Start with a page of focused writing about an incident that happened to you recently. Include plenty of material so that you can select the best details. Think of a topic statement that sums up the meaning of the experience. Now write an exploratory paragraph beginning with the topic sentence and including the

★Information from Philip S. Egan, *Design and Destiny: The Making of the Tucker Automobile.* On the Mark Publications, Orange, CA, 1989.

most interesting material from your focused writing. Read your exploratory draft aloud to someone else to get feedback. Add more details if needed. Write a final draft.

Writing Assignment II
Narrative Paragraph, Third Person

Write a paragraph telling how a person you know (either a friend or a famous person) tried to achieve a specific goal and either succeeded or failed. Include only the facts related to his or her goal. Do not try to tell a whole life story. Begin with an exploratory draft; then write a final edited paragraph. Stay on the specific topic.

Description: Telling About Persons, Places, and Objects*

THREE RULES FOR WRITING GOOD DESCRIPTIVE PARAGRAPHS

1. Limit Your Subject
2. Include Concrete Details
3. Arrange Your Sentences in a Spatial Sequence

Rule 1. Limit Your Subject

A descriptive paragraph can be about a large or small subject. If you want to describe the subject thoroughly, you must choose a very specific subject. If you want to describe a broad subject, you must concentrate on one of its characteristics. Either way, you must limit your topic. Here are some examples of limiting a large subject by choosing a physical characteristic:

Large Subject	*Reduced Subject*
My sister	My sister's face
My favorite city	The business district in my favorite city
My favorite building	The entrance to my favorite building

*Review adjectives and adverbs in Unit 5. See also Descriptive Essays in Unit 3.

Another way to limit is to select one characteristic of the subject rather than a physical part of it. The three large subjects could thus be limited in this way:

- My sister's taste in clothes
- The traffic problem in my favorite city
- The efficient use of space in my favorite building

Exercise
Limiting Descriptive Topics

Limit these topics in two ways—first by choosing a physical characteristic of the subject; second by selecting another characteristic.

General Subject	Physical Characteristic	Other Characteristic
Madonna	*Madonna's hair*	*Madonna's talent*
A Jeep Cherokee		
Seattle		
Tom Hanks		
Howard University		
Wall Street		

Rule 2. Include Sensory Details★

Most effective description is rich in details that appeal to the five senses. Don't forget that you can describe not only what you see, but also what you taste, feel, smell, and hear. Read the following paragraph and underline words that create sense impressions.

> Thanksgiving at my grandparents' house was always a delicious, uproarious occasion. When we arrived, the house was filled with the aroma of turkey, mince meat pies, and home-baked breads wafting from the oven. The shrieks of rowdy children tumbling over one another echoed through the downstairs rooms, and the bellow of a basset hound rang from the

★See Using Specific Language in Unit 4.

back steps. The antique armchairs and sofa were positioned with exquisite care, and the living room sparkled from hours of dusting, sweeping, and scrubbing. A familiar candelabra on the mantel added an extra light and warmth to the crackling fire in the fireplace. The dinner itself was a high point of the year, with bubbling conversation and laughter that never subsided long, with teasing of shy children by good-natured uncles, and the endless family gossip. The Thanksgiving turkey seemed more tender and juicy every year, and a child could wallow in mounds of mashed potatoes with huge dollops of gravy. Homegrown beans and peas, canned since the summer, along with tart cranberry sauce, filled stomachs so full that the hot dessert pies sat cooling on plates while youngsters poked halfheartedly at them.

Think of description as a way of sharing a whole experience with the reader. Don't hold back on the details; remember that the reader doesn't know anything about the experience until you share it with him or her. Choose specific words instead of vague or general ones.

Writing Assignment

Details in Descriptive Paragraphs

Write a paragraph describing a holiday at your home or the home of a relative. Include details that arouse at least three of the five senses. After you have finished, go back and find the words that convey sense impressions, and write which senses they refer to.

Rule 3. Arrange Your Sentences in Spatial Sequence

In the section on paragraph coherence, you already practiced using spatial sequence. In most descriptive paragraphs the details should be arranged to follow some physical direction—far to near, right to left, inside to outside, top to bottom, and so on. Read the next paragraph and identify what kind of spatial sequence its sentences follow.

As you approached the new stadium, you could see that it formed a huge square, except for a retractable roof located to the right that was mounted on rollers. The parking lot extending out from the front of the building and around to the left, together with the great height of the stadium, created the effect of a distant temple dedicated to the spirit of baseball. Once inside, past the ticket turnstiles, you faced what looked like an indoor shopping mall, with brightly lit stalls offering food, soft drinks, souvenirs, magazines, and pennants. As you entered the park itself, the sudden flood of sunlight dazzled your eyes, the thunder of the crowd overwhelmed your senses, and the great arc of the grandstand took your breath away. As you sat down you were greeted by an array of computer keys near your elbow that allowed you to order food and drinks from your seat. On the scoreboard you could watch gigantic closeup replays and action from the day's games in other cities. Never before had modern architecture and technology combined so well to give spectators a total immersion in the game.

As you probably could tell, this paragraph is arranged on an outside/inside scheme—a description first of the approach to the stadium, then of the entrance area, and finally of the park itself. Many other kinds of spatial sequence are possible.

Exercise

Spatial Sequence in Descriptive Paragraphs

In the following paragraph, the sentences are not in the right order. Read the paragraph as it is. Then renumber the sentences so that they follow an outside/inside order.

(1) Continuing to the living room, we discovered bare wood benches and chairs separated by piles of dusty pamphlets. (2) On proceeding up the front walk, we saw further homey touches such as the porch swing and the newspaper rack by the screen door. (3) Just as bare was the dining room, which contained neither table nor chairs, but only a large altar and one church pew. (4) From the street, the house where the religious cult lived looked like a normal suburban home. (5) The rest of the downstairs was as empty as if the owners had just moved out. (6) We first noticed the manicured look of the lawn and shrubbery and the fresh, clean appearance of the red bricks and white shutters. (7) Most intruders by this time would want to escape anyway. (8) Only on entering could we tell that the house was inhabited by a group of strange people. (9) Although we thought we could hear chanting voices and footsteps upstairs, it was impossible to see what was happening since the door to the stairway was locked. (10) The entrance hall was painted reddish purple, and a stained glass portrait of Satan stared at the entering visitor.

Writing Assignment

Spatial Sequence in Descriptive Paragraphs

Think of a place that is familiar to you, such as a bus or train station, a courtroom, a classroom, a shopping mall, a church, mosque, or synagogue, a supermarket, or a video arcade. Visualize the scene as specifically as you can, and brainstorm all the descriptive details you can remember. Arrange the items in two or three spatial categories, such as front, middle, back, or left, middle, right. Then write an exploratory draft, remembering to begin with a topic sentence in which a key word or phrase identifies the overall quality of the place. Read over your draft to find gaps that need transitional expressions. Make any improvements in word choice or grammar that are needed. Write a final draft.

Critical Thinking in Descriptive Paragraphs

Describing someone or something in words is not quite the same as taking a photograph. A person is not a camera that simply records scientifically what is in front of it. Each person perceives a given scene differently, influenced by his or her own experiences and mindset. A person who looks old to a teenager might seem young to an elderly person. One viewer might notice a person's clothes, another her hair, and a third the expression on her face. This does not mean they necessarily disagree, just that they emphasize different details and judge according to different standards. A homeless person might regard $30,000 a year as a big income, while Bill Gates might see it as near poverty—even though both would be thinking of the same number of dollars.

When you write a description, then, you are actively seeing and interpreting what you see. There is not just one correct description for a particular scene; two very different ones could both be valid. Both descriptions should, however, report the facts accurately and avoid distorting what the writer knows to be true. The difference will lie in how each writer interprets the meaning of the person or object being described.

Group Project

Critical Thinking in Descriptive Paragraphs

Together with your writing group, choose one of the photographs on the next page. Give the person an imaginary name, and write a paragraph in the third person (Betty is reading, Sam is worried), describing the person from the outside, how he or she looks, how he or she is positioned in the picture, and what he or she is probably thinking. (Remember to watch your S endings on verbs with a singular, third person subject: she look_s_, he talk_s_.) Read all of the paragraphs aloud and compare them. What did all of the paragraphs say that was the same? What differences are there? Have each writer try to explain why he or she had a different perception of the picture than other members of the group. Write a second draft of the paragraph, including ideas that may have occurred to you as a result of the group discussion.

Exposition: Comparing, Explaining, Defining, Classifying, Analyzing Cause and Effect★

COMPARATIVE PARAGRAPHS†

Creating paragraphs that compare people, places, experiences, or concepts is a valuable kind of writing practice. It will strengthen your ability to develop and analyze topics. Although few essays are devoted entirely to comparison, an experienced writer should be able to make clear, thoughtful comparisons whenever necessary.

When you compare, be sure to discuss both subjects together. Begin your paragraph with a topic sentence that mentions *both* persons or things, not just one. This way you will avoid the trap of discussing one, then the other, and leaving the reader to figure out how the subjects are similar or different. Which of these two sentences makes a better beginning for a comparison?

1. Making a film costs more than making a CD album.
2. Making a film is very expensive.

Either sentence might make a good topic sentence for a paragraph, but only Sentence 1 starts off with a comparison. We expect the writer to compare the costs of making films and making CD albums.

Three Kinds of Comparison

Parallels:	Pointing out similarities between two people or things
Contrasts:	Pointing out differences between two people or things
Comparison/Contrast:	Pointing out both similarities and differences between two people or things

The following three paragraphs illustrate the three main kinds of comparison. The first discusses the similarities between two countries, the second contrasts the differences between two sisters, and the third explores both the similarities and the differences between two jobs a student held. Notice that the topic sentences are focused and that they all make comparative statements.

★See the Expository Mode in Unit 3.
†Review adjectives and adverbs in comparisons in Unit 5.

Paragraph 1. Two Similar Subjects

As island monarchies, Japan and Great Britain have much in common. Both are small in land area but heavily populated, and both rely on the sea for food and imports. Each has a huge capital city that has played a major role in world affairs, and each has been in the forefront of industrial development. Although the surrounding ocean has enabled both to remain culturally isolated during some periods in history, the nearness of the continent has been the source of many wars over the centuries. Both peoples, in fact, derive from their neighboring continents, and their languages have close ties to continental languages—Japanese to Chinese picture writing and English to German and French. Over the centuries both nations have presided over great empires, both of which have disintegrated.

Paragraph 2. Two Different or Contrasting Subjects

My two sisters are so different in their attitudes toward work that it is hard to believe they come from the same family. Jill has always been a workaholic, while Joy always wanted to have a good time. When they were little girls, Joy would be skinning her knees in rollerblade races and begging Dad for money to buy candy while Jill was earning Mom's approval for her help with cooking and cleaning. In school Jill studied diligently and brought home stacks of homework. Joy, on the other hand, discovered that school was a social whirl and considered high grades the sign of a boring personality. In high school she was the favorite cheerleader; Jill was president of the honor society. Although Joy dropped out of college after two months, she has joined a country music group and expects to have a career on television without needing any higher education. Jill, with an M.B.A. and piles of honors, is heading up the corporate ladder.

Paragraph 3. Two Subjects That Are Both Similar and Different

My two jobs as coach of an amateur basketball team and as bartender required some of the same skills but offered different rewards. In both jobs I had to understand people and motivate them. The players needed cheering up when the team was losing, and customers at the bar told me their life stories, expecting me to be their psychoanalyst. Both jobs demanded cool control when tempers flared or fights broke out. Despite these similarities, the satisfactions from the two jobs were different. Besides the high pay, tending bar gave me the feeling that I had helped a few individuals and maybe given them a better outlook. Coaching, on the other hand, was volunteer work, but I received the satisfaction of inspiring teamwork and helping a whole group of kids grow together.

ATTENTION TO DETAIL

One important skill necessary in making good comparisons is the ability to notice many detailed similarities and differences. When beginning writers do not succeed in their efforts to compare, they often have not done enough brainstorming. They have found only a few similarities or differences and then given up. For practice, let's consider the similarities and differences between being in the army and working in an accounting firm discovered by a student named Steve. After really brainstorming, Steve thought of many similarities and differences.

Steve's Experience of Serving in the Army vs. Working in an Accounting Firm

Similarities	*Differences*
hard work in both	outdoor work in army; all indoors in firm
both required special training	hard basic training in army; short orientation period but learned on the job in accounting firm
worked mostly with men but with some women in both	military training tried to "make us men"; no emphasis on gender in company
had living quarters provided	lived in army barracks; lived at home when working
continued to learn in both situations	received electronics training in military; took night courses while working in firm
discipline needed in both	discipline imposed by officers in army; needed self-discipline to complete tasks in accounting
	physical and mental discipline in army; only mental discipline in accounting job
both provided upward opportunities	army would have required re-enlisting; accounting requires further degrees, which is my goal
dress code in both	uniform in military; conservative jacket and tie in business office
stayed in both about two years	assigned to many places in military; worked in same office in accounting firm
liked both experiences	hated military at first but got to like it; liked accounting job but started to get bored and wanted to move up

Exercise

Comparative Paragraphs

Choose the three sentences in the group below that would make good topic statements for comparative paragraphs.

1. Some people like snakes as pets.
2. Poodles are easier to train than Dalmatians.
3. Last summer was unusually hot.
4. My brother is less reliable than I am.
5. Knowing Spanish is more useful in business than knowing Latin.

Writing Assignment

Comparative Paragraphs

Brainstorm and make a list of the differences and similarities between yourself and another person close to you, such as a sibling, cousin, or friend. Make two lists: On the left write down all the similarities between yourself and the other person; on the right list the differences. Write an exploratory draft beginning with a comparative topic sentence such as "My sister and I are alike in our personal habits but very different in our career goals." Look over your work and read it aloud to a classmate. Decide what needs to be added, changed, or deleted. Revise and write a final draft.

Group Project

Comparative Paragraphs

Working with the members of your writing group, hold a brainstorming session on the similarities and differences between college and high school. Make two lists—one of similarities and one of differences. Then create a comparative statement for your topic sentence that provides a map for the paragraph, such as "College is a big change socially from high school but not much different academically." Finally, compose a group paragraph comparing college and high school. Pass the paragraph around, with one student after another adding a sentence. Look over your first draft; have the group recorder read it aloud. Decide as a group what needs to be added, deleted, or rearranged. Make revisions based on the group input. Write a final draft to read to the entire class.

"HOW TO" PARAGRAPHS*

Explaining how something happens or works is called **process analysis.** Explaining how to do something on the job is called **procedural writing.** Paragraphs of this kind follow a step-by-step plan and are not difficult to organize. However, they do demand great care: You have to be unusually clear and thorough. If, for example, you want to explain how to perform a certain computer applications procedure, such as using a spell check, you cannot make confusing statements or leave anything out; otherwise, the reader will be unable to do the procedure. We are used to giving instructions aloud, with the aid of gestures, tone of voice, and feedback from the listener. A writer can't use these devices. In a final draft, a writer's words have to say it all; he or she has no further chance to discuss what the reader does not understand. To guide the reader, use transitional words that refer to steps in a sequence, such as *first, next, then, after* and *finally.* Underline the transitional words in this "how-to" paragraph.

> *Doing your best on an essay examination requires a systematic approach. Before you do any writing, read the instructions and topics carefully so that you know how many topics you are to discuss and how much time you have for each. Next, choose your topic or topics according to your preparation and knowledge. Then, before actually writing, jot down the main parts of the essay and some of the important facts to support each main point. Only at this point are you ready to write. When you do write, be sure that your introductory paragraph includes a plan or "map" for your whole essay so that you and the grader will know just what you intend to cover. At last it is time to write the main body paragraphs and show how much you know about the subject. Be sure to include plenty of facts. If possible, end with a concluding paragraph that restates your chief ideas without repeating the words of the introduction. Finally, read your paper twice: once for errors in spelling, grammar, and phrasing, and once for revisions in content. If you have done all this, you may not earn an A, but you can feel confident that you have done your best.*

You also have to make sure that the reader can understand all of your terms. If you are writing for experts, use specialized terms; if you are writing for general readers, use understandable vocabulary and explain the meaning of all technical terms the first time you use them. Here is a paragraph explaining a process, how a particular emotional illness develops. Is the writer's vocabulary aimed at experts or general readers?

> *Anorexia nervosa is an emotional illness that leads some people, most often adolescent girls, to starve themselves. It develops in stages, begin-*

---

*See shifts of person and use of pronouns in Unit 5.

ning with normal dieting, often by people who are not much overweight in the first place. Social isolation leads to an obsession with food, weight, and exercise. If not treated at the beginning, the condition worsens to a stage in which victims may lose twenty percent of their weight, look like skeletons, have lowered pulse rate and body temperature, lose their menstrual periods, and have thinning hair. Next, in the acute stage, they may develop delusions about their bodies, imagining they are fat when they are terribly underweight, and go through rituals of excessive exercise and limited food intake. They become secretive and sometimes go on huge binges of overeating, after which they vomit the food to keep from gaining weight. Finally, some go into the chronic, or long-lasting stage, in which they can remain socially isolated and unhealthy for years. Some can even starve themselves to death if not given intensive psychiatric help.★

Group Project

"How To" Paragraphs

The diagram below is extremely simple, isn't it? Write a paragraph describing it. Give your description to someone who has not seen the figure. See if that person can follow your instructions and produce a perfect copy. Have your writing group, working together, draw a geometrical design, then write a paragraph instructing another group (which has not seen the diagram) how to draw it. Pass your paragraph to them and see if they can reconstruct your group's drawing from your instructions. Have them do the same for your group. No coaching: Each group's drawing must be done entirely from the written instructions. If errors occur, have the group discuss how you could change the instructions to make them more exact.

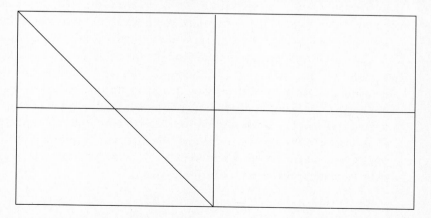

★Information from Steven Levenkron, *Treating and Overcoming Anorexia Nervosa*. New York: 1983. By arrangement with Wieser & Wieser, Inc., New York.

▶ Writing Assignment I

"How To" Paragraphs

Choose one of the following topics and write a "how to" paragraph. Remember to begin with a specific, clear topic statement and to develop your discussion step by step, using transitional words. First do a page of focused writing; then compose your paragraph. Revise and correct the final draft.

1. How to lose weight
2. How to behave during a job interview
3. How to choose a college
4. How to care for a cat
5. How to stop smoking
6. How to plan a wedding reception
7. How to earn high grades

▶ Writing Assignment II

Process Paragraphs

Write a paragraph explaining how some machine or apparatus works, how some condition like alcoholism or drug addiction develops, how people change when they become parents, or how students change when they go to college. Remember your reader: Write for the general reader, not the specialist.

DEFINITION PARAGRAPHS*

Writing a paragraph defining a term means more than giving a dictionary definition. Rather, the writer really discusses the word—what it means and what it does not. More than that, the writer discusses the experience, relationship, object, or idea that the word refers to. Defining *love,* for instance, is a way of discussing how people relate to each other; defining *success* is a way of discussing what people try to achieve in our society. In a good definition the writer includes examples, humor, or analysis to show the reader what the word really means.

Erich Fromm wrote a whole book defining *love,* for example. In *The Art of Loving,* he spent many pages examining the meaning of love, giving examples, describing types of love, identifying the characteristics of love, and distinguishing between real love and other feelings. That is an unusually long definition; in fact, it would be rare to find whole essays that do nothing but define a term. Defining terms, however, is a frequent practice in many kinds of writing. Learning to write accurate, thoughtful definitions will add a valuable component to your expanding repertoire of writing skills.

---

*See subject-verb agreement in Unit 5.

When you define a term, do not make a circular statement, as in this definition:

Love is the feeling you have when you are very fond of someone.

This statement is true, but it does not amount to much. It is almost like saying, "Love is the feeling of loving someone," or "Love is love." Think about the real meaning of the term, what it is and what it isn't, how you see it applied to real people and situations. Here is how Erich Fromm defined love. He identified four of love's necessary elements:

Beyond the element of giving, the active character of love becomes evident in the fact that it always implies certain basic elements, common to all forms of love. These are care, responsibility, respect, and knowledge.*

A definition usually places the term to be defined in a general category and then makes specific statements about its qualities or components.

Term	*Category*	*Description or Parts*
Love	Art	Care, responsibility, respect, knowledge

Here we can see how Dr. Fromm defined love: He said it is an *art* to be learned, like music, painting, or writing; then he identified its four main characteristics. Someone else might have called it a *feeling* or a *relationship* instead and described its parts differently. Here are two other definitions of love:

1. Love is a feeling that makes a person want to share another person's feelings and experiences.
2. Love is a relationship in which two people want to help each other grow and enjoy life.

Exercise 1

Definitions

Here are some one-sentence definitions. Underline the word or phrase that tells what category the term belongs in.

Example: A *shortstop* is a <u>baseball player</u> who stands between second and third base and catches ground balls and short fly balls.

---

*Erich Fromm, *The Art of Loving.* New York: Harper & Row, 1956.

1. A *soft sell* is a sales technique in which the salesperson uses tricky psychological methods to persuade the customer.
2. A *bomber* is a divorce lawyer who overpowers the ex-spouse's attorney and wins a lot of money for his client.
3. A *deadbeat* is a borrower who never pays back the money he or she owes.
4. A *browser* is a software program used to look at various resources on the Internet.

Definition paragraphs begin with one-sentence definitions and discuss the characteristics or parts of the thing being defined. You can see how the definitions just given could easily become topic sentences for whole paragraphs. Each needs examples or explanations to help the reader understand the term better. If we begin by defining *soft sell* as a sales technique in which the salesperson uses tricky psychological methods to persuade the customer, we would continue the paragraph by giving descriptions of some of these methods. We would tell how some salespeople flatter customers, pretend to agree with them, or make them think their purchase will give them prestige.

Here is a paragraph written by the famous author of a book on baby and child care, Dr. Benjamin Spock. Read the paragraph carefully and underline the term that he is defining.

> Much more dangerous than the open antagonism of one individual toward another...is the readiness of a majority of human beings to mistrust or hate whole groups of people with whom we have little or no acquaintance. Psychiatrists call this displaced hostility. It is derived from the antagonism that was first built up in all of us in early childhood toward family members. As we grew a bit older we sensed that since we were utterly dependent on them we must stay on the right side of them. And increasingly our parents and other teachers made us feel deeply guilty about hating them. So we learned to displace. In early childhood we are apt, in our society, to fear and hate witches, ogres, kidnappers, and other fiends that we hear about and that appear in our bad dreams. By the time we are six or eight we are ready to pick up and carry into adulthood the prejudices of the family and neighborhood against groups of real people. The less we know them in actuality the more easily we can imagine them as evil and fear and despise them.*

Dr. Spock's paragraph defines the term *displaced hostility* by explaining the feeling many people have toward groups, races, or nations they consider their enemies. He tells how this feeling originates in our childhood hostility toward family members and is later redirected toward strangers.

---

*From *Decent and Indecent*, Revised Edition, by Benjamin Spock. Copyright 1969, 1970 by James M. Houston, trustee. Used by permission of Dutton Signet, a division of Penguin Books USA Inc.

Exercise II

Definitions

Write one-line definitions for three of these terms:

Generation X	nerd	prerequisite
role model	hip-hop	elective course
superstar	virtual reality	gridlock

Writing Assignment

Definition Paragraphs

Use your imagination to write a paragraph defining one of the following terms. In your paragraph discuss the meaning of the term by analyzing, giving examples, expressing feelings, using personal experience, or identifying the sources of the concept. Remember, this is not a one-line dictionary definition, but a *discussion* of the term.

creativity	heroism	multiculturalism
beauty	intelligence	racism
courage	education	individualism
friendship	liberated woman	success

CLASSIFICATION PARAGRAPHS*

A paragraph can break down a large subject into categories. Writing paragraphs in which you classify subjects is good practice in clear thinking and organizing. Your main groups should belong in the same overall class but not overlap. Read the following sample paragraph, noticing the use of transitional words and the clear separation of categories.

Sample Paragraph

There are three main kinds of addiction: dependency on chemical substances, on patterns of activity or behavior, and on people. Addiction of the first type is familiar to everyone in the form of drug addiction and alcoholism. However, it also includes dependency on such substances as tobacco, coffee, and sedatives. Addiction to patterns of behavior includes excessive television watching, playing video games, gambling, eating, exercising, and sleeping. The third

*See Sentence Variety in Unit 4.

form of dependency is the immature reliance on and need for another person or persons, as opposed to a productive relationship in which both partners gain and contribute out of free choice. What characterizes all forms of addiction is an inability to function well without the habit, along with a destructive effect on the person's life and social relationships.

This paragraph explains that there are three kinds of addiction, and that they have certain things in common. The purpose of dividing a subject into categories is to understand it better. In this case, we understand what makes addiction undesirable, even when the addiction is to a good thing, like a relationship or exercise. Sometimes we can see something clearly only when we identify its different types. In biology, we divide animals and plants into many categories by a system called **taxonomy.** Biologists can name what species, genus, family, and so on a particular animal or plant belongs to. Such systems of classification help us understand many other things as well.

Try the following exercises to sharpen your powers of classifying.

Exercise I

CLASSIFICATION PARAGRAPHS

Identify three main groups in which all the people in the following list can be placed. List all of them under the appropriate headings.

Albert Gore	Richard Gere	Daniel Moynihan
Dwight Gooden	Carl Lewis	Lawrence Fishburne
Martin Lawrence	Pat Buchanan	Janet Reno
Robert Dole	Macaulay Culkin	Alfonse D'Amato
Monica Seles	Billy Dee Williams	Dennis Rodman
Dan Quayle	Marion Barry	George Foreman
Susan Lucci	Gary Shandler	Christine Whitman
Steve Young	Leslie Nielson	Dianne Feinstein
Wayne Gretzky	Boris Yeltsin	La Toya Jackson
Julio Iglesias	Sandra Bullock	Cal Ripken

Exercise II

Classification Paragraphs

Divide each of the following subjects into three categories—that is, identify three types of colleges, cars, and so on. Do not let the categories overlap.

Colleges: 1. private four-year colleges   2. state universities   3. community colleges

Movies	Professors
Cars	Stores
College students	Television programs
Friends	Politicians
Investments	Vacations

Writing Assignment

Classification Paragraphs

Write a paragraph explaining the three main categories of one subject in the preceding list. First do a brainstorming list including as many examples as possible; then, identify at least three main categories into which the examples fit. Write an exploratory draft describing these categories and providing an example of each. Read your paragraph aloud; write a final draft.

Group Project

Classification Paragraphs

Working with your writing group, choose one of the topics below and divide it into at least three categories. Have each member of the group identify a different category and write several sentences describing it. The group recorder should then assemble the separate sentences into one paragraph and read it aloud. Discuss the paragraph and suggest transition words and changes in sentence form to make it read as a unified, smoothly written paragraph. The recorder should write your final draft.

Types of students	Types of automobile drivers
Types of mothers	Types of shoppers
Types of teachers	Types of television watchers
Types of friends	Types of dressers

CAUSE AND EFFECT PARAGRAPHS*

Often in college assignments you will have to analyze the causes of something—inflation, wars, unemployment, drug addiction, scientific progress, or changes in fashion and artistic style. To write such examinations or term papers

---

*See subordinate conjunctions and fragments in Unit 5.

well, you will have to study the subjects and do research. To prepare now for such advanced writing, you can create paragraphs in which you explore such causes and effects by using information from newspaper reports, personal experiences, and what you have learned from parents and teachers. You can explore most issues intelligently without being an expert, but good analysis requires you to do more than express your opinion: You must support it with clear reasoning, facts, experience, and examples.

In cause/effect analysis, good writing cannot be separated from clear thinking. Use your common sense and keep an open mind. Remember a few guidelines:

Critical Thinking Rules for Cause and Effect Analysis

Rule 1. Don't jump to conclusions.

Do focused writing on your topic; brainstorm. Instead of settling for the first explanation that pops into your mind (usually the one that everyone automat-ically comes up with), test it. Could it be wrong? Could it be only one expla-nation among others?

Rule 2. Don't oversimplify.

Most important social problems and historical events have many origins. Con-sider indirect causes as well as direct causes. Remember that something occur-ring <u>after</u> something else is not necessarily <u>caused by it</u>. Don't treat a controversial opinion as a well-established fact.

Rule 3. Avoid making scapegoats.

When discussing the causes of a problem, try not to blame everything on the same old convenient villains. Television, for instance, is blamed for everything from poor school performance to violence in the streets and sex crimes. How do we know that it really is <u>the</u> cause, not just one of many causes? Is it the most important one?

Rule 4. Do your homework.

If you write an analytical paper for a specialized course such as sociology or his-tory, back up your statements with facts from the assigned readings or research. The instructor is interested less in your personal *opinion* than in your *conclusions* based on an analysis of what you have read.

In the following paragraph the writer began with a topic sentence and stayed on the topic by discussing one cause of crime. In what way, however, did he fail in this first draft to make a thorough analysis of the problem?

Poverty is the cause of crime. Poor people steal because they can't get money any other way. How can the government expect to get rid of crime when there are so many people without jobs or a decent income to live on? The cost of living keeps going up for poor people, and they have to go out and commit crimes to pay the rent and put food on the table. All the government has to do to eliminate the crime problem is provide jobs and housing for the poor. It's the government's fault that the crime rate keeps rising. People who have decent housing, food, and clothing do not commit crimes.

After getting feedback from readers, this writer discovered that he needed to make revisions, since many readers disagreed with some of his points. He realized that he had oversimplified the problem and made a scapegoat of the government. Not that he was completely wrong; he simply had to focus his argument better and support it with better reasoning.

Revision of Cause and Effect Paragraph

The writer then did a cluster to explore all the causes of crime he could think of (see following page).

Next he wrote a revised draft in which he recognized the complexity of the issue:

Poverty is often said to be the chief cause of crime. But the real cause cannot be poverty alone, since some very poor communities have little crime and since most poor people are not criminals. The greater problem is poverty in the midst of a rich society, a society in which crime has become a means of making quick money. Some people who become accustomed to a life of drug peddling, car stripping, or working for organized crime syndicates believe that they can rise out of poverty faster and farther through crime than by doing legitimate work. They look around and see many prosperous and some extremely rich people who did not necessarily work hard for their money, and they want to grab the easiest money they can get. Crime has become a major "career," with a nationwide annual income of more than $100 billion. As long as this situation continues, and as long as people born into poverty believe that crime offers as promising an "occupation" as anything else, the United States will continue to have an enormous amount of crime.

Police seen
as enemy

Crimes against
minorities condoned

Poor schooling

Distrust of law

Fantasies of
high lifestyle

Racism

Poverty

Unemployed teenagers

Ghetto conditions

Low self-esteem

Causes of Crime

Organized crime

Lure of glamour
and quick money

Slow court system

Drugs

Poor Enforcement

Need for money
to buy drugs

Drug lords
admired

Teenagers not
penalized

Light sentences

Not enough police

Writing Assignment

Cause and Effect Paragraphs

Do a page of focused writing on one of the topics below. Use this exercise simply to explore the range of your ideas on the subject. Look over your page and try to identify the precise cause or effect involved. Create a cluster in which you place the main cause (or effect, depending on the topic) in the middle and some secondary causes (effects) surrounding it. Then identify specific details associated with the secondary causes and write them in smaller balloons. Next, write a rough draft of a paragraph beginning with a precise topic sentence. Develop the paragraph in climactic sequence, using reasonable arguments and whatever facts you have. Read the paragraph aloud and get feedback from others. Revise and correct; write a final draft.

Suggested topics:
1. Why did a particular performer, performing group, or athletic team succeed?
2. Why did a particular product or program catch on with the public?
3. Why do so many people get divorced?
4. Why do many students drop out of high school (or college)?
5. Why do many teenagers smoke even though they know it will harm their health?
6. How does having children change people's lives?
7. How does being rich affect people's behavior and attitudes?
8. How does a college education improve the quality of a person's life?
9. How does American society benefit from having immigrants?
10. How does being unable to read limit a person's life?

Persuasion: Writing to Convince★

Writing that explains why the reader should believe something or why society should do something is called **persuasive writing.** In this kind of writing you are trying to change someone's opinion or give reasons why the opinion is correct. Here are some places you will find persuasive writing and speaking outside the classroom:

- political speeches and debates
- advertisements on television and in magazines
- editorials in newspapers and editorial comments on television
- arguments in private life
- business reports that recommend new policies
- lawyers' speeches in court
- sales pitches in automobile showrooms and stores
- books that recommend changes in laws or public attitudes

© 1998 by Addison-Wesley Educational Publishers Inc.

★See mixed sentences and pronouns and antecedents in Unit 5. See also The Persuasive Mode in Unit 3.

These kinds of persuasive writing and talking can range from a few words to a whole book. In writing persuasive essays, you will develop skills that strengthen your spoken and written communication.

Every attempt at persuasion can be boiled down to one topic sentence. The speaker or writer argues that something *should* or *ought* to be done. Persuasive paragraphs frequently use words like *should, ought, might, must, have to, could, probably, likely, possibly, certainly,* and *undoubtedly.* Such words measure what the writer thinks should be changed in people's attitudes or actions. These words signal *why* relationships—causes, effects, and consequences. They link motives and reasons to actions. Learn to use them correctly in your own paragraphs.

Here are some *why* statements and *should* statements that could serve as topic sentences for persuasive paragraphs:

1. High school graduates should work for a year or two before entering college.
2. Students should be allowed to earn credits for courses they can take on computers without attending classes.
3. The care of elderly people is the responsibility of their families, not the government.
4. Important laws should be passed by a public vote (referendum) rather than by the Congress.
5. Too much emphasis on athletics could damage the academic reputation of a college.
6. Elementary schools should provide activities for children until parents get off work in the evening.
7. Colleges should include computer skills as a requirement for degrees in all majors.

Critical Thinking Rules for Persuasive Writing

Rule 1. Be logical and fair.
Don't oversimplify or exaggerate. If you level with your readers, they will respect you and more likely be persuaded. Follow the Critical Thinking Guidelines in Unit 3, pp. 148–49.

Rule 2. Support your opinion.
You won't convince anyone if you just keep restating your opinion. You have to give facts, reasons, examples, testimony (other people's opinions), and personal experience to make a strong case.

Rule 3. Remember your readers.
They have the right to disagree and are not necessarily stupid if they do, so don't insult them. Consider the objections they might have to your position and try to answer their objections.

Which of these two statements is more persuasive?

    A. Karen excels in calculus because she comes from Colorado.

    B. Karen excels in calculus because she had excellent mathematics courses in high school.

<u>Sentence A violates Rule 1.</u> It is not a logical statement; the writer imagines a cause–and–effect connection that does not exist. Sentence B is logical. Excellent high school math courses often do prepare students to do well in college math.

Which of these statements is more persuasive?

    A. Women can never be good police officers; police work is not women's work.

    B. Women can be effective police officers. Commissioners' reports from five major cities show that female officers have performed as well as male officers.

<u>Sentence A violates Rule 2.</u> The writer states an opinion but does not back it up with evidence. Sentence B makes a claim, then backs it up with a fact. Sentence B is more persuasive.

Which of these statements is more persuasive?

    A. Foreign cars are usually more expensive to repair than American cars, because the imported parts cost a lot.

    B. Anyone who buys a foreign car is not only stupid but disloyal to the American way of life.

<u>Sentence B violates rule 3.</u> The writer insults readers who already own foreign cars without providing any support for the opinion. Sentence A makes a more careful claim and backs it up.

Which of the following two paragraphs provides more evidence to support the topic statement?

    A. *The mall on Palm Boulevard is a convenient place to shop. Last weekend my mother and I spent four hours there. We bought a pair of slacks for each of us, a clock radio, and a quartz watch. Then we had a terrific pizza at one of the restaurants. Later we just browsed around, looking at the boutiques and antique shops. There is a lovely indoor fountain with an artificial waterfall, into which we threw pennies for good luck. Mother felt really energetic that day because she had been down with the flu and was excited about getting out and enjoying the crowds for a while. After two hours, though, she began to get tired and so did I, because there was so much to do.*

B. *The mall on Palm Boulevard is a convenient place to shop. The wide variety of stores allows for one-stop shopping. There are two enormous supermarkets, a half dozen drug stores, fifteen clothing stores of different kinds, three furniture outlets, four sporting goods stores, a high-quality department store, two stationery shops, and fifty-three smaller retail shops of all kinds, from boutiques to coin and stamp shops. Parking is no problem, with a large free parking lot at each end of the mall and a small one with meters near the middle entrance. Benches are located every two hundred feet for the benefit of weary shoppers, and there is easy access to rest rooms. Customers who want to break for lunch have a choice of restaurants offering six different ethnic cuisines, and there are two fast food restaurants for those in a hurry. Mothers with small children can take advantage of an inexpensive child care service. And if you run short of money, four bank branches with twenty-four-hour cash machines allow you to continue shopping without leaving the mall. Nothing is missing that could make for easy, convenient shopping.*

The two paragraphs above show the difference between casually expressing an opinion and really backing it up with evidence. Paragraph A relies on personal experience more than factual evidence and even goes off the topic. It reads like a personal letter. A reader who does not know the writer personally wants to know the kind of information given in paragraph B, not gossip about the writer's personal life. The kind of evidence you include, then, depends on the point you are making and the sort of reader you hope to persuade.

Critical Thinking Exercise

Persuasive Statements

Explain whether each of these sentences seems persuasive. If not, explain what is wrong with it. In each sentence, identify the conclusion reached and the evidence or claim given to support it. In each case, ask yourself the following questions:

- Is the claim or evidence true?
- Does it actually support the conclusion?
- If it is true and supports the conclusion, is it adequate, or is more evidence needed?
- If the evidence does not make the conclusion convincing, what kind of evidence would make it convincing, or how could the conclusion be reworded to make it convincing?

1. The testimony must be false because it was given by a police officer, and police officers always lie on the witness stand.
2. You should get some advice from an experienced money manager before investing a lot of money, because inexperienced investors often make big mistakes.
3. Young people should not follow their parents' advice because the world has changed a lot since their parents were young.
4. Cigarettes should be made illegal because smoking harms people's health.
5. Beverly would make a good lawyer because she likes to help people.
6. The new situation comedy is excellent: The acting is outstanding, the events are believable, and the dialogue is hilarious.
7. Eileen has better taste than Judy because Eileen shops at more expensive stores.

Group Project

Persuasive Paragraphs

Working with your writing group, read the following two case studies. Discuss both situations with your group, considering all the options faced by the people in each case. Analyze the pros and cons of each alternative. Choose one of the case studies, and have each member of the group write a letter to Ms. Cruz or to Shirley and Mark advising them on what to do in their situation. Read your letters aloud and compare the reasons you each gave for your opinion.

Case 1

Ms. Cruz is the principal of a high school in a metropolitan area. A group of students has come to her requesting that the school distribute free condoms and include discussions of contraception, teenage sexual behavior, homosexuality, and AIDS in the required health education course. Ms. Cruz herself thinks that the course is behind the times because it says little about these topics, but she knows that some students and parents will object strongly. What should she do?

Case 2

Shirley and Mark have been married two years and live in Los Angeles. Both have career ambitions: He is a social worker employed by the city and has a private practice as a therapist; she works for a large educational software company. Shirley's firm wants to promote her and move her to Boston, where she will be in charge of a new project and will have a much higher salary. Mark knows that if they move to Boston he will eventually be able to get a job and set up a new private practice, but the move will set him back in his career. Shirley really wants to accept her company's offer. What should they do?

Revising Paragraphs: A Review

Creating effective paragraphs is a step-by-step process. First, you explore the range of the topic and your ideas about it by doing prewriting activities; then, you compose what seems to be a pretty good paragraph, but you still are not finished. Finally comes the challenging part: revising it to make it the best paragraph you can make it.

Paragraph revision can be of several kinds, depending on what the paragraph needs. The main types of revision are these:

- Revising the topic and topic sentence to give the paragraph a clear focus (see page 36)
- Revising unity to make the paragraph stay on the topic from beginning to end (see page 45)
- Revising organization to give the paragraph better coherence (see page 48)
- Revising development to make sure the paragraph says enough about the topic (see page 60)

You have already revised paragraphs in previous exercises. Now it is time to review these kinds of revision that paragraphs often need in order to make revision an important stage in all of your writing assignments.

REVISING THE TOPIC SENTENCE

Always check your paragraphs to be sure the topic sentences make clear statements and that the paragraphs really support the topics. In the paragraph below, revise the topic sentence to make it state exactly what the paragraph says.

Banks are really making large profits nowadays. Customers no longer have to wait in long lines to make deposits or withdrawals. Neither do they have to wait until the bank opens at 9:00 a.m. to make transactions, and you do not see people running at top speed to slip inside before the guard closes the door at 3:00 p.m. Now customers can do most of their business at automatic teller machines at any hour of the day or night. Because of the ATM machines, as well, bank patrons can easily keep track of their accounts, since at any time they can look up their current balance and see all the checks that have been cleared. Some customers also have bank cards that allow them to make payments directly from their accounts at stores and supermarkets without having to write checks or handle any cash. What is even more convenient is that now some customers do banking on their computers at home. They look up their account balances and even make electronic payments using their modems.

REVISING FOR UNITY

Read the paragraph below and underline the two sentences that are off the topic. Explain whether these two sentences should be eliminated or revised to make them relate to the topic and logically follow the sentences preceding them.

There are many good reasons why teenagers should not start to smoke. First of all, smoking pollutes the air and offends some of the people around them. Teenagers who smoke may have friends with health conditions like asthma who will suffer from the smoke. Another reason is that some students are athletes who have to stay in condition, and smoking will keep them from being in their best shape. Even more important, teenagers who smoke at an early age establish a pattern of substance dependency that includes alcohol and drug abuse, and teenagers usually do not realize how much easier it is never to start smoking than to give up such addictions later. Smoking is also a sign of an excessive need to conform. The latest fad is to wear rings on the nose and other parts of the body. Most teenagers who smoke are trying too hard to look grown up and impress their peers. The habit of always conforming to those around them then becomes an adult pattern that undermines their effectiveness as individuals. Equally important is the danger that teenagers will start ignoring hazards to their health and the health of others close to them. Smoking in restaurants is outlawed in most cities nowadays. Finally, smoking can be part of a generally irresponsible life style that involves many reckless habits like avoiding medical checkups, eating only junk food and driving under the influence of alcohol. Teenagers who smoke may think they experience no immediate harm from smoking, but all of these habits will get worse later and guarantee a shorter and less healthy life.

REVISING PARAGRAPHS FOR COHERENCE

Identify the organizing principle of this paragraph; then rearrange the sentences for effective organization, using transition words for a smoother sequence of statements.

Stephanie had some difficult times in college, but each year got better than the one before. Her senior year was the best of all; by this time she was doing well in her major, business administration, and she graduated with a 3.0 average and a 3.5 average in her major. She changed her major at the end of her sophomore year, so she had some problems with introductory courses and a required statistics course at the beginning of her junior year. She did manage to make progress by the

*second semester of that year. Her freshman year was very difficult,
because she had never lived away from home before, and it was hard
for her to adjust to living in a dormitory without her family nearby.
And she broke up with her boyfriend at the end of her first year, so
that just when she started getting adjusted, she had to put her life
back together emotionally. After living at home during the summer and
working in a gourmet store, she was able to face her second year with
much more confidence. As a sophomore, she actually began enjoying
college a lot for the first time.*

REVISING PARAGRAPHS FOR BETTER DEVELOPMENT

The following paragraph stays on the topic but does not develop it with enough
details. Brainstorm with your writing group and rewrite the paragraph, adding
examples and details to make it more informative, descriptive, and interesting.

*Television commercials are entertaining. All sorts of famous people
appear in them, saying and doing interesting things in unusual situations. You hear different kinds of music in commercials, from classical
to rap, and many famous musicians are used to make the commercials
more attention-getting. Many commercials are very funny because
they show unexpected things happening to ordinary-looking people.
Commercials also use plenty of animation, and they often include
children doing cute things.*

Review Exercise

Paragraph Revision

Read the paragraph below and identify any weaknesses you see in it. Consider whether it has an effective topic sentence, adequate development, smooth
transitions, and a coherent plan. Rewrite the paragraph, making all the
improvements that it needs.

*Attending college at night has as many advantages as disadvantages.
You may be tired when you go to class because you have been working
all day long, and you haven't had time to do all of your homework. Usually
there aren't any offices open either, so if you want to go see a counselor
or a dean or the financial aid office about a problem, you have to take
off work and go see them during the day. There aren't as many activities
for evening students to participate in, such as clubs and social groups.
Most of the classes in the evening are taught by part-time professors
who are less available for you to talk with outside class. Students in*

the evening are more mature. Usually they are older than day students,
and they take their work seriously. The selection of courses is not as
large in the evening as in the day. Parents who go to class during the day
have a child care center, but evening students have to find babysitters.
Still, I like going to college at night.

Computers and Paragraph Practice

Paragraph practice is especially well suited to word processing. Once you have learned the simpler commands of a word processing program, you become aware of the freedom you have to move large blocks of words anywhere you want. You can push phrases, sentences, and whole paragraphs around like hockey pucks. Like many students, however, you may at first feel bewildered by this power to rearrange your work and tend to concentrate instead on making smaller changes, such as correcting misspellings and grammatical mistakes. The prospect of reconstructing a whole essay by means of keyboard commands may seem too much to handle while you are still learning how to delete, insert, backspace, and so on.

For that reason, working with paragraphs can be excellent practice in learning to compose and edit with computers. You can see the whole paragraph on the screen while you are tinkering with it. You can even compare two versions of the same paragraph on the screen. Leave one as the original for comparison, copying it to the clipboard and reproducing it on your screen below the first. Then you can revise words, phrases, and sentences in the one below without worrying that you might lose something good in the process of editing.

This freedom to change without the fear of loss will enable you to make bigger changes and see the difference when you have finished. It will also allow you to add and insert material in an underdeveloped paragraph in a way that those who compose entirely on paper are often hesitant to do for fear of creating a messy copy. Working with paragraphs by themselves, you are much more likely to feel confident about making changes than with a whole essay because less computer expertise is required than in making major changes in a two- or three-page composition.

▶ Exercise

Practicing Paragraphs on a Computer

For extra practice in writing effective paragraphs, try revising some of the paragraphs you have composed while studying Unit 2. With each type of paragraph, try to improve your development by inserting additional relevant material. Try to rearrange the order of sentences whenever possible to improve effectiveness.

© 1998 by Addison-Wesley Educational Publishers Inc.

A. Narrative Paragraphs

Enter one of your narrative paragraphs on the screen; then insert additional sentences in the narrative in their proper chronological places. Next, delete one or two sentences from the narrative to see if you can improve the paragraph by removing less important details. Try to insert transition words like *then, next,* and *after that* where needed. Aim for the most effective sequence of sentences.

B. Descriptive Paragraphs

Enter one of your descriptive paragraphs on the screen. Identify vague, uninteresting, or inaccurate descriptive words and replace them with specific, vivid, and precise ones. Find phrases that lack descriptive words and insert effective ones. Add whole sentences if possible.

C. Expository Paragraphs

Enter one of the paragraphs you wrote in an expository pattern (comparison, definition, cause/effect, etc.) on the screen. Try to revise your sentence patterns and sentence length. If all of your sentences are short, combine several of them (see Unit 4 for sentence combining). If some are too long, break them up. If most of them follow the same pattern, rewrite several of them to lend variety to your style, or insert additional ones to break up the monotony. Keep on experimenting.

D. Persuasive Paragraphs

Enter one of your persuasive paragraphs on the screen. Try adding more statements to strengthen your argument. Experiment with changing the order of your arguments to achieve greater emphasis, putting the clinching point at the end.

Reminders About Writing Paragraphs

◆ **Identify paragraphs** by indentation at the beginning. Make them the right length (normally seven to twelve sentences for body paragraphs), and use them to help the reader recognize the parts of your essays.

◆ **Use topic sentences** with **key words** to identify the subject and the boundaries of each paragraph. The standard body paragraph begins with a topic sentence, although advanced writers often experiment with other patterns. To develop the habit of clear organization, practice writing body paragraphs that start off with topic sentences.

◆ Good paragraphs have **unity, coherence, transitions,** and **development.** Remember to make every sentence in a paragraph stay on the same topic and follow the sentence before it. Use transitional words and phrases to guide the reader, provide details to develop the paragraph enough to cover the topic.

◆ **Narrative paragraphs** are written in time sequence, with concrete details, transitional expressions, and correct verb tenses. When writing narratives, be careful to use correct verb forms, especially –ED endings, and do not shift verb tenses awkwardly between past and present. Use time markers to guide the reader.

◆ **Descriptive paragraphs** are written in spatial sequence, with limited topics and sensory details. Select descriptive words carefully, and use modifiers (adjectives and adverbs) correctly. In order to make your descriptive writing vivid, use specific, concrete words instead of general, vague ones. Use your thesaurus to remind you of possible synonyms.

◆ **Expository paragraphs** should contain thoughtful comparisons, clear process analysis, precise definitions, or logical explanations of cause and effect. Apply principles of critical thinking in your expository writing, and get feedback from readers to determine whether your explanations are clear.

◆ **Persuasive paragraphs** should convince the reader of an opinion through a reasonable presentation of arguments based on evidence. Apply principles of critical thinking in your persuasive writing, and avoid the traps of weak thinking, such as over-generalization, bias, lack of evidence, and oversimplification. Take a strong position, but show your open-mindedness by analyzing opposing views.

◆ **Practice writing paragraphs on computers** to improve your ability to develop and organize facts and ideas and to revise. Word processing is especially useful for paragraph practice because you can usually see your whole paragraph on the screen and watch as you make your revisions. Use the computer advantage to experiment with the wording, sentence patterns, content, and organization of your paragraphs. The habit of revision is your greatest asset in creating superior paragraphs.

UNIT

3

Writing Short Essays

Now that you have developed the ability both to write continuously for a page or two and to develop a specific point in paragraph form, you are ready to compose whole essays. To create superior essays, you must combine the skills you have been acquiring: developing and supporting your point, organizing material, and thinking critically. Like paragraphs, essays come in many lengths and categories. Some of them fit entirely into a single mode, but most combine several modes.

Recognizing the Essay

An **essay** is several pages of organized writing that makes one main point about a topic. It can be very long, but the essays you will practice will be about five to eight paragraphs, or about five hundred to twelve hundred words. Every college student should be able to plan, compose, revise, and proofread such essays.

Building Essays Out of Paragraphs

Paragraphs are the building blocks of essays. A successful essay contains the same elements as a good paragraph: *An essay should have a clear, limited main point; a logical arrangement; smooth, varied sentences; and correct spelling and grammar.* Like a paragraph, it should contain transitional words to signal relationships. It should have a recognizable beginning, middle, and end. However, it is not just a series of paragraphs strung together. The first paragraph makes a short introduction, the body paragraphs (there may be three, four, or five) discuss and illustrate separate supporting points, and the last paragraph briefly sums up and reaffirms the main point.

Here is a diagram of a two-page essay containing five paragraphs. This is a model you can use for many of your short essays. Notice its three main parts: the **introduction, body,** and **conclusion.**

Essay Diagram

Title	
Introductory paragraph arouses interest and states main purpose of essay. (3–4 sentences)	
Body paragraph #1 discusses first subtopic. (7–12 sentences)	Body paragraph #3 discusses third subtopic. (7–12 sentences)
	Short concluding paragraph sums up main purpose. (3–4 sentences)
Body paragraph #2 discusses second subtopic. (7–12 sentences)	
1	2

Study the following sample essay. It follows the diagram you just looked at, with an introduction, thesis statement, body, and conclusion. Write responses to assignments 1 through 5 in the Follow Up Exercise after the essay.

Sample Essay

Learning on the Internet

Introduction Some people think of the Internet as a huge videogame in which millions of "surfers" while away time skipping from one entertaining Web site to another with the flick of a mouse. While it is true that high technology provides unlimited opportunity for aimless entertainment, interactive technology also offers amazing new possibilities for serious learning. People can use the Internet intelligently for gaining knowledge, managing their money, pursuing special interests, and taking courses.

1st body paragraph One such use is information retrieval. Online access to reference material is becoming an unparalleled resource that will grow enormously in the next decade. Most standard reference works, such as dictionaries, encyclopedias, almanacs, thesauruses, telephone directories, and atlases are already available on the Internet, and more are being made available every month. Instead of having to make a trip to the library to find out information, you can look up encyclopedia entries, legal and political documents, word definitions, and telephone numbers in other cities without leaving your computer. No longer is there any reason to buy bulky, expensive reference works that take up space in your apartment or family room and become outdated in a year or two. Within a few years, even the most specialized and hard-to-find reference works will be available online. If your nine-year-old son is working on a geography project on India, he can look up articles in several encyclopedias using the World Wide Web. If you want to travel to central Europe, you can download maps from atlases to work out the details of your itinerary.

2nd body paragraph Another serious use for the Internet is money management. Many banks now have connections for customers to do much of their banking at home, looking up their balances, paying bills by computer, transferring money between accounts, and paying credit cards. Investors can get large amounts of information regarding stocks, mutual funds, and bond markets through a variety of services on the Internet as well. Prices on stocks are available almost up to the minute, and many conversation groups allow users to exchange financial advice. Books and magazines specializing in business, finance, and investing are now conveniently available online as well. Just as computers have almost created the "paperless office" in the business world, computers are bringing us near a "cashless" world of spending, saving, and investing.

3rd body Paragraph   For those who want to pursue a special interest, whether as part of their profession or as a hobby, the Internet offers access to a rapidly expanding number of special interest groups. These enable you to exchange opinions and information with others who share your interest, whether it is modern philosophy, Jane Austen, African-American films, or the Civil War. Electronic bulletin boards display the most recent announcements of events related to the subject and may provide more current information on recent developments in the field than you are likely to find anywhere else. Although such materials are not a substitute for good books on a subject, hypertext materials available on the World Wide Web combine sound, graphics, and written text in a way that a book cannot.

4th body paragraph   If you want to take courses for credit on the Internet, a number of colleges already offer that possibility, and many more are certain to follow. For people who find it inconvenient to live on a college campus or travel to one, courses by computer provide distance learning opportunities. Unlike correspondence courses of a generation ago, online courses sometimes allow for electronic communication between student and teacher, with virtual classrooms beginning to serve nearly the same function as actual classrooms. Furthermore, multi-media materials make the experience far more interesting and lifelike than any academic experience other than the classroom itself. Furthermore, colleges and high schools are now able to use distance learning technology to make available not only reference materials from around the world but also actual courses taught at remote campuses.

Conclusion   Of course you will always be able to use the Internet for downloading the latest jokes about lawyers or politicians, but serious users are already finding the resources of the Internet valuable and irreplaceable for more important purposes. As the number and variety of its services increase rapidly over the next few decades, serious applications of the Internet for reference purposes, money management, education, and research on special interests can only expand greatly.

> ## Follow-Up Exercise

Building an Essay

1. In your own words, state the main purpose of this essay.
2. Identify similarities between the introductory paragraph and the concluding paragraph.
3. Explain the differences between the introductory paragraph and the concluding paragraph.

4. Identify the subtopics of the body paragraphs (paragraphs 2, 3, and 4).
5. Explain the method used to develop the body paragraphs.
6. List five transitional words or phrases that signal connections between statements.

Practicing Thesis Statements*

The **thesis statement** is the sentence that explains the main purpose of an essay, much the way a topic sentence explains the purpose of a paragraph. Since the skills in writing thesis statements are similar to those used in writing topic sentences, this might be a good time to review the topic sentence in Unit Two, pp. 36–45. Like a topic sentence, a thesis statement can be just a short, simple sentence stating an opinion or attitude. It may, however, divide the main idea into two, three, or four parts. A thesis statement has to be broader than the topic sentence in a paragraph, since the thesis statement must cover the material for a whole essay.

Simple Thesis Statement:
People can use the Internet for serious purposes.

Developed Thesis Statement:
People can use the Internet intelligently for gaining information, managing their money, and taking courses.

Although a simple thesis statement is often satisfactory, a developed one provides a map for the rest of the essay and thus guides the reader more. Gaining information, money management, and taking courses are the subtopics for the body paragraphs in the sample essay. A simple thesis statement in this case would not guide the reader as clearly; it would not look forward to the topic sentences in the body paragraphs.

THESIS STATEMENTS MUST BE BROAD

Thesis statements must be broad enough to state the whole purpose of the essay. Why would the following sentence not make a good thesis statement for the sample essay?

---

*Since thesis statements often contain two or three items in a series, this is a good time to review parallelism, colons, and the use of commas in a series in Unit 5.

The Internet has over forty million users worldwide.

This is a specific factual statement. It does not provide a main idea or purpose for the total essay.

Exercise I

Thesis Statements

Identify which sentence in each pair might make a thesis statement for an essay:

1. A. The East Coast experienced a severe blizzard in 1996.
    B. Emergency response plans need to be improved in most large U.S. cities.
2. A. The Cowboys won the game 31 to 27.
    B. The game between the Cowboys and the Packers was full of suspense and unexpected reversals.
3. A. The current prison system lacks adequate means for rehabilitation and psychiatric counseling.
    B. The state prison at Capital City contains 1400 inmates.
4. A. Levels of alcohol in the blood can be tested by instruments.
    B. Drunken driving can be controlled better by strict law enforcement than by new legislation.
5. A. My vacation in Thailand was wonderful because I met some remarkable people and visited archaeological sites.
    B. I visited Thailand for two weeks in March 1996.

THESIS STATEMENTS MUST BE PRECISE

Although thesis statements must be broad enough to state the essay's main purpose, they should never be fuzzy or confusing. Remember that catchall words like *bad, good, nice, great, interesting,* and *thing* are not precise. What is good to one person is bad to another; what one person finds interesting another finds tedious. Try to find more precise key words for your thesis statements. Compare these two thesis statements:

A. *The Revenge of the Wimps* is a bad film.
B. *The Revenge of the Wimps* is a noisy, violent film with stiff acting and overused camera techniques.

Sentence A does not guide the reader much. It says only that the writer is going to make negative remarks about the film. Sentence B states what kind of objections the writer is going to make to the film.

Exercise II

Thesis Statements

Rewrite these sentences to make them more precise thesis statements:

Original Sentence: Reggie's first year in college was an important time in his life.

Revised Sentence: *Reggie's first year in college changed him from an adolescent to an adult.*

1. I had a good job last summer.

   _____

2. The neighborhood where I grew up was a nice place.

   _____

3. Working while going to college is a good idea.

   _____

4. Vacation Inn is a bad motel.

   _____

5. The courses at my college are interesting.

   _____

6. There are several things I don't like about television.

   _____

Group Project

Thesis Statements

Working with your writing group, compose precise, developed thesis statements for imaginary essays on these topics:

1. Teenagers and their parents

   Thesis statement: _____

_____

2. Television watching

    Thesis statement: _____

    _____

3. College courses

    Thesis statement: _____

    _____

4. Choosing careers

    Thesis statement: _____

    _____

5. Children and divorce

    Thesis statement: _____

    _____

Introductory Paragraphs

The first paragraph in an essay serves several purposes. Its main purpose is to let the reader know what the essay is about, usually in the thesis statement. Most writers, however, find starting with the thesis statement too abrupt. Instead, they lead up to the thesis statement in various ways. The three-step design of lead-in, tie-in, and thesis statement is a useful device for beginning writers.

STARTING WITH THE THREE-STEP DESIGN

Begin your paragraph with an effective **lead-in.** This attention-getter can be one of several types:

- A quotation or question
- A catchy remark
- A general, thought-provoking statement
- A surprising fact or statistic
- A problem or riddle

Be creative when you compose introductory paragraphs. Begin with a lively lead-in to capture the reader's interest; then find a way to focus that interest on the subject. The two or three sentences in which you do this are your **tie-in.** Finally, move smoothly from your tie-in to your thesis statement. The three-step design—lead-in, tie-in, thesis statement—will help you begin your essays successfully. As you become more experienced, you will find other effective ways to arrange your introductions.

The paragraph that follows serves as an introduction to an essay on the subject of computer technology in the office. Notice how it follows the three-step design for introductory paragraphs.

Model introductory paragraph:

"Future shock," a term from the title of a book by Alvin Toffler, means confusion caused by technological change. Nowhere is future shock more evident than in offices that have not kept up with recent advances in word and information processing. For the first time since the invention of the typewriter and the telephone, drastic changes in office procedures are occurring. Managers who hope to compete in today's business world must stay abreast of word processing software, electronic filing, computer networks, and new methods of communication.

Organized paragraphs like this do not result from your first efforts to write on a subject. First you must do plenty of prewriting to identify your main purpose and supporting details. Then you will need to write a rough draft of your introductory paragraph, perhaps even two or three, before you compose your final version.

HOW *NOT* TO BEGIN

If you try to compose an essay without any prewriting warm-ups, your introductory paragraph may have severe problems. For instance:

1. You may begin by apologizing for not knowing what to write:

In this essay I am supposed to write about the effect of computers. I don't own a computer and I'm not very good at word processing because I don't type very well. All I can say is that computers are very important and are here to stay. Every time I go into a magazine store, I see whole racks of magazines about computers. I wish I could understand everything they write about in those articles.

Compare this paragraph with the previous one about computers in the office. This one reads like a piece of focused writing; the writer is searching for something to say about the topic. The paragraph has no organization, no lead-in, and no thesis statement. Don't tell the reader what you don't know; explore what you *do* know through prewriting techniques until you find a good way to begin.

2. You may bore your reader by writing *too* much about what you are going to do in the essay:

> I am going to discuss computers in this essay. First, I plan to talk about how important computers are in today's world. My next paragraph will be about how computers are used in the home. Then I will discuss how computers are used in different kinds of businesses. Finally, I will stress how important computers will be in the future.

This writer has a clear plan but calls too much attention to it. No customer in a restaurant wants the chef to bring out all the recipes, pots, pans, and soup spoons used in preparing the food. Your reader also does not want to know the planning details. Leave the homework at home.

3. You may begin with grand, overblown statements that fail to lead into your thesis or contain any specific meaning★:

> Since the beginning of time human beings have invented new technological advances that have helped and hindered the progress of society toward perfection. In modern times of today, nothing has had a bigger impact on the way people live than one single invention: a machine called the computer. This machine will be remembered for all time.

Exercise

Introductory Paragraphs

Read the three sample paragraphs that follow. Identify the one that is carefully organized; find the *lead-in, tie-in,* and *thesis statement.* Explain why the other two would fail as introductory paragraphs.

A. Animals are one of the most important things on this earth. Animals have been around since human beings were created, and they come in millions of shapes and sizes. Most people could not live without animals, and many keep them for pets. If human beings ever get rid of the animals, it will be the worst crime in history. We should all be grateful for animals and learn all about them.

★If you find yourself having difficulty with this problem, study the section on wordiness in Unit 4.

B. Do animals have rights? In the past, we have heard about human rights, civil rights, and women's rights, but now for the first time we have groups demonstrating to protect the rights of animals. Such groups may strike some people as eccentric or silly, since we kill millions of animals for food, and we must sometimes perform experiments on animals to save human lives. But we should take seriously what the animal rights supporters are telling us: that other species have a right to exist and that we should stop unnecessary killing of animals and cruelty to them.

C. In this essay I am going to talk about the topic of animals. I once had a dog named Florence. It was sort of a poodle but it had big floppy ears. Otherwise, I haven't had much experience with pets, so I talked to my uncle about animals because he used to have a farm where he raised sheep and cows. He told me some funny stories about his animals that made me laugh out loud. Animals can be a lot more interesting than I realized, but I still don't know much about them.

Group Project

Introductory Paragraphs

Working with your writing group, practice writing an introductory paragraph. Choose an essay topic from the list below. Each member should then create a thesis statement for the whole essay. Read and compare your thesis statements. Once you have written thesis statements, each member should think of a lead-in that will arouse interest—remember to keep that first sentence short and lively. Now write the whole paragraph, perhaps four to six sentences—shorter than most body paragraphs. Read your first drafts aloud to one another. Check for words or phrases that need improvement and for errors. Write a final draft. Identify your lead-in, tie-in, and thesis statement in the paragraph.

1. Extracurricular activities in college: A benefit or waste of time?
2. College Curriculum: Should students be allowed to choose any courses they want?
3. Cheating on term papers and exams: Do many students do it, and why?
4. Safe sex: How can young adults protect themselves against sexually transmitted diseases?
5. Single parents: Can one parent raise children just as effectively as two?
6. Today's military: Why do young people join?
7. The etiquette of dating: Should women ask men for dates? Who should pay?

Concluding Paragraphs

Concluding paragraphs, like introductory paragraphs, are usually short. Although you can just stop when you run out of things to say in an essay, good writers usually make some concluding statements that leave the reader with a sense of completeness and a desire to think more about the subject. Like the opening, the ending of your essay should be dramatic, witty, imaginative, amusing, or thought provoking. It might be a question, a prediction, or a paradox. It should remind the reader of something you said at the beginning, but it should not merely repeat the information in the first paragraph. Think of the concluding paragraph as an upside-down version of the introductory paragraph. It may begin by reemphasizing the main idea (but not by restating the thesis sentence word for word) and end with statements that wrap up the discussion with humor, emotional appeal, or insight.

HOW *NOT* TO CONCLUDE

If you have not gone through the writing process sufficiently and really explored what you want to say on your subject, you may find yourself writing a concluding paragraph that is not a conclusion at all. Often you will need to write several pages in your exploratory draft before you discover your really original ideas. If you try to complete your essay in one hasty draft, your "concluding" paragraph may be the one in which these important new ideas finally come out. If this happens, either rethink the whole essay, using material from this "concluding" section as the main point of your essay, or rethink the concluding paragraph to make it fit the essay you have.

1. Do *not* use the concluding paragraph to introduce main ideas that are not supported in the essay. Consider this attempt at a conclusion to our imaginary essay on computers in the office:

> So we can see that computers have many benefits to offer businesses. This is why colleges should encourage students to take courses in computer programming and make sure all students have computer literacy. In fact, high schools ought to consider computer literacy a basic skill as important as reading, writing, and mathematics.

This paragraph jumps off the track. The essay is about computers in the office, but at the end the writer suddenly becomes interested in the implications of computers in education. The concluding paragraph is a bad place to change your topic, just when you should be stressing the points already made.

2. Another kind of conclusion that does not succeed in a short essay is the mechanical summary. Sometimes a very long piece of writing such as a book

or dissertation, especially if it is complicated, needs a summary to help the reader digest and remember the points made in it. In a short college essay, however, such a summary can bore the reader. Consider this paragraph as an ending to our essay on computers in the office:

> In summary, I have discussed in this essay some of the ways that computers make offices more efficient. The first way I discussed was electronic filing techniques. In the next paragraph I talked about word processing. Then I explained the advantages of high-technology editing. When you have read what I explained about these advantages, you will understand why it is important to know about computers if you work in an office.

This paragraph emphasizes the writer's plan when the focus should be on the topic itself. Give the reader a sense of order, and make some indirect reference to your opening, but don't overdo the repetition.

Sample Concluding Paragraph

Here is a more successful concluding paragraph to our essay:

> Knowing the equipment, filing techniques, and methods of writing and editing can be great a asset in today's office. Most offices across the country are rapidly replacing their outmoded procedures with computerized methods. Smaller companies may find the initial adjustment expensive, and some managers may feel anxious about giving up comfortable, old procedures. Nevertheless, the change pays off in the long run, and the pangs of change are easier to bear than the misery of suffering future shock while competitors hurry on ahead.

Note the use of the phrase *future shock* here. This phrase brings the essay full circle back to the beginning line of the essay (see page 106).

Group Project

Concluding Paragraphs

Look over the introductory paragraphs composed by members of your writing group in the previous exercise. Without actually writing a whole essay at this time, imagine that you have completed the body paragraphs on the topic. Now write an effective concluding paragraph that reaffirms your main thesis and broadens to suggest directions for further thought on the subject. End with a lively, thought-provoking finale. Read your first drafts aloud to one another and give one another feedback. Check your drafts for errors and ineffective words or phrases; revise, then write final drafts.

Modes of Developing Short Essays

In Unit Two you practiced writing paragraphs in the four rhetorical modes—narrative, descriptive, expository, and persuasive. Now you will apply the skills of development and organization you practiced in that unit in composing whole essays. Although the exercises in Unit 3 roughly parallel those in Unit 2, being grouped generally into the chief modes, you will not be merely repeating what you did in the previous unit. Essays not only require the writer to develop material much more extensively within a mode, they also may require the writer to borrow from one mode to develop another. A narrative essay may contain some description or analysis, just as a persuasive essay may contain elements of narration or description. In Unit 3 you are making more advanced use of the skills you acquired in Unit 2 and are becoming a more flexible, mature writer in the process.

The Narrative Mode: Telling About an Event

As you know from practice with narrative paragraphs, narration means telling a story. Like narrative paragraphs, narrative essays are arranged in time sequence, each paragraph marking one stage of the action. If you are telling about a trip you have taken, for instance, one paragraph might tell about planning for the trip, the next about getting to your destination, the next about what you did there, and another about your return. Although personal experiences happen in a steady flow of time, your paragraphs mark off the important phases of the experience, giving shape to the whole story. In your prewriting and exploratory draft, you need not pay close attention to each paragraph as a separate unit because you are engrossed in telling the story, but in the final draft be sure to divide your paragraphs wherever the story enters a different phase.

FIRST-PERSON NARRATION: TELLING ABOUT YOUR OWN EXPERIENCE*

You may choose to write in the **first person** in your narrative essay (*I, me, my*), telling about your personal experience.[†] First, brainstorm to collect interesting details about each phase of the experience. Narratives generally follow a before/during/after sequence; ask yourself questions about each stage to be sure you have included all the important facts. Here is an example of brainstorming done by a student as her first step in creating an essay about her experience of dropping out of high school, working, and finally going on to college.

----

*Review Narrative Paragraphs in Unit 2.
[†]Review personal pronouns and shifts of person in Unit 5.

Before

Question: Why did you drop out of high school?

Answer: I was bored. My friends were working and making money for clothes and going to parties. I wanted to be more grown up and live on my own. School was a drag.

During

Question: What was it like dropping out?

Answer: I thought it was cool at first. I got a job in the afternoons at a video store and worked on weekends at a movie theater. I made enough money to start enjoying my life.

Question: How did you afford to pay the rent?

Answer: My mom let me live at home for six months. She was so mad at me for dropping out of school that she kicked me out after that. First she thought she could make me go back to school, and then when she couldn't she thought that by making me leave she would prove she was right.

Question: Is that what happened?

Answer: Almost. It was harder making it on my own than I thought, but I did it for a while.

Question: How did you survive after you moved out of your mother's house?

Answer: My friend Sharon was renting an apartment and her roommate moved out, so I moved in with her. It was still hard to pay the rent, but it was fun at first. We gave parties and hung out with guys. I started working more hours to buy the clothes I needed.

Question: Did you miss school? Were you sorry you dropped out?

Answer: I missed some of my friends, but I didn't miss school. I wasn't sorry I dropped out. I am now, sort of. But I learned a lot by doing what I did.

Question: What made you decide to further your education?

Answer: I started getting tired of the work. It was hard getting up early every morning, especially if I was out late the night before, and my job was boring anyway. I started to realize that this is what I would be doing fifteen years from now if I didn't get more education.

Question: When did you go back to school?

Answer: I didn't. After my roommate started hanging out with some really dead-end friends, I really got worried about my future. I signed up for tutoring for the equivalency diploma test and started doing a lot of studying on my own. After eight months, I took the test and got my equivalency diploma. I was still only nineteen. I was shocked that I failed the test. Then I felt like giving up, but I didn't know where to go, so I studied some more and got some help from my high school guidance office. They told me where I could get more tutoring at nights, and I studied real hard all and took the test again in the spring. This time I passed.

After

Question: How did you get into college?

Answer: I knew I wouldn't get into a four-year college where I would need a high average, so I signed up at a community college.

Question: What were your plans?

Answer: I didn't know what I wanted to study, but I knew I had to do something that would get me higher paying jobs. At first I started as a liberal arts major. Then I wanted to get some kind of specialized training that would get me a good job after I graduated. I found out about physician's assistant programs and computer programming.

Question: How did you make up your mind?

Answer: I kept taking basic courses and went to the career counseling office to find out about job prospects and talk to counselors about what I might be good at.

Question: What did you do next?

Answer: I finally decided I wanted to be a medical social worker and work in a hospital. So I transferred to a four-year college that has a major in sociology and social work. If I do well I want to get a master's in social work.

Question: Do you think you would have done better if you had stayed in school?

Answer: No, because I wasn't grown up enough to get much out of it. I wouldn't have learned very much then and maybe wouldn't have wanted to go to college. I had to find out how hard it was making a living at low-paying jobs before I really wanted to further my education. Some of my friends who stayed in school still haven't gone to college and they mostly didn't get good jobs. Some of them are married and have kids, but most of the others went to college and expect to get high-paying jobs later.

Question: What did you learn from your experience?

Answer: I found out that you can make mistakes, and they don't wreck your life. They do mess you up for a while, but you have to go on, and if you have the right attitude and try hard, you can succeed even if you make some mistakes. Sometimes they aren't really mistakes because you have to do what you do at the time, even if other people think it's a mistake.

Like most brainstorming, this exercise produced plenty of ideas and facts than could be used in an essay, but it all needs to be put together into a continuous story. The next step is to write an exploratory draft using some of the brainstorming material, leaving out some of it, and adding details where needed.

EXPLORATORY DRAFT

Why I Went to College

When I was in high school, sixteen years old, I was so bored that I dropped out of school. Most of my friends were working and buying good clothes and jewelry and going to parties, and I wanted to enjoy my life more. I didn't think it made any sense to study about the Civil War and algebra or French because they didn't mean anything to me and they wouldn't get me a job later anyway. So I stopped going to school. For a while I pretended to be going to school so my mom wouldn't suspect it, but finally I just dropped out completely and told her I was going to get a job. Mom just about killed me when I told her. She was sure I was going to get pregnant and move in with some guy and probably commit crimes, but after a while she got over it, and I kept on living at home while I worked afternoons in a video store and had a job in a movie theater on weekends. She thought she could force me to go back to school and yelled at me every day about it, then she tried to convince me that it would make me happier if I went back. Finally she realized nothing was going to work that way, so after six months she kicked me out. She thought I would learn the hard way and go back to school. A television show she saw talked about using "tough love," which means don't spoil your kids if they have an attitude, just make them find out how to tell right from wrong by not having their parents to give them everything they want. I knew I wanted to live on my own, so I asked my friend Sharon if I could room with her. She had her own apartment and we were good friends. It was still hard to pay the rent even with two jobs, but it was fun at first.

We gave parties and hung out with a lot of guys. I started working more hours during the week so I could have money left over for clothes and other things I needed. I got tired by the end of the week and wasn't so sure what to do next. I didn't miss school, but I missed some of my friends that I saw in school, and my jobs were getting boring.

I always had a hard time getting up in the morning, especially if I was out late the night before. I began to realize that if I didn't do something, I would be doing the same thing fifteen years from now. I also could see that just changing jobs wasn't the answer because without any more education I would not be able to make much more money than I was making. My roommate began hanging out with some friends who were involved with drugs, and I started to get worried about my future.

I knew I would have to get more education if I wanted to do anything with my life. I didn't want to go back to high school because it made me feel like a little kid to do that, and I already felt like I was grown up. I signed up for some tutoring for the equivalency diploma test. I studied at nights and on weekends and eight months later I took the test. I was shocked when I failed the test. Then I felt like giving up, but I couldn't stand just working at a boring job for the rest of my life, so I went back to the guidance office at my high school to get help. They wanted me to come back to school, but I wasn't going to, so they helped me get better help to pass the equivalency test. This time I studied real hard and took the test in the spring, and this time I passed. That meant I could go to college. They told me in the guidance office that I wouldn't get into a four-year college because of my high school record, but I could go to a community college first and see how I could do.

That sounded like a good idea, so I started college. I was still nineteen, so I didn't feel much older than the other students. Some of them were twenty-five, and one woman who was divorced was thirty-seven and just starting college.

I was a liberal arts major at first. I didn't know what to study but I knew I had to learn something that would get me better paying jobs. I thought specialized training was necessary, and I found out about physician's assistant programs and computer science. I took basic courses for two semesters like math and English and chemistry. Then I went to the career counseling office, where they gave me some tests about my abilities and interests, and I talked to counselors about what I should study. After taking a course in psychology I decided that I wanted to be a social worker and work in a hospital or clinic. Since I had high grades, I applied to a four-year college that has a major in sociology and social work. I was accepted, and I am now in my junior year. I want to go on and get my master's in social work.

Sometimes I wonder if I would have done better if I had stayed in school, but I wouldn't have learned very much and probably wouldn't have wanted to go on to college. I had to find out how hard it was going to be for me without an education and then I really wanted it. I look at some of my friends who did stay in school, and some of them still haven't gone to college and they mostly didn't get good jobs. Some of them are married and have kids, too.

I found out from my experience that it can be okay to make mistakes and they don't always wreck your life if you don't give up. If you have the right attitude and try hard, you can succeed even when you make some mistakes. Sometimes they aren't really mistakes because they are what you have to do at the time, even if other people think it's a mistake. You have to do what works for you.

REVISING NARRATIVE ESSAYS

On rereading this essay in rough draft, the writer could see that there are some problems with the way it is organized and divided into paragraphs. Although there is a before-during-after sequence, some paragraphs are very short, and others are not divided in logical places. The writer decided that she would have to arrange her material so that each paragraph would mark a new step in the story. First she would tell about dropping out of school, then about moving away from her parents' home, next about living on her own. At that point, she realized, there were quite a few steps left: handling problems that started to happen, taking and passing the equivalency test for her General Equivalency Diploma, entering college, and finding a major and a new direction in life. Each of these phases in the story needed to have its own paragraph to tell about it completely.

Critical Thinking in Narrative Essays: Finding Your Main Idea

Points to Remember

- Identify the purpose of your narrative in your thesis statement. While revising your draft, be sure to identify your purpose clearly.
- Be sure that every paragraph not only tells about a stage in your story but also contributes to developing the main point.
- Consider suggesting your main idea in your title, and be sure it comes through in your introduction and conclusion.
- Get feedback from your writing group to be sure that your main idea comes across to the reader.

Even narrative writing requires critical thinking. A narrative tells a story, but every story has a meaning; most stories have several meanings. Often the best way to identify the meaning of your narrative is to read it aloud to a group and see how others interpret it. The meaning of your story, after all, is what it says about everyone's experience, about life in general. The writer of this essay got feedback from her group and decided that her most important idea was that she had become a stronger person even though she had made some mistakes because she had learned from them. So she decided to put this idea into her title and make it a thesis statement in her first paragraph. In the first draft the story reached a point at the end, but it was not clearly supported and developed throughout the story. Here is a revised draft with better organization, unified paragraphs, and a clearer main point that is introduced in the first paragraph and developed throughout the essay:

SAMPLE ESSAY: NARRATIVE MODE

Learning from Your Mistakes

Lead-in   Most people think of high school dropouts as losers. They think that not graduating from high school means that you will never make anything of yourself and you will probably end up on welfare or become a criminal. But sometimes when you make a mistake like dropping out of school, you can learn from your experience and make your life better. That's what happened to me after I left school. *Maybe I took a wrong turn in my life, but my future will be better because I was able to get back in the right direction.*

Thesis statement

Paragraph 2: Dropping out

When I was sixteen, I was so bored that I dropped out of school. Most of my friends had jobs so they could buy clothes and jewelry and go to parties, so I wanted to enjoy my life the way they did. It didn't seem worthwhile to study about the Civil War and algebra or French because these subjects wouldn't help me get a job. When I couldn't stand it anymore, I stopped going to school. For a while I pretended to be going to school so my mom wouldn't suspect it, but finally I dropped out completely and told her I was going to get a job. At first she wanted to kill me when I told her. She was sure I would get pregnant, move in with some guy, and turn into a drug addict or criminal. After about a week she got over it, and I kept on living at home while I worked afternoons in a video store and in a movie theater on weekends. She thought she could force me to return to school by yelling at me every day about it; then she tried to be nice and convince me that I would be happier if I did.

Paragraph 3: Moving out

Finally she realized that nothing would work that way, and she kicked me out. She thought I would learn the hard way and go back to school. She saw a television show that talked about "tough love," which means not spoiling your kids if they have an attitude and making them learn right from wrong by trying to make it without their parents' help. The idea didn't make me change my mind. I knew I wanted to live on my own, and I was determined to make it work. My friend Sharon had her own apartment, so I asked her if I could move in with her, and she agreed.

Paragraph 4: Enjoying life on my own

For a while, I had a new, exciting life. Although it was hard paying the rent even with two jobs, it was fun. We had parties and hung out with guys and went where we wanted any time we felt like it. I felt like an adult, making my own decisions about what to wear, what to eat, and how to spend my spare time. I started to work longer hours so I could buy the clothes I wanted, and sometimes I got tired, but I knew I was living the life I wanted and wasn't going back to school.

Paragraph 5: Problems

After about a year and a half, though, it became harder to get up every morning, especially after staying out late the night before. By the end of the week, I sometimes was completely exhausted, and it was hard to enjoy going to parties. Although I didn't miss school, I did miss some of my classmates. Then my roommate began to hang out with some friends who were into drugs, and I got worried. I had to make a change. I realized that if I didn't do anything, I would be doing the same kind of work fifteen years later. Changing jobs wouldn't help because without more education, I could never earn much more than I was making.

Paragraph 6: The equivalency test

It was time to do something. It would make me feel like a child to go back to school after living like an adult on my own. So I signed up for tutoring for the equivalency diploma test. After eight months of studying in the evenings and on weekends, I took the test. I was shocked to find out that I failed it. Then I felt like giving up, but I knew I couldn't stand to work at a boring job for low pay all my life, so I went back to the guidance office at my high school for help. I knew they would try to convince me to return to high school, but I refused, and they told me how to get better help with the equivalency test. This time I studied really hard and passed the test four months later.

Paragraph 7: Starting college

That meant I could go to college. Maybe dropping out would not hold me back so much after all. The guidance counselors at school said I wouldn't get into a four-year college, but I could start at a community college and transfer later. That sounded like a good idea, so I started college. As a freshman I felt self-conscious because I was already nineteen, but soon I learned that many of the students at community colleges are older. Some of them were twenty-five, and one woman in my psychology class had just gotten divorced and was coming back to college; she was thirty-seven. I realized that one reason I didn't like high school was that everyone treated me like a child. Now I was really a grownup, and my classmates were mostly older than I was.

Paragraph 8: Choosing a major

Uncertain what to study at first, I became a liberal arts major. I took basic courses like math, English, psychology, and chemistry for two semesters while thinking about my future. I wanted to get some kind of specialized training that would help me get a high-paying job. I found out about physician's assistant programs and computer science. Then I went to the career counseling office, where they gave me some tests to see what my abilities and interests were, and the counselors talked with me about what career I should choose. Since I liked my psychology course and got an A in it, I thought I would like to pursue a career related to psychology. I decided to become a social worker and work in a hospital or clinic. That would require at least a bachelor's degree and maybe graduate work. Since my grade point average was now very high, I applied to a four-year college that has a combined major in psychology and social work. I was accepted, and now I am in my junior year and plan to get my master's in social work.

Conclusion: What I learned

Sometimes I wonder if I would have done better if I had stayed in school. Maybe it was a mistake to drop out, but I wouldn't have learned much and probably wouldn't have wanted to go on to college when I graduated. I had to learn by working how much I needed and wanted a college education so I could get a really good job. Some of my friends who did stay in school have not gone on to college and they mostly did not find good jobs. Some of them are married and have children already. Looking at myself now in comparison to my friends, I believe that I did what was right for me. I learned that you can make mistakes and come out all right if you work hard and don't give up. Sometimes what seems like a mistake at the time turns out to be for the best.

Follow-Up Exercise

First-Person Narration

1. In your own words, state the main thesis of this essay. Explain what it says about experiences of your own or of your friends.
2. Explain how the author's experiences support this thesis statement.
3. Identify the similarities and differences between the introductory paragraph and the concluding paragraph.
4. Explain how the author organized the essay. Why did she put the body paragraphs in the order they are in? Explain what each paragraph contributes to the story.

Writing Assignment

First-Person Narration

Think of a change you have made in your life. Follow the stages of the writing process to create an essay about the experience. First, brainstorm or do focused writing to explore the facts and impressions you remember and group the material into stages—before, during, and after. Then look over your prewriting activities. What did the experience teach you? Write an exploratory draft in which you mainly try to tell the important facts and experiences. Put this rough draft away and look at it again a day or two later. Read it aloud to someone else; you and your listener together may be able to recognize your main idea and your attitude toward the experience. (The writer of "Learning from Your Mistakes" was obviously somewhat partly troubled by what happened, but she was proud of her achievement and ended on a positive note.) Once you have a clear idea of your main point and your paragraph groupings, write the organized second draft.

THIRD-PERSON NARRATION: TELLING ABOUT A PUBLIC EVENT

Third-person narration means telling about an event from the outside, either as an observer or as a researcher who has collected facts about the event. Factual narratives of this kind include news reports, magazine articles about important events, and books of history and biography. Short stories and novels are also third person narratives in which the events are imaginary. As a college student, you will no doubt write essays and term papers that either tell about historical events or trace the lives of famous people.

As in first-person narration, third-person narration should be based on a clear arrangement of paragraphs. As always, you should have an interesting lead-in and conclusion, and each body paragraph should focus on a single stage of the action. Sentences should follow smoothly one after the other with occasional transitional expressions like *next, after, then, soon, later,* and *meanwhile.*

When doing a narrative essay on an event, be sure to collect your important facts first and do some focused writing to explore your thoughts about the event.

SAMPLE NARRATIVE: WRITING ABOUT THE OKLAHOMA BOMBING

Let us consider, as an example, writing a short essay that will tell about the bombing in Oklahoma City in April 1995. Before trying to write a whole exploratory draft, let's collect some of the main facts about the event. All of us remember some of the main things that happened, but to be sure we are accurate and possibly discover a few details we didn't know about, we should always make use of available sources in the library, such as newspapers or magazines. If we look, for instance, at the reports from the *Time Daily News Summary,* we find the following facts:

Brainstorming the Facts

- At 9:02 in the morning on April 19, 1995 a bomb nearly destroyed the Alfred Murrah Federal Building in Oklahoma City.
- Of the 550 people in the building, at first about 300 were not accounted for. Remembering the World Trade Center bombing, many people suspected Islamic terrorists were responsible, especially because it appeared that a car bomb was used.
- Furthermore, the Islamic Society of North America had just had a conference in Oklahoma City.

- To most people's surprise, the two suspects taken into custody by the FBI turned out to be crewcut Americans belonging to the right-wing paramilitary fringe, Timothy McVeigh, and Terry Lynn Nichols.

- McVeigh, Nichols, and Nichols' brother James Douglas Nichols were linked to the Militia of Michigan, a recently founded group that blamed the government for the Branch Davidian disaster at Waco, Texas, which had also occurred on April 19 two years before.

- In the meantime, three Middle Eastern men held as suspects in Dallas were released, as was a Palestinian man brought back from London.

- The President and the First Lady attended a memorial service on Sunday, April 23 for the people killed in the blast. Eventually the number of dead would be put at 168.

- Americans had strongly conflicting attitudes about what to do next. There was wide support for tighter gun control, but at the same time, many Americans expressed anger at what they saw as the oppressive power of government and still supported gun ownership.

- Most Americans were deeply upset that the violence had come from within, not from an outside terrorist organization.

- Rescue efforts began immediately and continued for weeks. At the time of the blast, survivors within the building, including the injured themselves, even a man who had lost an arm and another who had fallen six stories, tried to help the injured. Efforts focused intensely on the day care center on the second floor, where many were already dead and a few remained to be rescued.

- Groups came to help from everywhere. The Oklahoma City police and local firefighters were joined the first day by the National Guard and the Air Force, as well as a special urban rescue team from Arizona. 100 doctors, about to leave for a vacation, all turned around and rushed to help. Churches, the Boy Scouts, the international relief group Feed the Children, the Red Cross, and hundreds of private volunteers helped care for survivors by donating blood, helped parents find and identify children, and provided every imaginable item needed for rescue and relief.

- Exactly a week after the blast, at 9:02 a.m., everything and everyone in the Oklahoma City area and in other towns and cities throughout the country observed a moment of silence in memory of the tragedy.

- Commentators throughout the country began to search for lessons to be learned from the explosion. Some mentioned the danger of "paranoid" thinking; others called for a toning down of the rhetoric of hatred and rage often expressed on the media, especially talk radio. Some congressional figures called for a closer look at the Branch Davidian disaster and wanted to investigate the Bureau of Alcohol, Tobacco, and Firearms for its alleged invasions of citizens' privacy.

- President Clinton asked Congress for more power to oppose terrorism through such means as hiring more federal agents, requiring public identification of explosive materials, and allowing the military to participate in law enforcement.
- As usual, both political parties looked for ways to see the tragedy as a confirmation of warnings they had already issued: The Democrats warned of right-wing paranoia, and the Republicans warned of the anger caused by the federal government enraging citizens by its invasions of their private lives.
- The chief suspect, Tim McVeigh, turned out to be a fairly intelligent young man who went to school in Lockport, New York, near the border of Canada. He had served in the army and had no criminal record and had wanted to be a computer programmer. No one recalled him as seeming dangerous or threatening.★

There are obviously many interesting facts about the event. Before trying to create an essay out of them, we should group the facts into some related categories. For this purpose, a clustering diagram may be useful. See the clustering diagram opposite:

The cluster shows that the topic contains many aspects, some of which we do not want to explore. Still we don't have a main point. Perhaps an exploratory draft will reveal one.

Exploratory First Draft

On Wednesday, April 19, 1995 at 9:02 a.m. an explosion rocked downtown Oklahoma City, leaving the Alfred Murrah Federal building in ruins. Many people in the building were killed immediately. Disbelief, panic, and terror ran through the surrounding area, as survivors struggled to escape, not knowing whether another blast might soon follow. Some tried to help others, and parents of children in the day care center on the second floor hysterically tried to find out what had happened to them. The explosion was so huge that it destroyed nine floors of the federal building and blew out windows blocks away. Hours later, more than half of the 550 people in the building had still not been accounted for, and scenes of anguish were everywhere, as victims were rushed to hospitals. The world saw and remembered the photograph of a large firefighter carrying the limp body of one-year-old Baylee Almon.

★Information from the following articles in *Time: News Summary,* April 19, 25, 26, 28, 1995; Nancy Gibbs, "The Blood of Innocents," *Time* cover story, May 1, 1995; Richard Lacayo, "A Moment of Silence," *Time* cover story, May 8, 1995; and George J. Church, "Justice: The Matter of Tim McVeigh," *Time,* August 14, 1995.

All day long and for weeks afterward efforts at rescue and relief continued. Four hundred people volunteered to help sort and pack relief materials. The Oklahoma City police and firefighters were joined by a special urban

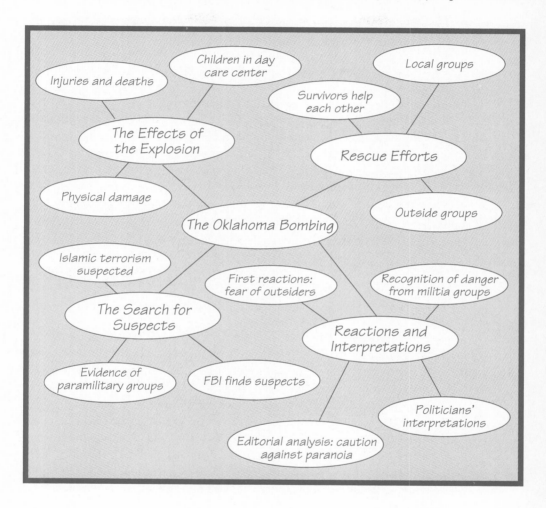

rescue force from Arizona, the National Guard, and the Air Force. The Red Cross, the global relief agency Feed the Children, and even the Boy Scouts got into the act. 100 doctors, about to go on a retreat in Houston, cancelled their vacation and flew back to help. At the time of the blast, some of the injured themselves, including one man who had lost an arm and another who had fallen six stories, tried to help others. Frantic efforts were made to find and remove children from the second floor, but many had been killed. One woman, pinned in a foot of water under steel girders, could be rescued only by having her leg amputated below the knee. Although the stories of suffering, agonizing grief, pain, and terror were everywhere, the heroic responses of people in the area were inspiring.

The public immediately assumed, wrongly, that the act had been done by Islamic terrorists. Not only did the blast resemble the explosion at the World Trade Center, but there was a large Islamic population in the Oklahoma City area, and there had been a convention there of the Islamic Society of North America. Suspects, including two Middle Eastern men held in Dallas and a Palestinian man brought back from London, were held for questioning. Anger at anti-American terrorists and fear of foreign conspiracies ran through the country. Only after considerable FBI investigation did it become apparent that the act had been committed by all-American young men with crewcuts who hated the government and blamed it for the Branch Davidian debacle at Waco, Texas, exactly two years before the explosion in Oklahoma City. Timothy McVeigh and his friend, Terry Lynn Nichols, were taken into custody, and it became clear that they, along with Nichols' brother, James Douglas Nichols, were linked to a paramilitary anti-government group in Michigan called the Militia. McVeigh, it turned out, was an intelligent young man who grew up in Lockport, New York, near the border of Canada. He had been a good student in high school and served creditably in the army. Nothing about him suggested the stereotyped terrorist, and his anti-government opinions resembled those of many who were victimized or shocked by the bombing.

The reactions of Americans to the bombing were extreme but complicated and confusing. When it was no longer possible to focus hatred on an alien conspiracy, Americans, though united in their outrage at the act itself and their sympathy for the victims and their families, were divided sharply over the meaning of the act. Some, including President Clinton, called for a toning down of the extremist rhetoric on the media, particularly talk radio. Many people saw the event as proof of the breakdown of law and order in our society, and President Clinton called on Congress to step up the fight against terrorism, including hiring more federal agents, requiring the public labeling of explosives, and allowing the military to assist in law enforcement. Some commentators talked of the dangers of "paranoia" in American political attitudes, while others blamed the government for the Waco disaster which, in turn, they believed proved how justified many citizens are in their hatred of the government. As usual, the political parties reacted by seeing the disaster as confirming what they had often warned about. The Democrats saw it as the result of right-wing extremism and unrestrained conservative rhetoric. The Republicans called for an investigation of the Waco disaster and redoubled their efforts to convince the public that the government is too large and invasive.

The bombing was like no event in living memory, and Americans did not find it easy to sum up its meaning in a way everyone would accept. The controversy over gun control, already intense, became even more so. Disagreements about the role and function of government continued at a higher pitch, and the fear of dangerous terrorists among our own, instead of replacing the fear and distrust of aliens, was only added to it. Perhaps the only lesson it is safe to draw from the bombing is that everyone was left feeling less safe than ever. Now it seemed that anyone could be a terrorist; worse than that: Anyone could be a victim.

When we read over this draft, we realize that although we have put a lot of interesting material into it and have a general sequence moving from the bombing itself through rescue attempts, the efforts to catch the perpetrators, the reactions and aftermath, the paragraphs are a little mixed up. Some are too small and undeveloped; others are very large and too cluttered with details. Even more important, we haven't quite stated a clear main idea. But, as often happens in an exploratory draft, we may have discovered one in the process of writing.

Main Idea

The Oklahoma bombing taught us that no one is totally safe from violence: A terrorist can be anyone, and, what is worse, anyone can be a victim.

Now we can try for a revised final version in which each paragraph contributes clearly to this main idea, and all of the details are included for a purpose.

Revised Draft

IT COULD BE ANYONE

Wednesday morning, April 19, 1995, began like any ordinary day among ordinary people in the heart of the country. By nine o'clock children were already playing in the day care center on the second floor of the Alfred Murrah Federal Building in Oklahoma City. About 550 people, mostly federal employees and clients, were busily engaged in everyday work. It was a day when ordinary people were to learn that the extraordinary could happen to them, and that they could prove to be extraordinary themselves.

Two minutes after nine, a bomb exploded in front of the federal building, turning this peaceful world of middle America into what one witness described as a scene out of Dante's hell. The blast destroyed nine floors of the building, blew out windows for blocks around, killed many people instantly, and created hours of panic, disbelief, and terror in which anguished parents sought desperately for their children, and injured victims, including one man who had fallen six stories and another with his arm blown off, tried to help others escape. Viewers around the country suffered with the victims, particularly because of the many children killed and injured by the explosion. The world would never forget the photograph of the large firefighter desperately but futilely carrying the limp body of one-year-old Baylee Almon.

Although the people and the circumstances were ordinary, the response to the emergency was not. Heroic efforts to rescue, aid, and identify victims began immediately and continued for weeks. Ordinary people rose to the occasion in extraordinary ways. Four hundred people volunteered help in sorting and packing relief materials; volunteers gave blood. The Red Cross, the global agency Feed the Children, and even the local Boy Scouts got into the act. The Oklahoma City police and fire departments were joined by a special urban rescue force from Arizona, the National Guard, and the Air Force. A group of 100 local doctors, who had just flown to Texas for a retreat, cancelled their vacation and flew back immediately to help. Risking great danger, crews worked urgently but carefully to find and rescue every single living victim. One woman, pinned under steel girders in a foot of water, could be rescued only by having her leg amputated below the knee. Everywhere there were stories of everyday people enduring unreal terror, grief, pain, and anguish—and everywhere there were stories of selfless courage reminiscent of war films and ancient sagas.

The public assumed, wrongly, that the perpetrators had to be satanic outsiders. The first thought was Islamic terrorists. Not only did the blast resemble the one at the World Trade Center, in New York, which had been created by Islam terrorists, but there was a very large Islamic population in Oklahoma and there had even been a convention of the Islamic Society of North America recently in Oklahoma City. Suspects, including two Middle Eastern men held in Dallas and a Palestinian man brought back from London, were questioned. Anger at anti-American terrorists, a fear of conspiracies, and a general distrust of foreigners ran through the country with the news of the bombing.

Soon, however, it became clear that the primary suspects were not "them" but "us." The FBI took into custody two all-American young men, Timothy McVeigh and Terry Lynn Nichols. The chief suspect, McVeigh, a tall young man with a crew cut, turned out to be an intelligent high school graduate from Lockport, New York, who had been a good student and served creditably in the army. Nothing about him suggested the demonic conspirator, except that the paramilitary group to which he and Nichols were linked, the Michigan Militia, hated the government and blamed it for the Branch Davidian debacle that occurred at Waco, Texas, exactly two years before the Oklahoma City explosion. But many Americans, including some victimized by the blast, shared similar opinions if less extreme feelings.

No longer able to focus hatred against a single outside enemy, Americans' reactions became divided and confused. Everyone continued to express outrage at the act itself and sympathy for the victims. Many people saw the event as proof of a breakdown of law and order, and President Clinton called on Congress to step up the fight against terrorism by hiring more federal agents, requiring the public labeling of explosives, and allowing the military to assist in law enforcement. Some leaders, including the President, called for a toning down of rhetoric in the media, particularly hate speech on talk radio. Some commentators talked of the danger of "paranoia" in American political attitudes, while others tended to blame the government for creating hatred through such behavior as its handling of the Waco disaster. The political parties predictably claimed that the tragedy confirmed what they had been saying all along. The Democrats blamed it on right-wing extremism and unrestrained conservative rhetoric; the Republicans on a government that is too large, invasive, and inept. No one, however, could blame the tragedy on "un-American" attitudes or activities.

No one could remember an event quite like the Oklahoma bombing. Americans have been unable to sum up its meaning in a simple way that everyone will accept. Oklahomans could be proud of the courage and sympathy many ordinary people demonstrated during the emergency. But around the nation, controversies tended to be heightened by the disaster: The gun control question became more fiercely debated, with both sides redoubling their efforts. Disagreements about the role and function of the government continued at a higher pitch than ever before. The fear of alien terrorists and distrust of foreigners did not subside; another fear was simply added to it. Perhaps the only lesson everyone agrees on is that Americans, whose fear of violence has already grown considerably, feel less safe than ever. The bombing made it clear that a terrorist could be anyone; worse than that, anyone could be a victim. Terror had become ordinary.

Follow-Up Exercise

Third-Person Narration

1. In your own words, state the thesis of this essay. Explain how the story illustrates that thesis.
2. Identify the connection between the introductory paragraph and the concluding paragraph.
3. Identify the topic of each body paragraph. Explain how each body paragraph moves the action one stage further.
4. Explain how details of the event support the topic of each body paragraph.
5. Explain whether your reaction to the news reports of the bombing was similar to those described in the essay.

Group Project

Third-Person Narration

Working with your writing group, brainstorm together the facts of some recent event that you all know about. Have the group recorder jot down every important fact and detail concerning the event that your group can think of. Next, collect a few news articles about it, using either newspapers or news magazines in the library or news resources on the Internet. Meet again and share your information, selecting the facts that are most important. Each member should then plan and compose an exploratory draft telling his or her version of the event. Read your drafts aloud and help each other discover what the main theme of each draft is. Try to state the main idea of your essay before you write the next draft. Help one another identify the main sections of each essay and plan paragraphs. Compose organized drafts; read them aloud for revisions and errors. Write carefully edited final drafts. Identify your printed sources at the end of the essay. If possible, have all of the essays printed together as a group newsletter: Preparing your work for publication helps you take pride in doing your best.

Note: Remember that *when you use printed sources, you must use quotation marks if you quote word for word, and you must identify sources for any facts or ideas you use.* Although this project is not a formal research paper, when you do write research papers in advanced courses, be sure to use the correct form for identifying your sources and to provide a list of sources, called a **bibliography,** at the end of your paper.

Writing Assignment

Third-Person Narration

Interview an older relative, such as a grandparent, who can tell you about life in an earlier generation. Ask this person to tell you about some interesting event that happened to your family a long time ago, such as immigrating to America, your grandparents meeting and getting married, a family business being set up, the family's experiences in wartime, its survival in hard times, or some other amusing, frightening, or moving experience.

Take plenty of detailed notes. Even better, use a tape recorder. Look over photographs or old letters if there are any. Remember that you should have far more material than you will actually use. Once you have all the material, list the facts in chronological order. Try some prewriting activities such as clustering or focused writing. Write an exploratory draft, mainly concentrating on telling the story and bringing out vivid details. Put the draft aside; then read it a day or two later. Think about the meaning of the experience and compose a thesis statement expressing the meaning. Look over your paragraph divisions and reconsider your paragraph planning. Write a final draft.

The Descriptive Mode: Telling About a Place or Person★

Descriptive essays, although they may contain elements of other kinds of writing, are intended chiefly to give a mental picture of a place, person, or object. As in descriptive paragraphs, be sure to use vivid, specific details and arrange your material in spatial sequence. This means that each paragraph, except the introduction and conclusion, will concentrate on one part or feature of the subject you are discussing. As in all essays, your thesis statement, preferably located near the end of the introductory paragraph, should state an idea that holds the whole description together. It will indicate what parts or features of the subject (the place, person, or object) the essay will discuss, and some point it makes.

TELLING ABOUT A PLACE

Describing a place, whether it is a small area such as your room or a large geographical area like the Caribbean islands (as in the sample essay that follows), requires thought, organization, and supporting details. Therefore you should expect to go through the stages of the writing process. The details will not arrange themselves; you have to group them into spatial categories by either outlining, making lists, or clustering. You should expect to do one or two rough drafts before you get the arrangement and the details right.

Critical Thinking About Descriptive Essays

When you write a descriptive essay, you are primarily trying to present a place, object, or person to the reader exactly as it is. However, as with narrative essays, some important critical thinking is necessary to write effective description. Every description is influenced by the writer's own perspective, and the reader's perspective influences how he or she interprets it (see descriptive paragraphs in Unit Two). Using critical thinking can help you become aware of your own perspectives and biases.

 Furthermore, critical thinking is needed to help you identify the purpose of your description. If you do not have an interesting main idea about the place you are discussing, try focused writing, clustering, or other prewriting activities to explore your thoughts and impressions before you compose an organized essay. Listening to feedback from others is the best starting point for applying critical thinking to your descriptive writing. After they have heard you read your exploratory draft or focused writing aloud, what ideas do the members of your writing group find in it? What main idea can you find in these suggestions? How can you use each body paragraph to describe a different aspect of this main idea?

★Review the use of adjectives and adverbs in Unit 5. See also Using Specific Language in Unit 4.

Before writing the following essay describing the Caribbean islands, the writer first created a cluster that helped her clarify her mental picture of the subject. In doing this, she also discovered her main thesis and some of the relationships between subtopics. After studying her cluster and reading her essay, answer the follow-up questions after the essay.

SAMPLE ESSAY: DESCRIPTIVE MODE

ISLANDS OF DIVERSITY

Many people picture the islands of the Caribbean the way they see them in travel commercials. They imagine gleaming hotels and tourists lounging under beach umbrellas. Although the islands do offer tourists some of the best beach vacation opportunities in the world, only people who have spent time living and traveling in the Caribbean are likely to know the amazing diversity of the cultures contained in these islands. Each of the three major regions has its special kind of diversity.

The most northerly of the Caribbean group are the Bahamas, a group of over 700 islands extending from the waters just east of Miami for about 750 miles to the southeast. The Turks and Caicos Islands mark the furthest point of this group. Having once been a British colony, the Bahamas show extensive British influence but contain many other cultural influences, most notably the impact of African culture and speech. The predominant religions are Protestant and Catholic, and the people are 85% of African descent and 15% of British, Canadian, or U.S. descent. Despite their proximity to the United States, the culture of the Bahamas has a distinctively British character from having been a British colony for almost two hundred years.

Still more culturally diverse is the largest group of Caribbean islands, called the Greater Antilles. The four large islands that make up this group—Cuba, Hispaniola (containing Haiti and the Dominican Republic), Jamaica, and Puerto Rico—stretch in an arc parallel to the Bahamas from the western tip of Cuba just below Florida for more than one thousand miles to the east and south. These islands illustrate the great cultural and linguistic diversity of the region. Cuba, the Dominican Republic, and Puerto Rico show the impact of early Spanish dominance in the Caribbean, whereas the predominant language in Haiti is French creole, and Jamaicans are primarily English speaking. These four islands contain about ninety percent of the Caribbean population and the widest cultural diversity. Some of the place names, including *Cuba, Haiti,* and *Jamaica,* come from the names given these islands by the native peoples (later called Arawaks) who first populated the Greater Antilles, and certain farming methods still in use today descend from these peoples. In addition to the European cultural influences, cultural and linguistic traditions from Africa are evident throughout the Greater Antilles, especially in Haiti and Jamaica; in Jamaica particularly, one also sees the cultural impact of people descended from India and China, whose ancestors arrived as indentured workers in the 1800s.

Curving southward and eastward from the Virgin Islands just east of Puerto Rico all the way to Trinidad and Tobago near the coast of Venezuela is the third group called the Lesser Antilles. The northern arc of islands in this group are called the Leeward Islands, and the southern group the Windward Islands. Among the many small islands in Lesser Antilles are Antigua, Dominica, Martinique, St. Lucia, Barbados,

St. Vincent, and Grenada. In this region the Amerindians called the Caribs, after whom the Caribbean is named, survived into the 1700s. The Spaniards paid less attention to the Lesser Antilles than to the larger islands to the north and west; consequently the Dutch, British, and French exerted greater influence. Some of these islands changed hands frequently as a result of frequent wars among the European powers. As a result, the cultures of these islands reflect rich complexity in their place names and varied dialects, their religions, and their cultural traditions. The influence of peoples from India is noticeable as well, particularly in Trinidad, where Hindu temples and Muslim mosques are numerous, and the people of Indian descent are nearly as numerous as those descending from Africa. Beyond Trinidad, along the coast of Venezuela to the west are the so-called ABC islands, Aruba, Bonaire, and Curaçao. Here the Dutch influence in the Caribbean remains in evidence, along with a small number of descendants of the Arawaks and traces of their cultural traditions.

Because of the flourishing trade and communication between the islands of the Caribbean and its history of colonialization by numerous European powers, this region contains one of the world's richest, most diverse collections of languages, religions, musical and artistic styles, and cultural festivals. Perhaps it is this mixture that accounts not only for its magnetic appeal to tourists but also for its current blossoming of outstanding poets, novelists, painters, and musicians. In its blending of the old and the new, of many races and cultures, the Caribbean is the most concentrated example of what the Western Hemisphere offers to the world.

Follow-Up Exercise

Description

1. How did this student arrange her paragraphs in spatial sequence?
2. What main idea ties the essay together?
3. How does the concluding paragraph connect to the introductory paragraph?
4. What is the topic of each body paragraph?

Group Project

Description

Both of the following pictures portray a man and a woman, one standing, the other seated. Discuss with your writing group how the spatial arrangements and body language in both pictures make the viewer think about the relations between

the two people. After brainstorming with your group on the pictures, choose one of the pictures and make a list of as many details and ideas as you can. Then each member of the group should do some focused writing on the meaning of the picture, thinking especially about its spatial layout. Read the focused writing aloud to each other. Write exploratory drafts, in which you organize your description into parts: foreground vs. background, or left side, middle, and right side. Share feedback; then revise your drafts, adding details where needed and using precise, vivid adjectives to describe what you see. Write final drafts.

Writing Assignment

Description

Write a short essay of about five paragraphs describing the town where you live or the college campus where you study. Remember that you must limit such a broad topic by focusing on one controlling idea about the place. (Notice how the essay on the Caribbean concentrates on highlighting the diversity of the region.) Divide your description into two, three, or four body paragraphs, each one describing one section of the place you are writing about. Remember to practice what you have learned about introductory and concluding paragraphs.

PORTRAYING A PERSON

Another important kind of descriptive essay is the portrait of a person. While resembling the one-paragraph description of a person that you have practiced, the essay portrait is longer and fuller. It will succeed best if you discuss several characteristics of the person, possibly bringing out one in each body paragraph. The thesis statement should introduce these characteristics. A descriptive thesis statement might read, "Mary is one of the most sensible, ambitious, and resourceful members of the freshman class." One body paragraph would discuss how sensible she is, one would discuss how ambitious she is, and the final one would discuss how resourceful she is. Be sure to focus on a central idea that all the subtopics will support, such as your admiration for the person in his or her successful pursuit of a career, or some such general concept. Notice how the author of the following essay develops one main idea, that his favorite teacher's combination of strictness and caring helped many students succeed. All of the details in the essay support this idea.

SAMPLE ESSAY: PORTRAYING A PERSON

Read the following essay and answer the questions after it. Notice the way the writer uses details to reveal the personal qualities of his favorite teacher.

UNFORGETTABLE MISS BESSIE*

Carl T. Rowan

She was only about five feet tall and probably never weighed more than 110 pounds, but Miss Bessie was a towering presence in the classroom. She was the only woman tough enough to make me read *Beowulf* and think for a few foolish days that I liked it. From 1938 to 1942, when I attended Bernard High School in McMinnville, Tenn., she taught me English, history, civics—and a lot more than I realized.

I shall never forget the day she scolded me into reading *Beowulf.* "But Miss Bessie," I complained, "I ain't much interested in it."

Her large brown eyes became daggerish slits. "Boy," she said, "how dare you say 'ain't' to me! I've taught you better than that."

"Miss Bessie," I pleaded, "I'm trying to make first-string end on the football team, and if I go around saying 'it isn't' and 'they aren't' the guys are gonna laugh me off the squad."

"Boy," she responded, "you'll play football because you have guts. But do you know what *really* takes guts? Refusing to lower your standards to those of the crowd. It takes guts to say you've got to live and be somebody fifty years after all the football games are over."

I started saying "it isn't" and "they aren't," and I still made the first-string end—and class valedictorian—without losing my buddies' respect.

During her remarkable 44-year career, Miss Bessie Taylor Gwynn taught hundreds of economically deprived black youngsters—including my mother, my bother, my sisters and me. I remember her now with gratitude and affection—especially in this era when Americans are so wrought-up about a "rising tide of mediocrity" in public education and the problems of finding competent, caring teachers. Miss Bessie was an example of an informed, dedicated teacher, a blessing to children and an asset to the nation.

Born in 1895, in poverty, she grew up in Athens, Ala., where there was no public school for blacks. She attended Trinity School, a private institution for blacks run by the American Missionary Association and in 1911 graduated from the Normal School (a "super" high school) at Fisk University in Nashville. Mrs. Gwynn, the essence of pride and privacy, never talked about her years in Athens; only in the months before her death did she reveal that she had never attended Fisk University itself because she could not afford the four-year course.

At Normal School she learned a lot about Shakespeare, but most of all about the profound importance of education—especially for a people trying to move up from slavery. "What you put in your head, boy," she once said, "can never be pulled out by the Ku Klux Klan, the Congress or anybody."

---

*Carl T. Rowan, "Unforgettable Miss Bessie." Reprinted with permission from the March 1985 *Reader's Digest.* Copyright © 1985 by The Reader's Digest Association., Inc.

Miss Bessie's bearing of dignity told anyone who met her that she was "educated" in the best sense of the word. There was never a discipline problem in her classes. We didn't dare mess with a woman who knew about the Battle of Hastings, the Magna Carta and the Bill of rights—and who could also play the piano.

This frail-looking woman could make sense of Shakespeare, Milton, Voltaire, and bring to life Booker T. Washington and W.E.B. DuBois. Believing that it was important to know who the officials were that spent taxpayers' money and made public policy, she made us memorize the names of everyone on the Supreme Court and in the President's Cabinet. It could be embarrassing to be unprepared when Miss Bessie said, "Get up and tell the class who Frances Perkins is and what you think about her."

Miss Bessie knew that my family, like so many others during the Depression, couldn't afford to subscribe to a newspaper. She knew we didn't even own a radio. Still, she prodded me to "look out for your future and find some way to keep up with what's going on in the world." So I became a delivery boy for the Chattanooga *Times*. I rarely made a dollar a week, but I got to read a newspaper every day.

Miss Bessie noticed things that had nothing to do with schoolwork, but were vital to a youngster's development. Once a few classmates made fun of my frayed, hand-me-down overcoat, calling me "Strings." As I was leaving school, Miss Bessie patted me on the back of that old overcoat and said, "Carl, never fret about what you *don't* have. Just make the most of what you *do* have—a brain."

Among the things that I did not have was electricity in the little frame house that my father built for $400 with his World War I bonus. But because of her inspiration, I spent many hours squinting beside a kerosene lamp reading Shakespeare and Thoreau, Samuel Pepys and William Cullen Bryant.

No one in my family had ever graduated from high school, so there was no tradition of commitment to learning for me to lean on. Like millions of youngsters in today's ghettos and barrios, I needed the push and stimulation of a teacher who truly cared. Miss Bessie gave plenty of both, as she immersed me in a wonderful world of similes, metaphors and even onomatopoeia. She led me to believe that I could write sonnets as well as Shakespeare, or iambic pentameter verse to put Alexander Pope to shame.

In those days the McMinnville school system was rigidly "Jim Crow," and poor black children had to struggle to put anything in their heads. Our high school was only slightly larger than the once-typical little red schoolhouse, and its library was outrageously inadequate--so small, I like to say, that if two students were in it and one wanted to turn a page, the other one had to step outside.

Negroes, as we were called then, were not allowed in the town library, except to mop floors or dust tables. But through one of those secret Old South arrangements between whites of conscience and blacks of stature, Miss Bessie kept getting books smuggled out of the white library. That is how she introduced me to the Brontes, Bryon, Coleridge, Keats and Tennyson. "If you don't read, you can't write, and if you can't write, you might as well stop dreaming," Miss Bessie once told me.

So I read whatever Miss Bessie told me to, and tried to remember the things she insisted that I store away. Forty-five years later, I can still recite her "truths to live by," such as Henry Wadsworth Longfellow's lines from "The Ladder of St. Augustine":

The heights by great men reached and kept
Were not attained by sudden flight.
But they, while their companions slept,
Were toiling upward in the night.

Years later, her inspiration, prodding, anger, cajoling and almost osmotic infusion of learning finally led to that lovely day when Miss Bessie dropped me a note saying, "I'm so proud to read your column in the Nashville *Tennessean.*"

Miss Bessie was a spry 80 when I went back to McMinnville and visited her in a senior citizens' apartment building. Pointing out proudly that her building was racially integrated, she reached for two glasses and a pint of bourbon. I was momentarily shocked, because it would have been scandalous in the 1930s and 1940s for word to get out that a teacher drank, and nobody had ever raised a rumor that Miss Bessie did.

I felt a new sense of equality as she lifted her glass to mine. Then she revealed a softness and compassion that I had never known as a student.

"I've never forgotten that examination day," she said, "when Buster Martin held up seven fingers, obviously asking you for help with question number seven, 'Name a common carrier.' I can still picture you looking at your exam paper and humming a few bars of 'Chattanooga Choo Choo.' I was so tickled, I couldn't punish either of you."

Miss Bessie was telling me, with bourbon-laced grace, that I never fooled her for a moment.

When Miss Bessie died in 1980, at age 85, hundreds of her former students mourned. They knew the measure of a great teacher: love and motivation. Her wisdom and influence had rippled out across generations.

Some of her students who might normally have been doomed to poverty went on to become doctors, dentists, and college professors. Many, guided by Miss Bessie's example, became public-school teachers.

"The memory of Miss Bessie and how she conducted her classroom did more for me than anything I learned in college," recalls Gladys Wood of Knoxville, Tenn., a highly respected English teacher who spent 43 years in the state's school system. "So many times, when I faced a difficult classroom problem, I asked myself, *How would Miss Bessie deal with this?* And I'd remember that she would handle it with laughter and love."

No child can get all the necessary support at home, and millions of poor children get *no* support at all. This is what makes a wise, educated, warm-hearted teacher like Miss Bessie so vital to the minds, hearts and souls of this country's children.

Follow-Up Exercise

Portraying a Person

1. Name two or three key words that describe Miss Bessie's character. How does Carl Rowan illustrate these characteristics by what Miss Bessie does or says?
2. This essay is mostly descriptive. Identify what other mode of writing is used extensively as well. Explain why the author uses this other mode to support his purpose of portraying Miss Bessie.
3. Identify descriptive details that help you visualize Miss Bessie. Identify other details that show her attitudes and goals as a teacher.
4. Explain how Carl Rowan's relationship to Miss Bessie changed when he grew older. What caused this change?
5. Explain how the social situation in Carl Rowan's childhood affected him. Why did this situation make Miss Bessie even more important as an influence on him?

Writing Assignment

Portraying a Person

Think of a person who has influenced you because of what he or she said and did. Do some focused writing or other prewriting activities to collect details about how this person looked, talked, and acted. Try to remember memorable statements the person made that you can quote directly. Brainstrom for details that will give the reader a vivid picture of the person and his/her character. Write a first draft organized around the influence of this person on your life. Put the essay away for a while. Take it out later and read it to another student or to your group for feedback. Do a final draft.

The Expository Mode: Discussing an Issue

In English composition courses and in other college courses as well, you will have to write essays about social issues. These will allow you to make use of what you know about writing "how" and "why" paragraphs. Such essays usually include several modes that you have practiced in your paragraph writing. Although chiefly expository, such essays may also contain narration, description, and persuasion. You have been practicing these modes separately, but it is well to remember that in expository writing you will often combine several of them to support your points.

Expository essays on social issues may cover any number of topics, but they tend to fall into several broad categories such as the following:

- Schools and education
- Crime and the justice system
- Children and child rearing; conflicts between generations
- Marriage, divorce, and living together without marriage
- The media and their effect on our lives
- Moral questions: for example, abortion, assisted suicide, teenage sexuality
- Medical problems such as AIDS and substance abuse
- The economy
- Environmental issues (chemical and nuclear waste, air and water pollution)
- College and professional sports
- The civil rights movement and the women's movement
- Foreign policy
- Technological change and its effects

These are, of course, broad categories, not topics for essays. The topics you write about, whether you choose them or they are assigned to you, will be much more specific. You have been exposed to all of these general concerns through news broadcasts, editorials, television documentaries, magazine articles, books, and general conversation. In some advanced courses you will study such issues systematically and have to write about them using source material. For now, however, we are concerned with your ability to write intelligently about social issues using your own experience and your general knowledge as a concerned citizen.

A reasonably well-informed citizen should be able to write an effective essay on any of the foregoing subjects without specialized research. We are speaking here of the kind of article or letter to the editor that appears frequently in newspapers and magazines, not the heavily documented research paper that might appear in a scholarly magazine or be assigned in an advanced seminar. You do not need to be an expert to express an opinion and back it up with evidence. What you *do* need is a clear main point and the ability to organize your ideas effectively. How you organize depends on the kind of essay you are writing. There are several common patterns for expository essays; we will look at a few.

ESSAYS BASED ON EXAMPLES

One of the simplest methods of developing and organizing expository essays is **multiple illustration,** or **enumeration.** This means supporting the main point in a series of examples that illustrate it. This method allows you to draw on your own experience or on the experience of people you know, or to furnish examples from your reading. Each example may be a small story or description of a situation that proves your main point. College examination questions often call on students to provide examples from their reading in the course to illustrate some thesis. In composition courses as well as popular magazines, lively personal essays may use multiple examples to discuss a social issue like single parenthood, computerized dating, forced retirement, or teenage runaways in an amusing or emotionally moving way.

Remember a few pointers when writing essays of this kind:

- Be sure that your examples all support the point—it is easy to get into an interesting story and lose the point you are making, ending up with a long piece of gossip.
- Think about the order of your examples, putting the most important, dramatic one last.
- Vary your examples—although they all support one main idea, the way they do it should differ in order to hold the reader's interest.
- Make connections between the examples by using transitional phrases like "another example," "a still more exciting case," "a third incident that illustrates the point," and so on.

Here is a short plan for an essay using multiple examples:

Main Point: *People sometimes achieve greatness by overcoming physical illnesses or handicaps.*

Examples:
1. Demosthenes, the ancient Greek leader, became a great speaker by overcoming his speech handicap.
2. Theodore Roosevelt became a great military and political leader by overcoming his childhood asthma.
3. Helen Keller, though deaf, mute, and blind, overcame these handicaps to become a great public figure.
4. Jim Abbott, although born with only one hand, became a pitcher for the California Angels and the New York Yankees.

Exercise

Multiple Examples

Write sentences about famous people whose lives make good examples of the main point.

Main point: *Young celebrities such as rock stars, television actors, and athletes sometimes cannot handle sudden fame and destroy their careers through drug abuse, alcohol, or self-destructive behavior.*

Examples (Write complete sentences like the ones in the four examples above):

1. _____

2. _____

3. _____

4. _____

5. _____

SAMPLE EXPOSITORY ESSAY: MULTIPLE EXAMPLES

Read the following essay, identifying its main thesis and the examples used to support that thesis. Do the follow-up exercise after the essay.

SCHOOLS: AN UNIMPORTANT ROLE?*

Given the lack of fit between gifted students and their schools, it is not surprising that such students often have little good to say about their school experiences. In one study of 400 adults who had achieved eminence in all areas of life, researchers found that three-fifths of these individuals either did badly in school or were unhappy in school. Few MacArthur Prize fellows, winners of the MacArthur Award for creative accomplishment, had good things to say about their precollegiate schooling if they had not been placed in advanced programs. Anecdotal reports support this. Pablo Picasso, Charles Darwin, Mark Twain, Edvard Grieg, Stephen Vincent Benét, Oliver Goldsmith, and William Butler Yeats all disliked school. So did Winston Churchill, who almost failed out of Harrow, an elite British school. About Oliver Goldsmith, one of his teachers

---

*Ellen Winner, *Gifted Children: Myths and Realities.* Reprinted by permission of BasicBooks, a division of HarperCollins Publishers, Inc. Copyright © 1996 bt Ellen Winner.

remarked, "Never was so dull a boy." Often these children realize that they know more than their teachers, and their teachers often feel that these children are willful, arrogant, inattentive, or unmotivated.

Some of these gifted people may have done poorly in school because their gifts were not scholastic. Maybe we can account for Picasso in this way. But most fared poorly in school not because they lacked ability but because they found school unchallenging and consequently lost interest. Yeats described the lack of fit between his mind and school: "Because I had found it difficult to attend to anything less interesting than my own thoughts, I was difficult to teach." As noted earlier, gifted children of all kinds tend to be strong-willed nonconformists. Nonconformity and stubbornness (and Yeats's level of arrogance and self-absorption) are likely to lead to conflicts with teachers. This is what happened with Jacob, Peter B., and Alex. Children like this often educate themselves informally. They read a lot, they join after-school math clubs, or they work on the school newspaper. These experiences can be far more instructive than regular classes. "I always learned more out of school than in," said one MacArthur Prize fellow. This comment echoes Darwin, who said, "I consider that all I have learnt of any value has been self-taught."

When highly gifted students in any domain talk about what was important to the development of their abilities, they are far more likely to mention their families than their schools or teachers. A writing prodigy studied by David Feldman and Lynn Goldsmith was taught far more about writing by his journalist father than his English teacher. High-IQ children in Australia studied by Miraca Gross had much more positive feelings about their families than their schools. About half of the mathematicians studied by Benjamin Bloom had little good to say about school. They all did well in school and took honors classes when available, and some skipped grades. But they often knew more math than their teachers, and in elementary school their mathematical abilities usually went unnoticed. In the best situations, the teacher recognized their ability but could not teach at this level and simply sent the child off to the library to learn independently. While any group of people picked at random might describe their school experiences negatively, it is distressing to hear such evaluations from individuals with the kinds of minds that schools are supposed to nurture.

Follow-Up Exercise

Multiple Examples

1. In your own words, state the author's thesis. In a few sentences, state why you agree or disagree with her thesis.
2. Make a list of the famous people named as examples. Identify as many of them as you can.

3. Identify passages where the author refers to studies of people who were not famous. Explain whether these examples prove the same point as the examples of famous people

4. Give some examples, either of famous people or of people you know personally, that support or refute the author's thesis.

5. Explain what overall point the author is making about the schools. Can you think of other types of students who seem not to like school? Explain what you think might be done to make the schools better serve all types of students.

Group Project

Multiple Examples

Working with your writing group, choose one of the topics listed below and do a brainstorming session to identify as many examples as you can of people to illustrate your topic. The group recorder should make a list of all the suggestions. Each member of the group should then write an exploratory draft describing three of these examples. You may want to include bad examples as well as good ones. Read your drafts aloud and discuss them. Consider each other's feedback; write a revised draft.

1. Describe the qualities of an effective leader and illustrate them with three examples.

2. Discuss the qualities of a good film by using at least three examples.

3. Identify the traits of effective parents and illustrate them using at least three examples.

4. Explain what courage is by using at least three examples from real life.

PROBLEM/SOLUTION ESSAYS*

Essays in which you propose solutions to problems involve careful thinking and require clear, organized writing. Such essays may propose solutions to personal problems, problems on the job, or large social or political problems. Writing successful essays of this kind requires critical thinking as part of your prewriting and composing process. While planning a problem/solution essay, be sure you have explored the whole range of the topic before writing. Ask yourself questions like these:

---

*Review subject/verb agreement in Unit 5.

1. What kind of problem am I trying to solve? Is this an ethical, psychological, economic, social, or political problem?
2. Why does this problem have to be solved? What will happen if it is not?
3. What are all of the possible ways of trying to solve this problem?
4. Which solution do I think is the best?
5. Why will the other ones not be as effective?
6. Why will mine prove the most successful?

Here is a sample problem for you to analyze. First read the statement of the problem and offer your solution. Then read the analysis afterward and the model student essay. Which elements of the problem did you overlook when you first reacted to the problem? What possible solutions did not occur to you? Did you think of any not mentioned?

Statement of Problem

Andrea has been working for a year and a half in a clothing store. She has been happy with her working conditions, her co-workers, and her salary. About a month ago, however, she began to realize that the store's owner has been engaged in a major fraud: He buys cheap imitations of name brand dresses, jeans, shirts, and sweaters with false labels and sells them for genuine name brands at a huge mark-up. What should Andrea do?

 ## Critical Thinking Analysis

1. What Kind of Problem Is This?

This is mainly an ethical problem because Andrea knows that she is working for a partly criminal operation. There are possible economic and psychological implications for Andrea as well.

2. Why Must This Problem Be Solved?

Andrea's conscience will not let her ignore this scam. Equally important, she is working her way through law school and wants to become a criminal attorney, so she doesn't want to be part of an illegal operation or have such a fact on her record.

3. What Are the Alternatives?

There are many possibilities, some of which Andrea would not consider. She can ignore the problem and hope it won't be discovered. She can ignore the problem and quit her job, hoping to get another good one. She can quit her job and report the fraud to the police or the Better Business Bureau. She can keep her job and report the fraud, either anonymously or as a whistle-blower. She can confront her boss, either to demand that he stop or to blackmail him for more money. She can ask her co-workers for advice, or she can consult her friends, family, or religious counselor.

4. Which Solution Is the Best?
Your answer to this question depends partly upon your own values, priorities, and personality.

SAMPLE ESSAY: SOLVING A PROBLEM
Read the sample essay below, identifying the different parts of the essay and noticing how the author organized it. Then do the follow-up exercise after it.

SPEAKING UP FOR WHAT YOU BELIEVE

My friend Andrea taught me a lesson about having the courage to stand up and tell the truth no matter what. Most people would not have the nerve to do what she did, and when she told me about it, at first I thought she was crazy. After thinking about it, however, I decided that she did the right thing. She is a good role model that other people should imitate.

Andrea worked in a clothing store in her neighborhood until last year. She liked her job because she was getting a good salary, and she liked the other salespeople. She was getting so good at recommending the right sizes, styles, and colors to customers that they always came back to her for advice. She earned two raises in a year and a half and her job was helping to pay her way through law school.

One day last March she was shocked to discover that the owner of her store was a crook. While some name brand items were being delivered, she admired some of them, and one of the deliverymen laughed and told her confidentially that they were all cheap imitations. At first Andrea didn't believe him, but when she looked at them closely and saw the low prices the owner was paying, not to mention the huge mark-up he was getting, she realized it had to be true.

Right then she panicked because she didn't know what to do. She didn't want to be part of a big scam because she always tried to be honest, and she resented the owner for getting so much money by cheating customers. She was afraid that if she said anything he might take revenge against her, but if she didn't do anything, somebody might report the fraud, and she could get caught up in the crime. As a future lawyer, she didn't want anything illegal or even suspicious on her record.

She thought over some of her alternatives. She felt like quitting her job, but she needed the income. She wanted to confront the boss immediately, but she was sure he would fire her and make up a phony reason that would hurt her chances for getting other jobs. She thought of becoming a whistle-blower by taking the story to the local television station, but then she was afraid no other employers would want to hire her because she would look like a troublemaker.

She finally decided to talk to all the other salesworkers during their lunch hour and convince them that they should all go with her to the boss and demand that he stop cheating customers. Some of the other workers didn't want to do anything about it and got angry when she kept insisting that they join her. But finally she convinced them that if they didn't do anything, somebody would eventually find out and report the fraud, at which point the store would be closed down, and they would all lose their jobs, maybe even be arrested.

So they all met with the boss and made their demands. At first he denied that he was doing anything illegal; then he tried to laugh it off, saying that everyone else was doing the same thing. Then he got angry because they wouldn't back down, and he told them that they were getting good salaries from the same money and had no right to complain. They still wouldn't let him have his way, so, to their surprise, he shrugged and said okay, he would stop doing it, but they would have to take a ten percent salary cut because he couldn't afford to keep paying them what they were making when he started losing some of his profits.

So, the problem was solved, in a way. Some of the other workers were very angry with Andrea for a while because they had to take a pay cut, but a few others backed her up and praised her for standing up for what she believed in. A year later she got a better job as a clerk in a law firm. I still wonder where she got the nerve to stick her neck out. I told her she has a lot of courage and will make a good criminal lawyer.

Follow-Up Exercise
Problem Solving

1. This essay is primarily expository because it analyzes a problem. Identify the paragraphs which contain the following: the explanation of the problem, the description of possible solutions, the account of how Andrea solved the problem, and the outcome.
2. Explain why this essay could also be called a narrative essay.
3. Explain how Andrea's situation influenced the decision she made.
4. Tell what you think you would do in a similar situation and why.

Group Project

Thinking Critically About Problem Solving

Have your writing group choose one of the three case studies below. Let each member select one of the four critical thinking questions on pp. 144–145 and write an answer to it as it applies to the case chosen. Read your answers aloud. Discuss the person's alternatives and try to determine which one would be best. Each member should then write a draft for an essay explaining the problem and proposing the best solution to the problem. Read your drafts aloud and discuss the problem again. Write final drafts.

A. Frank is looking out his apartment window one evening when he sees two men attacking an elderly woman across the street. Frank is an able-bodied young man; he does not have a gun. What should he do?

B. Audrey picks up her paycheck one Friday and notices that the amount is much too large—about twice as much as she is supposed to be getting. Her firm is very large and has hundreds of employees, so the error might not be noticed, if it is an error. What should Audrey do?

C. While John is working on his term paper for sociology, he overhears a friend, who is on the baseball team with him, bragging that he paid someone to write his term paper for him. John knows that his friend needs a very high grade in sociology to remain eligible for baseball and keep his scholarship. What should John do?

SOLUTIONS TO SOCIAL PROBLEMS

Essays about social problems require a larger perspective than ones about personal problems. As a student you will probably be asked at some time to write an essay proposing a solution to one of our society's many problems. Assignments like this may be given not only in English courses but in the social sciences such as psychology or sociology. In such essays, you are expected to use critical thinking and display an understanding of the methods of analysis used in the social sciences. You may be expected as well to show knowledge of the facts related to the problem and even have to do research for the assignment. You may find an outline helpful in planning the major parts of this kind of essay. However, do not try to make an outline for your essay without first exploring the range of your knowledge and opinions on the problem through prewriting activities. *Critical thinking in particular is crucial in the prewriting stages of an essay of any kind.* In creating a problem/solution essay, or any other type of essay, try to follow these guidelines.

Critical Thinking Guidelines

Expository writing, to be effective, must be based on critical thinking. Read the guidelines below and check your essays for effective content based on clear, open-minded thinking free of biases and illogical traps.

1. Be Clear About Your Main Point

Distinguish carefully between your main idea and subordinate ideas, and establish the boundaries of your discussion. Does this discussion include all educational institutions, all colleges, or just your college? Does it include all men and women, just women, just single women, or just young single women?

2. Judge on the Evidence

Get all the facts you can and base your main point on the evidence. But be sure that your evidence really supports the point you are making. Beware of overgeneralizing from a small amount of evidence ("I know that all athletes are poor students because two of my friends on the baseball team failed their courses last semester"). And don't assume that because certain facts occur together, one necessarily causes the other ("Sandra always writes on blue paper, and Sandra gets As; I'll get As too if I write on blue paper").

3. Consider All Alternatives

Choose your main point by first considering all the possible points of view and eliminating the others—not by jumping to conclusions. If you are suggesting a solution to a problem, consider all the possible solutions first. If you are analyzing a cause or effect, be aware that there may be a combination of causes and effects for most social problems. If you are trying to persuade, answer some of the opposing points.

4. Divide Your Topic into Parts

Don't oversimplify; break your topic into components to discuss it carefully in all its complexity. What are the aspects of the problem? Why must it be solved? What suggestions have already been thought of and tried? Why will yours succeed? The problem of homelessness, for example, includes other problems such as unemployment, high rents, substance abuse, and mental illness. One simple solution may not work for all of these problems.

5. Be Aware of Biases, Especially Your Own

Everyone has biases, some of them favorable, some unfavorable, and since we're human, we won't get rid of all of them. However, biases hinder effective writing, causing us to fix our gaze on only one part of a problem and to see it from only one perspective. A reader can always detect a closed-minded, dogmatic writer and will usually respond negatively to biased arguments.

6. Don't Confuse Strong Emotion or Strong Language with Strong Argument

Powerful writing often expresses strong emotion and uses powerful language, but some very bad writing does the same. Strong feelings and extreme words should be justified by the force of the points you make and the evidence you use to support them.

7. Spend Time with Your Topic and Discuss It with Others

Don't state your main argument without giving your ideas time to develop. What you think about your subject may change after you have thought it over for a day or two and read some articles about it. Unless you have to write an essay in class without knowing the topic beforehand, don't try to throw it together in a hurry. If you have a writing group in your class, use other students' opinions to help you develop all sides of the topic.

> ## Group Project

Using the Critical Thinking Guidelines

Working with your writing group, discuss and analyze each of the following passages of student writing. In each passage, decide whether the statements are convincing. Identify which of the guidelines the passage follows or violates. Rewrite the passages that seem to be lacking in critical thinking and make them more logical and convincing.

A. Teachers should give less homework and assign shorter reading assignments. All the students I know go to college and have jobs at the same time. We don't have time to write long papers or read whole chapters of textbooks and still have time for social activities. If they want us to do a lot of work, they should let us turn it in when we want to and not lower our grades for lateness.

B. The way to solve the problem of terrorism is to stop letting so many foreigners into the country. People who form conspiracies to blow up airplanes or buildings hate America and they always get their ideas and training from terrorists in other countries.

C. The problem of teenage pregnancy can be solved easily: All schools have to do is teach children and teenagers to say no to sex and to have good values. Teenagers experiment with sex and get pregnant because they have an attitude, and that's because schools are too permissive.

D. I don't want to have a career in computers because computer types are boring nerds who are interested only in video games, Web pages, and the speed of their modems. I can't imagine working around people like that.

E. The problem of increasing college costs will require several approaches at once. Some colleges may have to reduce their most expensive programs and lower their tuition, and others may have to pursue more aggressive fund raising. Some students may have to attend less expensive public colleges, families will have to begin saving earlier for college, and the government should provide more low-cost loans.

OUTLINING ESSAYS ON SOCIAL ISSUES*

Essays on social issues, such as problem/solution essays, can be more demanding in their content than essays based mostly on personal experience, even though the writing process involved is similar. You may find that making an outline will help you keep ideas grouped effectively. Essays of this kind often can be organized into three main parts:

1. Establishing the need for a solution
2. Considering various proposals
3. Stating and defending the best proposal

Leaving out any of these parts will inevitably weaken your essay.
 An outline for a problem/solution essay might look like this:

I. **Introductory paragraph** stressing the urgency of the problem and indicating the kind of solution you will propose
II. **Body paragraphs**
 A. Paragraph explaining the need at length and possibly analyzing how the problem arose
 B. Paragraph discussing other proposed solutions and showing why they will not work
 C. Paragraph (or two) explaining your solution in detail and showing why it will work
III. **Concluding paragraph** reemphasizing the need for change and stressing the effectiveness of your solution, possibly warning what will happen if your proposal is not implemented.

SAMPLE ESSAY: SOLVING A SOCIAL PROBLEM

Read the essay below, noticing how it follows the problem/solution essay outline. Write responses to the follow-up exercise after the essay.

---

*See Outlining in Unit 1.

CAN THE JURY SYSTEM BE SAVED?

Since the Rodney King trial and the trials of O.J. Simpson and the Menendez brothers, one hears nothing but loud complaints about the jury system. The question no longer is whether the current jury system works well but whether it can be saved at all. Many people would just like to get rid of it, and those who favor keeping it assume that it needs to be drastically reformed. Although no system of justice will be satisfactory in every case, and certainly none will be perfect, the current system can be improved to make it the best overall system possible in a democratic society. To do that, we need to make changes in the pool of jurors, the methods of jury selection, and the procedures for using juries in trials.

Those who support the current system overlook the ways the current system fails the jurors themselves and thwarts the effort to attain real justice. Those who would like to eliminate the present system haven't been able to propose any other system that would not be worse. For example, a system in which judges make all the decisions might work in some cases, but it would put all the power in the hands of those who appoint judges and almost guarantee corruption. Having a body of professionally trained and hired jurors might seem appealing, too, but the same problem would arise: Who would prevent them from being bought off or threatened by rich or powerful people? Systems of this kind might work better than the current one for a short time, but they would become less and less democratic and fair as time went on.

The current system can be improved. First, the jury pool must be widened. One of the complaints people make when they attack jury decisions is that the jury was biased. Attorneys sometimes try to get the venues of trials changed to better their chances of getting a jury sympathetic to their clients. Americans are supposed to be guaranteed the right to a trial by a jury of their peers, but often the members of a jury are far different in every way from the defendant—in income, race, religion, and attitudes. Can they still be called peers? One way to improve the system is to draw from a wider pool of potential jurors. In the past some groups of professional people, for example, have never been in jury pools, and others could easily be excused. Furthermore, it is customary to draw jurors only from the county in which they live, making it possible for a particular jury to be biased because of their common experiences. It might be possible to draw jurors from larger areas and create juries with more mixed backgrounds.

When juries are picked by the lawyers on both sides, the process becomes a game of mind-reading and reading of body language. Nowadays experts in jury selection hire themselves out to assist lawyers in picking jurors likely to be favorable to their clients. Although the two-sided battle might be expected to result in a balanced jury, in many cases it simply awards the victory to the lawyer who is shrewder or more persistent. If a client cannot afford a good lawyer, the other side may pick a jury strongly biased against him. Courts in some countries allow far fewer removals of jurors by attorneys, leaving the process more to chance than to the manipulations of expensive lawyers and expert advisers. The more removals each side is allowed, the longer the pre-trial game lasts, and the more tired and impatient everyone becomes. Limiting the game would help.

Still more important is the fact that most people would do anything to stay off a jury in an important case. Even a moderately important case can last for a much longer period than most people are willing to stay away from their jobs, or, at worst, be sequestered. A publicized case is far worse, and one involving organized crime could be dangerous for jurors. Reforms friendly to jurors would make it easier for the courts to get balanced, competent juries. In cases that threaten to drag on too long, a limited number of hours should be allotted to each side, and the jury should be promised a time limit for the trial. In publicized cases, jurors should not be allowed to make contracts for books or interviews about the trial, so that those on the case are concentrating on the case itself, not what they can get out of it. Jurors who serve on difficult, prolonged cases should be excused from future jury duty for a long period in the future so that all jurors have an incentive to sit on such cases. Electronic means should be used where possible to convey information about the trial to jurors at their homes or places of business on matters that do not require their presence. And it should not be necessary to have a unanimous decision in order to reach a decision of guilt or innocence. Almost nowhere else do we ever try to get unanimous decisions—in companies, sports, or families, and we often elect presidents and members of Congress with less than majorities. Nine or ten out of twelve jurors should be enough. That way juries would not be kept in endless deliberation because of one or two irrational individuals.

All of these changes have some problems to them, but the current system has much worse problems, and other systems that have been proposed simply do not fit in a democratic society. It is better to work with the system we have and improve it than to give up and accept its faults or throw it out and accept a truly unjust system. Some of the most publicized cases like the Menendez brothers and the O.J. Simpson criminal trial, after all, are one a million. What happened in them is not at all like what happens in typical cases, and these are the ones we should worry about, not the few we see on television.

Follow-Up Exercise
Problem/Solution Essay

1. In your own words, state the thesis of this essay. Underline the sentence in the essay that best states the thesis.
2. Identify which paragraph or paragraphs describe the nature of the problem.

3. Identify which paragraph or paragraphs explain the alternative solutions that have been proposed.
4. Tell how many proposed improvements the author suggests, and identify them.
5. Explain how the concluding paragraph is connected to the introductory paragraph.

Writing Assignment

Problem/Solution Essays

Identify a problem at your college, such as racism on campus, the rising cost of tuition, fraternity hazing, cheating on exams and term papers, snobbishness between different groups of students, a high dropout rate, problems with registration and financial aid, problems with course selection and curriculum, or problems with extracurricular activities or the athletic program. Discuss this problem with friends to explore the range of opinions about it. Do two pages of focused writing expressing your thoughts about the problem—what is causing it, who is responsible, and what should be done about it.

Once you have explored your thoughts, brainstorm the separate aspects of the problem. First, list everything you can about the problem itself—its causes, why it has to be dealt with, whom it affects, whether it is getting worse, and so on. Then list all the possible solutions, including any suggested by friends. Finally, identify the one solution that seems most likely to work, and write down everything you can about it.

At this point you should have the basis for a working draft of a problem/solution essay. Make a rough outline of your paragraph plan before you begin. You may not follow this outline exactly, because new ideas may come as you compose (always be open to new ideas even if they force you to reconsider your outline). Write your exploratory draft using the outline as a general guide only. Put the essay aside for a day or two; then look at it again. Read it aloud to friends for their feedback. If they disagree, use their disagreement as an opportunity to dig deeper into the subject, either to strengthen your point with better evidence or to modify your point. Revise your organization if revision is needed. Write a final draft.

ESSAYS BASED ON AN AUTOBIOGRAPHICAL EXAMPLE*

Another method of developing an expository essay is by means of your own experience. An autobiography is a story you write about your own life. Development by autobiographical example means using experiences from your own

---

*If you have not done so already, review verb tenses in Unit 5.

life to support a point. If you have ever been the victim of discrimination because of race, sex, or religion, you could use the experience to illustrate how prejudice manifests itself in our society. If you have had experience with the courts, you could use it to discuss the legal system. Many topics are suited to this method. Adoption, divorce, immigration, upward mobility, hospital care, problems in the schools, and issues regarding jobs and unemployment can all be discussed effectively by means of autobiographical examples. Of course, you have to have enough experience to discuss the issue effectively. Everyone, for instance, has plenty of experience with the schools, but not everyone can use personal experience to discuss adoption or immigration. Such essays can be vivid and forceful, sometimes humorous. However, it is easy to get off the track and forget that your main purpose is to discuss only one issue. *Be sure to state your main point early in the essay, and use topic sentences to focus your paragraphs on supporting points.*

SAMPLE ESSAY 1: AUTOBIOGRAPHICAL EXAMPLE

Read the following essay, noticing how the author tells about her own experience, not just to tell a story but to analyze a social issue. Write responses to the follow–up questions after the essay.

WORKING WHILE ATTENDING COLLEGE

With the cost of college nowadays, you almost have to be rich to finish a degree without working at least part of the time. When I came to New York City from Guyana, South America, I thought it would be easy to get a nursing degree and pursue the career of my choice. It turned out to be much harder than I expected, working full-time and taking classes at night. A two-year nursing degree is taking much more than two years, but I have discovered that you can turn the problem of working full-time while attending college into a big opportunity to improve your life.

First of all, you have to learn how to live with a double schedule. When I first came to this country, I got a full-time job in a bank, thinking that I would work only part-time when I began my studies. Instead, I quickly realized I could not afford to pay my rent and other expenses without working full-time. This meant I would have to maintain a forty-hour or more work week and fit my courses in whenever I could. Luckily, the community college I wanted to attend had just opened an evening nursing program that allowed me to take courses in the evenings and on weekends. On paper, this looked like a good schedule, but I was shocked to learn that I had no time for social activities or shopping, and very little for homework. The first semester I slept only five hours a night and became so tired that I thought I wouldn't make it. To make matters worse, I suffered stomach pains just before midterm exams and was afraid I would end up in the hospital. Fortunately, it was just heartburn, and I was able to take some medication and not have to drop out of college. By the end of the first term, I was sure that with enough determination I would reach my goal.

A working student also has to overcome academic difficulties and make sensible choices. I didn't expect problems with my courses because I had always been good in school. Since English was the main language in my schools at home, I was able to pass proficiency tests in reading and writing, and I knew I would do all right in speech and writing courses. Math was never my strong point, however, and I found out that I would have to take a remedial math course before enrolling in the math course for nursing students. I also discovered that since I had not taken chemistry in high school, I would have to complete a college chemistry course before beginning the science courses like anatomy and physiology in the nursing sequence. Most working students also find out as I did that since they have very little time for homework, they have to reduce their course loads. The nursing degree that I had planned to complete in four semesters was obviously going to take four, maybe five or six years. But I was determined.

Here I am in my third year, not as far along as I had hoped. But I have discovered that many of my classmates also work full-time, and we see many advantages to being a working student. We are more mature and self-disciplined because we carry our work habits over to our studies. We concentrate harder than some of the younger, nonworking students, and teachers seem to show us more respect, partly because we are used to being serious and punctual and getting work done. We also have more life experiences to relate to our courses in sociology, literature, and psychology. Instead of cramming knowledge into our heads in a few overloaded semesters in an ivory tower situation, we continually relate what we study to our lives and work. By taking longer to earn degrees, we have time to assimilate what we learn and develop our awareness from one semester to the next. While it's true that we don't have much time for socializing or extracurricular activities, we do learn to make friends quickly in classroom situations and make the most of our social opportunities between classes.

Most of us working students probably wouldn't have chosen to work full-time while attending college, but we didn't have that choice. Still, many of us have been able to turn a disadvantage into a big opportunity. When I finish my studies next year, I will enter the career of my choice better prepared to work in it than I could have been any other way. I have learned to use my time efficiently. Having balanced work and study, I will be able to balance work and child care when I have a family. I have acquired the attitude of lifelong learning instead of the get-it-over-with attitude of some nonworking students. Working full time while going to college can make you a better learner, a better worker, and a better person.

Follow-Up Exercise
Autobiographical Example

1. State in your own words what social issue the author is analyzing. Tell what her main thesis is, and identify the sentence that best states it.
2. Identify the topics of paragraphs two and three. Explain how they support the main thesis of the essay.
3. Explain how the author uses her own experience to support her topic statements in paragraphs two and three.
4. State the topic of paragraph four and explain how the author develops it.
5. In a few sentences, state why you agree or disagree with the author's main thesis.

SAMPLE ESSAY 2: AUTOBIOGRAPHICAL EXAMPLE

Read the following essay, noticing both the personal narrative in it and the opinion that the author is supporting by telling about his own life. Write responses to the follow-up exercise after the essay.

BILINGUAL EDUCATION*

Richard Rodriguez

Supporters of bilingual education today imply that students like me miss a great deal by not being taught in their family's language. What they seem not to recognize is that, as a socially disadvantaged child, I considered Spanish to be a private language. What I needed to learn in school was that I had the right—and the obligation—to speak the public language of *los gringos.* The odd truth is that my first-grade classmates could have become bilingual, in the conventional sense of that word, more easily than I. Had they been taught (as upper-middle-class children are often taught early) a second language like Spanish or French, they could have regarded it simply as that: another public language. In my case such bilingualism could not have been so quickly achieved. What I did not believe was that I could speak a single public language.

Without question, it would have pleased me to hear my teachers address me in Spanish when I entered the classroom. I would have felt much less afraid. I would have trusted them and responded with ease. But I would have delayed—for how long postponed?—having to learn the language of public society. I would have evaded—and for how long could I have afforded to delay?—learning a great lesson of school, that I had a public identity.

---

*From *Hunger of Memory* by Richard Rodriguez. Reprinted by permission of David R. Godine, Publisher, Inc. Copyright © 1982 by Richard Rodriguez.

Fortunately, my teachers were unsentimental about their responsibility. What they understood was that I needed to speak a public language. So their voices would search me out, asking me questions. Each time I'd hear them, I'd look up in surprise to see a nun's face frowning at me. I'd mumble, not really meaning to answer. The nun would persist, "Richard, stand up. Don't look at the floor. Speak up. Speak to the entire class, not just to me!" But I couldn't believe that the English language was mine to use. (In part, I did not want to believe it.) I continued to mumble. I resisted the teacher's demands. (Did I somehow suspect that once I learned public language my pleasing family life would be changed?) Silent, waiting for the bell to sound, I remained dazed, diffident, afraid. Because I wrongly imagined that English was intrinsically a public language and Spanish an intrinsically private one, I easily noted the difference between classroom language and the language of home. At school, words were directed to a general audience of listeners. ("Boys and girls.") Words were meaningfully ordered. And the point was not self-expression alone but to make oneself understood by the others. The teacher quizzed: "Boys and girls, why do we use that word in this sentence? Could we think of a better word to use there? Would the sentence change its meaning if the words were differently arranged? And wasn't there a better way of saying much the same thing?" (I couldn't say. I wouldn't try to say.)

Three months. Five. Half a year passed. Unsmiling, ever watchful, my teachers noted my silence. They began to connect my behavior with the difficult progress my older sister and brother were making. Until one Saturday morning three nuns arrived at the house to talk to our parents. Stiffly, they sat on the blue living room sofa. From the doorway of the other room, spying the visitors, I noted the incongruity—the clash of two worlds, the faces and voices of school intruding upon the familiar setting of home. I overheard one voice gently wondering, "Do your children speak only Spanish at home, Mrs. Rodriguez?" While another voice added, "That Richard especially seems so timid and shy."

That Rich-heard!

With great tact the visitors continued, "Is it possible for you and your husband to encourage your children to practice their English when they are home?" Of course, my parents complied. What would they not do for their children's well-being? And how could they have questioned the Church's authority which those women represented? In an instant, they agreed to give up the language (the sounds) that had revealed and accentuated our family's closeness. The moment after the visitors left, the change was observed. "*Ahora,* speak to us *en inglés,*" my mother and father united to tell us. At first, it seemed a kind of game. After dinner each night, the family gathered to practice "our" English. (It was still then *inglés,* a language foreign to us, so we felt drawn as strangers to it.) Laughing, we would try to define words we could not pronounce. We played with strange English sounds, often overanglicizing our pronunciations. And we filled the smiling gaps of our sentences with familiar Spanish sounds. But that was cheating, somebody shouted. Everyone laughed. In school, meanwhile, like my brother and sister, I was required to attend a daily tutoring session. I needed a full year of special attention. I also needed my teachers to keep my attention from straying in class by calling out, *Rich-heard*—their English voices slowly prying loose my ties to my other name, its three notes, *Ri-car-do.* Most of all I needed to hear my mother and father speak to me in a moment of seriousness in broken—suddenly heartbreaking—English. The scene was inevitable: One Saturday morning I entered the kitchen where my parents were talking in Spanish. I did not realize that they were talking in Spanish however until, at the moment they saw me, I heard their voices change to speak English. Those *gringo* sounds they uttered startled me. Pushed me away. In that moment of trivial misunderstanding and profound insight, I felt my throat twisted by unbounded grief. I turned quickly and left the room. But I had no place to escape to with Spanish. (The spell was broken.) My brother and sisters were speaking English in another part of the house.

Again and again in the days following, increasingly angry, I was obliged to hear my mother and father: "Speak to us *en inglés*." (*Speak.*) Only then did I determine to learn classroom English. Weeks after, it happened: One day in school I raised my hand to volunteer an answer. I spoke out in a loud voice. And I did not think it remarkable when the entire class understood. That day, I moved very far from the disadvantaged child I had been only days earlier. The belief, that calming assurance that I belonged in public, had at last taken hold. . . .

My awkward childhood does not prove the necessity of bilingual education. My story discloses instead an essential myth of childhood—inevitable pain. If I rehearse here the changes in my private life after my Americanization, it is finally to emphasize the public gain. The loss implies the gain: The house I returned to each afternoon was quiet. Intimate sounds no longer rushed to the door to greet me. There were other noises inside. The telephone rang. Neighborhood kids ran past the door of the bedroom where I was reading my schoolbooks—covered with shopping-bag paper. Once I learned public language, it would never again be easy for me to hear intimate family voices. More and more of my day was spent hearing words. But that may only be a way of saying that the day I raised my hand in class and spoke loudly to an entire roomful of faces, my childhood started to end.

Follow-Up Exercise

Autobiographical Example

1. State Richard Rodriguez' main point about bilingual education. Explain whether you agree or disagree with it. What does he believe to be the main purpose of school?

2. Describe the personal experiences he uses to support his main point. Tell why you think these experiences do or do not support the point convincingly.

3. Write definitions of the following words: *diffident, intrinsically, incongruity, accentuated.* Try to figure them out from the way Rodriguez uses them; then look them up in the dictionary.

4. Do you think there is any way Rodriguez as a child could have learned English well without the painful loss of family intimacy he describes? Explain your opinion.

Writing Assignment

Autobiographical Example

Basing your choice on your own experience, select one of the following topics for an essay using autobiographical example to support the main idea.

1. Discrimination in our society is still present.
2. Working full time teaches you a lot about yourself.
3. Military service changes your life in many ways.
4. The schools are not what they should be.
5. Hospitals are not as safe and efficient as we think.
6. Becoming a father (mother) changes your life.
7. Learning about religion affects your values.

Since this essay will be chiefly in narrative form, start with a focused writing exercise in which you tell everything that comes to mind about your experiences with this subject (hospitals, schools, parenthood, and so on). Once you have as much material as you can gather, think about what you want to say. What have you learned from your experience? Be as specific as you can. To say that the schools are bad, for instance, is an overgeneralization. In what way are they bad? Is your experience typical?

Once you have a thesis statement, write an exploratory draft. Try to stay on the point throughout the draft, and divide your experience or experiences into clearly identifiable phases or events. Put this draft away for a day or two. Then read it aloud to someone else to see if that person responds with similar experiences from his or her life. If that person disagrees with your point, perhaps you need to sharpen the point or modify it. If you have a strong point, you will probably get an "I know what you mean" response. Using feedback from your listener and your own critical eye, revise your draft as needed to make the main point clear and the paragraphs distinct and unified. Write a final draft.

The Persuasive Mode: Enumerating Reasons*

One reliable pattern of organization for argumentative essays is the series of reasons. You express your main idea in the thesis statement, then give three or four reasons why you hold that opinion. One reason should be discussed in each body paragraph. This method produces an extremely clear arrangement, but it is not necessarily simple. You may want to support each reason in a different way—a small story for one, facts for another, analysis of cause and effect for a third. The overall plan, in other words, is simple, but there is plenty of room for variety in the ways you develop the parts. As a result, you will need to be careful about making smooth transitions between body paragraphs and seeing to it that all three or four reasons really do support your thesis. A final concern is the sequence of reasons: which comes first? second? last? Usually, the most convincing reason should come last, in the most emphatic position.

SAMPLE ESSAY: ENUMERATING REASONS

Read the following essay, noticing how the author supports his opinion by listing several arguments in support of it. Then write responses to the follow-up exercise after the essay.

CURFEWS ARE FOR PARENTS TO SET†

Geoffrey Canada

One reason I was able to grow up in the South Bronx of the 1950's and 1960's without getting into trouble was that I lived under a curfew. The penalty for violating the curfew was swift and severe. Although I got to plead my case—a watch didn't work, the train was running late— the judge was seasoned and cynical (she had heard it all before). The usual verdict: guilty. The sentence: confinement to the apartment, when I wasn't at school, for a whole week.

This curfew was set, of course, by my mother, who raised four sons by herself. Like my mother, I am a strong believer in curfews. But I don't believe cities or states should impose them.

The calls for teen-age curfews by President Clinton and Bob Dole and, earlier this month, by Thomas V. Ognibene, a New York City Councilman, are part of a disturbing trend. Though New York doesn't have a curfew, most big cities now do. Increasingly, politicians are viewing the problems of youth solely through the prism of crime and punishment.

Indeed, while violent adult crime is falling in many big cities, youth crime and violence are generally on the rise. At the same time, the pop-

---

*Review the discussion of persuasive writing in Unit 2.

†Geoffrey Canada. "Curfews are for Parents to Set", *New York Times,* July 23, 1996, A19. Reprinted by permission of the *New York Times.*

ulation of children in the 5- to 8-year-old range has risen by more than 20 percent over the past decade. So by the year 2005, the thinking goes, we may have an explosion of violence led by young people—including children who are being called "superpredators." The result: almost all proposals for young people involve "getting tough"—prosecuting juveniles as adults, for example.

So what is wrong with official curfews? Many of the biggest American cities have them on the books. Dallas has reported that a curfew has helped reduce crime significantly. (No accurate data exist on the effectiveness of curfews nationwide.) But there are plenty of problems with curfews.

The wrong people impose them. At a time when many people are clamoring for less government, why pass curfew laws that usurp the rights of parents to raise their children as they see fit? Families are a better context for kids to learn that freedoms come with responsibilities. Each year, I had to renegotiate my curfew with my mother; the older I got, the later the curfew. If there was a dance or a party, I got special permission from her, not the police, to stay out late. As a high school senior, I worked in a factory after classes and didn't get home until 11 P.M. My mother was skeptical about my ability to juggle work and school. But she gave me permission to try, with the proviso that if my grades dipped or I didn't get up on time, the job was over. My freedom to stay out late, for fun or work, depended on my maturity and on meeting the expectations of my mother and my teachers.

Curfews create a new category of criminal behavior. These are tough times for young people. Guns claim thousands of their lives; schools are failing (some are even falling down). Jobs are hard to find in minority communities. Yet programs have been cut: summer employment, health and mental health services and after-school centers—even though children are more likely to get into trouble between 3 P.M. and 6 P.M. than at any other time, according to a report issued last year by the National Center for Juvenile Justice. The last thing kids need is a new way to be negatively classified—as delinquent curfew-breakers.

Curfews may worsen community problems with police and racism. If you are a person of color and male, you invariably have a story to tell about police harassment or worse. I have my own stories. Will curfews be enforced uniformly? Many in the African-American and Latino communities doubt this. In New York City, police abuse in their neighborhoods includes the use of excessive force and the death of suspects in custody, according to an Amnesty International report issued last month.

A curfew won't work if adults do not support it because they think the police act unfairly. Besides, it puts police in a tough situation. Can *you* tell the difference between a 19-year-old (who may be exempt from a curfew) and a 17-year-old (who may not be)? A law that gives police the right—indeed, requires them—to stop people on the basis of their perceived age is an invitation to trouble.

I know that some parents need help with their children. I also know that when help is offered, parents respond. If political leaders really want to help, they should stop cutting resources for youth. Until then, if you want to know about curfews, before you talk to the President or a city councilman, talk to my mother.

Follow-Up Exercise
Enumerating Reasons

1. In your own words, state the main thesis of the essay. Identify the sentence in the essay that best expresses this thesis.
2. Tell how many reasons the author gives in support of his thesis. State each one separately and tell how he supports each one.
3. Explain how the author also uses autobiographical narrative as part of his argument.
4. Tell how the concluding paragraph is connected to the introductory paragraph.
5. Explain which of the author's reasons seems most convincing to you and why.

Writing Assignment
Enumerating Reasons

Choose one of the following statements as a thesis for an essay. (You may take the opposite side if you prefer.)

1. Homeowners should be required to own guns to protect their families and property.
2. Colleges should not have required courses—students know what courses they need and are interested in.
3. Parents should raise boys and girls the same way, giving them the same toys, games, advice, rules, and discipline.
4. Women should wait to get married and have children until they have had time to enjoy life and have established their careers.
5. Life in a small town is better than life in a big city.

After you have chosen the topic, list all the reasons you can think of to support your opinion. Try to list five to ten. If you cannot think of more than one or two, try doing focused writing on the subject to loosen up your thinking. You might also try listing reasons why people have the opposite opinion and then list your responses to those reasons.

When you have gathered more than enough reasons, analyze the list. Pick out the three or four that seem to you the most important. List them in climactic sequence, with the most important—the clinching one—last. Write an exploratory draft using this list, with one paragraph for each reason. Explain each reason clearly and use examples to illustrate some of them. Read your rough draft aloud to get feedback on your ideas. If the other person disagrees at any point, see if you need to strengthen your argument with a better explanation or examples. Be sure you have an effective introduction and conclusion. Write a final draft.

The Persuasive Mode: The Dialogue Pattern

Still another effective method of developing an opinion on a social issue is the dialogue pattern. You will often see this method in editorials. The writer will state an opinion held by some person or group that he or she disagrees with; then the writer will use the rest of the editorial to reply to that opinion. The result is either a long answer to one opinion or a pro-and-con discussion in which the writer takes up several opinions of the opposition and answers them one by one.

This method is especially effective for the most controversial issues, ones that demand open-mindedness and fairness. By taking up the arguments of the other side, the writer demonstrates reasonableness and a grasp of the issue. To write this kind of essay well, you must be able to answer the best objections from the other side. It is tempting to use the "straw man" technique of mentioning only opinions that you can easily knock over, while ignoring really convincing ones.

Organizing an essay of this kind is not difficult if you include three or four opinions held by the other side. Include one in each body paragraph and refute each one effectively. The pattern is much like the series-of-reasons method: Arrange the body paragraphs so that the arguments build up from the least to the most important. Each paragraph can be developed in its own way. When you answer one objection from the other side, you may find a personal example to be your best means of support; when you answer the next, you may use logical analysis, and so on.

Critical Thinking on Controversial Issues: The Dialogue Pattern

Understanding a controversial issue requires a close look at arguments presented on both sides. Just as a jury has to hear both sides before rendering a verdict, you should study arguments on both sides before developing your own argumentative essay on a controversial topic. In the process, you may become confused and feel like President Harry Truman when he used to complain that he wanted a one-armed adviser—one who wouldn't always say, "On the one hand . . .; on the other hand. . . ." Despite the temporary uncertainty, however, once you explore the issue, you will eventually come to a strong, well–informed position; one that is genuinely yours.

Group Project

Critical Thinking on a Controversial Issue

Working with your writing group, do the following:

1. Read the article below on the death penalty, "How Capital Punishment Affirms Life," written in 1985 by former Mayor of New York City, Ed Koch. Notice how the writer replies in different ways to opinions held by those who disagree with him.

2. Make a list of Koch's points favoring the death penalty. On the other side of the page, make a list of the opposing points (against capital punishment) that he attempts to disprove.

3. Next, read "Talking Points on the Death Penalty," a list of points published recently on the Internet by a group in Washington State opposed to capital punishment. Identify any arguments against the death penalty not already on your list, and add them to your list.

4. Discuss the death penalty in the light of any real cases you have read about or films like *Dead Man Walking* that dramatize the human experience of capital punishment. Discuss with your group which three or four arguments on each side are the most convincing. Identify several arguments on both sides that seem biased, illogical, or otherwise unconvincing.

5. Have each member of your group do several pages of focused writing explaining why he or she agrees with several of the strongest points on one side.

6. Read your focused writing aloud and give each other feedback on what each writer has argued most persuasively and what he or she may have left out. Revise your first drafts to strengthen your arguments and respond to opposing opinions. Read the revised drafts aloud for further feedback; revise them for style and grammar, and write final drafts.

SAMPLE PERSUASIVE ESSAY: THE DIALOGUE METHOD

HOW CAPITAL PUNISHMENT AFFIRMS LIFE*

Edward I. Koch

Last December a man named Robert Lee Willie, who had been convicted of raping and murdering an 18-year-old woman, was executed in

---

*Edward I. Koch, "How Capital Punishment Affirms Life." Reprinted by permission of *The New Republic*. Copyright © 1985, The New Republic, Inc.

© 1998 by Addison-Wesley Educational Publishers Inc.

the Louisiana state prison. In a statement issued several minutes before his death, Mr. Willie said: "Killing people is wrong. . . . It makes no difference whether it's citizens, countries, or governments. Killing is wrong." Two weeks later in South Carolina, an admitted killer named Joseph Carl Shaw was put to death for murdering two teenagers. In an appeal to the governor for clemency, Mr. Shaw wrote: "Killing is wrong when I did it. Killing is wrong when you do it. I hope you have the courage and moral strength to stop the killing."

It is a curiosity of modern life that we find ourselves being lectured on morality by cold-blooded killers. Mr. Willie previously had been convicted of aggravated rape, aggravated kidnapping, and the murders of a Louisiana deputy and a man from Missouri. Mr. Shaw committed another murder a week before the two for which he was executed, and admitted mutilating the body of the 14-year-old girl he killed. I can't help wondering what prompted these murderers to speak out against killing as they entered the deathhouse door. Did their newfound reverence for life stem from the realization that they were about to lose their own?

Life is indeed precious, and I believe the death penalty helps to affirm this fact. Had the death penalty been a real possibility in the minds of these murderers, they might well have stayed their hand. They might have shown moral awareness before their victims died, and not after. Consider the tragic death of Rosa Velez, who happened to be home when a man named Luis Vera burglarized her apartment in Brooklyn. "Yeah, I shot her," Vera admitted. "She knew me, and I knew I wouldn't go to the chair."

During my twenty-two years in public service, I have heard the pros and cons of capital punishment expressed with special intensity. As a district leader, councilman, congressman, and mayor, I have represented constituencies generally thought of as liberal. Because I support the death penalty for heinous crimes of murder, I have sometimes been the subject of emotional and outraged attacks by voters who find my position reprehensible or worse. I have listened to their ideas. I have weighed their objections carefully. I still support the death penalty. The reasons I maintain my position can be best understood by examining the arguments most frequently heard in opposition.

1. *The death penalty is "barbaric."* Sometimes opponents of capital punishment horrify with tales of lingering death on the gallows, of faulty electric chairs, or of agony in the gas chamber. Partly in response to such protests, several states such as North Carolina and Texas switched to execution by lethal injection. The condemned person is put to death painlessly, without ropes, voltage, bullets, or gas. Did this answer the objections of death penalty opponents? Of course not. On June 22, 1984, the *New York Times* published an editorial that sarcastically attacked the new "hygienic" method of death by injection, and stated that "execution can

never be made humane through science." So it's not the method that really troubles opponents. It's the death itself they consider barbaric.

Admittedly, capital punishment is not a pleasant topic. However, one does not have to like the death penalty in order to support it any more than one must like radical surgery, radiation, or chemotherapy in order to find necessary these attempts at curing cancer. Ultimately we may learn how to cure cancer with a simple pill. Unfortunately, that day has not arrived. Today we are faced with the choice of letting the cancer spread or trying to cure it with the methods available, methods that one day will almost certainly be considered barbaric. But to give up and do nothing would be far more barbaric and would certainly delay the discovery of an eventual cure. The analogy between cancer and murder is imperfect, because murder is not the "disease" we are trying to cure. The disease is injustice. We may not like the death penalty, but it must be available to punish crimes of cold-blooded murder, cases in which any other form of punishment would be inadequate and, therefore, unjust. If we create a society in which injustice is not tolerated, incidents of murder—the most flagrant form of injustice—will diminish.

2. *No other major democracy uses the death penalty.* No other major democracy—in fact, few other countries of any description—are plagued by a murder rate such as that in the United States. Fewer and fewer Americans can remember the days when unlocked doors were the norm and murder was a rare and terrible offense. In America the murder rate climbed 122 percent between 1963 and 1980. During that same period, the murder rate in New York City increased by almost 400 percent, and the statistics are even worse in many other cities. A study at M.I.T. showed that based on 1970 homicide rates a person who lived in a large American city ran a greater risk of being murdered than an American soldier in World War II ran of being killed in combat. It is not surprising that the laws of each country differ according to differing conditions and traditions. If other countries had our murder problem, the cry for capital punishment would be just as loud as it is here. And I daresay that any other major democracy where 75 percent of the people supported the death penalty would soon enact it into law.

3. *An innocent person might be executed by mistake.* Consider the work of Hugo Adam Bedau, one of the most implacable foes of capital punishment in this country. According to Mr. Bedau, it is "false sentimentality to argue that the death penalty should be abolished because of the abstract possibility that an innocent person might be executed." He cites a study of 7,000 executions in this country from 1893 to 1971, and concludes that the record fails to show that such cases occur. The main point, however, is this. If government functioned only when the possibility of error didn't exist, government wouldn't function at all. Human life deserves special protection, and one of the best ways to guarantee that protection is to assure that convicted murderers do not kill again. Only the death penalty can accomplish this end. In a recent case in New Jersey, a man named Richard Biegenwald was freed from prison after serving 18 years for murder; since his

release he has been convicted of committing four murders. A prisoner named Lemuel Smith, who, while serving four life sentences for murder (plus two life sentences for kidnapping and robbery) in New York's Green Haven Prison, lured a woman corrections officer into the chaplain's office and strangled her. He then mutilated and dismembered her body. An additional life sentence for Smith is meaningless. Because New York has no death penalty statute, Smith has effectively been given a license to kill.

But the problem of multiple murder is not confined to the nation's penitentiaries. In 1981, 91 police officers were killed in the line of duty in this country. Seven percent of those arrested in the cases that have been solved had a previous arrest for murder. In New York City in 1976 and 1977, 85 persons arrested for homicide had a previous arrest for murder. Six of these individuals had two previous arrests for murder, and one had four previous murder arrests. During those two years the New York police were arresting for murder persons with a previous arrest for murder on the average of one every 8.5 days. This is not surprising when we learn that in 1975, for example, the median time served in Massachusetts for homicide was less than two and a half years. In 1976 a study sponsored by the Twentieth Century Fund found that the average time served in the United States for first-degree murder is ten years. The median time served may be considerably lower.

4. *Capital punishment cheapens the value of human life.* On the contrary, it can be easily demonstrated that the death penalty strengthens the value of human life. If the penalty for rape were lowered, clearly it would signal a lessened regard for the victims' suffering, humiliation, and personal integrity. It would cheapen their horrible experience, and expose them to an increased danger of recurrence. When we lower the penalty for murder, it signals a lessened regard for the value of the victim's life. Some critics of capital punishment, such as columnist Jimmy Breslin, have suggested that a life sentence is a harsher penalty for murder than death. This is sophistic nonsense. A few killers may decide not to appeal a death sentence, but the overwhelming majority make every effort to stay alive. It is by exacting the highest penalty for the taking of human life that we affirm the highest value of human life.

5. *The death penalty is applied in a discriminatory manner.* This factor no longer seems to be the problem it once was. The appeals process for a condemned prisoner is lengthy and painstaking. Every effort is made to see that the verdict and sentence were fairly arrived at. However, assertions of discrimination are not an argument for ending the death penalty but for extending it. It is not justice to exclude everyone from the penalty of the law if a few are found to be so favored. Justice requires that the law be applied equally to all.

6. *Thou Shalt Not Kill.* The Bible is our greatest source of moral inspiration. Opponents of the death penalty frequently cite the sixth of the Ten Commandments in an attempt to prove that capital punishment is divinely proscribed. In the original Hebrew, however, the Sixth Commandment reads "Thou Shalt Not Commit Murder," and the Torah

specifies capital punishment for a variety of offenses. The biblical viewpoint has been upheld by philosophers throughout history. The greatest thinkers of the 19th century—Kant, Locke, Hobbes, Rousseau, Montesquieu, and Mill—agreed that natural law properly authorizes the sovereign to take life in order to vindicate justice. Only Jeremy Bentham was ambivalent. Washington, Jefferson, and Franklin endorsed it. Abraham Lincoln authorized executions for deserters in wartime. Alexis de Tocqueville, who expressed profound respect for American institutions, believed that the death penalty was indispensable to the support of social order. The United States Constitution, widely admired as one of the seminal achievements in the history of humanity, condemns cruel and unusual punishment, but does not condemn capital punishment.

7. *The death penalty is state-sanctioned murder.* This is the defense with which Messrs. Willie and Shaw hoped to soften the resolve of those who sentenced them to death. By saying in effect, "You're no better than I am," the murderer seeks to bring his accusers down to his own level. It is also a popular argument among opponents of capital punishment, but a transparently false one. Simply put, the state has rights that the private individual does not. In a democracy, those rights are given to the state by the electorate. The execution of a lawfully condemned killer is no more an act of murder than is legal imprisonment an act of kidnapping. If an individual forces a neighbor to pay him money under threat of punishment, it's called extortion. If the state does it, it's called taxation. Rights and responsibilities surrendered by the individual are what give the state its power to govern. This contract is the foundation of civilization itself.

Everyone has his or her rights, and will defend them jealously. Not everyone, however, wants responsibilities, especially the painful responsibilities that come with law enforcement. Twenty-one years ago a woman named Kitty Genovese was assaulted and murdered on a street in New York. Dozens of neighbors heard her cries for help but did nothing to assist her. They didn't even call the police. In such a climate the criminal understandably grows bolder. In the presence of moral cowardice, he lectures us on our supposed failings and tries to equate his crimes with our quest for justice.

The death of anyone—even a convicted killer—diminishes us all. But we are diminished even more by a justice system that fails to function. It is an illusion to let ourselves believe that doing away with capital punishment removes the murderer's deed from our conscience. The rights of society are paramount. When we protect guilty lives, we give up innocent lives in exchange. When opponents of capital punishment say to the state, "I will not let you kill in my name," they are also saying to murderers: "You can kill in your own name as long as I have an excuse for not getting involved."

It is hard to imagine anything worse than being murdered while neighbors do nothing. But something worse exists. When those same neighbors shrink back from justly punishing the murderer, the victim dies twice.

BRAINSTORMING THE OPPOSITE SIDE: TALKING POINTS AGAINST THE DEATH PENALTY

The points below are not intended to be an organized essay; they are separate arguments from a list created for public distribution by a group opposed to the death penalty. Use them as brainstorming points to help you explore the topic before writing your essay. Which of these points and facts seem most convincing to you? Do you think that any of them successfully refute arguments put forward in Edward Koch's article? Are there any that he does not discuss?

TALKING POINTS ON THE DEATH PENALTY*

What Do We Do About Crime If There Is No Death Penalty?

1. We are all concerned about crime, and would like the rate of crime to be reduced. The death penalty, however, is not an effective deterrent to crime.

—While the individual executed would certainly not commit another crime, research indicates the death penalty does not serve as a general deterrent to crime, that is, having the death penalty does not reduce the overall rate of crime.

—Murder rates are lower in states that have abolished the death penalty. In 1990, there was an average of 5.0 homicides per 100,000 population in states that had abolished the death penalty. In death penalty states without executions, the homicide rate was 6.0 per 100,000. The highest homicide rates were in death penalty states with executions: 9.7 homicides per 100,000.

—While murder rates have indeed increased everywhere in the past ten years, they have increased more in states with the death penalty.

—There have been many studies on the impact of the death penalty on the homicide rate; these studies have found no conclusive evidence that the death penalty acts as a deterrent. The reason is simple. The overwhelming majority of murders are irrational and passionate acts. Murder most often occurs during an uncontrolled rage or while under the influence of alcohol or drugs. The threat of a possible death sentence has little effect on a person incapable of rational thought. Those relatively few who plan their crimes rarely think they will be caught.

2. Alternatives to the death penalty do exist.

—One alternative to the death penalty is not having the death penalty at all. This alternative is practiced in a number of states and in every industrialized European country.

—In Washington, those found guilty of aggravated first degree murder may also be sentenced to life without the possibility of parole, a new

---

*"Talking Points on the Death Penalty." Washington Coalition to Abolish the Death Penalty, September 1995. Reprinted with permission.

sentence established that is different than what is commonly thought of as a life sentence. Life without parole means life without parole.

—While life without parole clearly may be considered by some as cruel, it still leaves people with their lives: the prisoner still has opportunities to make meaningful changes in his/her life, to make contributions to society, to relate to family. Moreover, if a person sentenced to life without parole is later found to be innocent, that person can be released. There is no way to give life back to someone who's been executed.

—There is public support for alternatives to the death penalty. When pollsters give alternatives to the death penalty, such as 25 year minimum sentences with restitution to the family of the murder victim, support for the death penalty decreases dramatically.

—If we really want to decrease the level of violence, we should consider alternatives to the death penalty such as support services for children and family, good community mental health programs available to all who need them, training in conflict resolution, etc.

The Death Penalty as an Ultimate Punishment

3. There is a sense that those convicted of the death penalty have acted outside the boundaries of acceptable human behavior. In this way, the death penalty appears justified. But for us to then kill those people puts us in the same moral position as they are in—we become killers. The death penalty is wrong because it makes us killers.

4. By killing those who kill, we teach that killing is sometimes right.

5. The people on death row did not get there on their own. All of us—their families and communities—share the responsibility of making them people who could consider committing the brutal acts they committed. It's not fair for these individuals alone to take the punishment.

6. The death penalty is the punishment in only a few murders. About 20,000 murders occur in the U.S. every year. Of those, only about 200 are selected as death penalty cases.

7. It's difficult for us to imagine a murderer ever going on to lead a good life. In fact, however, research has proven that those who commit murder are generally less likely to re-offend than most other prisoners. Studies of those who were on death row who were later released because of court decisions prove this fact.

8. There are, of course, individuals who have killed more than once and whose crimes especially horrify us. They are not, however, typical of the individuals on death row. . . .

Religious Arguments

9. While the Hebrew Bible (Old Testament) provides for the death penalty, it also calls for incredible safeguards, making the death penalty rare and almost impossible to carry out.

10. The major, mainstream Christian denominations have rejected the death penalty (Catholic, Lutheran, Presbyterian, UCC). Their understanding of the Christian tradition is that God commands them not to kill, but to forgive and trust that redemption and healing are possible.

Cost of the Death Penalty

11. Because executions are irreversible, death sentences will almost always be appealed. It may take a long time to execute a person, but we can never bring an innocent person back to life. If we replace the death penalty with an alternative, the new system will likely be quicker and less expensive.

12. Research on the death penalty indicates that death sentences cost the state more than life imprisonment. This is because death penalty trials are more expensive than other trials—more attorney time is required, more experts are generally used, the trial is more complex and takes more time, and there is an automatic appeal period (whether anyone wants it or not).

13. Florida has spent an average of $3.2 million for each person it has executed since 1972. The comparable figure for Texas is $2 million per case that has gone through all levels of appeal. The cost of executing Ted Bundy was at least $6 million.

14. The death penalty draws away resources from other areas of criminal justice and prevents us from finding more effective ways of reducing crime. While the death penalty is a popular symbol of a "get tough on crime" stance, it has proven worthless as a solution to the problem of violent crime. States whose resources and energies are not drained by the use of capital punishment are able to develop more effective methods of reducing violence.

15. We should not, of course, make decisions about the value of a person's life simply based on cost. But the figures make it clear that "saving money" is not a valid excuse for supporting the death penalty.

16. The death penalty has a number of costs. The money we spend is only one of them. The other "costs" of the death penalty are our inability to use the resources spent on the death penalty for more effective criminal justice initiatives; the execution of innocent people; and making us a society of killers.

Writing Assignment

The Dialogue Pattern

Find a magazine or newspaper article, preferably an editorial, that expresses a strong opinion you disagree with. List the main point of the article and the supporting reasons. Across from these write your own opposing opinions on each point. Add to your list any further points you can think of on your side. If you have difficulty thinking of sufficient reasons to support your opinion, try a non-stop writing exercise to explore your thoughts on the subject.

   Once you have sufficient ideas, write a first draft of an essay using the dialogue method. Begin with an introduction identifying the writer and article you are opposing, as well as its main point. State your opposing point. Base the body of your essay on a series of rebuttals to the main arguments given in the article. Add any important points on your side not considered in the article, and write an effective conclusion. As always, read your rough draft aloud to someone else, preferably a small group of other students, to get as much feedback as you can. Use the feedback to strengthen arguments that need more support and to better explain arguments that are unclear. Reread your first draft to be sure you have represented your opponent's opinion correctly and organized your material effectively, saving your strongest argument for the last. Write a final draft.

Group Project

The Dialogue Pattern

Working with your writing group, supply counter arguments to each of the arguments presented on these topics. Each of these exercises contains a main thesis and some supporting points. Across from each point, have your group recorder write in arguments on the opposite side based on your discussion. After completing the exercises, choose *one* of them as the basis for an essay. Each writer should do an exploratory draft; then all members of the group should read their drafts aloud and discuss the pros and cons of the issue further. Write final drafts. Remember: You need not agree with one another. Two essays on opposite sides of an argument can be equally good.

1. **Thesis Statement:**
   Drugs should be legalized in the United States.

   Opposing Thesis Statement:
   Legalizing drugs would make the drug problem worse in the United States.

   Supporting Points:

   A. Legalizing drugs would reduce drug-related crimes and violence.

   B. We can't stop drug traffic—it is too widespread.

   C. People have a right to make their own choices, even harmful ones.

   Opposing Points:

   A. _____
      _____

   B. _____
      _____

   C. _____
      _____

D. Legalizing drugs would make drug use less exciting; there would be less addiction.

D. _____
_____
_____

E. We tried making alcohol illegal in the past; that did not work, and keeping drugs illegal does not work either.

E. _____
_____
_____
_____

F. The government would collect taxes on the legal sales of drugs.

F. _____
_____

2. **Thesis statement:**
Women should not serve in the military.

Opposing Thesis Statement:
Women improve the military significantly.

Supporting Points:

Opposing Points:

A. Women are not as strong as men in combat and other military work.

A. _____
_____

B. Women are needed at home during wartime.

B. _____
_____

C. Women would be more emotional in war situations.

C. _____
_____

D. Women might get pregnant and drop out.

D. _____
_____

E. Having women around would distract men from their duties.

E. _____
_____

3. **Thesis Statement:**
Pornographic videos, magazines and telephone services are harmless entertainment and should be permitted.

Opposing Thesis Statement:
Pornography promotes violence and harms society by degrading both sex and women.

Supporting Points:

Opposing Points:

A. People have a right to whatever forms of entertainment they choose.

A. _____
_____
_____

B. Pornography has not been proven to be harmful.

B. _____
_____

C. Many serious films, books, and
works of art are "pornographic."

C. _____
_____

D. Denial and ignorance of sexuality
does more harm than pornography, which helps educate people.

D. _____
_____
_____

4. **Thesis Statement:**
Young people should not have
sex before marriage.

Opposing Thesis Statement:
Sexual experience before marriage is
morally and socially acceptable.

Supporting Points:

A. The only safe sex today is celibacy
before marriage

B. Sex is right only with the person
you want to spend your life with.

C. The purpose of sex is to bear
children, which should happen in
marriage.

D. Sex before marriage is often
psychologically harmful, especially
for young teenagers.

E. Premarital sex tends to make
marriages fail.

Opposing Points:

A. _____
_____

B. _____
_____

C. _____
_____
_____

D. _____
_____
_____

E. _____
_____

Writing Activity for Extra Practice

Fifteen Topics for Persuasive Essays

Making use of all you have learned about the writing process, write a well-
developed, organized, and convincing essay expressing your opinion on one of
the topics below. Explore the topic through the prewriting methods that work
best for you, write a first draft based on your prewriting activities, get feedback
from others on your arguments and examples, revise your work, and write a
final draft.

1. Should there be mandatory drug testing on all jobs?
2. Should people who have AIDS or are HIV positive be guaranteed the
right to keep their jobs and not be turned down for new jobs?
3. Should the government control what people can say on the Internet?
4. Should smoking be banned in all public places?

5. Should state and city universities admit all high school graduates?
6. Should a teenager who gets pregnant have an abortion, keep her child, or put it up for adoption?
7. Should the reports of Unidentified Flying Objects be taken seriously?
8. Should parents of adolescent criminals be sentenced to fines or other criminal punishments?
9. Should homosexual people be allowed to get married?
10. Should affirmative action continue to be practiced in college admissions and hiring?
11. Should young adults have to put in two years of public service in place of military service?
12. Should the United States remove all barriers on imports of foreign products even though some countries restrict our exports to their countries?
13. Should prostitution be legalized, taxed, and regulated?
14. Should public school children have to wear uniforms?
15. Should the United States increase or decrease the number of immigrants it admits?

Revising Essays: A Review

In the process of writing essays, revising is almost as important as composing itself. You have already done several kinds of revision in this unit and are already aware of the extent to which revision can improve the content and organization of your essays. Before continuing to Unit 4 where you will work on revising your word choice and sentence patterns, let's review the kinds of revision you should make in your earlier drafts. Revision of essays includes the following:

- Revising the thesis and thesis statement to give the essay a clear focus (see pages 102–105).
- Revising development to be sure the essay covers the main purpose thoroughly (see pages 111–125).
- Revising for critical thinking to be sure that your arguments are logical and persuasive (see pages 116, 129, 144–150, 163–164).
- Revising for unity and coherence to make sure everything in the essay supports the main thesis and sentences and paragraphs are in the right place (see pages 115–116, 150, 160, 163).

Group Project

Practice with Revision

Read the two essays below. Both of them have been developed beyond the prewriting stage but still need to be revised. Take a look at the marginal notes and handwritten comments calling for revisions of the kinds listed above. Working with your writing group, choose one of the essays, and discuss the suggestions for revision. Create a revised draft that improves the essay by using both the written suggestions and your own judgment about what the essay needs.

Essay 1

English Spoken Here

Interesting lead-in, but can you tie it into your thesis better?

Overgeneralized statement

Is there a topic sentence?

Thesis sentence; put it in 1st paragraph.

Paragraph needs a clear topic and more development.

Many places in the United States, especially in big cities, you can hear people speaking dozens of languages, and you often see signs and advertisements in other languages. Even some automatic teller machines allow you to make transactions in five or six languages. All of this may be good for the people who speak those languages, but what about speaking English? Shouldn't these people learn English the way everybody else always did?

If I went to live in one of their countries, I would have to learn how to speak the language of that country. Why do they expect to come here and not have to learn English? A law should be passed making English the only official language of the United States. That way everybody would have to do all their business in English, and we would all be able to understand each other.

What happens if a nurse or doctor doesn't understand what a patient is saying? Or what if your cab driver can't understand your directions and takes you to the wrong part of town?

This paragraph has two topics: school and government business.

English should also be the official U.S. language so that all classes in school will be taught in English. Imagine what it's going to be like for teachers if they have to speak to students in seventeen languages. How is anyone going to learn anything without being able to read their textbooks and talk in class in English? Bilingual classes are supposed to help students learn English faster, but they never work; all they do is let students avoid learning English for years. Also, all government business should be in English, and ballots should be in English. Think how confusing it is when somebody in a trial doesn't speak English and they have to use translators. How do we know that the translator is telling us exactly what the person says?

Is your thesis about bilingual education or English as an official language?

When my parents came to this country, they didn't speak any English either, but after five years they learned to speak and read it very well. It was hard for them at first, but they took adult education classes and worked in jobs where they didn't have to use English at first, and after a while they were able to get along very well. That's what America is all about. Bilingual education isn't the answer; everybody should learn English.

Comments

This is a promising draft, but it needs some major revisions. First of all, your thesis seems to be that the U.S. government should pass a law making English the official language. Stick to that point only (bilingual education and the use of foreign languages in banking and other businesses are a little off the topic). So far, however, you haven't supported the thesis that English should be the official language strongly enough. Can you give a supporting reason in each of your body paragraphs? (Remember, by the way, that your body paragraphs ought to be 7-12 sentences each, not just one or two.) What are some of the benefits of such a law? There are good arguments to support it, but it is very controversial. Can you answer some of the objections? The example of your parents' experience is a good one, but you say that for five years they were using their first language; how would an English-only law have benefited them?

A good exploration draft, but you can make it a much better essay by clarifying and developing your thesis, and arranging your arguments sequentially.

Essay 2

When Is the Right Time to Start a Family?

OK lead-in, but is this an introductory paragraph?

It's not quite clear which side you're on; is there a thesis statement?

A lot of my friends are waiting to get married and have children until they are in their late twenties or early thirties. I think they are doing the right thing because it's hard to support a family nowadays with the high cost of living, and both parents have to work just to make ends meet. Some guys are too immature to settle down before they are older, and a lot of young women aren't ready either to give up their freedom in their early twenties. Most people nowadays need a college degree to get ahead, and it takes a long time to finish a degree because most students have to work to afford college. On the other hand, if you wait too long, you may have more trouble finding the person you want to marry, and sometimes younger women have an easier time getting pregnant. People I know who have gotten married later usually make better choices of mates and have marriages that last better. This is because both the husband and wife are more mature and they have dated other people and know what sort of person they want to share their life with. People in their thirties are usually better parents too because the babies are not interrupting their social life or their education as much, and they are ready to take care of them better. Not only that, but they know more about psychology and how to relate to children.

what is the topic of this paragraph?

I know some people who were good parents when they were nineteen or twenty, and I've known some older parents who acted like teenagers and never took care of their kids the way they should. But I think that for most people it's better to wait until you are finished with your education and start your career. Also if you want to try life on the wild side for a while when you're young, it's too soon to take on family responsibilities that you aren't able to handle yet. Half of today's marriages end in divorce, and this is more likely to happen when the husband and wife are very young.

Interesting historical background, but how does it support your thesis?

People used to get married a lot younger, but in those days they didn't need a college education to get ahead, and women usually didn't work outside the home. There was no need to wait because people usually married someone their families wanted them to marry. Today, when you are making your own choice of a lifetime spouse and a parent for your children, you should be sure you know who's right for you and who will make a good parent. You aren't likely to know that until you have had a chance to get an education and work for a while.

Again, are you changing your opinion?

With the high cost of living today, you also need to save up money before you start a family. Besides that, most students nowadays have college loans to pay off. However, some couples that wait to get married until they are over thirty are so involved with their careers that they don't have time for each other, not to mention time for children. People like that probably should start earlier. Not everybody should do the same thing. For most people, though, it's a lot smarter to wait until you are really ready before you have children. Once they are here, you can't say that you made a mistake and don't want to be a parent after all. It's not the same for men as it is for women. Men don't have to worry about the "biological clock," and they can become fathers at any age. Women don't usually want to wait until they are forty before they start having children, although some of them do. It's a different world now, and people can do what they want to do.

Why bring up a new topic at the end?

Comments

You have a lot to say about this subject, and you can see both sides of the issue. However, let's start with your main thesis: You are supporting the idea that it's a good idea not to marry too early, but sometimes you seem almost to be arguing the other side. Could you include a clear, firm thesis statement in the first paragraph that leaves no doubt about your position?

© 1998 by Addison-Wesley Educational Publishers Inc.

You can answer some of the objections from the other side later. What about an introductory paragraph? In your first paragraph, you seem to be trying to cover most of the issue all at once. How about separating your argument into body paragraphs that each argue a different reason for couples to wait until they are ready to get married? How about an example or two from your own experience to support some of these points? In your last paragraph, instead of concluding, you bring in some new ideas that either ought to be developed earlier or omitted. Should these be discussed earlier? This essay will be much more effective with clearer organization and a consistent main thesis.

Computers and Essay Writing

In this book you have been encouraged to focus on the writing process, that is, to think of an essay as the result of many stages of development. When you write by hand or on a typewriter, this means you produce many *drafts,* each one better developed, organized, and written than the last. Every time you wrote something about the topic, whether you were doing focused writing, clustering, a rough draft, or a final draft, you left separate sheets of paper that could be looked at and compared with one another.

Writing on a computer is different. It is possible to do all your prewriting on the screen and all your composing on one document that you can keep revising, rearranging, and correcting as many times as you want. You can, if you wish, wait to print it out only when you have the final document exactly as you want it. This means that you have separate drafts only if you decide to print the hard copy. If you have limited access to a printer; therefore, you may tend to avoid printing out your document until the point at which you do not want to revise it any more.

The trouble with that approach is that you are likely to do less revising of the whole document, since you will be conscious of the screen as a unit of writing rather than the page or the whole essay. Equally important is that working alone at a computer you are more likely to neglect input from classmates and other readers, and possibly from your teacher. Unless the teacher or tutor confers with you as you work or asks for a copy on disk, you may be tempted to avoid the ongoing feedback from readers that you should be getting at all stages of your work. The physical arrangements of computers tend to encourage writers to mind their own business, unless they are working on an interactive network. It seems much more natural to show handwritten work to the person sitting next to you or to read it aloud to a small group. However, collaborative reading, listening, and responding is just as important whether you write on a computer, or you compose longhand. No machine can take the place of human interaction in the writing process.

Although the computer can be a miraculous tool for helping you produce a perfect finished document, don't expect it to do the creative work for you. Use it to the maximum for those aspects of your work where you find it helpful—the spell check, the capacity for changing words or phrases, or the larger capacity for rearranging large chunks of text. If there are points at which you find that it seems to get in your way—if, for instance, you simply MUST write your first draft long-hand—remember that the computer is a tool, not an end in itself.

Exercise I

Computers and Essay Writing

As an exercise in developing your relationship with the computer, try this com-parison: Do one essay assignment entirely without using the computer; use longhand or a typewriter for the whole process from prewriting activities to final draft. Then do a similar assignment entirely on the computer, from prewrit-ing activities through the final revised and proofread document. Ask yourself these questions:

1. When I did the essay assignment without the computer, at what points did I find myself frustrated and impatient, writing too cautiously for fear of making a mistake and having to redo a whole page or make messy corrections?
2. When I did the whole process on the computer, at what points did I feel out of touch with my own writing because the machine felt impersonal? Was there any point at which I wanted to tear out a sheet of lined paper and begin writing?

For you and all writers in today's world of electronic communications, the important question is, what combination of speaking, handwriting, composing on the computer screen, and working with printouts will allow you to produce your best essays? Only you can discover the answer.

> ### Reminders About Writing Essays
> ◆ **Build essays out of paragraphs, with short introductory and concluding paragraphs and well-developed body paragraphs**. Although the structure of your essay should not be too obvious to the reader, it should be clear to you. Be sure that you can explain what your intention is in every part of the essay.

◆ Learn to write effective **thesis statements** that will guide the reader and make your main purpose clear. An effective thesis statement must be broad enough to be divided into subtopics and developed in several paragraphs but specific enough for you to discuss it thoroughly in your essay. In a short essay, a good place for your thesis statement is the end of your introductory paragraph, although advanced writers place thesis statements in other places as well.

◆ **Narrative essays** present personal experiences or public events in chronological order. Make each paragraph carry the story one step further in time, and use transitional expressions between and within paragraphs to create continuity. Avoid shifting verb tenses, and watch verb forms in the past tense, especially–ED endings. Your story should have a point to it, but this point may emerge as you are writing your first draft. Your revised drafts will often bring out this point more.

◆ **Descriptive essays** portray persons or places, using vivid, sensory details and varied supporting paragraphs. Although physical details are important, description also involves capturing the essential character, meaning, or spirit of a person or place. In your prewriting activities and first draft, search for this overall quality and put it into your thesis statement in revised drafts. Each paragraph should make a distinct contribution to the overall purpose, describing either a physical part or area or a separate quality of the person or place. Descriptive writing usually requires multiple revisions to improve descriptive wording and organization.

◆ **Expository essays** should explain and analyze social issues so that the reader understands them better. Principles of critical thinking are important in expository writing. Explore all important aspects of the topic by discussing it with others, reading, and doing sufficient prewriting activities. Look up background facts if needed. Avoid oversimplifying complex issues and be sure to include any necessary steps in analysis or explanation. Since clarity is all-important in expository writing, get feedback from readers to be sure you have communicated exactly what you wanted to.

◆ **Persuasive essays** should present a strong argument based on several kinds of support. Learn to employ several methods, such as enumerating examples, enumerating reasons, or using the dialogue pattern to organize arguments. Be sure that your main purpose comes across effectively—not only the main point but what you want readers to feel and think about what you say. Avoid logical fallacies, especially oversimplification and overgeneralization, and try not to come across as dogmatic or prejudiced. Above all, show that you understand arguments on the opposite side and can answer them.

◆ **Composing essays on computers** presents different opportunities and challenges than composing on paper. Instead of several drafts, you have a single document on file which you can change many times in large and small ways. Experiment to see what combination of writing on paper and word processing works best for you. Since the opportunities for revising are now much greater than in the past, word processing presents additional responsibilities for writers who want to do their best.

U N I T

4

Improving Your Writing Style

You have now learned and practiced prewriting and paragraph composition. You have also composed short essays and revised the plan, content, and organization of your work. Now we will turn to techniques for improving the effectiveness of your language, including your choice of words and your sentence patterns. To write vividly and forcefully you must be able to turn monotonous, flat prose into writing that catches and holds the reader's interest. This means taking what you thought was already a "final draft" and making it still better.

Improving Your Revised Drafts

In the previous units you have learned to work with a topic through several phases of the writing process. Moving from prewriting to formal composition, you have composed essays and revised them by adding descriptive details, supporting facts and ideas, and by organizing them into well-fitted parts. In this unit you will work on another kind of revising, which comes later in the writing process: **improving your style by choosing effective words and phrases and by creating varied, well-constructed sentences.** Although an effective style may be part of your writing at any stage, you should pay special attention to revising your style on your second drafts (unless you are writing on a computer and have made many changes on one document instead of doing two drafts). At that point, most of your planning and composing is done, and whatever changes in style you make will probably remain in the final draft. It is tempting to stop when you are satisfied with your content and organization, but remember: *The difference between mediocre writing and superior writing often lies in stylistic revision.*

Here is an example of a reasonably good first draft that needs alterations to bring it to life. Where is it too vague? Where is the language not vivid enough? What is wrong with the sentences?

First Draft

Moving out of my parents' house was a big deal. I had to find a place to live. A job had to be found and my daily responsibilities had to be taken care of. I never realized until then how much my parents had done for me. I couldn't use the family car anymore, so I rented a van. I packed all the stuff that I owned and got myself moved, but it was a huge mess. I soon discovered how expensive living on your own is, but I got used to my new life-style and I was glad I decided to move.

How have the words and sentences been improved in the revised draft below?

Moving out of my parents' house was both difficult and challenging. Although it was hard finding a new apartment, landing a job and meeting daily responsibilities, I learned to appreciate how much my parents had done for me. Not being able to use the family car anymore, I had to rent a van and transport my clothes, books, and stereo equipment to my new residence. After surviving this exhausting, chaotic ordeal, as well as the shock of realizing how expensive independent living can be, I began a new phase in my life and quickly adjusted to my new lifestyle. I made the right decision at the right time.

What are the main differences between the draft and the revised version? What makes the revision better than the earlier draft? Which words have been changed? How have the sentences been improved?

Read the following draft. This short essay is on a subject the writer had been reading about and thus knew something about. It is much more developed than the short passage you just read; however, its words and sentences can also be improved.

Sample Draft

Music and Art Courses in College

Note sentence beginnings: almost all start with the subject of the main clause.

Some colleges require music or art courses for all students, and some require them only for liberal arts students. Other colleges let students take courses in music and art if they choose to. Some students support the idea of music and art courses, and some do not, but there are many benefits for all students who take such courses. They can improve their career skills, improve their general knowledge, and improve their enjoyment of culture.

Some students don't want to take courses in art or music. Some of these students believe that art and music courses are for students with specialized skills and specialized interests. These students claim that they should be able to choose courses that they need to further their progress toward their careers. They often are afraid that they will get low grades in music or art courses, and they don't know as much about these subjects as students who major in these areas. They also sometimes think that they will be bored by having to learn about music and art.

Use of passive voice weakens some statements

Note the rather flat vocabulary

One of the good things these students are taught in art and music courses is the improvement of their thinking skills and knowledge they will get from studying art or music. Art and music make students use their imaginations and think with their feelings and senses and not just learn facts from memory. This kind of thinking makes them better able to understand many other things and to become better at some of the skills they may need in their other courses and on their jobs. College graduates will be employed where they will be expected to carry on interesting conversations on many topics and have interesting ideas and share aesthetic values. If they are given a lot of general knowledge, they will succeed in presenting their ideas and communicating with well-educated people. They will also become better parents and their children will be exposed to better cultural opportunities.

Music and art also teach students to value creativity and to be creative themselves. Being creative will help them be more effective in their careers and more interesting in the way they spend their time. Most people spend too much time watching television and videos and not being creative. They should spend more time being creative, and they will lead more interesting lives. In their jobs they need to be creative just as much. People who get ahead in companies and other places of employment are the ones who create new approaches and ideas. Art and music courses can teach them to be creative this way.

People who take courses in the arts appreciate the qualities that make our lives more beautiful, interesting, and worth living. They enjoy life more and teach their families to appreciate the things that help people enjoy life more. Making money is important and necessary, but how we spend our money is also important. Having a good income but living a boring life is not good enough. How we spend our time is just as important as how we spend our money. The quality of our lives is just as important as the quantity of our wealth. Studying art and music is an important way to make our lives better.

Note lack of variety: one short sentence after another

The writer of this essay has done a good job in many ways. She has made some good points about her subject and organized her ideas into paragraphs. She has stayed on the general topic and maintained a clear main point. Her sentences are clear and easy to read, and her vocabulary is college level, even including such terms as "aesthetic values."

Why is this not a first-rate finished essay? If this writer asked for readers' feedback on the language of the essay, she might find that some words are repeated too often. She might also discover that her sentences, although clear, are somewhat monotonous and need more variety. Sometimes her phrases are wordy and some sentences are too long and involved. In short, the style of her essay can be improved quite a bit.

Revised Version

Why Paint and Fiddle?

Because music and art can be fun, some students doubt that they belong in serious, required courses. Although many colleges require fine arts courses for all liberal arts students, and some even for all students, a lingering suspicion exists that such "luxury courses" belong as electives for talented undergraduates with special interests. Nearly all students, when they take such courses, however, find themselves opening up to a new range of interests and gaining skills and benefits they never expected. Courses in music appreciation, the history of art, or jazz dance enhance students' general knowledge, career skills, and aesthetic enjoyment.

Sentences do not all begin with the main clause; better variety

Convinced that the fine arts require special talent, many students avoid music and art courses entirely. In addition, undergraduates intent on fulfilling their career aspirations often dismiss art and music as irrelevant to their vocational goals. Anxious about maintaining their grade point averages, they may fear competing with students who have special musical or artistic training. Above all, many students expect to be bored by courses in which they will analyze paintings or listen to operas, possibly disliking as well the prospect of being surrounded by nonconformist, "artsy" students and professors. By yielding to these doubts, they may miss out on some of the richest, most enjoyable educational opportunities of their lives.

Length of sentences varies, alternating between long and short.

Contrary to the notion that the arts speak only to the specialized few, students discover that studying chamber music or impressionist painting enriches their general knowledge and teaches them to think. Music and art open a window on the real world that reveals many new ideas about society, human nature, and history. Even more important than factual knowledge, however, is the way in which students learn to think by using their imagination, emotions, and sense perceptions. Such thinking enables them to understand human relationships, cultural values, and society. Surprisingly, it even prepares them to succeed in their world of employment, where they must relate to other educated people, understand cultural variety, and present their ideas effectively. As parents, they will urge their children to play instruments, paint, dance, or sing and take them to museums and concerts.

Word choice is more precise and vivid; stronger verbs in active voice

Most important, music and art teach students to value creativity and to be creative themselves. Their creativity will enhance their careers and enrich their personal lives. Unlike the many Americans who waste hours every day staring at mindless television programs, they will participate actively in improving the aesthetic quality of their homes and their communities. Not only will their personal lives be more interesting, but they will seek resourceful solutions to problems in their jobs and in their society. People who succeed in their careers and lead in their communities are the ones who create new approaches much the way artists explore new forms and styles.

Students who take courses in the arts are not just "fiddling around." They are learning to appreciate what makes our lives more beautiful, interesting, and worthwhile. They and their families will eventually enjoy life more, and they may even succeed better at their jobs. Making money is necessary, but how we spend our money and our time is equally important. Art and music enrich the quality of our lives, which matters just as much as the quantity of our capital.

The language in this version is much better than in the previous draft. Notice the specific improvements mentioned in the marginal comments. The words are less repetitive and better chosen, and the sentences are more varied.

Group Project

Revision

The following paragraph contains repetitions, poorly chosen words, and boring sentence patterns. In your writing group, discuss what needs to be done to improve the language of the paragraph. Have your group recorder write down each sentence with the revisions your group agrees upon. When you have improved the whole paragraph, have your recorder read it aloud.

Eating Right for a Healthy Life

Most people have some bad ideas about what they should eat to be healthy. Some people think that they will be healthy if they just go to a health food store and don't eat a lot of junk food. But most people will do better if they know more about what foods will really make them healthy. For example, they need to know that they should consume only about 2000 calories a day, which is less than most people eat, and no more than 20 percent of the calories should come from fat. Many people think that eating a lot of red meat is good for them, but actually such foods as grains, vegetables, fruit, and fish are a lot better for your health than red meat, which has a lot of fat. Also, egg yolks and liver have a lot of cholesterol. This is not good for your health either. Many desserts, like cheesecake and pecan pie, are bad for your health because tons of calories and a lot of fat are contained in them too. Most people think that eating lots of proteins is important for their health, but most people already get more than enough protein in the foods they eat, and they should start eating more carbohydrates and vitamins and other nutriments instead. Green vegetables, fruit, cereals like oat bran, fish, and chicken (without the skin) are included in a good diet, and fruit juice, milk, and water are to be consumed frequently to make for a healthy life. Food guides are published by the government that can be used to give you advice on how to eat right to be healthy. If they are used properly, and common sense is applied, your health will be assured.

Questions to Help You Revise:

1. Which words and phrases are repeated too often? What new ones can you replace them with?
2. Which sentences are in the passive voice? Which sentences are too long and loose? Which are too choppy? How can you rewrite them?
3. Which words are too vague or convey the wrong tone? What better words can you suggest?

Exercise

Revision

Rewrite the following passage to improve its sentence patterns and choice of words.

Writing Your Resume

Having a good resume is very important. It is important for it to look good and to make a good impression. To create the right impression, it should be done on a computer and a laser printer, and it should be done carefully. Your spelling and grammar should be checked with care, and all the important information should be included. For most jobs, your work history will be the most important part of your resume, so you should put that first. List the jobs that you have held in reverse chronological order, starting with the most recent one. Most employers will want to know not only where you worked but also what you did on the job. They will be impressed if you include some brief descriptions of your accomplishments on each job. Positive action words like *created, developed, directed, encouraged,* or *expanded* should be used to show that you were an active person in each job. For most jobs, you should also include your educational history. This means identifying any degrees you have earned and the colleges where you earned them. Emphasize any facts about your education that might help you get the job you are applying for, and leave out anything (such as the dates you received degrees or courses of study unrelated to the job) that you think might hurt your chances or detract in any way; you may have extracurricular activities or volunteer activities that will help you get the job you are applying for, so be sure to include these as well. You do not have to include personal information such as your age, marital status, and ethnicity, but you may want to include any personal information that you think will help you get the job you want. When you have completed your resume, check it over several times to correct any errors in spelling or grammar, and have someone else check it over too. You may want to have it done professionally to create an impressive format. When you're sure it is ready, don't fold it and mail it, but deliver it to your prospective employer in person.

Improving Your Choice of Words

In the process of revising paragraphs and essays, as in the previous exercises, concentrate above all on the whole shape and development of your revised draft. Once you are satisfied with the essay as a whole, it is time to improve it by concentrating on your diction, or choice of words. The most noticeable difference between an acceptable but uninteresting essay and one that makes the reader want to read it again and again is usually a powerful use of words. Choose words that are precise, appropriate in connotation, specific, economical, vivid, and idiomatic.

BEING PRECISE

Legal, scientific, and medical writing must be precise for professional reasons, but all writing is more effective when the words convey exactly the right meaning. You know how infuriating it is when you ask for directions and someone tells you your destination is "down the road a piece" or "a few miles from here." You need more precise directions. Similarly, in writing, make careful statements. Be especially careful with words like *all, everybody, nobody, most, many, some,* and *a few.* In conversation we casually throw around remarks like "Everybody knows that song." We don't take such remarks literally, but you should not write casual statements about serious issues. "Everybody wants stricter enforcement of drug laws" is not a careful statement. "Most people" would probably be an accurate phrase in this statement; "many people" or "some people" would be too weak.

Be careful also to choose the correct transitional expressions and connective words. Don't use *and* as a catchall connective instead of *but, therefore,* or some other connective. "Police sometimes react too quickly, *and* they don't have enough training" is less precise than "Police sometimes react too quickly *because* they don't have enough training." Avoid using *which* or *in which* vaguely in place of *and* or other connectives. "Teenagers face many temptations today, *in which* they often get into trouble" is awkward and imprecise. A better statement might be "Teenagers are often in difficult situations *in which* they suddenly need help." Some writers often misuse *whereas,* treating it as an all-purpose transitional word. The correct use of *whereas* is to show a contrast, as in the statement "The state law permits turning right on a red light, *whereas* the city ordinance prohibits it." Do not use it carelessly, as in "The government should do something about the homeless, *whereas* inexpensive public housing should be built and counseling should be provided."

As you learn new vocabulary, do not be afraid to use it in your writing. Just be sure to check the meaning in a dictionary first. When you begin noticing a particular new word in your reading, you may guess at the meaning—and guess wrong. "This will *exacerbate* the condition"; "This will *alleviate* the condition." Which word do you want? What is the difference between *uninterested* and *disinterested?* between *discreet* and *discrete?* What does it mean to *defer* payment? What exactly do we refer to as a *story,* a *novel,* a *poem,* or a work of *prose?* What does it mean to *rationalize?* Is that different from *being rational?* When should you write *infer* and when should you write *imply?* What is the difference between *compose* and *comprise?* These are just some of the hundreds of fine distinctions made by careful writers. If you hope to be a careful writer, you must always have a dictionary at hand, especially when you edit.

Exercise I

Choosing Precise Words

The underlined words or phrases are imprecise or incorrect as used. Use common sense and a dictionary to help you determine more precise equivalents. Write them in the blanks.

Example:

appraised   The senator was <u>appraised</u> of the results of the election.

_____ 1. The presence of heavily armed police only <u>alleviated</u> the crowd's anger.

_____ 2. Food served in fast-food restaurants is more nutritious than most people think, <u>and</u> the problem is that it is highly caloric.

_____ 3. <u>Most</u> people believe in astrology and witchcraft.

_____ 4. Both parties in the labor dispute agreed to submit the decision to an <u>uninterested</u> third party.

_____ 5. <u>All</u> of the members of Congress put their constituents' wishes before the needs of the nation.

_____ 6. Biology majors must take at least three courses in subjects not related to science, <u>whereas</u> two must be in the humanities.

_____ 7. Lucie <u>rationalized</u> that she could afford to pay no more than $700 for rent.

_____ 8. The writer is <u>inferring</u> that she really does not believe the government's statistics.

_____ 9. When Donna pointed out his mistake, Frank <u>extracted</u> his statement.

_____ 10. The patient's stomach was badly <u>extended</u> from the internal pressure.

USING CORRECT CONNOTATION

Connotation is what a word suggests; **denotation** is what it means literally. Blue, red, green, and gray denote certain colors, but they all connote something else—blue, sadness; red, radicalism or anger; green, envy or illness; and gray, indistinctness (a gray area). In effective writing one chooses words for their implied meanings and associations as well as for their factual meanings. *Love, adoration, affection, devotion, liking,* and *friendship* all mean approximately the same thing, but each word suggests a different emotional quality. *Debate, argue, quarrel,* and *clash* all refer to differences of opinion but suggest different degrees of feeling. Some words are more formal than others: *before, previously,* and *hitherto* all refer to the past, but each one is more formal than the one before. Most of us would never use *hitherto* in conversation.

In college writing, faulty connotation may result from not finding the right voice and tone. If your writing shuttles between casual street remarks and formal statements, your word choice will be erratic. An essay that contains words such as *hitherto, reciprocal, charismatic,* and *extraneous* will sound funny if it also contains expressions like *cop out, cool, booze,* and *dude.* Some words may also have offensive connotations; *gal,* for instance, has a sexist connotation that *women* does not. *Spinster* used for a single woman has both sexist and old-fashioned connotations. Words may have favorable neutral or negative connotations. *Bureaucrat,* for example, may refer to an office worker in a large organization, but it can also suggest a person who merely follows orders without being humanly involved in his or her work. *Government employee* does not have a negative connotation of this kind. Be sure that the words you choose have the connotations appropriate to your intention and tone.

USING YOUR DICTIONARY AND THESAURUS

Choosing words with the correct meaning and connotation means using your dictionary and thesaurus. When revising later drafts, have your thesaurus and dictionary handy. The thesaurus will give you a list of *synonyms,* or words similar in meaning to the one you want to select. (The major word processing programs, like *WordPerfect* and Microsoft *Word* contain thesaurus icons that allow you to call up synonyms with a single mouse command.) The dictionary will give you not only the precise meaning or meanings of a word you choose, but also, for some words, an explanation of the differences in connotation between that word and near synonyms.

For example, suppose you want to write the sentence, "I disagree with this writer's *belief* about legalizing drugs." You are not satisfied with the word *belief,* so you look in *Roget's Thesaurus* to find synonyms to consider. You come up with the following possibilities: *opinion, sentiment, feeling, sense, impression, reaction, notion, idea, thought, mind, thinking, way of thinking, attitude, stance, posture, position, mind-set,* and *point of view.*★ Out of this group, the word *opinion* sounds better, so you look it up in the dictionary, which offers you the following explanation:

★*Roget's International Thesaurus,* ed. Robert L. Chapman. New York: HarperCollins; Fifth Edition, 1992. p. 660.

syn   OPINION, VIEW, BELIEF, CONVICTION, PERSUASION, SENTIMENT mean a judgment one holds as true. OPINION implies a conclusion thought out yet open to dispute <each expert seemed to have a different *opinion*>. VIEW suggests a subjective opinion <very assertive in stating his *views*>. BELIEF implies often deliberate acceptance and intellectual assent <a firm *belief* in her party's platform>. CONVICTION applies to a firmly and seriously held belief <the *conviction* that animal life is as sacred as human>. PERSUASION suggests a belief grounded on assurance (as by evidence) of its truth <was of the *persuasion* that everything changes>. SENTIMENT suggests a settled opinion reflective of one's feelings <her feminist *sentiments* are well known>.★

Looking over this explanation, you probably would decide that *belief* was not the best word, since it implies loyalty to a party or religion. Words like *persuasion* and *sentiment* probably wouldn't fit the statement perfectly either: *Persuasion* is still a kind of *belief,* and *sentiment* suggests emotion more than judgment based on evidence. Although one could have a *conviction* about legalizing drugs, your hunch that *opinion* is the best word seems right: The author has an *opinion* ("a conclusion thought out yet open to dispute") about legalizing drugs.

Exercise

Connotation

Explain why each of the underlined words has the wrong connotation for its use in the sentence. Write a more appropriate word in the blank.

Example:

assistants   I admire the mayor for appointing high quality inferiors. (*Inferiors suggests that the mayor's appointees are unqualified.*)

_____   1. After the refreshments were served, the executives decided to <u>split.</u>
_____   2. The police commissioner told the officers to stop <u>griping</u> about the regulations.
_____   3. The Senate <u>quarreled about</u> the bill for two hours.
_____   4. The SWAT team approached with extreme caution so that the sniper would not suddenly go <u>wacko.</u>

★*Merriam-Webster's Collegiate Dictionary.* Springfield, MA: Merriam-Webster, Inc.; Tenth Edition, 1993. p. 815.

_____ 5. Two female attorneys encouraged all the <u>gals</u> in the audience to consider law as a profession.

_____ 6. Eddie Murphy starred in a <u>mirthful</u> film.

_____ 7. Martin Luther King, Jr., was America's most <u>notorious</u> civil rights hero.

_____ 8. Cooking a pot roast dinner made Stanley feel <u>homely.</u>

_____ 9. After the long wait, the diner <u>leered</u> at his salad angrily.

_____ 10. The ball-carrier <u>sidled</u> head-on into the defensive linemen.

Group Project

Connotation

Read the following paragraph and discuss with your group why each of the italicized words is not appropriate in tone or implied meaning. Decide together on a more suitable substitute for each one.

When President Kennedy (1) *nicknamed* the United States a "nation of immigrants," he was (2) *hinting* at the fact that all United States citizens, except native Americans, descend from ancestors who (3) *meandered* here from other countries. Among the earliest (4) *bunches* were the English, the Dutch, the French, and the African Americans, who had to endure the horrors of the Middle Passage. During the (5) *center* of the nineteenth century a wave of immigrants (6) *sneaked* here from Ireland, England, Germany, and Scandinavia. These groups (7) *infiltrated* rapidly across the newly opened territories in the Midwest and the West. The next (8) *humongous horde* to (9) *show up* came from Italy, Austria Hungary, Poland, and Russia. These immigrants, arriving from 1870 to the 1920s, found most of the farmland already (10) *snatched* and tended to (11) *coagulate* in the large cities. In recent (12) *eons,* few of our immigrants have come from Europe. In the 1980s, for instance, about half our legal immigrants came from the western hemisphere, with Mexico (13) *forwarding* the largest number and the Caribbean countries providing another sizable group. Asia has been a (14) *novel* source of immigrants recently; of the more than seven million immigrants to the United States in the 1980s, 37 percent, or about 2.7 million, came from Asia. European immigrants, once the largest group, (15) *contracted* to 10.4 percent in the 1980s.

USING SPECIFIC LANGUAGE

Whenever possible, use specific words instead of general ones and words that appeal to the five senses instead of abstract ones. Rather than "large," write "six feet four, weighing three hundred pounds." Instead of "loud noise," write "a piercing car alarm." Use a more identifiable term like "1992 Oldsmobile" in place of the general word "car." In descriptive writing especially, choose specific adjectives and nouns that create sense impressions: A "blue spruce" can be visualized specifically, whereas the word "tree" conveys a vague impression at best. In expository writing, try to make statements that evoke a personal response through specific examples instead of statements that make impersonal generalizations. When you find yourself about to write, "The American family is less cohesive than it used to be," stop and think up a statement that the reader will respond to more personally, such as, "Most American children are lucky to see their parents one hour a day."

Compare the two paragraphs below. The first is written in vague language that does not show imaginative selection of words that appeal to the senses. The second, richer in specific, sensory words, was written by the well-known author Maya Angelou:

Vague

We lived in a big house. We had a lot of people renting rooms from us; they were all different from one another. Some were workers, and others were prostitutes. One couple talked with me until the husband went away. Then the wife became shy. There was also an old couple who were boring.

Specific

Our house was a fourteen-room typical San Franciscan post-earthquake affair. We had a succession of roomers, bringing and taking their different accents, and personalities and foods. Shipyard workers clanked up the stairs (we all slept on the second floor except Mother and Daddy Clidell) in their steel-tipped boots and metal hats, and gave way to much-powdered prostitutes, who giggled through their makeup and hung their wigs on the door-knobs. One couple (they were college graduates) held long adult conversations with me in the big kitchen downstairs, until the husband went off to war. Then the wife who had been so charming and ready to smile changed into a silent shadow that played infrequently along the walls. An older couple lived with us for a year or so. They owned a restaurant and had no personality to enchant or interest a teenager, except that the husband was called Uncle Jim, and the wife Aunt Boy. I never figured that out.*

---

*Maya Angelou, *I Know Why the Caged Bird Sings.* Used by permission of Random House, Inc., copyright © 1969.

Recognize the difference between general, somewhat specific, and highly specific language:

General	*Somewhat Specific*	*Highly Specific*
vehicle	car	Porsche
animal	dog	bull terrier
medical worker	nurse	geriatric nurse
sports	track and field	400-meter hurdles

Exercise I

General and Specific Language

Fill in the blanks with general, somewhat specific, and highly specific terms:

	General	*Somewhat Specific*	*Highly Specific*
1.	educational institution	_____	Georgia State University
2.	food	dessert	_____
3.	_____	planet	Mars
4.	news medium	news magazine	_____
5.	celebrity	_____	Michael Jackson
6.	_____	soft drink	Pepsi-Cola
7.	state	_____	Indiana
8.	country	African country	
9.	book	_____	Webster's Dictionary
10.	_____	skyscraper	Sears Tower

Exercise II

General and Specific Language

Revise these sentences using specific, concrete words in place of general, abstract words:

1. Maxine lived in a large building and worked in a small business not far away. She took public transportation to work.

    _____

    _____

2. Ernie participated frequently in sports. He liked several of them, but was outstanding in one. He won awards in that sport.

3. People who are addicted to various substances can do a number of things to get over their addictions.

4. Inez took a rather long vacation to several islands; she enjoyed a number of activities while she was there.

5. When you live in a big city, you get used to scary sights, loud noises, and unpleasant encounters.

Group Project

Using Precise and Specific Language

Along with your writing group, analyze the two pictures following. What do the details of each picture show about American life? What feeling does the appearance of the people and the location express? With your group, brainstorm and collect impressions and details. Choose one of the pictures, and have each group member write an exploratory draft describing it. Exchange drafts and underline words that could be replaced with more precise, specific, and vivid words; notice verbs and adjectives especially. Write final drafts, paying special attention to your choice of effective words.

REDUCING WORDINESS

In your prewriting and composing, you have worked hard to develop **fluency,** which means to be able to write many words without too much hesitation and awkwardness. Now it may seem like a step backward to try to *reduce* the number of words in your final drafts. Here we want to distinguish between effective words and wasted words. Well-chosen words add to the meaning and power of your essays; "deadwood" or clutter, as some editors call wasted words, gets in the way. Expert writers make words count more than beginners do; they improve their rough drafts by shortening them without changing the meaning or reducing the coverage. This is what you will do as your final step in learning to be a good editor of your own writing. If the instructor assigns a five–hundred–word essay, aim for about seven hundred words first. In your prewriting and writing of a rough draft, you should not be concerned about wordiness; it will hamper your flow of words and ideas. When the time comes to edit, however, your essay should be long enough that you can pare down the excess words and still fulfill the assignment.

Wordiness is a loose, repetitious way of writing. It can have several causes. Carelessness may cause a writer to overlook repetitions and wasted words. Or trying too hard to sound impressive can lead to the use of formulated, wasted phrases. Quite often, wordiness comes from lack of experience in reading good writers. Many writing students, in fact, do not realize that good writing is concise. Just as an expert swimmer or runner knows how to get the most speed and distance with the least effort, an expert writer learns to get the most mileage out of each word and sentence.

Here is an example of wordy writing:

In modern times of today, the majority of Americans in our society, by and large, have come to recognize that our senior citizens are in need of quite a number of kinds of help and assistance that they are not receiving as of yet.

The following would do much better:

Most Americans now realize that the elderly need many kinds of help that they are not receiving.

This sentence has only seventeen words, in contrast to the forty-four words of the first sentence, and it makes the point much more clearly. If you look back at the wordy statement, you will find that none of the extra twenty-seven words adds anything to the meaning. These words are like wood chips to be cut away from the block by the carver.

You will be a more concise writer and better editor if you learn to spot the common patterns of wordiness. Although editing, unlike grammar, cannot be reduced to rules to be learned and errors to be corrected, conciseness (the opposite of wordiness) can be learned through practice. Here are some of the common faults of wordiness:

- Useless repetitions, called **redundancies.** "Modern times of today" is a wordy way of saying "now." "Help and assistance" is saying "help" twice.
- Vague phrases and false connectors. "By and large" sounds like a transitional phrase but really serves no purpose.
- Roundabout substitutes for simple words. "As of yet" means "yet"; "on the basis of the fact that" means "because."

Writing clean, direct sentences does not necessarily mean writing short sentences or using short words. Sometimes using complicated sentences and long words is the best way, even the only way, to express particular ideas. But use these *only* if they are the best; otherwise, keep your sentences simple and straightforward.

Here is a list of wordy phrases commonly used by careless writers; more concise equivalents are on the right.

Wordy Phrase	*Concise Word or Phrase*
due to the fact that	because
with respect to	about
in terms of	about
in this day and age	nowadays
hurried quickly	hurried
in all probability	probably
at that point in time	then
conduct an investigation	investigate
blue in color	blue
circular in shape	circular
there are many students who join	many students join
it is my belief that	I believe that
inside of the house	inside the house
has a preference for	prefers
in my opinion I feel that	I think that
In Alice Walker's story, "Everyday Use," she writes	In "Everyday Use" Alice Walker writes
he is the kind of person who likes to play chess	he likes to play chess

▶ Exercise 1

Wordiness

Rewrite the sentences below to remove wordiness:

1. It was inside of the house that I was frightened on account of the fact that it was my belief that someone was there.

   _____

   _____

2. Elba's joy and happiness with respect to her mother's arrival was due to the fact that they had not been able to see each other for months.

   _____

   _____

3. Leonard made up his mind to conduct a survey that would include many first year students as to their opinions with regard to drugs.

   _____

   _____

4. In the short story by Shirley Jackson entitled "The Lottery," the author tells a story about a small rural town somewhere in the country.

_____

_____

5. It is my intention in this essay to give an analysis of a number of the ways many people often use in the effort to cover up their true hidden motives.

_____

_____

Exercise II

Wordiness

Read the paragraph below and underline the wordy phrase in each sentence. Then rewrite the paragraph with each wordy phrase omitted or replaced with a more concise one.

> Of all the anxiety disorders, phobias are the most common of them all. More than one out of ten people will experience phobias at some point in time in their lifetimes. This is due to the fact that there are many objects and situations that can trigger phobias. People with phobias may, in point of fact, fear heights, airplane flights, driving, dogs, snakes, closed spaces, open spaces, shopping malls, or social situations. What causes the fear, by and large, is not immediate danger but something irrationally associated with the object or situation. In the opinion of most therapists, they believe that behavior therapy can usually help eliminate phobias. Therapists help people with phobias confront rather than avoid the situations in which they experience and feel anxiety. There are a number of people who have acute panic attacks. In these cases therapists have a tendency to prescribe medications to block the attacks. Although anxiety disorders do not endanger people's physical health, they can, as a matter of fact, limit their lives severely.

Exercise III

Wordiness

Look over your previous paragraph and essay assignments. Make a list of the ten most frequent wordy phrases you have used, and write next to them more concise equivalents. Then choose the assignment that seems wordiest and rewrite it. Try to reduce it by at least twenty percent.

USING THE ACTIVE VOICE FOR STRENGTH*

Difference Between Active Voice and Passive Voice

In the **active voice,** the subject *does* the acting:

$$\overset{\text{s}}{\text{The radio}} \overset{\text{v}}{\text{blasted}} \text{ hard rock music on the bus.}$$

The radio blasted hard rock music on the bus.

In the **passive voice,** the subject *receives* the action:

Loud rock music was heard by everyone on the bus.

Both active and passive voice are correct English, but too-frequent use of the passive voice weakens writing. Sometimes in news reports and business writing, the passive voice may be best because who is doing the action is not important:

1. Three more suspects were taken into police headquarters for questioning in the continuing search for the mass murderer.
2. The machines were shipped to the Denver branch on Monday.

We do not need to know who took the suspects into custody or who shipped the machines. However, use of the passive is *not* effective in most writing.

Weak Writing	Strong Writing
Kim was invited by Raymond to model for him.	Raymond invited Kim to model for him.
The truth was suddenly realized by both contestants at once.	Both contestants suddenly realized the truth at once.

Exercise 1

Using the Active Voice

Convert these sentences from passive voice to active voice.

Example: The turnoff for Route 287 was finally reached by Carla.

Active voice: *Carla finally reached the turnoff for Route 287.*

1. The poem was read aloud in class by Margaret.

    Active voice: _____

---

*See the use of participles with passive voice in Unit 5.

2. The Yankees were beaten by the Tigers in the playoffs.

    Active voice: _____

3. The moon was landed on by the Apollo 11 crew in 1969.

    Active voice: _____

4. Her personal computer was given to Edith by her parents.

    Active voice: _____

5. Many letters have been sent by me to your office.

    Active voice: _____

The following paragraph is in the passive voice. Read it, and then read the revised version in the active voice. Notice how the active voice gives the paragraph strength.

Passive Voice

Instructions were given to the class by the teacher in how to use the computer keyboard for word processing. The keyboard was unknown to Doris, and she was bewildered by all the symbols. She was assured by Sue, who sat next to her, that her fears would be overcome when the meaning of the symbols had been explained by their teacher to her. The lecture was listened to carefully by her, and notes were taken. Soon the class was told by the instructor to copy and edit a piece of writing on the computer. Everyone in the class was helped by an assistant, and a grasp of the editing techniques was quickly had by all. When the editing was finished by everyone, the results were fed into the printer, and a copy of the work was received by every student.

Revised Paragraph in Active Voice

The teacher gave instructions to the class in how to use the computer keyboard for word processing. Doris did not know the keyboard, and the symbols bewildered her. Sue, who sat next to her, assured her that she would overcome her fears when the teacher had explained the symbols to her. She carefully listened to the lecture and took notes. Soon the instructor told the class to copy and edit a piece of writing on the computer. An assistant helped everyone in the class, and all quickly had a grasp of the editing techniques. When everyone had finished the editing, the teacher fed the results into the printer, and every student received a copy of the work.

Exercise II

Using the Active Voice

Read the following paragraph, noticing that it is entirely in the passive voice. Rewrite the whole paragraph in the active voice.

> The meeting was called by the boss for Monday at 10:00 a.m. Cynthia, Walter, and Eva were scheduled to make presentations to the clients who had been invited to attend. Cynthia's department was considered by the boss to be the most crucial to the deal; therefore her presentation was made first. It was received with enthusiasm by the new clients, and Cynthia was praised for her work. Cynthia was followed by Walter, whose project was also greeted with praise, and then Eva was introduced. The clients were surprised by the project planned by Eva because such a sophisticated use of the World Wide Web as a sales medium had never been seen in their companies. At first skepticism was aroused by her presentation, but after the clients' questions had been answered, a large amount of enthusiasm was generated, and the deal was concluded.

USING STRONG, VIVID VERBS*

One key to forceful writing is selecting verbs that do heavy work for you. All words count, but verbs are especially important. Pick your verbs as you would pick a pair of designer jeans. As one clothing store used to advise customers, "Select, don't settle." A flat, boring, vague verb can numb the reader. A vital, specific verb can make a sentence crackle, sing, or snarl. Be on the lookout for the flat, catchall verbs that do not create pictures—words like *move, look, go,* and of course *is.* Read some of your previous writing, circling the verbs. Do you come up with nothing but *has, have, are, does, do,* and *looks?* If so, you are still singing on one or two notes. Use the whole scale. Instead of *looks,* try *stares, gazes, gapes, ponders, peers, surveys, contemplates,* or *leers.* Notice the difference between flat, vague verbs and vivid ones in these examples:

1. The runner *moved* to the left, *went* to the right, and *went* through three tacklers for a first down.
2. The runner *feinted* to the left, *veered* to the right, and *ploughed* through three tacklers for a first down.

1. Eleanor *looked* at the photograph for five minutes, *looked* out the window, and then *watched* the other students writing.
2. Eleanor *studied* the photograph for five minutes, *glanced* out the window, and then *glared* at the other students' writing.

---

*You may want to review finding verbs, subject-verb agreement, and verb tenses in Unit 5.

1. Norman *said* hello to the news vendor, *said* good morning to the bus driver, and *said* a few words to the attractive girl sitting next to him on the bus.

2. Norman *greeted* the news vendor, *tossed* a "good morning" to the bus driver, and began *flirting* with the attractive girl sitting next to him on the bus.

Underline the verbs in the following passage. Notice how the writer, Dr. Haim G. Ginott, in his book *Between Parent and Teenager,* has chosen specific verbs instead of repeating *is, does,* or *goes.*

> Teenagers need privacy; it allows them to have a life of their own. By providing privacy, we demonstrate respect. We help them disengage themselves from us and grow up. Some parents pry too much. They read their teenagers' mail and listen in on their telephone calls. Such violations may cause permanent resentment. Teenagers feel cheated and enraged. In their eyes, invasion of privacy is a dishonorable offense. As one girl said: "I am going to sue my mother for malpractice of parenthood. She unlocked my desk and read my diary."*

Group Project

Using Effective Verbs

Read these sentences aloud with your group; decide, through group discussion, what vivid, precise verb should replace the vague one in each sentence.

Example: Sandra *looked* at the dress with disgust.
Rewrite: *Sandra glowered at the dress with disgust.*

1. Robert <u>went</u> to the police station for help.
2. The students <u>were</u> in the lounge.
3. The van <u>moved slowly</u> through heavy traffic.
4. The announcement <u>said</u> that the Japanese ambassador had been kidnapped.
5. A geriatric nurse <u>has</u> many responsibilities.
6. The dancers <u>moved</u> to the loud music.
7. One driver <u>said</u> that he would sue the cab driver who ran into his Porsche.
8. The half-conscious patient <u>looked</u> at the ceiling.

---

*Haim G. Ginott, *Between Parent and Teenager.* Copyright © 1969, Avon books, 1971. Used by permission of Dr. Alice Ginott.

9. The ice hockey players <u>moved</u> across the ice.
10. Misty blue–green mountains <u>were</u> in front of them.

USING IDIOMS CORRECTLY

Idioms are fixed phrases or combinations like "out of order," "keep an eye on," "take your time," or "out of the question." These phrases often do not make sense if you analyze them word by word, but people who grow up speaking English (all other languages have idioms too) learn the meanings of idioms by habit. Careless writers may, however, occasionally write phrases that are not idiomatic, and students who have learned English as a second language often have some difficulties with idioms. When you edit your writing, check to see that your phrasing matches the natural phrasing of American speech. If you learned English as a second or foreign language, you may need extra practice with spoken English to become more secure in your grasp of idioms. A dictionary of American idioms may speed the process. All students, however, are likely to have a little trouble with idiomatic word combinations that involve advanced vocabulary. The most common problems occur in matching verbs with prepositions. For instance, we say that a person is accused *of* a crime, charged *with* a crime, convicted *of* a crime, and sentenced *to* ten years in jail. Here is a list of some common errors in idiom:

Not Idiomatic	*Idiomatic*
He was angry at his boss.	He was angry with his boss.
I bought the car off Paul.	I bought the car from Paul.
The horse is not capable to run.	The horse is not capable of running.
She was bored of the party.	She was bored with the party.
The discussion centered around politics.	The discussion centered on politics.
I am concerned for your grades.	I am concerned about your grades.
We went in search for the cat.	We went in search of the cat.
I differ from you on that subject.	I differ with you on that subject.
She was born at Denver.	She was born in Denver.
A cassette deck is preferable than a radio.	A cassette deck is preferable to a radio.
Fish is superior than red meat.	Fish is superior to red meat.
A cheetah has twice the speed as a dog.	A cheetah has twice the speed of a dog.
Sandra was not interested to go along.	Sandra was not interested in going along.
Poor health prevented him to do it.	Poor health prevented him from doing it.

Exercise I

Idiomatic Usage

One of the following sentences is correct; write C in the blank next to it. In the other blanks, write the word that will correct the unidiomatic expression in the sentence. Circle the unidiomatic expression.

_____ 1. Vodka has twice the alcohol content as beer.

_____ 2. You may become bored of going to the library every day.

_____ 3. President Clinton is interested in holding a press conference.

_____ 4. The Democrats differed from the Republicans about the budget appropriations for child care.

_____ 5. The singer is healthy and capable to give a great concert.

_____ 6. The weather forecast should not prevent farmers to plant early this year.

_____ 7. Far superior than a new law would be a public relations campaign.

Exercise II

Idiomatic Usage

The paragraph below contains eight expressions that are not idiomatic. Circle these phrases and write the correct idiomatic phrases above them.

Plea bargaining is a method used by the courts to speed up the process of law enforcement. When a person is charged of a crime, he or she has the option to pleading guilty or not guilty. If the plea is not guilty, a trial must take place, and the person may receive a severe sentence or go free, according on the jury's decision. To avoid the time-consuming procedures of jury trials, judges often have defendants to plead guilty in exchange for a lighter sentence. Those who defend plea bargaining point out that holding complete trials for all persons accused with crimes would overwhelm the system and bring it to a halt. In the other hand, critics insist that plea bargaining never produces perfect justice.

That is, if the defendant is guilty, he or she should not get off by a light sentence, whereas if he or she is innocent, pleading guilty for avoiding a harsher sentence is unjust. It is up to judges, prosecutors, and defense attorneys to make the system work as justly as possible.

If English Is Not Your First Language

For writers who learn English as a second or foreign language, idiomatic usage can be a bigger problem than grammar. Features of English such as word order, the use of articles (*a, an,* and *the*), the use of verb tenses, omitted D and S endings, and idiomatic phrasing often trouble speakers of English as a second language. This problem arises because such patterns come mostly from speech habits, not from memorized rules. As a non-native speaker, unless you have an exceptional command of spoken English, you will find errors of this kind turning up occasionally in your writing. A few such errors are not important, but they can seriously mar your writing if they happen often.

To improve your idiomatic usage, seek the help of a tutor and get plenty of practice in speaking and listening to English. Make it a point to read English aloud, especially your own writing. Do not expect one writing course to solve such problems entirely; learning to speak and write a second language is a gradual process. You can, however, progress faster by recognizing some of the patterns of error that often appear in ESL writers' compositions.★

Improving Sentence Effectiveness

Have you ever read a story, article, or book that had a powerful effect on you—left you touched, delighted, angered or convinced? What do you think made the writing come alive with feeling and purpose? In part, it may have been the mysterious element of originality.

Each writer's imaginative gift is his or her own, and not everything about the best writing can be taught in a classroom. However, most stylistic effects boil down to choice of words, which you have been practicing, and sentence effectiveness, which you will be practicing next. Improving sentence form will make your style forceful and varied.

★For work on these grammatical patterns, see the following ESL sections in Unit 5: subjects and verbs, p. 243, plural forms, p. 278, verb tenses, p. 308, modifiers, p. 322, mixed sentences, p. 343.

AVOIDING REPETITION

Although some repetition of words, phrases, and sentence patterns is necessary to good writing, too much repetition will set the reader snoring. Several techniques will help you achieve sentence variety: using pronouns to avoid repeating nouns, varying your sentence beginnings, and using all three basic sentence types.

Using Pronouns to Avoid Repeating Nouns★

What is wrong with this passage?

> Yvette is my next-door neighbor. Yvette has three children, ages six, eight, and twelve. I first met Yvette when I moved into the apartment house where Yvette lived. Yvette didn't wait for me to come over to introduce myself; instead Yvette showed up right there at my door with a present to welcome me to the new building. That's what I like about Yvette—Yvette always thinks of others first.

In this passage, the writer always refers to her neighbor with one word, Yvette. She never uses the pronouns *she* or *her* instead. Read the passage again and say *she* or *her* wherever you think it would break up the repetition effectively. (Note: it is not a good idea to replace <u>every</u> reference to the name with *she* or *he;* that can become boring too. Read the improved passage, with *she* and *her* substituted to avoid repeating *Yvette* too often:

> Yvette, my next-door neighbor, has three children, ages six, eight, and twelve. I first met her when I moved into the apartment house where she lived. Yvette didn't wait for me to come over to introduce myself; instead she showed up right there at my door with a present to welcome me to the new building. That's what I like about her—she always thinks of others first.

The original passage names Yvette eight times. How many times does the name occur in the revised passage? _____

▶ Exercise

Using Pronouns

Read the following passage and notice the repetitious references to Felicia. Rewrite the passage, eliminating repetition by substituting *she, her,* or *hers* in place of the name. Leave just enough references to the name so that the passage reads clearly.

_____
★Review the use of pronouns in Unit 5.

Felicia likes writing very much. Whenever an interesting idea or a strong feeling comes to Felicia, she takes out her journal and writes a page or two expressing what is on her mind. Although Felicia is studying business management, she hopes to make writing an important part of Felicia's life. Felicia has written three short stories and has begun a novel, and Felicia hopes to publish her work within a few years. Felicia knows that it is not easy making a living as a writer, but Felicia does expect to make some money from her fiction. She has already talked with one literary agent, who has assured Felicia that after he has read Felicia's completed novel, he will probably take Felicia on as a client.

VARYING SENTENCE BEGINNINGS*

One of the most common faults of inexperienced writers is to begin nearly all sentences the same way. Look over some of your previous writing—your paragraphs and essay exercises. Did you begin most of your sentences with the subject followed by the verb?

Sentences can begin many ways, not always with the main subject and verb. One of the most familiar patterns is the monotonous repetition of "I did," "I saw," "I went," and so on, in essays about a personal experience.

Read the following sample passage:

I used to live in a neighborhood where many of the kids committed minor crimes. I thought stealing fruit from an open stand or jumping turnstiles in the subway was a sign of courage and intelligence. I never worried much about what would happen if I got caught doing these things. I wanted to learn from the older kids how to get away fast and how to fool the police. I thought I was leading the life of a legendary outlaw until my cousin was arrested.

It is easy to fall into this "I, I, I" pattern without noticing it. Remember that there are many other ways to begin a sentence.

Ways to Begin Sentences Other than with Main Subject and Verb

<u>Begin with an introductory phrase or clause</u>

Examples:
In my neighborhood, there were many kids who committed minor crimes.
When my family moved to St. Louis, there were many kids in my neighborhood who committed minor crimes.

---

*Review the use of commas after introductory parts and subjects and verbs in Unit 5.

<u>Begin with a participle or participle phrase</u>

Participles are verb forms, usually ending in –ing or –ed, that serve as modifiers, such as a *used* car or a *burning* building. Sometimes phrases are built on participles, such as "*embarrassed* by his remarks," or "*realizing* that the audience disagreed." See more discussion of participles in Unit 5.

Examples:

Baffled, he stepped back and looked carefully at the entrance.

Influenced by the example of my friends, I began to commit minor robberies.

Ignoring the possible consequences, I ventured into a life of minor robberies.

<u>Begin with an appositive</u>

An appositive is a short identifying word or phrase placed next to the thing or person it identifies. Appositives most often come after the noun they identify, as in the following: "Sandra, *the editor of the newspaper,*" or "Leonard, *the father of the child.*" However, they can come before the noun, as in the examples below. For more on appositives, see Unit 5.

Examples:

Winners from the beginning of the season, the team set a college record.

A skilled thief at the age of ten, I took pride in my daring and expertise.

Learn to use these sentence beginnings to break up monotonous patterns. Many of your sentences will begin with the ordinary subject/verb combination, but some variety will make your writing more lively and readable. Read the revised version of the original passage.

In my old neighborhood there were many kids who committed minor crimes. Influenced by their example, I ventured into an early career of robbery. I ignored the possible consequences of stealing fruit from open stands or jumping subway turnstiles. A skilled thief at the age of ten, I took pride in my daring and expertise. From older kids I learned how to get away fast and fool the police. Not until my cousin was arrested did I begin to question the wisdom of trying to become a legendary outlaw.

Exercise I

Sentence Beginnings

Rewrite the following sentences so that they begin with an introductory phrase or clause, a participle, or an appositive.

Group I: Introductory Phrases and Clauses

Example: I found a wonderful Mexican restaurant two blocks away.

Rewrite: _Two blocks away I found a wonderful Mexican restaurant._

1. Stephanie was lucky to find an apartment with two bathrooms near 94th Street.

   Rewrite: _____

2. Most of the jobs had already been filled by the time Steven applied.

   Rewrite: _____

3. The old grocery store began to lose business when a new supermarket opened across the street.

   Rewrite: _____

Group II: Participles★

Example: The driver noticed a problem with the engine while turning the corner.

Rewrite: _While turning the corner, the driver noticed a problem with the engine._

1. May did her math and Spanish homework after taking a shower.

   Rewrite: _____

2. Roberto, knowing that he had a good chance to win, pulled into the lead.

   Rewrite: _____

3. The boat, abandoned a year ago by its owner, was now half submerged.

   Rewrite: _____

Group III: Appositives†

Example: Mr. Rogers, who has been a popular television figure for many years, criticized some of the new commercials.

Rewrite: _A popular television figure for many years, Mr. Rogers criticized some of the new commercials._

1. The candidate, a former member of the CIA, insisted on the importance of classified information.

★Review participles in Unit 5.

†See the use of commas with appositives in Unit 5.

Rewrite: _____

2. My sister, who is an ardent supporter of children's rights, joined a new lobbying group.

   Rewrite: _____

3. The professor, a graduate of Purdue University, was an expert on agricultural technology.

   Rewrite: _____

Exercise II

Sentence Beginnings

Rewrite the following paragraph, eliminating boring repetition by varying the beginnings of sentences.

> Herbert is a totally independent person. He refuses to take advice from anyone, even when he is wrong. He was an only child, and his parents let him do whatever he wanted. He learned to have his own way as a result. He goes his own way around his friends, and he expects them to do whatever he wants. He sometimes likes to look at pretty girls with his friends, and he always decides which ones they will try to pick up and where they will go. He once ignored his girlfriend's advice that he should stop hanging out on weekends until exams were over, and he was put on probation. He likes to give advice to other people and criticize them, but he is hypersensitive toward criticism himself. He will get into big trouble someday if he doesn't stop being such a know-it-all.

VARYING SENTENCE LENGTH AND TYPE*

Good writing depends on sentence variety. Learn to vary both the length and pattern of your sentences. Some students try to "play it safe"—escaping grammatical errors by writing only short, simple sentences. As a result, their style becomes immature and blunt. Others have the opposite problem: They launch into sentences without much attention to form and create long, tangled, shapeless monstrosities that are too complicated to revise. Be realistic: You can't expect to compose sentences as complicated as those of Henry James or James Baldwin without planning or careful revision. Neither should you underestimate your ability and settle for short, flat, monotonous sentences.

---

*See Unit 5 for more on simple, compound, and complex sentences.

Sentence length and type have to be studied together. In order to revise a passage written in short, choppy sentences, you have to know how to form longer sentences.

Here is an example:

Bungee jumping appeals to a lot of people. It is one of the most thrilling sports. It looks very dangerous. Some people have been killed at it. But this was caused by equipment failure. Many people claim it is perfectly safe. Some states have made it illegal. This seems unfair. After all, parachuting is legal. It is just as dangerous.

This passage is written in very short sentences, all of which contain only one subject-verb combination. Such sentences are grammatically defined as *simple sentences*. To rewrite the passage in more varied sentences, some short and simple, others longer and more complicated, we must also include some *compound* and *complex* sentences. Compound sentences combine two main clauses joined by a semicolon or a comma and a short connective word like *and* or *but*. Complex sentences combine one main clause with one subordinate clause beginning with a word like *because, when, although,* or *which*.

Notice the difference:

Bungee jumping, which looks very dangerous, appeals to people because it is one of the most thrilling sports. Some people have been killed at it, but this was caused by equipment failure. Many people claim it is perfectly safe. For states to make it illegal, as some have done, seems unfair; after all, parachuting, which is just as dangerous, is legal.

In this revised passage, the first sentence is complex, the second compound, the third simple, and the fourth compound-complex.

Exercise

Varying Sentence Length and Type

The following passage is written in short, simple sentences. Rewrite it so that some of the sentences are a little longer and constructed in the form of compound or complex sentences.

Virtual reality is a computer term. It refers to a sense of three-dimensional reality. This is created by computer images. Usually these are seen through headsets. Virtual reality may be induced by different types of programs. They may be used for anything from video games to training for surgeons or astronauts.

The opposite problem of writing long, tangled sentences usually comes from a lack of planning or revision. If you find yourself frequently getting lost in sentences that are much too long or complex, you should learn to break them up into clearer statements of moderate length. Here, for example, is the kind of sentence you may produce if you're not careful:

> Of all the sightings of unidentified flying objects, many are not very believable, such as the ones about people being abducted by little creatures that look like E.T. and kidnap the people and take them into their space platforms and perform brain operations on them or impregnate them with sperm from outer space so that they will give birth to half-human, half-extraterrestrial babies, but some of the reports of seeing flying objects are hard to dismiss as just optical illusions or weather conditions because they come from level-headed people with scientific training.

This sentence is much too long and overloaded. Rather than merely revise it a little, the writer should break it up into several shorter sentences:

> Many of the sightings of unidentified flying objects are not very believable. For example, people have claimed that they were abducted by little creatures that looked like E.T. and taken to space platforms where they were subjected to brain surgery. Some women have even claimed that they were impregnated by extraterrestrials and gave birth to babies that were half-human and half from outer space. Other reports of UFOs, however, are hard to dismiss as mere optical illusions or weather conditions because they come from level-headed people with scientific training.

This passage is now four sentences of varying length and type. Of course, many other revisions of the original passage are possible, but almost any good one would have to begin by breaking up the long, stringy sentence into several shorter ones.

> ## Exercise

Avoiding Long, Tangled Sentences*

Rewrite the long sentence below as a more effective passage made up of three, four, or five sentences of varying length and type:

> "ER" appeals to television viewers because it shows not only many of the crises and frustrations that occur in modern hospitals where not only doctors and nurses but also patients have to cope with problems like AIDS, child abuse, and domestic violence, which are becoming familiar to many average Americans and also because the program shows characters in real-life situations

---

*Review run-together sentences and comma splices in Unit 5.

like trying to adopt a child, having a fist fight in a parking garage, and trying to train a new employee who has a bizarre attitude, and most of all because the program is full of sudden, unexpected incidents and unpredictable behavior.

Combining Sentences to Improve Your Style★

Sentence combining is something all writers do, often unconsciously, to show relationships between ideas and to make their writing more effective. Combining can be simple or complicated. It includes both adding elements to simple statements by using connecting words like *and* and inserting within simpler statements modifying words or phrases (a procedure called **embedding**). Advanced writers learn to pack much material into their clauses and sentences; beginners tend to write in short, simple statements or to string long ones together loosely.

Sentence-combining exercises can start you on the road to acquiring this density and complexity. In simple terms, *sentence combining means taking short kernel (or core) sentences and fitting their essential facts together into more developed statements.*

For example:

Kernel Sentences	The painter did a job. The job was careless. The job was messy. The messiness and carelessness were embarrassing.
Developed Sentence	The painter did an embarrassingly careless and messy job.

We have packed in the facts from the kernel sentences to make one mature statement. We embedded *careless* and *messy* as adjectives before the noun *job* and *embarrassingly* as an adverb describing the adjectives *careless* and *messy.* Being able to do this kind of combining is indispensable to writing varied, mature, and readable English. Studying grammar alone will not give you this skill. It comes partly from your familiarity with the phrasing and rhythm of English, which you have gained from speaking, reading, and hearing the language. You can improve the skill you already possess by doing sentence-combining exercises that help you recognize the varied possibilities for expressing a thought.

There is never just one way to combine a series of kernel sentences, although in some exercises one way may seem much better than the others and some possibilities may sound awkward. In the previous example, there are other possible combinations. Are these two as good as the first?

★Review fragments; run-together sentences; comma splices; and simple, compound, and complex sentences in Unit 5 to be sure you combine sentences grammatically.

1. The painter did a job that was embarrassingly careless and messy.
2. The job done by the painter was so careless and messy that it was embarrassing.

These took more words to say the same thing as the first sentence. While this does not necessarily mean that the first way was best, we all like economy. The short-est, most compact way is often the best, as long as it is not awkward or unclear.★

Exercise I

Combining Sentences

The following groups of kernel sentences have been combined into pairs of developed sentences. Circle the letter of the sentence you prefer in each case. Explain to a classmate why you prefer it. Is it smoother, more condensed, or freer of grammatical errors than the other one?

> The dancer gave a performance.
> The performance was graceful.
> The performance was skillful.
> The grace and skill were remarkable.

Developed Sentences
A. The dancer gave a remarkably graceful and skillful performance.
B. It was remarkable how graceful and skillful the dancer's performance was.

> The student wrote an essay.
> The student was ambitious.
> The essay was long.
> The essay was involved.
> The writing was rapid.

Developed Sentences
A. The student who was ambitious wrote an essay that was long, involved, and rapidly written.
B. The ambitious student rapidly wrote a long, involved essay.

> The road changed.
> The road was bumpy.
> The road was made of dirt.

★Review adjectives and adverbs in Unit 5 before doing the next exercises.

The change was unexpected.
The change was into a broad highway.

Developed Sentences

A. The bumpy dirt road unexpectedly changed into a broad highway.

B. The dirt road, which was bumpy, changed suddenly into a broad highway.

Exercise II

Combining Sentences

Write your own developed sentences using the kernel sentences given. Write two possible sentences for each group; circle the letter of the one you think reads more smoothly.

The teacher gave a test.
The test was short.
The test was easy.
The shortness and easiness were surprising.

Developed Sentences

A. _____

B. _____

The campers erected a tent.
The tent was green.
The tent was made of canvas
The tent was large.
They erected it carefully.

Developed Sentences

A. _____

B. _____

The story came to an end.
The story was about ghosts.
The story was thrilling.
The end was abrupt.
The end was shocking.

© 1998 by Addison-Wesley Educational Publishers Inc.

Developed Sentences

A. _____

B. _____

> Travis learned hip hop.
> He learned from other teenagers.
> The teenagers performed at parties.
> They performed in films.
> Travis watched them perform.

Developed Sentences

A. _____

B. _____

> Jennifer selected an umbrella.
> She selected it carefully.
> The umbrella was beautiful.
> The umbrella was plaid.
> The umbrella looked expensive.

Developed Sentences

A. _____

B. _____

In these exercises you have either *added* parts by joining them with *and* to the main sentences or *embedded* parts by fitting them tightly into the sentences as modifiers. You should also be able to use **free modifiers** sometimes to make your sentences more varied. A free modifier is a descriptive word or phrase that reads as an extra element, interesting and informative but not essential. The same descriptive elements can sometimes be used either way:

Embedded	The dancer gave a *remarkably graceful, skillful* performance.
Free	The dancer's performance, *remarkably graceful and skillful,* received tremendous applause.

The second way sounds more sophisticated, doesn't it? That does not mean that it is better, but by knowing how to use options you can make your style more interesting.

For practice, convert the embedded modifiers to free modifiers in this sentence.

1. The *heavy, lumbering* dump truck rolled gradually to a stop.
2. The dump truck, _____ , rolled gradually to a stop.

FREE AND EMBEDDED MODIFIERS*

Free modifiers are groups of words—nouns, verbs, or adjectives—that can be placed in different parts of the sentence. They are called free because they are movable; the same cluster may be located before the main statement, in the middle of the main statement, or after the main statement. A free modifier is added to enliven or add color to the main statement.

Suppose we begin with a main statement:

Michael took extra courses in the summer.

Now we add a free modifier: *hoping to graduate in three years.* This modifier can be placed at the beginning:

Hoping to graduate in three years, Michael took extra courses in the summer.

Or it can be placed in the middle:

Michael, *hoping to graduate in three years,* took extra courses in the summer.

It can also be placed at the end:

Michael took extra courses in the summer, *hoping to graduate in three years.*

Exercise 1

Combining Sentences with Modifiers

Write two developed sentences for each exercise. Use embedded modifiers in one sentence, free modifiers in the other.

Example:

Ted's girlfriend was waiting.
She was waiting at the cafe.
His girlfriend was intelligent

---

*See dangling and misplaced modifiers in Unit 5. Sometimes a free modifier will not fit correctly in one of the possible positions. See also correcting by subordinating in Unit 5.

His girlfriend was charming.
She waited patiently.

Embedded modifiers: <u>Ted's *intelligent, charming* girlfriend was waiting patiently</u>
<u>at the cafe.</u>

Free modifiers: <u>Ted's girlfriend, *intelligent and charming,* was waiting patiently at</u>
<u>the cafe.</u>

The poodle came running.
The running was toward his owner.
The poodle was trimmed.
The trimming was exquisite.
The poodle was perfumed.

Embedded modifiers: _____

Free modifiers: _____

The car was parked.
The parking was near the school.
The car had been stolen.
The car had been stripped.
The car was new.

Embedded modifiers: _____

Free modifiers: _____

The wedding took place.
It was in a ballroom.
The wedding was large.
The wedding was planned.
The planning was careful.

Embedded modifiers: _____

Free modifiers: _____

The sequoias towered.
They were in the forest.
They towered above the other trees.
They were ancient.
They were awesome.

Embedded modifiers: _____

Free modifiers: _____

Exercise II

Combining Sentences with Modifiers

On a separate sheet of paper, combine these kernel sentences into developed sentences; write two versions of each set.

The parties lasted.
The lasting was often.
The lasting was until 3:00 a.m.
The parties were given.
The giving was by Scott and Zelda Fitzgerald.
The parties were wild.
The parties were unforgettable.

The stories appeal.
The stories are by Edgar Allan Poe.
The stories are short.
The stories are bizarre.
The stories are macabre.
The appealing is to readers.
The readers are in the millions.
The readers are today's.

The stories contain crimes.
The crimes are grotesque.
The stories contain events.
The events are supernatural.
The stories are among thrillers.
The thrillers are the earliest.
The thrillers are psychological.
The thrillers are about detectives.

Child abuse is a problem.
The problem is widespread.
The problem is in our society.
The problem requires action.
The action is from our communities.
The action is from our legislatures.

Exercise III

Combining Sentences with Modifiers

Rewrite this paragraph in better style by combining the choppy sentences into more developed ones.

My friend Laverne is an impressive person. She is impressive because of her style. She is impressive because of her activities. She is impressive because of her goals. Her style of dressing is beautiful. It is also up to date. Her clothes always look elegant. They also look expensive. But they really aren't expensive. That is because she knows how to shop. She also has many activities. She knows how to do silkscreens. She also knows how to do landscape photography. She can play golf. She can play racquetball. She can play tennis. She does all of these like an expert. It is not surprising that she has high goals. She wants to graduate from college. She wants to do this with honors. She wants to graduate with a major in biology. She later wants to earn a master's degree. This will also be in biology. Later she wants to become an oceanographer. This job will allow her to travel. It will also keep her interested for many years. It will also give her satisfaction. This is because such work is important. It is important to the future of the environment.

WHO, WHICH, AND THAT CLAUSES*

Clauses that begin with *who, which,* or *that* are called **relative clauses**, meaning that they **relate to**, or **describe**, some person or thing just before them in the sentence. Two kernel sentences can sometimes be combined by turning one of them into a relative clause:

Kernel Sentence	Some people drive to work every day. These people don't want the price of gasoline to rise.
Developed Sentence with Relative Clause	People who drive to work every day don't want the price of gasoline to rise.

The same thing can be done with things instead of people using *which* or *that* instead of *who:*

Kernel Sentences	Some companies receive government contracts. These companies face bureaucratic regulations.
Developed Sentence with Relative Clause	Companies that receive government contracts face bureaucratic regulations.

Some clauses use prepositions like *in, to, for, of,* and *from* before *which* or *whom.* Learn to use these patterns as well:

---

*Review the use of commas to separate *who* and *which* clauses in Unit 5. See also use of verb forms in relative clauses and the use of *who* and *whom.*

Kernel Sentences	You spoke to a woman in the elevator. The woman is our Saturday afternoon newscaster.
Developed Sentence with Relative Clause	The woman to whom you spoke in the elevator is our Saturday afternoon newscaster.

Exercise

Combining Sentences With Relative Clauses

Combine these kernel sentences into developed sentences using who, which, or that clauses:

1. Some students wait until the last minute to study for exams. These students rarely earn high grades.

Developed Sentence:

_____

2. Some colleges have developed work-study programs. These colleges have flourished in a tight economy.

Developed Sentence:

_____

3. Robert Frost is known as a New England poet. He was actually born in San Francisco.

Developed Sentence:

_____

4. Some people appear on television talk shows. These people often have a film or book to promote.

Developed Sentence:

_____

5. For some people correct spelling is easy. These people often learned to read early.

Developed Sentence:

_____

6. From some countries raw materials are exported to the United States. These countries suffer economic losses when the dollar increases in value.

Developed Sentence:

_____

7. Brochures were sent to some customers. These customers can receive free six-month subscriptions.

Developed Sentence:

_____

HOW, WHEN, WHERE, AND WHY COMBINATIONS

You can often combine kernel sentences by **subordinating**,★ which means turning one kernel sentence into a **subordinate clause**. Here is an example:

| _Kernel Sentences_ | Utility bills are high during the summer. Air conditioning consumes a large amount of electricity. |

The first statement is the base sentence; the second explains _why_ the first is true. Transform the second into a subordinate clause by using _because._

| _Developed Sentence_ | Utility bills are high during the summer _because_ air conditioning consumes a large amount of electricity. |

In such combinations, the base statement is a **main clause**. It contains a subject and verb (bills _are_) and stands by itself as a complete statement. The other statement becomes a **subordinate clause**. It also has a subject and verb (air conditioning _consumes_) but cannot stand by itself. Rather, it tells how, where, when, or why the main statement is true. Subordinate clauses begin with introductory words called **subordinate conjunctions** like these:

_____

★Clauses using _who, which,_ and _that_ also subordinate by using these relative pronouns; they are called **relative clauses**. To check your grammar while using subordinate clauses to combine sentences, review subordinate conjunctions and fragments in Unit 5.

after	if
although	since
as	until
as if	when
because	where
before	while

Notice that more than one subordinate conjunction may be possible in the same combination:

> Utility bills are high during the summer, *when* air conditioning consumes a large amount of electricity.
>
> Utility bills are high during the summer, *since* air conditioning consumes a large amount of electricity.

Exercise I

Combining Sentences by Subordinating

Combine these kernel sentences into developed sentences by subordinating.

Kernel Sentences	The original date of the performance was changed. The original date conflicted with commencement exercises.
Developed Sentence	The original date of the performance was changed *because* it conflicted with commencement exercises.

1. Politicians lose their credibility with the public. Politicians make wild promises.

Developed Sentence:

_____

2. Drivers should be especially alert. Drivers approach busy intersections.

Developed Sentence:

_____

3. Actors in soap operas are sometimes attacked in public. The characters they play do ugly or immoral things on the screen.

Developed Sentence:

_____

4. The marathon run is named after an ancient Greek city. The Athenians defeated the Persians at that place.

Developed Sentence:

_____

5. Reading modern poetry is difficult. Its meaning is usually hidden.

Developed Sentence:

_____

6. You can learn a lot about the process of your writing. Other people share their impression of it with you.

Developed Sentence:

_____

7. Sandra has decided to wait to get married. She will be thirty-five years old at that time.

Developed Sentence:

_____

> ## Exercise II

Combining Sentences by Subordinating

These groups are more complicated than the preceding ones. All of them need subordination, but you may want to use other forms of combining as well.

Kernel Sentences	Some elderly people are at a disadvantage. They are on fixed incomes. Inflation keeps reducing their spending power.
Developed Sentence	Elderly people who are on fixed incomes are at a disadvantage because inflation keeps reducing their spending power.

1. Teenage pregnancies can be tragic. The mothers have babies to care for. They are not much more than babies themselves.

Developed Sentence:

_____

2. Alcoholism has been a menace for decades. It has increased sharply in recent years. It now affects one out of ten American adults.

Developed Sentence:

_____

3. Marijuana used to be considered harmless. Recent studies have shown its serious long-range effects. These include damage to the lungs, heart, and reproductive system.

Developed Sentence:

_____

4. Pornography has become offensive in big cities. It overwhelms the business districts with signs and pictures. These pictures are of explicit sexual acts. Sometimes these acts include children.

Developed Sentence:

_____

5. Gambling can be a form of light entertainment. For some people it is an addiction. This addiction destroys their personal lives. It reaches a certain point. At this point they cannot control it.

Developed Sentence:

_____

Extra Practice

Combining Sentences

These sentences are too simple and boring. Combine each pair into a more developed, mature sentence.

1. Darryl waited impatiently for the race to begin. He was clutching the steering wheel and muttering to himself.
2. Yvonne waved to her boyfriend. She noticed he had left his Sony Walkman on the counter.
3. Sally owns an enormous dog. It looks like a monster from *Jurassic Park* and terrorizes her friends.
4. Many teachers thought the students' evaluations of them were fair. Some teachers thought students were unfair to teachers who gave them low grades.
5. As he entered the dugout, the catcher made an obscene remark to a noisy spectator. This noisy spectator had been heckling him for three innings.

Improving Your Style with a Word Processor

Word processing has made it easier to create a concise, readable, lively style, but a computer won't do all the work for us. With word processing, it is easy to try a sentence three or four ways and look at all the options before we decide which is best, and we don't have to rewrite the entire page to do so. The ability to shift sentences or paragraphs around—insert, delete, change, and correct without limit—before we put the document on paper is a great advantage—but only for the person who knows how to revise. The computer only follows orders. As writers, <u>we</u> still have to decide which verb is more emphatic, which phrase sounds better, and which version of a sentence is more effective. Knowing how to use keyboard commands to delete, insert, move, and correct words and phrases is the necessary beginning, but the more important skill is knowing how to explore and select options.

To put it another way, word processing is an amazing tool, but only a tool. Whether you write on your own personal computer or work in a computer classroom, remember that you must not only use that tool efficiently but also develop a reliable sense of word choice, phrasing, and sentence patterns. Using a computer, learn to do the following:

- Revise your word order and sequence of sentences. Consider the possibility of creating a more powerful effect by rearranging your statements.
- Explore sentence options, using the skills practiced in sentence combining to try out several patterns based on the same kernel sentences. You can write three or four versions of a sentence, choose one, and delete the rest.
- Really consider your diction, looking at each verb, noun, adjective, and adverb to consider whether another might be more precise, concrete, vivid, or accurate in connotation. Use the skills you have practiced in this unit regarding word choice.
- Eliminate wordiness. Learn the pleasure of deleting wasted words and condensing wordy phrases to create a cleaner, more readable copy; it is one of the joys of writing. In addition, it is now possible to get help with

editing from word processing programs. Be cautious about what you expect, however. The state of the art in style checks is still not advanced enough for you to gain much from such checks unless you already have a strong command of grammar and revision skills. Most style checks will give you information only about the average length of your sentences and items like the frequency with which you use the passive voice. More sophisticated style checks will question your use of particular phrases, but you are the final authority. The computer will not improve your style; it will only help make you more conscious of your stylistic habits.

As programs become more sophisticated, however, these aids will become more and more useful as learning tools. You probably know how to use a spelling check, and you probably also realize that, instead of making you a lazy speller, it forces you to notice the words that you habitually misspell, thus making you a better speller. So will it eventually be with style checks—they will give you some of the feedback that a good writing instructor might give you. At present, however, they fall short of the stylistic comments you will receive from a good teacher and other readers.

Reminders About Improving Your Style

◆ Once you are satisfied with the content and organization of an essay, revise it to improve the choice of words and the form of your sentences. Revise several times for specific kinds of improvements.

◆ **Improve your choice of words** to make them more precise. Use a large dictionary that explains the slight differences in word meanings so that the words you choose mean *exactly* what you mean, not just approximately what you mean. Study vocabulary to give yourself a larger repertoire of words from which to choose. Become familiar with the often-misused words.

◆ Choose words with the **correct connotation**. Use your thesaurus and a large dictionary to consider all the possible choices of important words. Study the explanations in the dictionary of the slight differences in the connotations of words with similar meanings. Read the works of good writers to acquire a larger vocabulary and a finer sense of their subtle shades of meaning.

◆ Prefer **specific language** over vague words and phrases. Check your essays to find flat, vague verbs, nouns, and modifiers. Replace them with more specific, concrete words that focus your meaning and create sense impressions.

◆ **Reduce wordiness** for direct impact. Eliminate redundancies and replace roundabout phrases with concise, direct ones.

◆ Use the **active voice** and **vivid verbs** for strength. Avoid the passive voice except when the doer of the action is unknown or when you want to emphasize the receiver of the action by putting it first in the sentence. Remember that verbs should carry the force of your writing more than modifiers.

◆ Make your phrasing sound natural by **using idioms correctly**. Check your writing to make sure that you have used the correct word combinations and fixed phrases. If English is not your first language, learn idioms by speaking and reading English frequently, and study a dictionary of American idioms.

◆ Avoid repetition by **using pronouns** and by **varying your sentence beginnings and sentence patterns**. If you find yourself starting sentence after sentence with the subject followed by the verb, revise the patterns to create better rhythm and variety.

◆ **Practice sentence combining** to attain greater maturity and creativity in your style. A developed style comes less from writing long sentences than from concentrating meaning into each phrase and weaving sentence parts together gracefully and tightly.

◆ Improve your style by **using word processing to explore vocabulary and sentence options**. Use the resources of your word processing program to improve your style. The grammar check will caution you about the overuse of passive voice, the length of your sentences and other features in your writing. The program thesaurus is much easier to use than a thesaurus in book form.

UNIT

5

Proofreading Your Writing and Reviewing Grammar

This is the last unit because proofreading your revised drafts to eliminate all mistakes in grammar and spelling should always be your last stage in the writing process. Basic mistakes can destroy the effectiveness of an essay that has been created carefully through the stages of prewriting, composition, and revision. However, grammar is not just a kind of polish applied to the last draft: It is part of the writing process at all stages. Good writers must become proficient enough that whenever they write, even in prewriting activities, most of their words are spelled correctly and have correct endings, and most of their sentences are complete and correct. If you do not improve your mastery of grammar and spelling enough, not only will you leave many errors in all drafts, but you will be unable to proofread your revised drafts effectively.

Therefore, Unit 5 offers you a chance to work intensively on whatever aspects of grammar and spelling cause you difficulties. In this unit, practice until your grammar, proofreading, and spelling reach the same high level as the other writing skills you develop while working on the earlier units.

Proofreading and Correcting the Revised Essay

Proofreading for errors in typing, punctuation, spelling, and grammar is most important on the next-to-last draft. The final copy that you turn in should be letter perfect and without correction marks. On the earlier drafts, you need not spend time making minor corrections, since you will probably change or remove many passages later. In fact, proofreading too soon may make you resist making revisions later, because you won't want to "ruin" your handiwork. Save the really detailed corrections for the late stages. Make a final draft as if you were going to hand it in; then proofread this draft and make final corrections for the one you *really* hand in. This way you will have an almost perfect copy of your own for safekeeping.

Proofreading requires extremely close attention, not the careless attention we usually give to television programs and advertisements. As you read your work slowly aloud, you will learn not to mentally correct errors—that is, to read the way you meant the passage to be without noticing little words left out, endings omitted, words repeated, apostrophes missing, letters reversed, and so on. As you do the grammatical exercises in this unit, you will become more expert at recognizing errors. While proofreading, remember these points:

Proofreading Hints

- **Read aloud slowly.** Most writers are tempted to skim over their work silently. Force yourself instead to read carefully, pointing to every word. Some professional writers even read their work backward to avoid rushing over mistakes. Try it.

- **Know yourself.** What mistakes do you always make? Do you make certain spelling mistakes? Drop *S* and *D* endings? Leave out small words? Run sentences together? Leave fragments? When you know your own habits, you will know the corrections your writing is most likely to need.

- **Proofread several times.** When writing at home, proofread once carefully after you have written the essay. Then put the essay away for a day or two and proofread it again. You will often catch mistakes that you overlooked the first time.

- **If English is not your first language, watch for patterns.** Look for missing articles (*a, an,* and *the*), errors with verb tenses (especially progressive tenses using -ing forms), and incorrect word order.

Try copying the following passage exactly as it is on the page:

> NOW IS THE TIME FOR
> FOR ALL GOOD MEN TO
> TO COME TO THE AID
> THEIR COUNTRY.

Did you notice the two repeated words and the one left out? When you read passages with which you are familiar, you tend to overlook slips like this. When you read your own writing, you are even more likely to overlook errors.

Exercise

Proofreading

The passage that follows contains simple writing mistakes: words left out, words accidentally repeated, wrong punctuation, simple misspellings. Circle the mistakes; then rewrite the passage, correcting as many mistakes as you can.

Trash Talking on Radio and Television

In today's society they are many people who makes hateful statement on radio and television. They don't care whose feelings are hurt by there negative comments on the media. Since they no that expressing anger and hate attract more attention then expressing intelligent opinions, they try to be as insulting as they can to all sorts of groups. Sometimes they put down woman or minorities sometimes they attack homosexual or immigrants. They think nobody will do anything about their remarks. Because censorship violates the right to free speech guaranteed in the Constitution. Once in a while one of these announcer go to far and looses his job, but others just go right on making the same prejudice comments as before. Its difficult to find a way to to stop this abuse of the airways without making people give up their right to here what they want or watch what they want. One of the worse result of this trash talking is that children

often listen to it and imitates what they hear, later when they grown up they

maybe full of negative attitudes.

Reviewing Basics

Correcting your writing does require knowledge of grammar. When college students say they are "terrible with grammar," however, they are usually exaggerating. When you speak English correctly, you are following most of the important grammatical rules. You do not have to relearn grammar from the ground up, but correcting your writing may require you to study some features of grammar that you are uncertain about. In this unit you will review the major kinds of writing errors and concentrate on learning how to correct them, especially the ones that give you the most trouble.

Diagnostic Test

Name _____

The following test will give you an idea of your strengths and weaknesses in grammar, punctuation, and spelling. You can then use Unit 5 for explanation and practice in the areas where you require the most improvement. Bear in mind, however, that correcting grammatical mistakes on a short answer test is not the same as correcting them in your writing. **Correct grammar must be incorporated into your whole writing process, especially in the final proofreading stage.** Always notice your instructor's marks and comments on your writing, and listen to your classmates' feedback to identify your strengths and weaknesses.

Part One: Sentence Divisions
In each group of sentences, only one is correct—a, b, or c. Write the letter of the correct one in the blank.

1. ______   a. The senator changed his campaign strategy because the polls showed he was losing.
   b. The senator changed his campaign strategy, the polls showed that he was losing.
   c. The senator changed his campaign strategy. Because the polls showed that he was losing.

2. _____ C _____
   a. Although Veronica had a degree in accounting. She wanted to be a novelist.
   b. Although Veronica had a degree in accounting; she wanted to be a novelist.
   c. Although Veronica had a degree in accounting, she wanted to be a novelist.

3. _____ b _____
   a. The curtain was about to rise, Miguel felt nervous and impatient.
   b. Before the curtain rose, Miguel felt nervous and impatient.
   c. Miguel felt nervous and impatient. While waiting for the curtain to rise.

4. _____ C _____
   a. Nursing students must earn at least a B in chemistry. Also take two semesters of anatomy and physiology.
   b. Nursing students must earn at least a B in chemistry then they must take two semesters of anatomy and physiology.
   c. Nursing students must earn at least a B in chemistry. Then they must take two semesters of anatomy and physiology.

5. _____ b _____
   a. Talk shows appeal to most television viewers they combine scandal, gossip, and psychological revelations.
   b. Talk shows, combining scandal, gossip, and psychological revelations, appeal to most television viewers.
   c. Talk shows appeal to most television viewers. Because they combine scandal, gossip, and psychological revelations.

6. _____ A _____
   a. The restaurant lowered its prices to attract more customers; soon it was filled to capacity.
   b. The restaurant lowered its prices to attract more customers, soon it was filled to capacity.
   c. The restaurant, which had lowered its prices to attract more customers. Soon was filled to capacity.

7. _____ b _____
   a. Sonia called an 800 number. Trying to get help with her malfunctioning computer.
   b. Sonia called an 800 number to get help with her malfunctioning computer.
   c. Sonia called an 800 number; to get help with her malfunctioning computer.

8. _____ A _____
   a. Exercise is good for your health; it improves the lungs, heart, and circulatory system.
   b. Exercise is good for your health, it improves your lungs, heart, and circulatory system.
   c. Exercise improves your lungs, heart and circulatory system. Which is good for your health.

9. _____C_____
   a. Attending a community college can be the best choice for some older students. Especially if they have to work full time.
   b. If they have to work full time. Attending a community college can be the best choice for some older students.
   c. Attending a community college can be the best choice for some older students, especially if they have to work full time.

10. _____C_____
   a. The study of other cultures is required in most colleges it allows students to evaluate their own culture from a new perspective.
   b. The study of other cultures is required in most colleges, it allows students to evaluate their own culture from a new perspective.
   c. The study of other cultures is required in most colleges because it allows students to evaluate their own culture from a new perspective.

Part Two: Verb Forms, Endings, and Agreement
Write the correct form in the blank provided.

___use___ 11. People who (use, uses, used) the Internet have access to information about current events, finance, and popular culture.

___live___ 12. One of this year's lottery winners used to (lives, live, lived) in Bosnia.

_____ 13. Moving to Portland was the best thing that ever (happen, happens, happened) to Charles.

_____ 14. Either the business curriculum or the physician's assistant program (is, are, were) expected to attract the most students.

_____ 15. Tourists (spend, spends, spent) millions of dollars last year visiting Washington, D.C.

_____ 16. A successful student usually sits near the front and (ask, asks, asked) questions frequently.

_____ 17. Last year this same laptop computer (cost, costs, costed) twice what it does today.

_____ 18. There (is, are, was) two film directors living in the building.

_____ 19. Auditions for the band (use, uses, used) to be held in the gymnasium.

_____ 20. Representatives are (suppose, supposed) to live in their own districts.

Part Three: Spelling
If the word or phrase is correct, write C in the blank; if not, write the correctly spelled word in the blank.

_____ 21. beginning

_____ 22. definitly

_____ 23. neccessary

_____ 24. their my neighbors

_____ 25. younger then you

_____ 26. seperate

_____ 27. commited

_____ 28. a guilty conscious

_____ 29. develope

_____ 30. received

_____ 31. responsability

_____ 32. its my turn

_____ 33. take alot of time

_____ 34. occuring

_____ 35. it dosen't make sense

Part Four: Punctuation

If the sentence is punctuated correctly, write C in the blank. If not, circle the spot where a punctuation mark is missing or incorrect and write the correct mark in the blank. No sentence has more than one punctuation error.

_____ 36. The store sold treadmills, weightlifting equipment sneakers, and clothes for working out.

_____ 37. Expecting an appearance by Michael Jackson the crowd started to clap rhythmically.

_____ 38. The college council took the following actions lowering the number of credits for a degree, adding a new program in criminal justice, and eliminating the speech code.

_____ 39. A conference of educators was held in Toledo Ohio in February 1996.

_____ 40. Mark Twain wrote "Never put off till tomorrow what you can do the day after tomorrow."

_____ 41. Leonard had many skills, which included computer programming, writing poetry, filmmaking, and speaking Russian.

_____ 42. Eileen wanted to be an investigative journalist, however, her friends encouraged her to choose an easier profession.

_____ 43. Salman Rushdie, the author of *The Satanic Verses* has remained in hiding for several years.

_____ 44. Some athletes, most notably Magic Johnson and the late Arthur Ashe have brought public attention to the AIDS crisis.

_____ 45. Videotapes of Hollywood films are widely available nevertheless, filmgoers continue to fill the theaters whenever new movies appear.

Part Five: Pronouns, Parallelism, Mixed Sentences, and Modifiers

If the sentence is correct, write C in the blank. If a word or phrase is incorrect, circle it and write the correct word or phrase in the blank.

_____ 46. The freshmen are untrained, but they play as good as the seniors.

_____ 47. Sharon is dependable, knowledgeable, and has compassion for others.

_____ 48. There is almost no difference between you and I.

_____ 49. Reading her e-mail messages, the computer screen suddenly went blank.

_____ 50. All married graduate students are required to submit his student aid information.

_____ 51. Kendra and Susan decided they could make a music video by theirself.

_____ 52. Her and her brother both take their vacations in January.

_____ 53. The college administration decided that the budget won't allow for no more free tutoring.

_____ 54. If you read the introduction careful, you will find the answer to your question.

_____ 55. You will pass this course easy if you just study these notes.

_____ 56. By withholding love from the infant made her depressed and anxious.

_____ 57. Designer drugs have become popular among the wealthy; it is being used widely in Europe and Asia, as well as the United States.

_____ 58. Cars powered by electricity may someday be inexpensive to own, convenient to drive, and not making much noise.

_____ 59. The commencement speaker urged students to strive for success, support their families, and help those less fortunate than themselves.

_____ 60. Most employees do more better work if they feel secure in their jobs.

Possible Score: _____60_____   Your Score:_____

How Words Work: Recognizing Parts of Speech

We can label all words according to the way we use them in sentences. The eight labels we use are called the **parts of speech.** They include **nouns, pronouns, verbs, adjectives, adverbs, prepositions, conjunctions,** and **interjections.** Since we often need to use these labels when talking about grammar, you should study the list below and familiarize yourself with any of these terms you do not already know.

NOUNS: Refer to Persons, Objects, Places, or Ideas

Nouns come in two categories, **common nouns** and **proper nouns.** **Common nouns** are <u>general</u> words for persons, objects, places, or ideas: *student, beeper, corner, advantage.* Do not capitalize common nouns. **Proper nouns** are <u>specific</u> names of persons, objects, institutions, places, or ideas: *Jerry Seinfeld, Pepsi Cola, Venezuela, Protestantism.* Always capitalize proper nouns.

Nouns also come in two forms, **singular** and **plural. Singular nouns** refer to one person, object, place, or idea: *a student, a beeper, the corner, an advantage.* (If English is not your first language, don't forget to write the article *a* or *the* before singular nouns.) **Plural nouns** refer to two or more persons, objects, places, or ideas: *students, beepers, corners, advantages.* (Don't forget that most plural nouns take –s endings.)

PRONOUNS: Take the Place of Nouns

Prounouns come in five categories: **personal pronouns, indefinite pronouns, relative pronouns, interrogative pronouns,** and **demonstrative pronouns.**

Personal pronouns include all forms of *I, we, you, she, he, they,* and *it,* as well as the reflexive pronouns *myself, ourselves, yourself, yourselves, himself, herself, themselves,* and *itself.*

Indefinite pronouns are words that refer to a number of persons or things, like *everyone, something, all, many,* and *each.*

Relative pronouns introduce clauses that relate to or modify other parts of a sentence. These pronouns include the forms of *who,* as well as *which* and *that.*

Interrogative pronouns, used to begin questions, include *who, which,* and *what.*

Demonstrative pronouns point out persons, places or things; they include *this, that, these,* and *those.*

VERBS: Designate Action or State of Being

Action verbs include words like *swim, drive, dance,* and *write.* **State of being verbs** include *be* (in all its forms—*is, was, were,* etc.), *seem, become,* and similar words.

Verbs can take different forms, depending on number and tense. Exercises on verb forms later in this unit will help you learn how to use the correct verb forms and verb endings.

ADJECTIVES: Describe or Modify Nouns

Some adjectives, like *green, prodigious, beautiful,* and *happy,* tell what kind of person or thing is being described. Others, like *twenty, few,* and *innumerable,* tell how many persons or things are being described. And a few adjectives, like *this, that, these,* and *those* (which can also be pronouns when they stand alone), identify which person or thing is being described. Adjectives can take comparative and superlative forms in comparative statements. See the section on modifiers later in this unit.

ADVERBS: Describe Verbs, Adjectives, or Other Adverbs

Adverbs can designate how, when, or where an action occurs. Many adverbs, like *quickly, permanently,* and *happily,* are formed by adding *-ly* endings to adjectives. Like adjectives, adverbs can take comparative and superlative forms. See the section on modifiers later in this unit.

PREPOSITIONS: Small Words or Word Combinations that Show Relationship or Direction

Prepositions include words like *in, of, on, above, beneath,* and *through,* as well as combinations like *by means of, on behalf of,* and *in regard to.* **Prepositional phrases,** such as *of the students, in the film,* or *with an attitude,* contain prepositions and their objects (the nouns or pronouns that come after them). Identifying prepositional phrases will help you recognize the grammatical structure of sentences. See the section on subject–verb agreement in this unit.

CONJUNCTIONS: Connectors that Link Words, Phrases, or Clauses

Coordinating conjunctions (*and, or, nor, but, yet, so,* and *for*) join equal parts, such as two words (bread *and* butter), two phrases (above the ankles *but* below the knees), or two clauses (she wanted to apply for the job, *yet* she had doubts about it). Coordinating conjunctions are used to join parts of **compound sentences.** See the section on **run-on sentences** in this unit.

Correlative conjunctions, such as *either/or, not only/but also,* and *both/and,* are used in combination to join words, phrases, or whole clauses. See the section on subject/verb agreement later in this unit.

Subordinating conjunctions, such as *because, when, if, although,* and *since,* connect **main clauses** with **dependent clauses** in **complex sentences.** See the sections on fragments and run-together sentences in this unit.

INTERJECTIONS: Inserted Exclamations

These are short words like *oh, well, yes,* and *sure,* and phrases like *good heavens!* or *good grief!* that are put at the beginnings of sentences to express strong feeling or surprise. Put commas or exclamation points after them.

Subjects and Verbs

To understand sentences, learn to spot subjects and verbs.

The Subject

The subject names the person or thing the sentence is about:

> The whole *family* uses the new personal computer.
> The *videotape* belonged to the school library.
> *Jay Leno* became host of the "Tonight Show" in May 1992.

The Verb

The verb is the word that shows action or being:

> The whole family *uses* the new personal computer.
> The videotape *belonged* to the school library.
> Jay Leno *became* host of the "Tonight Show" in May 1992.

Every sentence must have at least one subject and verb that go together. A sentence states that someone or something does or is something. If the subject or verb is missing, the sentence is not complete. Underline the subjects and circle the verbs in these sentences:

1. The excited crowd waited for the singers to appear.
2. Seven students majoring in sociology traveled to Ghana.
3. The legal voting age in the United States is eighteen.

IDENTIFYING SUBJECTS

In most sentences, subjects appear at or near the beginning. Subjects can be nouns (words that name persons, places, or things):

> the *campus*   *Detroit*   two *actresses*   my *car*   academic *subjects*

Subjects can also be pronouns (words that stand for nouns):

> *I*   *you*   *she*   *he*   *it*   *we*   *they*

Sentences with Noun Subjects

> The *space shuttle* orbited the earth before descending.
> A *degree* in hotel management makes you eligible for the job.
> *Sex education* in schools raises heated controversies.

Sentences with Pronoun Subjects

> *We* discovered a new way to drive to New Orleans.
> *She* entered a bicycle race.
> *You* know the difference between discipline and child abuse.

Exercise I

Identifying Subjects

Underline the subjects in these sentences. Two of the sentences have no subjects and are therefore incomplete; write F in the margin next to these two fragments.

1. The first book on the list was about Latin America.
2. I know four people who have made their own films.
3. A few retired members contributed large sums of money.
4. Specially trained experts defused the incendiary bomb.
5. Reaching the warning track near the left field wall.
6. Next Monday you will have to pay $29.95 for the videotape.
7. During the negotiations over the hostages in Peru.

Exercise II

Identifying Subjects

Underline the subject of each sentence in the following paragraph. One sentence is incomplete because it lacks a subject; circle the number next to that fragment.

(1) We no longer stereotype people because of their sex. (2) Little girls do not have to limit their interests to paper dolls and toy sewing machines. (3) Little boys are not confined to toy guns, trucks, and erector sets. (4) Today's parents have become more concerned about the individuality of their children than about their children's conformity to stereotypes. (5) Teenagers, too, are less rigid in adopting "feminine" or "masculine" roles than in the past. (6) In most high schools, you will now find a large number of girls majoring in chemistry or mathematics. (7) And even playing aggressive sports, like lacrosse and basketball. (8) Furthermore, in most families, both parents share in wage earning as well as housework and caring for children. (9) In fact, few adult activities can be labeled "men's work" or "women's work" nowadays. (10) In the place of stereotyped roles, people are now adopting living patterns suited to their individual abilities and needs.

 ## If English Is Not Your First Language

Unlike some languages, **English requires that you actually name the subject in every sentence.** The only sentences from which the subjects are omitted are commands ("Look over to your left") or requests ("Please bring me a floppy disk"). In these *imperative sentences,* as they are called, the word *you* is understood to be the subject.

In English, we cannot say, "Is raining" or "Is time for lunch," as in some languages. We say, "<u>It</u> is raining" or "<u>It</u> is time for lunch."

We cannot say, "Is a good day for shopping." We say, "<u>This</u> is a good day for shopping."

In some languages, the verb forms in such sentences indicate the subjects, but in English sentences of this type, the subjects must always appear.

Neither is it correct in English to name the subject twice by using a pronoun after the noun subject. We do not write, "<u>My brother he</u> likes to play racquetball." The correct form is either "My brother likes to play racquetball" or "He likes to play racquetball."

Exercise III

Identifying Subjects (For ESL Writers)

Some of the sentences below have subjects missing. If the sentence is correct, write C in the blank. If the subject is missing, write an X over the place where the subject belongs, and in the blank write a word that would be a good subject. If the sentence has an incorrect double subject, write an X over the subject and cross out the extra one.

Example:

_it_	The students thought $\overset{X}{}$ was a difficult test.
_____	My sister $\overset{X}{\text{she}}$ belongs to a neighborhood church.

_____ 1. Beverly she decided to ask her boss for a raise.
_____ 2. Is not the right answer to the question the student asked.
_____ 3. Was snowing yesterday, so we stayed home.
_____ 4. Was not a good reason to knock him down.
_____ 5. The coach he was fired even though the team had a good year.
_____ 6. Sometimes will be hard to find the right Web site.
_____ 7. Is hard to use this book because it has no index.

Writing Assignment

Identifying Subjects

Do a page of focused writing on the topic of the way different groups of students dress on your campus. Do not concentrate on grammar while writing; just fill up a page and stay on the topic. Afterward, go back and underline the subject or subjects in every sentence. Did you find any sentences without subjects? Rewrite these sentences with subjects added.

MULTIPLE SUBJECTS

Sentences may contain two subjects connected by *and* or *or*, or three or more subjects that form a list, or series. Writers often make mistakes in grammar if they fail to recognize these multiple subjects.

Sentences with Two Subjects

> *Betty* and *David* went to see a horror film.
> My *brother* and *I* bought tickets in the lottery.
> *You* and *we* disagree about methadone treatment.

Sentences with Three or More Subjects

> The *heart*, the *lungs*, and the *reproductive system* may be affected by the use of marijuana.
> *Buddhism, Christianity*, and *Judaism* have much in common.
> *Cecil, Marylou, Rachel*, and *I* eat lunch together.

HARD-TO-FIND SUBJECTS

Some subjects are hard to identify.

Subjects in the Middle or End of the Sentence

A. Across from the diner was Sam's auto parts *store*. (This sentence begins with a descriptive phrase, "across from the diner," and ends with the subject, *store*.)

B. There are probably many *answers* to your question. (*There* is only a position word, never a subject; in sentences beginning with *there*, the subject usually comes after the verb.)

Verbal Subjects

Verbals are verb forms that can be used as subjects in place of nouns or pronouns; they may be infinitives (*to dance, to write*) or gerunds (*dancing, writing*).

A. *Moving* away from home was difficult for Sharon.

B. *To find* your sister in this crowd is going to be difficult.

In these sentences, *moving* and *to find* are verbals that serve as subjects.

Whole-Clause Subjects

Sometimes whole groups of words, called *noun clauses,* can serve as subjects; they often begin with *what* or *that:*

A. *What I would prefer* is a high-paying job with no responsibilities.

B. *That you like rock music* is no secret to your friends.

In these sentences, *What I would prefer* and *That you like rock music* are clauses that serve as subjects.

You-Understood Subjects

In sentences that give commands or make requests, the subject is understood to be *you,* but is not included in the sentence:

A. Tell me the rest of the story when we get home.
B. Turn left at the light and follow Route 84.

In both these sentences, *you* is understood to be the subject.

Exercise I

Identifying Subjects

Underline the subjects in the following sentences. If the sentence is a command or request, write *you* in the blank. Two of the sentences are incomplete because they lack subjects; write F in the blanks next to these fragments.

_____ 1. There is a fashion show in the student union this afternoon.

_____ 2. Television, newspapers, and magazines compete for money from sponsors.

_____ 3. Finish your A.A. degree before continuing on to a four-year college.

_____ 4. A series that included documentaries on World War I, the Great Depression, and the rise of fascism.

_____ 5. Located next to the drive-in bank was an electronics store.

_____ 6. Later in the afternoon a wedding and reception are scheduled.

_____ 7. Sonia, Stanley, and I use the same online shopping service.

_____ 8. Angered by the news report, listeners bombarded the station with calls.

_____ 9. Lacrosse, racquetball, and rock climbing continue to be Ellen's favorite sports.

_____ 10. Having safe working conditions, fringe benefits, and congenial co-workers.

Exercise II

Identifying Subjects

Underline the subjects of the sentences in the following paragraph. One sentence is incomplete; circle the number next to it. If the subject is understood, write *you* above the number

(1) Having a credit card has its advantages and disadvantages. (2) In the first place, using the card for purchases is obviously quick and convenient. (3) Clothes, cosmetics, airline tickets, and liquor can be bought speedily with a credit card. (4) Another benefit is the use of a major credit card for personal identification. (5) Giving the credit card bearer confidence when traveling or working. (6) We all, however, are tempted to abuse the privilege of buying on credit. (7) What causes the biggest problem is that we ignore our financial

situation when making purchases. (8) As a result, what was a small convenience can lead to a troublesome debt. (9) Don't get a credit card unless you are sure you can keep your expenditures under reasonable control. (10) Then the advantages of having a credit card will outweigh the disadvantages.

Writing Assignment

Identifying Subjects

Compose a paragraph of seven to twelve sentences, keeping in mind what you have learned about topic sentences, development, and unity. In this paragraph describe how people shop at some store or mall with which you are familiar. Tell how they decide on purchases, what they buy, and how they relate to the employees. Remember to use vivid and precise words. After composing the paragraph, underline the subject or subjects of every sentence, being sure that no sentences are left incomplete because they lack subjects.

IDENTIFYING VERBS

Action and Being Verbs

Verbs are the words that tell about action or being. In many sentences they come directly after the subject:

>   s   v
> Both contestants <u>answered</u> the final question correctly. (action verb)

>   s   v
> The challenger <u>was</u> ahead by $1500. (verb of being)

Sometimes, however, verbs can come before subjects or they can be separated from subjects; they can even appear at or near the ends of sentences:

>   v   s
> Nearby <u>was</u> a store that sold comic books for collectors. (verb before subject at the beginning of the sentence)

>   s   v
> The audience, bored by the sloppy performance, <u>booed</u> loudly. (verb near the end of the sentence, separated from the subject)

Exercise I

Identifying Verbs

Underline the verb in each of the following sentences. It may be an action word (*throws, dances, swims,* etc.) or a word of being (*is, are, was, were*). One sentence is incomplete because it lacks a verb. Write F in the margin next to it.

1. Action movies usually give Ronald a headache.
2. What is so appealing to him about special effects and violence?
3. His girlfriend Cindy prefers documentaries on television.
4. A woman with a wide knowledge of history and sociology.
5. She knows all about the women's movement and the civil rights movement.
6. Her favorite historical figure is Eleanor Roosevelt.
7. Ronald usually prefers books about the history of science.

Exercise II

Identifying Verbs

Underline each subject and circle each verb in the following sentences. One sentence in the paragraph lacks a verb; circle the number next to it.

(1) Many people have trouble with debt. (2) The bills for their credit cards, car payments, and college loans come in every month. (3) Their total debts accumulate into an insurmountable pile. (4) Sometimes they resort to experts for advice on how to cope with their debts. (5) With such professional help these people often manage their finances better. (6) Every month they pay more than the minimal required amount on their credit cards. (7) They also negotiate for lower interest rates on lines of credit. (8) Their college loans on manageable repayment plans as well. (9) In addition, a bad credit record can be improved with the right planning. (10) Intelligent management of a person's debts and credit record will make his or her life easier and happier.

MULTIPLE VERBS

Many sentences have more than one verb matched with the same subject. To avoid errors, you must be able to identify all the main verbs:

Mary *left* early and *took* a cab home
Oscar *feinted* to the left, *crossed* rapidly to the right, and *fired* a jump shot from the foul line.

Exercise III

Identifying Verbs

Underline the verbs in these sentences; be sure not to ignore the second or third verb in the sentence. One sentence is incomplete because it lacks a verb; write F next to this fragment.

1. Cable television provides good reception and offers extra program choices.
2. Hot weather lures many people outdoors but produces sunburn.
3. Along with accounting and marketing, Susan wanted to take a course in economics but later changed her mind.
4. He attends conferences and often makes presentations at them.
5. After the last day of registration but before the first day of the semester.

HELPING VERBS

Verbs often take **helpers** (*is* going, *should be* working, *has* applied, etc.), or **auxiliaries,** as they are called. Usually the helping verbs come right before the main verbs, but sometimes there are words separating them.

Be, Have, and Do: The Most Common Helping Verbs

Forms of **be** (*is, are, was, were*), **have** (*have, has, had*), and **do** (*do, does, did*) are the most common helping verbs.

> The prices of designer jeans *are* going wild.
> Sally *has* gone to five aerobics classes this week.
> *Did* you see the shell collection in the science building?

Fixed-Form Helpers

The many other helping verbs do not have changing forms like *be, have,* and *do.* These fixed-form (unchanging) helpers often appear next to main verbs:

can	might	should	could	must
will	may	shall	would	

> The prices of personal computers *will* drop soon.
> We *could* arrange to meet on Wednesday afternoons.
> I *can* always give you a call tomorrow.

Exercise IV

Identifying Verbs with Auxiliaries

Underline the complete verbs—both the main verbs and the helpers—in these sentences. One sentence is incomplete because it lacks a verb; write F next to this fragment. (Note: do not underline *not* and *never;* they are not verbs or helpers.)

1. Some students had never seen a silent film.
2. The job was considered the best one in the company.
3. Before the application deadline in February. F

4. Has your cousin ever lived in Chicago?
5. A state university would offer a large number of majors.
6. In the manual you will find the most frequently asked questions.
7. All swimming instructors must learn cardiopulmonary resuscitation.

VERBALS: THE FAKE VERBS

Writers often leave sentences incomplete because they mistake verbals for main verbs.

The man in the back row *wearing* a yellow necktie.

Is this a complete sentence? If you answered yes, you may need to review the difference between verbs and verbals. Verbals are forms made from verbs but used for other purposes. *Wearing* in this sentence is only a descriptive word; "wearing a yellow necktie" describes the man, but it doesn't say what he does.

The man in the back row wearing a yellow necktie *lives* in Utah.

Now we have a complete sentence with a verb telling what the man does. Verbals can be verb forms ending in *ing* (called **present participles** or **gerunds**), forms ending in *ed* (called **past participles**), or forms with *to* in front of them (called **infinitives**).

Fragment:	The car *approaching* the intersection.
Sentence:	The car approaching the intersection *slowed* down in time to avoid an accident. (verb added)
Fragment:	The prices *listed* on the menu.
Sentence:	The prices listed on the menu *do* not *include* dessert.
Fragment:	*Pitching* against left-handed batters.
Sentence:	Pitching against left-handed batters *is* his specialty.
Fragment:	*To express* yourself effectively before an audience.
Sentence:	To express yourself effectively before an audience, you *should learn* the techniques of public speaking.

Exercise 1

Identifying Subjects and Verbs

Underline the subjects and circle the verbs in the following sentences. Be sure to include helping verbs. Three sentences are incomplete because they contain verbals but no main verbs. Write F in the margin next to each of these.

F 1. A good reason to visit Jamaica during the Easter vacation.
2. The cheerleaders formed a pyramid and waited to be photographed.
3. We have collected fifteen articles on alcoholism for the file.
F 4. Investigating crimes committed with stolen handguns.
5. The unemployment rate has risen and fallen unpredictably.
F 6. The distance measured by telescopes in orbit.
7. Does Mara know anything about Japan?
8. Stretching exercises are helpful before distance running.
9. Parents of troubled teenagers should be expert listeners.
10. Lost articles at the airport are kept in the security office.

Exercise II

Identifying Subjects and Verbs

Underline the subjects and circle the verbs in the following paragraph. One sentence has deliberately been left incomplete; circle the number next to it.

(1) Many people lose their jobs in today's economy. (2) Receiving a pink slip can be a devastating experience. (3) However, certain survival techniques will help you overcome the destructive effects of being laid off. (4) First of all, you should not give up too quickly. (5) Your boss may be willing to reconsider his or her decision. (6) If not, there is still often some room for negotiation of details concerning your termination. (7) Next, your financial situation must take priority. (8) There are usually ways to rearrange your payment schedules to creditors. (9) An optimistic attitude toward finding another job will help enormously in the next phase of your life. (10) With the help of a financial manager, you can probably scale down your monthly costs and bring your budget into manageable proportions. (11) Being optimistic about your chances, always remembering your strongest assets and true abilities. (12) A systematic job search and lots of persistence will eventually lead to another, and sometimes better, employment opportunity.

Group Project

Identifying Subjects and Verbs

Brainstorm with your writing group about the courses you are taking this semester. Then have each member write a rough draft of a paragraph telling about what is going on in one of his or her courses. Exchange drafts; each writer should then underline the subject or subjects of every sentence and circle the verbs. Compare drafts to see if you agree about identifying subjects and verbs;

are there any missing subjects or verbs? Write a final draft of the paragraph, being sure that every sentence has a subject/verb combination.

Fragments

You have already been identifying some fragments, or incomplete sentences, in the previous exercises. Fragments are fake sentences; they begin with capital letters and end with periods, but lack some necessary part.

TELLING THE DIFFERENCE BETWEEN FRAGMENTS AND SENTENCES

In the previous exercises, either the subject or the verb was missing from the fragments. Some fragments, however, are incomplete because a word at the beginning turns them into subordinate clauses.

A whole sentence can be called a *main clause:*

> s   v
> The <u>siren</u> <u>was making</u> an ear-splitting noise.

A **subordinate,** or **dependent clause** also has a subject and verb but begins with a word like *because* or *when,* which makes the whole clause incomplete. It becomes a modifying part of a sentence:

> Because the siren was making an ear-splitting noise

To make it complete, you must add a main clause:

> subordinate clause   *main clause*
> Because the siren was making an ear-splitting noise, *the nearby residents*
> *evacuated the area.*

SUBORDINATE CLAUSES AND SUBORDINATING CONJUNCTIONS

The **subordinating conjunctions** are words that turn main clauses into subordinate clauses. If you begin a sentence with one of these words, you must add a main clause to complete the sentence.

Subordinating Conjunctions

after	for as long as	when
although	if	whenever
as	just as	where

because	since	whereas
before	though	wherever
even though	unless	while
ever since	until	

SUBORDINATE-CLAUSE FRAGMENTS

Remember that clauses beginning with these words are not sentences but fragments.

> Because the bus splashed mud on Tina's jeans.
> Although the three brothers grew up in different families.

To make such fragments complete, add a main clause:

subordinate clause   main clause

Because the bus splashed mud on Tina's jeans, *she bought a new pair.*

subordinate clause   main clause

Although the three brothers grew up in different families, *they attended the same school.*

Exercise I

Subordinate-Clause Fragments

Some of the following sentences are complete; others are fragments. The fragments may have subjects or verbs missing, as in the previous lesson, or they may begin with subordinating conjunctions. Underline the subjects and circle the verbs in the complete sentences. Write F next to the fragments.

1. The yeti in Tibet, the alma in the Soviet Union, Sasquatch (or Bigfoot) in the northwestern United States, and the Chinese Wildman all hairy monsters resembling human beings.

2. The skunk ape, a foul-smelling creature that has surprised trappers and fishermen in Florida since the 1920s.

3. While the Missouri monster, named Mo-Mo, is also an apelike figure that has frightened people since the 1960s.

4. Nessie, or the Loch Ness monster, being the most famous of all monsters and one of the oldest, the first report occurring in the sixth century.

5. The beast of Truro, a large creature resembling a mountain lion, was sighted in Cape Cod, Massachusetts, in 1981 and blamed for the deaths of several cats.

6. The coelacanth, hauled in off the South African coast in 1938, was not really a monster but a species of fish once thought to be extinct for millions of years.

7. A monster in Argentina said to drag people into the water called the iemisch.

8. The nandi bear, in Africa, a beast that purportedly eats only the brains of its victims.

9. Champ is the name of a long-necked monster seen occasionally in Lake Champlain ever since it was first sighted by the lake's discoverer, Samuel de Champlain, in 1609.

10. Because the kraken, first reported in 1752, was supposed to be large enough to drag whole ships under water.*

Exercise II

Subordinate-Clause Fragments

All of the following sentences begin with subordinating conjunctions from the list on pp. 252–253. Five of them are complete sentences because they have main clauses as well as subordinate clauses. Five are fragments. Underline the main clause in each complete sentence; write F next to each fragment.

1. Because our electoral system is rather complicated, many people do not understand how we elect a president.

2. Although many people believe they are voting for a presidential candidate on election day.

3. When they go to the polls, American voters actually choose members of the electoral college.

4. Unless members of the electoral college violate a long tradition, they all vote for the candidate who won the most votes in their state.

5. Because this system makes it possible in a close race for a candidate who got the most popular votes to lose the election.

6. If no candidate receives a majority of the electoral votes, the House of Representatives chooses a president.

7. Whenever the electoral system comes up for discussion, especially during a closely contested election.

8. After the election of 1824, for instance, in which no candidate won a majority, the House of Representatives chose John Quincy Adams, who had come in second in the popular vote.

---

*Information from Daniel Cohen, *The Encyclopedia of Monsters.* New York: Dodd, Mead, 1982.

9. Since the electoral system is not a perfect example of government "by the people."

10. For as long as we have been electing presidents in the United States.

ADDED-CLAUSE FRAGMENTS

Subordinate clause fragments often occur as an afterthought, an incomplete statement added to complete the thought of a previous sentence but left to stand by itself:

Sentence Followed by Added–Clause Fragment

He was an entertaining teacher. One who ran his sociology class like a television talk show.

Corrected Version with Two Complete Sentences

He was an entertaining teacher. He ran his sociology class like a television talk show.

Corrected Version with Parts Combined into One Sentence

He was an entertaining teacher who ran his sociology class like a television talk show.

When correcting added–clause fragments, first check to see whether the fragment can be combined with the sentence before it; usually, it can. If not, rewrite the fragment as a complete sentence; this usually means removing the subordinate conjunction (*because, when, if,* etc.) or changing the *who, which,* or *that* to *he, she,* or *it.*

► Exercise

Added-Clause Fragments

Each item below contains two statements. If both are complete sentences, write C in the blank. If one is a fragment, either rewrite the pair as a single combined sentence or rewrite the fragment as a complete sentence.

Example: I lost half my research paper. Because my computer was infected with a virus.
Correction: *I lost my research paper because my computer was infected with a virus.*

1. Computer viruses are just like biological viruses. Because they spread from one computer to another by contact.

   _____

   _____

2. Your computer could be described as getting "sick." When it picks up a virus carried by a floppy disk.

   _____

   _____

3. A famous virus is called the Michaelangelo virus. One which is designed to take effect on March 6, the birthday of the artist.

   _____

   _____

4. Such viruses can be carried from a floppy disk to your computer's hard disk. Where they corrupt or erase data, causing you to lose large amounts of material.

   _____

   _____

5. Viruses can lie hidden in your files. Until they become activated on predetermined days.

   _____

   _____

6. Protective software has been designed to detect and remove viruses. Although many of these programs are effective, they are seldom foolproof.

   _____

   _____

7. One problem is that new viruses keep appearing frequently. Many of which succeed in escaping the anti-virus programs.

   _____

   _____

ADDED-PHRASE FRAGMENTS

Another kind of fragment that occurs frequently is the **added-phrase fragment.** This may be a phrase beginning with a verbal (an *-ing* word or infinitive such as *to go, to read,* etc.), or it may be a prepositional phrase, even a string of prepositional phrases.

–ing Word Fragments

The last three miles of the race proved to be hilly and dangerous. *Leaving only the most daring motorcyclists in the race.*

Sarah decided not to go to the party on Friday night. *Being exhausted by the overtime work she had put in at her job on Thursday.*

Fragments Beginning with To

Christopher knew the one thing he wanted most of all in life. *To establish his own computer retail outlet.*

Prepositional Phrase Fragments

Eileen had many happy memories of her summer experiences. *In the Caribbean, in Venezuela, and along the coast of Florida.*

Connecting Fragments

In each of these examples, the added-phrase fragment really belongs to the sentence preceding it. Usually such writing can be corrected by connecting the fragment to the preceding sentence:

1. The last three miles of the race proved to be hilly and dangerous, *leaving only the most daring motorcyclists in the race.*
2. *Being exhausted by the overtime work she had put in at her job on Thursday,* Sarah decided not to go to the party on Friday night.
3. Christopher knew the one thing he wanted most of all in life: *to establish his own computer retail outlet.*
4. Eileen had many happy memories of her summer experiences *in the Caribbean, in Venezuela, and along the coast of Florida.*

Bear in mind that not all word groups beginning with *to,* with *-ing* words, or with prepositional phrases have to be fragments. A sentence may begin with one of these phrases and then have a main clause after it, forming a complete statement. We could even use one of the added phrase fragments from the preceding examples as the beginning of a complete sentence:

To establish his own computer retail outlet, Christopher borrowed money from a commercial bank.

As with dependent-clause fragments, the beginning word or phrase may warn you that you may have a fragment, *but you must look at the whole sentence to see if it is complete.*

Exercise I

Added-Phrase Fragments

If the sentence or sentence group is complete, write S next to it. If it contains a fragment, write F.

_____ 1. To dramatize the sufferings of Dust Bowl farmers during the Great Depression, John Steinbeck wrote a novel called *The Grapes of Wrath*.

_____ 2. Zora Neale Hurston wrote a novel called *Their Eyes Were Watching God*. To portray a young black woman's search for love in rural Florida.

_____ 3. Mark Twain ends *Huckleberry Finn* with his hero about to "light out for the territory." Leaving the reader to wonder what will become of Huck in later life.

_____ 4. In World War I, in the Spanish Civil War, and in World War II, Ernest Hemingway served as a war correspondent. Collecting material for his novels and short stories as well.

_____ 5. Observing wealthy upper-class New Yorkers with a realistic eye, Edith Wharton wrote novels that won acclaim in the early twentieth century.

_____ 6. Henry James portrayed the dilemmas of highly sophisticated, educated Americans. Striving to find a cultural identity while living and traveling in England, France, and Italy.

_____ 7. In *Invisible Man,* Ralph Ellison depicts the efforts of a young black man to adjust to, as well as to change, American society. With its many forms of obvious and subtle racism.

_____ 8. J. D. Salinger, in *The Catcher in the Rye,* portrays the hostilities, resentments, and insecurities of an adolescent in the 1950s.

_____ 9. F. Scott Fitzgerald's main character in *The Great Gatsby* embodies the wild life-style of the rich during the Jazz Age. Throwing lavish parties attended by movie stars and riding around in a chauffeur driven Rolls-Royce.

_____ 10. Saul Bellow portrays the humorous but also sad and self-defeating lives of urban people in our time. Focusing especially on middle-class people in Chicago and New York.

Exercise II

Added-Phrase Fragments

Create complete sentences using the fragments at either the beginning or the end. Be sure every sentence has a main clause.

Example:

Fragment: *with both rooms still left unpainted.*
Sentence: Sam knew he would need the rest of the week to finish decorating his apartment, *with both rooms still left unpainted.*

1. Fragment: in her courses, her social life, and her music

   Sentence: _____

2. Fragment: to change careers at the age of thirty-two

   Sentence: _____

3. Fragment: making the lecture even more difficult to follow

   Sentence: _____

4. Fragment: for the sake of her two children

   Sentence: _____

5. Fragment: hoping for a major role but expecting a smaller one

   Sentence: _____

Group Project

Added-Clause and Added-Phrase Fragments

Working with your writing group, have each writer compose seven sentences using the phrases or clauses below. Compare your sentences and discuss any that appear to be fragments.

1. especially the advanced courses
2. with the engine still running
3. after winning the dance competition
4. because some of the parts were missing

5. while looking for the remote control
6. who knows how to find whatever she wants
7. in order to graduate in four years

ADDED-VERB FRAGMENTS

Our last category of fragments is the type created by adding a second or third verb to the same subject in a sentence—but without joining the extra verb or verbs to the sentence. One subject in a sentence can have two or more verbs (we call these **compound verbs**), but all verbs must be in the same sentence with their subject. If you break them off and try to start a new sentence with them, you will automatically create a fragment.

Fragment: Sharon glanced out the window at the park. *And shrieked as she spotted her boyfriend kissing another woman.*

Correction: Sharon glanced out the window at the park *and shrieked as she spotted her boyfriend kissing another woman.*

In this example, *shrieked* is a second verb that matches the subject *Sharon* (*glanced* is the first verb). Both *glanced* and *shrieked* belong in the same sentence with their subject *Sharon.* If a period is placed after *park,* as in the first example, the remaining words create a fragment that has no subject (who shrieked?).

Remember that every sentence must have a subject and verb that go together. Therefore, to correct added-verb fragments, you can simply drop the period and join the fragment to the preceding sentence, where it belongs. It is also possible to correct the fragment by adding a subject to match the verb:

Sharon glanced out the window at the park. *She shrieked* as she spotted her boyfriend kissing another woman.

Exercise I

Added-Verb Fragments

Some of the passages that follow contain fragments; others are complete. Write F next to the fragments, C next to those that are correct.

_____F_____   1. Many people nowadays are interested in space exploration. But do not know very much about outer space.

_____   2. Most people cannot tell the difference between a planet and a star by looking at them over a period of time. They do not know that a planet changes its position continually.

_____   3. Some people also underestimate the vastness of space. And imagine that we could travel to other stars in a week or two.

_____   4. Comets and meteors also cause a lot of confusion. And lead people to think of them as the same.

_____   5. Comets appear small in the night sky. But can be millions of miles long.

_____   6. Meteors are usually about the size of a pea. But they seem large because they burn up in our own atmosphere.

_____   7. The Hubble space telescope has stirred up new interest in space. And revealed exciting evidence about distant galaxies.

Exercise II

Added-Verb Fragments

Correct the following fragments either by attaching them to the preceding sentences or by adding subjects to make them complete.

Fragment: Barbara waited for her cousin to offer to help with the dishes. And then gave up and did them herself.

Correction: Barbara waited for her cousin to offer to help with the dishes and then gave up and did them herself.

Alternate correction: Barbara waited for her cousin to offer to help with the dishes. Then she gave up and did them herself.

1. Fragment: Fred watched soap operas all afternoon. And went to a movie in the evening.

   Correction: _____

2. Fragment: Jessica prides herself on being able to predict the Dow Jones average a month in advance. And once impressed her economics professor by getting it exactly right.

   Correction: _____

3. Fragment: Films and books that attack famous, highly respected people often arouse controversy. But earn fortunes for the people who make or write them.

   Correction: _____

4. Fragment: Mastery of spelling requires a combination of ear and eye training. And can be acquired by most people only through frequent practice.

   Correction: _____

5. Fragment: The country singers could drive to Nashville in about six hours. Or spend twice as much and get there in an hour by air.

Correction: _____

THREE WAYS TO CORRECT FRAGMENTS

1. Connect fragments to the sentences that precede or follow them.
2. Add subjects or verbs to make fragments complete.
3. Add main clauses to make fragments complete.

Connect the fragment to the preceding sentence:

Fragment: The students sat in small groups. And read their papers aloud to one another.
Correction: The students sat in small groups and read their papers aloud to one another.

Add a subject or verb to make the fragment complete:

Fragment: The shell of the missile fell to earth. And landed in a woods in Kentucky.
Correction: The shell of the missile fell to earth. It landed in a woods in Kentucky.

Add a main clause to make the fragment complete:

Fragment: After Stanley and Evelyn quarreled about her getting a job.
Correction: After Stanley and Evelyn quarreled about her getting a job, Stanley got one himself.

In your own paragraphs and essays, one of the easiest ways to correct fragments is to join them to sentences next to them. Fragments are often pieces of longer sentences that were mistakenly broken off; usually they can be reattached to the sentences in front of them. Just be sure that the resulting sentence is not too long and complicated. To check for fragments, read your essay carefully as if it were a list of sentence exercises, taking each sentence one at a time. Notice especially the *beginning* of each sentence. Does it have a subject and verb? If so, does it start with a main clause or a subordinate conjunction?

Review Exercise I

Correcting Fragments

In each of the following passages, underline the fragment. Then rewrite the passage with the fragment attached to the sentence before or after it, whichever makes sense.

Example:
Courses in technical writing are useful. <u>If you become a skilled technical writer</u>. You will find many job openings, usually at high pay.

Rewrite, with fragment attached to the sentence after it:
Courses in technical writing are useful. <u>If you become a skilled technical writer</u>, you will find many job openings, usually at high pay.

1. Euthanasia, or mercy killing, has become increasingly controversial. Some people believe that it is justified. When a patient is terminally ill and in pain.
2. Some people object that any intentional taking of life is wrong. Because life is sacred even when a person is not happy. Therefore they support laws prohibiting euthanasia.
3. Before taking a simple-minded stand on the issue. We should study the difference between several types of euthanasia. We may then decide that we accept some forms and not others.
4. One type is ending the use of life-support machines. For patients in pain and beyond hope of recovery. Cases of this kind have already been disputed in courts.
5. If a patient's death is possible only through a direct act such as administration of a lethal drug. Euthanasia becomes much more controversial. Some people still will argue that it is morally better to relieve suffering than prolong it.
6. When a patient is not conscious, euthanasia is especially open to dispute. One way to simplify the problem is use of the "living will." Stating that if the person is injured or ill beyond recovery and is unconscious, death would be preferable to remaining in a coma.
7. The big moral question is whether life itself is the highest priority. Or whether life without hope or consciousness should be terminated. Obviously people with different philosophies will continue to disagree on the answer.

Review Exercise II

Quick Drill on Fragments

Do this drill quickly to review the difference between fragments and complete sentences. Write F next to a fragment and S next to a complete sentence.

1. People in the suburbs who take car pools to work.
2. After allowing for inflation and changes in international exchange rates.
3. Along the highway were many annoying billboards.

_____ _F_ _____   4. Because Spanish I has no prerequisite.
_____ _S_ _____   5. We usually go skiing in Vermont in February.
_____ _F_ _____   6. Except for those who travel by bus.
_____ _S_ _____   7. The governor and his wife appearing on camera together.
_____ _F_ _____   8. When spring comes, the water level rises.
_____   9. During the last episode of a soap opera I saw recently.
_____   10. Having passed the bar, she felt exhilarated.

Group Project

Fragments

Have each member of your writing group look through his or her entire set of writings up to this point in the semester, including freewriting and focused writing as well as organized paragraphs and essays. Write down every fragment you can find, and exchange them with one another. Correct the fragments of one of the other members. As a group, discuss all examples over which there is disagreement.

Simple, Compound, and Complex Sentences

To be able to recognize and correct the next groups of sentence errors, you should review the three main types of sentences. Sentences can be **simple, compound, or complex:**

Simple sentences have one main clause, with one subject-verb combination:

> s v
> Tony works after school in a restaurant.

Compound sentences★ have two main clauses joined together; each clause has its own subject-verb combination:

> s v   s v
> Stephanie buys lottery tickets every week, but Frank spends his money
> on compact disc recordings.

Complex sentences have one main clause and one (sometimes more than one) dependent clause. Each clause has its own subject-verb combination. The dependent clause can come before or after the main clause:

★See commas before conjunctions in compound sentences later in Unit 5.

Main clause before dependent clause:

         s   v

Irene usually gives money to the homeless people in her neighborhood
           s   v

because she feels sorry for them.

Main clause after dependent clause:

           s   v

Because Irene feels sorry for the homeless people in her neighborhood,
s   v

she usually gives them money.

Exercise

Simple, Compound, and Complex Sentences

Identify each sentence that follows by writing S (simple), CD (compound) or CX (complex) in the blank next to it.

1. _____ The American family has changed in the last twenty years.
2. _____ When our grandparents were growing up, they lived in traditional nuclear families.
3. _____ The nuclear family includes the father, the mother, and their children.
4. _____ There are still many nuclear families, but many other kinds of nontraditional families also exist.
5. _____ Because the divorce rate has increased, many families are headed by one parent.
6. _____ If current trends continue, most American families will be nontraditional in one way or another.
7. _____ Some people think that nontraditional families are healthy; others believe that traditional families are better for children.

Run-Together Sentences

Every sentence should end with a period, exclamation point, or question mark. A run-together sentence occurs when a writer goes right through the end of the sentence like a driver running a red light.

I watched the man enter the bank suddenly I realized he was planning a hold-up.

In this sentence, "enter the bank suddenly" looks like it goes together as a phrase, and it is easy to miss the cutoff point between sentences. Reading more carefully, we see that we have two sentences, not one:

I watched the man enter the bank. Suddenly I realized he was planning a hold-up.

If two sentences are closely related, you may want to put them together in a compound sentence instead of separating them. Do not run them together, and do not put just a comma between them; use a semicolon, as in this sentence. Use a semicolon also in sentences joined together by long connectives like *however, therefore, meanwhile, consequently,* and *nevertheless.* These are called conjunctive adverbs; put semicolons before them when they connect main clauses in compound sentences and commas after them.

Examples: Run-Together Sentences Corrected Two Ways

Run-together sentence	A many-colored float rolled slowly toward midfield it was circled by cheerleaders and a marching band.
Corrected as two separate sentences	A many-colored float rolled slowly toward midfield. It was circled by cheerleaders and a marching band.
Corrected with semicolon	A many-colored float rolled slowly toward midfield; it was circled by cheerleaders and a marching band.
Run-together sentence	The tenants sent many letters to the landlord about the lack of heat and electricity however he did not reply for two weeks.
Corrected as two separate sentences	The tenants sent many letters to the landlord about the lack of heat and electricity. However, he did not reply for two weeks.
Corrected with a semicolon	The tenants sent many letters to the landlord; however, he did not reply for two weeks.

Exercise I

Separating Run-Together Sentences

The following paragraph contains five run-together sentences. Rewrite the paragraph, separating the run-together statements with periods or semicolons, *not with commas.*

(1) Lasers are now being used for many purposes for instance they serve as surgical tools in operations on the skin, eyes, and blood vessels. (2) Lasers also have many military uses they can guide bombs to their targets or pierce

metal surfaces. (3) In communications, lasers are used in new types of pho-
tographic systems some sound devices, such as walkie-talkies, employ lasers.
(4) Both art and industry now make extensive use of laser beams, and corporations have discovered countless industrial uses. (5) For instance, lasers have
dramatically improved welding techniques, drilling, and cutting everything
from gems and metals to fabric and paper can be cut with laser devices. (6)
Lasers once seemed a remote form of new technology soon, however, we
may have lasers in our appliances at home. (7) Yesterday's miracle may become
tomorrow's commonplace.

Exercise II

Separating Run-Together Sentences

The following sentences were written by students. One of them is correct;
the others are run together. Separate the run-together sentences by periods or
semicolons.

1. I returned home from my job that evening my mom was sitting in the living room crying.

2. American families have changed tremendously for example today there are a lot of families with two wage earners.

3. This is what my father says all the time he sounds like a broken record, but I've grown accustomed to hearing him.

4. The educational system in my country makes students work harder than students in America do especially in science maybe that is because they need more scientists there.

5. I have one older sister and an older brother the other siblings are younger than me.

6. During my teenage years I took life for granted my grades were satisfactory and I had a part-time job after school.

7. I finished high school and started looking for a job unfortunately I couldn't find one that I wanted.

8. The first stage of his disease was denial this was when he heard the diagnosis but didn't believe it was happening to him.

9. *My aunt is sixty-seven years old, but no one would believe it if they saw her in action.*

10. *After the exam, I felt relaxed and satisfied it was easier than I expected, and I thought I did well.*

Comma Splices

In previous exercises you have been warned not to put a comma between the two statements in a run-together sentence. This common mistake is called the **comma splice.**

Comma splice: We arrived at Danceteria before the main crowd, then we decided to look for a good film near Times Square.

Correct: We arrived at Danceteria before the main crowd. Then we decided to look for a good film near Times Square.

CORRECTING COMMA SPLICES

Correct comma splices the same way you would correct run-together sentences. Separate the main clauses with a semicolon, or divide them into two separate sentences with a period.

A third way to correct either run-together sentences or comma-spliced sentences is by *joining the main clauses with a connecting word and a comma.* The connecting words to remember are called **coordinating conjunctions.**

Coordinating Conjunctions
Use these short connecting words, with commas before them, to join main clauses:

> , and
> , but
> , or
> , nor
> , yet
> , so
> , for★

★You may want to use a familiar device to remember this list of connecting words: The first letters of these words spell out FANBOYS (*For, And, Nor, But, Or, Yet, So*).

Compare this comma-spliced sentence with the correct one using a comma with a conjunction.

Comma splice: The retail price of the dress is $41.95, the wholesale price is $25.
Correction: The retail price of the dress is $41.95, but the wholesale price is $25.

Ways to Correct Comma-Spliced and Run-Together Sentences
1. Divide the two statements into separate sentences.
2. Use a semicolon between the statements.
3. Join the statements with a comma and connecting word.

Here is an example of the same comma-spliced sentence corrected all three ways.

Comma splice: Sandra enjoys soap operas, she never misses an episode of *General Hospital.*
Correction: Sandra enjoys soap operas. She never misses an episode of *General Hospital.*
Correction: Sandra enjoys soap operas; she never misses an episode of *General Hospital.*
Correction: Sandra enjoys soap operas, and she never misses an episode of *General Hospital.*

Exercise I
Comma Splices

Correct the following sentence in three ways.

Emil attends the University of Texas, he is finding the work difficult but interesting.

1. Separate sentences:

_____

_____

2. With semicolon:

_____

_____

3. With connecting word and comma:

_____

_____

Exercise 11

Comma Splices

Each of the following sentences has a comma in the middle. If the sentence is correct, write C in the blank; if it contains a comma splice, rewrite the sentence using a semicolon or divide it into two sentences.

1. Most Latin American countries became independent early in the nineteenth century, at that time the Spanish Empire had become weakened.

   _____

   _____

2. Because many Latin American cities refused to recognize Napoleon's brother Joseph as their leader, the control that Spain once held over the New World began to slip.

   _____

   _____

3. In 1817 Jose de San Martin helped Chile gain independence, he led his army in a heroic climb over the Andes.

   _____

   _____

4. Brazil became independent in 1828, it was still called an "empire" until 1889.

   _____

   _____

5. When Simon Bolivar defeated the Spanish at Boyaca in 1819, Colombia also joined the emerging group of independent nations.

   _____

   _____

6. In 1823 the United States proclaimed the Monroe Doctrine, this declaration warned European powers against further colonization in the Americas.

   _____

   _____

7. Although the Monroe Doctrine became a permanent policy, some opponents have claimed that it should also have guaranteed nonintervention by the United States in Latin America.

_____

_____

Exercise III
Comma Splices

The sentences below were written by students. Correct each comma splice by one of three methods: (1) Use a semicolon, (2) divide into two sentences, or (3) add a short connective word. One sentence is correct; leave it as it is.

1. In our communities there are many people who need jobs, therefore better training should be available to help them pursue their careers.

2. In my brother's home my nephew watches violent programs on television all the time, as a result he is starting to adopt loud and violent behavior.

3. Some people believe that there needs to be more awareness of the subject of sex among teenagers, they believe that sex education should be taught in the schools.

4. Forty years ago parents used to think that it was all right to use physical force to discipline their children, but nowadays that is called child abuse.

5. After that experience I started liking my own company, I discovered a few things about myself.

6. This move to the other office was not by choice, she had to do it.

7. At the party I saw someone I knew, we both went to the same high school.

8. The first years of their marriage were fun and exciting, then something happened that made her realize things weren't going so well.

9. Ricki Lake has a lively and flamboyant style, this appeals to an adolescent audience.

10. *Parents are the most important role models, people whose parents are alcoholics and drug abusers sometimes grow up to do the same thing themselves.*

Review Exercise

Comma Splices and Run-Together Sentences

Rewrite these sentences, separating the main clauses in one of these ways: (1) into two sentences, (2) with semicolons, or (3) with commas and short connectives. If a sentence is correct, write C next to it.

1. Most people have heard of the main laws of science and the social sciences, they should recognize, however, that the laws of nature are usually more precise than those of human behavior.

2. Kepler's law explains the motion of the planets around the sun, most students of astronomy master it early in their studies.

3. Darwin proposed the theory of evolution in 1859, then he explained its meaning for mankind in *The Descent of Man* in 1871.

4. Einstein's theory of relativity is generally known to be the basis for atomic energy, however, not many people understand it.

5. Another well-known theory in the social sciences is Gresham's law this law states that currency of low value drives currency of high value out of circulation.

6. There are also theories of linguistics Grimm's law and Verner's law, for instance, explain patterns of change in spoken language.

7. Some amusing "laws" have been concocted to explain social phenomena; Parkinson's law, for example, states that work expands to fit the manpower available.

8. The Peter Principle describes the workings of status levels, or hierarchies, it states that workers are promoted until they reach their "level of incompetence," where they remain in jobs they perform poorly.

9. Computer experts refer to Moore's Law, named after Gordon Moore, a co-founder of Intel, this law says that the speed of personal computers doubles every 18 months.

10. Perhaps the most reliable principle describing modern society is Murphy's law, which states that whatever can go wrong will go wrong.

Correcting by Subordinating

A fourth way to correct run-together sentences and comma splices is to subordinate one statement to another. This means to turn one of the main clauses into a subordinate clause. Do this by adding one of the subordinate conjunctions like *because* or *when* to one of the main clauses or by beginning one of the main clauses with *who, which,* or *that* (making that clause a **relative** subordinate clause).

Run–together sentence:

The students felt nervous they had an examination that morning.

Correction by subordinating one clause:

The students felt nervous *because* they had an examination that morning.
The students, *who* had an examination that morning, felt nervous.

Exercise I

Subordination

Correct the sentences that follow by making one main clause a subordinate clause. Use *although, because, if,* or *when* to subordinate one clause, or use *who, which,* or *that* to make it a relative clause.

1. Some experts once predicted that computers would make books obsolete, this has not happened so far.

   _____

   _____

2. The computer age began in the 1960s, this age has brought an increase in book publication.

   _____

   _____

3. The use of computers has actually increased the number of books many of them have been written about computers.

   _____

   _____

4. Books on word processing appear every month they have become too numerous to count.

   _____

   _____

5. Other areas of activity besides publishing expand as well, computer technology has an impact on them.

_____

_____

6. Teachers once feared they would be replaced by computers, they have discovered that their role is even more important than before.

_____

_____

7. Computers have enhanced rather than eliminated the teacher's job, teachers now can use computers to relieve them of meaningless drills.

_____

_____

Exercise II

Subordination

Five of the sentences in the paragraph below either contain comma splices or are run-together sentences. Rewrite the paragraph with these sentences corrected by means of subordination. Refer to the list of subordinating conjunctions on pp. 252–253.

(1) Scientists disagree about what caused the dinosaurs to become extinct. (2) One theory is that the dinosaurs vanished about 65 million years ago, an asteroid crashed into the earth. (3) Plants, the dinosaurs' main food supply, may have died out the collision darkened the sky for months. (4) Geologists believe that such a catastrophe might have eliminated half of all life on earth. (5) They have even found a layer of underground clay containing iridium, an element often present in objects from outer space, matching the period when the dinosaurs disappeared. (6) There is evidence to support the asteroid theory, some scientists think that the dinosaurs died out gradually. (7) Some evidence indicates that the dinosaurs became extinct before the collision supposedly occurred, the asteroid theory cannot be considered proven. 8) It is possible that a change of climate, especially a cooling off, was the cause. (9) An asteroid collision may have been just one of several factors that brought the extinction of many species during that period. (10) More exact methods of dating fossil records can be discovered we may know more certainly just what happened.

Subject-Verb Agreement

In the present tense, use the correct form of the verb to match the subject. Singular subjects take singular verbs:

s   v
<u>Paula</u> usually <u>arrives</u> on time.

Plural subjects take plural verbs:

s   s   v
<u>Paula</u> and <u>Richard</u> usually <u>arrive</u> on time.

Hint

Verbs in the singular take the *s* ending in the present, unless *I* or *you* is the subject.

	Singular	*Plural*
First person:	I write	We write
Second person:	You write	You write
Third person:	She, he, it writes	They write

SINGULAR AND PLURAL SUBJECTS

Learn to tell the difference between singular and plural nouns. Most nouns form the plural by adding *s* or *es* to the singular:

Singular Nouns	*Plural Nouns*
one ticket	three tickets
a computer	both computers
my shoe	my shoes
Susan's typewriter	Susan's typewriters

Some nouns form their plurals in unusual ways. Some change their spelling instead of adding *s:*

Singular	*Plural*
a woman	four women
the man	those men
one child	all my children
your foot	both your feet
a mouse	two mice

Some stay the same in singular and plural:

one deer	a herd of deer
a big fish	a school of fish
a pet sheep	hundreds of sheep

Words ending in *f* or *fe* may change the *f* to *v* before adding *es:*

one half	both halves
one life	many lives
his wife	several wives

But in some words the *f* remains:

a steep roof	many roofs
definite proof	a number of proofs

Words ending in *o* sometimes take *s* and sometimes *es:*

hero	ten heroes
this tomato	ten tomatoes
one stereo	several stereos
my radio	our radios

Words ending in *y* usually change the *y* to *i* before *es:*

a large company	many companies
a new secretary	two new secretaries

But those with vowels before the *y* just add *s:*

a good play	three good plays
a new toy	some new toys

Hint
Use your dictionary to find the plural forms of nouns that you are uncertain about. If no plural is listed, you should add *s* or *es.*

Exercise I

Singular and Plural Subjects

Write *singular* or *plural* after each noun:

1. tests _____
2. scientists _____
3. bus _____
4. guitars _____
5. videodisc _____

6. hamburgers _____
7. professor _____
8. section _____
9. experiences _____
10. parent _____

▶ Exercise II

Singular Subjects

Write singular nouns as subjects in the following sentences.

1. A _____ always eats a lot.
2. One _____ is not enough.
3. Every _____ knows how to read.
4. Each _____ belongs in the class.
5. This _____ looks like a winner
6. My _____ works in a large corporation
7. That _____ matches your shoes.

▶ Exercise III

Plural Subjects

Write plural nouns as subjects in these sentences.

1. Many _____ think they know everything.
2. Some _____ like to cause trouble.
3. Three _____ have new cars.
4. All of the _____ belong in the Hall of Fame.
5. Most _____ have several charge accounts
6. Very few _____ are open on Sunday.
7. A large number of _____ have gotten loose.

▶ Exercise IV

Singular Subjects

The following list contains ten subjects in the third person singular. Circle these ten. Then write ten sentences using them as subjects, remembering to use the *s* form of the verb in every sentence.

he	I
the store	your opinion
my shoes	her dress
that dog	our reasons
a test	seven women
two books	this corner
they	it
she	the game

If English Is Not Your First Language

When you form plurals in English, only the nouns change their forms, never the adjectives modifying them. In some languages, adjectives take endings according to whether the nouns they modify are singular or plural, and even according to the way the nouns are used (as subjects, objects, etc.). You may find English simpler in this feature than your first language. You don't have to remember any forms of adjectives; just remember not to stick *s* endings on them:

Wrong: *others* students
Right: *other* students

Wrong: *expensives* books
Right: *expensive* books

Exercise V

Plural Subjects (For ESL Students)

If the sentence has an incorrect form, adjective, noun subject, or verb, write the correct form in the blank. If the sentence is correct, write C in the blank.

Example:

*older*   The olders members of the team want to meet with us.

_____ 1. Four youngs parents are in the waiting room.
_____ 2. The extra hamburgers seems to be meant for the children.
_____ 3. The others pictures look as if they need touchups.
_____ 4. Some of the special award are presented by the mayor.
_____ 5. Many intelligents animals are able to imitate human behavior.
_____ 6. Most of the new shows have high ratings.
_____ 7. Successful filmmakers usually works hard.
_____ 8. Every year many Asians tourists visit San Francisco.
_____ 9. The historically importants buildings are shown on the map.
_____ 10. Three special insurance plans contain that clause.

FINDING AND CORRECTING ERRORS IN AGREEMENT

Most errors in subject-verb agreement involve missing *s* endings on nouns or verbs. Sometimes writers put *s* endings where they should not be.

Incorrect singular: My sister Lucia *insist* on doing her best.
Correct form: My sister Lucia *insists* on doing her best.

Incorrect plural: Those people always *argues* with foreign visitors.
Correct form: Those people always *argue* with foreign visitors.

Exercise I

Correcting Errors in Agreement

Some of the verbs in the following sentences agree with their subjects; some do not. If the verb is correct, write C in the blank; if not, write the correct form.

_____ 1. Wise investing depend upon several factors.
_____ 2. It involves your income, needs, and willingness to take risks.
_____ 3. Some people invests their money only in stocks.
_____ 4. Other opportunities also exists.
_____ 5. Municipal bonds, mutual funds, and term savings accounts all offer investment advantages.
_____ 6. The right kind of investment for you mean considering several elements.
_____ 7. Tax benefits from municipal bonds appeals to some investors.
_____ 8. Stocks present possibilities for high income but with high risk.
_____ 9. The investor who wants to avoid risks often choose mutual funds.
_____ 10. Corporate bonds also offer high income possibilities but with greater risk than municipal bonds.

Exercise II

Correcting Errors in Agreement

The following paragraph contains errors in subject–verb agreement. Underline the subject of every sentence and circle every verb. Write the correct verbs above the wrong ones.

(1) Stanley arranges his day in three segments. (2) He usually devote the whole morning to his classes. (3) He always concentrate very hard on his work. (4) On Mondays, Tuesdays, and Thursdays mathematics and sociology occupy most of his time. (5) On Wednesdays and Fridays his schedule include Spanish and English literature. (6) In the afternoon, from noon until 4:30, his job at the student union

take up all his time. (7) He always works at a cash register, where he receives payments for tickets to football and basketball games. (8) In the evening he and his friends often goes to parties, discos, or movies. (9) His life keep him active and socially busy, and he needs the weekend to rest and do his homework.

SPECIAL PROBLEMS WITH AGREEMENT

Forms of *Be, Have,* and *Do*

The common helping verbs *be, have,* and *do* present special difficulties with agreement because they have more forms than other verbs. Instead of just adding an *s* ending, *be* has these forms:

	Singular	*Plural*
First person:	I am	We are
Second person:	You are	You are
Third person:	He, she, it is	They are

Note: In the **past tense,** *be* is the only verb that can cause agreement problems because it has two forms:

She was   They were

    Have has two forms in the present: *has* for third person singular and *have* for all other subjects.

    Do also has two forms: *does* for third person singular and *do* for all the others. Be careful about *don't* and *doesn't* as well.

> ## Exercise I

Be, Have, and Do

If the verb is correct, write C in the blank; if not, write the correct form.

_____ 1. Parents who doesn't join the program will lose out.
_____ 2. Marisol thinks she have the best voice in the choir.
_____ 3. One of the old buildings are going to be renovated.
_____ 4. Some of the artists does their work in the studio.
_____ 5. The first day of June has a special meaning for us.
_____ 6. Ricardo and Tony is distantly related.
_____ 7. Practice sessions has taken up too much time.

_____   8. Each lecture in the series is going to last one hour.

_____   9. Several fathers does their shopping together.

_____   10. Elizabeth always have a positive attitude.

Exercise II

Be, Have, and Do

Underline all incorrect forms of *be, have,* and *do* in the following paragraph. Write the correct forms above the wrong ones.

People has to face many pressures on holidays. Those who entertain a lot has to send invitations to friends and relatives, prepare food, and decorate their homes. On some holidays, especially Christmas, giving gifts are in order, so many people does a lot of shopping and has to worry about choosing, wrapping, and mailing presents. On religious holidays, churches, synagogues, and mosques are full of worshippers practicing their religion. Loneliness and depression is widespread during major holidays, especially among the elderly, who is often far away from their relatives. Many families has to plan and pack for vacation trips during the holidays, and the crowded hotels and highways is usually a source of difficulty for them. Patients in hospitals, inmates in penitentiaries, and children in foster homes is likely to feel more isolated during holidays than at other times because they does not share the holiday festivities with their families. The financial and emotional pressures of the holidays has an effect on the rates of suicide, crime, and mental illness. Although most experts is likely to agree that the importance we place on holidays does some harm, few of us is going to stop observing and enjoying our favorite holidays. The pleasures of holiday parties

and vacations is too great for us to abandon.

Exercise III

Be, Have, and Do

Fill in the correct forms of *be, have,* and *do.*

1. Over the years, human beings _____ fantasized about life on
   other worlds.

2. One of the most important steps in the search for extraterrestrial life
   _____ Galileo's use of the telescope to identify the moons of
   Jupiter and the rings around Saturn.

3. Later astronomers, such as Percival Lowell in Arizona, thought they
   _____ able to detect such features as canals on Mars.

4. Although such speculations _____ proven to be false, the search
   for life beyond earth _____ since become even more exciting.

5. The Mars landing in 1976 _____ intended to provide evidence
   of organic matter on the Red Planet; although it _____ not succeed in doing that, it provided important knowledge.

6. Exciting new evidence of microscopic life forms on a meteorite from Mars
   _____ announced by NASA scientists in 1996. Such discoveries
   always _____ to be confirmed by other scientists.

7. In 1996, as well, astronomers at last _____ able to claim that they
   _____ proven that planets exist outside the solar system.

Subjects That Come After Verbs

Some of the sentences in the preceding exercises may have made you stop and
think. You could not always just choose a verb that "sounded right." Such difficulty
is likely to occur in sentences that do not follow the ordinary subject–verb–object
order. Sometimes the verb comes before the subject; when it does, you can choose
the right verb form only by finding the subject and matching the verb with it.

Verbs come before subjects in several kinds of sentences:.

1. Questions containing reversed word order:

> $\overset{v}{\underline{Are}}$ there any new $\overset{s}{\underline{students}}$ here today?

> Why $\overset{v}{\underline{have}}$ the $\overset{s}{\underline{lights}}$ been turned off?

2. Sentences beginning with *there* or *here* place the verb before the subject:

> There $\overset{v}{\underline{have}}$ to be many $\overset{s}{\underline{reasons}}$ for her decision.

> Here $\overset{v}{\underline{is}}$ an exciting $\overset{s}{\underline{picture}}$ of her as a teenager.

3. Sentences beginning with descriptive phrases sometimes place the verb before the subject:

> Behind the door $\overset{v}{\underline{were}}$ three armed $\overset{s}{\underline{men}}$.

> Sprayed on the walls $\overset{v}{\underline{was}}$ an angry $\overset{s}{\underline{message}}$.

Notice that in such sentences you should not try to match the verb with the word right before it so that the combination sounds right. You must find the subject *after* the verb. In the last sentence, not the *walls were* but the *message was* sprayed on the walls.

Exercise I

Subjects That Come After Verbs

Underline the subject in each sentence and circle the correct verb form in parentheses:

1. There (is, are) several important terms used in economics.
2. Among the most familiar (is, are) *inflation* and *recession*.
3. Probably the simplest of all economic terms (is, are) the word *money*.
4. How simple, however, (do, does) the many conceptions of money prove to be?
5. (Is, Are) all forms of payment, including checks, credit cards, and traveler's checks, to be considered money?
6. Among other cultures (is, are) such kinds of currency as shells, beads, gold, and animals' teeth.
7. In the ancient world there (was, were) still other forms of money, such as goods and services.

Exercise II

Subjects That Come After Verbs

Circle the incorrect verb forms and write correct ones in the blanks. Write C if the sentence is correct.

_____ 1. Why has amateur videotapes become important in the news?

_____ 2. Before videotapes there was the Zapruder film of the assassination of President Kennedy.

_____ 3. More recently there has been many examples of amateur videotapes becoming part of famous news stories.

_____ 4. Among the most influential of all were the videotaped scenes of Rodney King being beaten by police officers in Los Angeles.

_____ 5. On television news there is often glimpses of accidents, storms, or crimes caught by amateurs' videocameras.

_____ 6. How have the use of such tapes affected the media, the courts, and the attitudes of the public?

_____ 7. Do everything that happens turn into a form of entertainment when it is filmed for television?

Group Project

Subjects That Come After Verbs

Have the members of your writing group look through their previous writing, both free and focused writing and organized pieces. Write down as many sentences as you can find in which the subjects appear after the verbs. Exchange lists with one another. Each member should underline the subject in each sentence and check to see if the verb forms are all correct. The whole group should discuss all sentences over which there is disagreement.

Special Subjects

Some subjects are hard to match with verbs because they seem to be plural but are singular grammatically or because they are singular when used one way and plural when used another.

Singular Pronouns	*Singular/Plural Words*
everyone	all
anyone	half
someone	some
everybody	most
anybody	more
somebody	

Write *everyone has* some kind of special talent, not *have. Each, either,* and *one* are also singular, even though they are often followed by plural phrases. *Each of the students is* (not *are). Either of the women has* the right to participate (not *have).*

Some words are singular when they refer to amounts and plural when they refer to numbers.

All of the money *has* been spent (singular—an amount).
All of the visitors *are* required to wear passes (plural—a number).

Exercise

Special Subjects

Choose the correct form of each verb in parentheses; underline the subject before writing the verb in the blank.

1. Despite the enormous wealth in America, many still _____ (be) unemployed in the big cities.

2. According to federal reports, almost half of working-age residents in the largest cities _____ (be) neither employed nor looking for work.

3. Most of the young people in their late teens _____ (do) not have either part-time or full-time jobs.

4. In some cities only about one out of three men and women between sixteen and nineteen years of age _____ (be) in the labor force.

5. Each of the unemployed _____ (have) a reason for not working; it may be lack of skills, psychological problems, dependence on drugs or alcohol, or unavailability of jobs.

6. Some economists _____ (do) not give us hopeful predictions, because improved economic conditions do not seem to improve these unemployment figures.

7. All of the experts _____ (be) in agreement that the source of the problem is deeply rooted in our changing society.

Group Nouns

Nouns that refer to groups of people present a special problem: Words like *army, family, team, jury, chorus, union, committee, company,* and *organization* seem to be plural because they refer to many people. However, these nouns have plural forms (*armies, families,* etc.), so the singular forms should be used with singular verbs: An *army marches* on its stomach; or The *team* has won eleven games this season. When you refer to such words as single units, using the singular form, use singular verbs as well. However, when you use the word to refer to the individual members of the group, it is permissible to use a plural verb. Some writers find it awkward and not strictly correct to write: The *team are* taking their places on the field. It is less objectionable to write: The *players are* taking their places; or The *members* of the team *are* taking their places. Just be sure to tell the difference between the group as a unit (singular) and as separate individuals (plural).

> **Exercise**

Group Nouns

Circle the correct verb form in each sentence.

1. The committee (has, have) reached its decision.
2. Our family (has, have) an unusual kind of annual reunion
3. The army (has, have) just published a new training manual.
4. The players in the band (don't, doesn't) usually leave their instruments in the rehearsal room.
5. The company (is, are) making its projections for the next year.
6. The union (schedule, schedules) a meeting every Wednesday.
7. The members of the jury sometimes (disagree, disagrees) violently with one another.

Verbs Separated from Subjects by Prepositional Phrases

What are prepositional phrases? They are phrases made out of the little relational words like *in, of, with,* etc. Some of the most common prepositions are listed below:

about	between	on
above	by	onto
across	for	over
along	from	past
among	in	through
at	into	to
before	like	toward
behind	next to	under

beneath   of   with
beside   off

A verb will often be separated from its subject by a prepositional phrase. Do not be confused by such phrases. *A subject cannot be part of a prepositional phrase.* If you try to match the verb with a word next to it, sometimes you may miss the subject and choose the wrong verb form. Notice the difference:

1. The <u>names are</u> in alphabetical order.

2. <u>One</u> of the names on the list <u>is</u> out of place.

In sentence 2, the subject *one* is separated from the verb *is* by two prepositional phrases, "of the names" and "on the list." You must mentally cross out these phrases and match the subject with the verb: "One ... is out of place."

Exercise I

Verbs Separated from Subjects

In the following sentences underline the subject, cross out the prepositional phrase or phrases between the subject and verb, and circle the verb that matches the subject.

Example: The <u>cars</u> ~~in the lot across the street~~ (is, (are)) for sale.
1. Some customers in the neighborhood (find, finds) the food prices too high.
2. One of the stations on the express line (has, have) been closed for a week.
3. Testing for HIV (involve, involves) taking a blood sample.
4. The Baptists, along with two other denominations, (has, have) gained membership.
5. Long-lasting parties with techno-music and funky clothes (is, are) called raves.
6. Economic progress in central European countries (has, have) been steady.
7. A stimulating environment with caring family members (is, are) necessary to an infant's development

Compound Subjects: *And* versus *Either/Or*
Two or more subjects joined by *and* take a plural verb:

Kentucky <u>and</u> Massachusetts <u>have</u> good teams this year.
Marisol <u>and</u> Kevin <u>are</u> my best friends.

Joining two subjects with *either ... or,* however, does not make the subject plural. A statement with *either ... or* says that only one person does the action:

> Either *Jack* or *Melanie* <u>is</u> going to videotape the performance.

This sentence takes a singular verb because it says that one person <u>is</u> going to do the videotaping. Notice, however, that *either ... or* sometimes joins plural subjects; then of course the verb is plural:

> Either *students* or *visitors* <u>are</u> in the cafeteria.

A rare sentence may contain one singular and one plural subject joined by *either ... or.* This usually is awkward, so try to avoid it; if you can't, the rule is to make the verb agree with the subject nearer to it:

> Either *Donald* or his *sisters* <u>are</u> going to represent the family at the ceremony.
> Either the *players* or the *coach* <u>has</u> to take the blame for the loss.

Exercise 1

Compound Subjects

Underline the subjects and circle the correct verbs in these sentences.

1. Either Deirdre or Suzanne (belong, belongs) in that role.
2. Either a keystroke or a click of the mouse (was, were) enough to alter it.
3. Either Nigeria or Liberia (send, sends) diplomats.
4. Coffee, tea, and orange juice (is, are) served on the flight.
5. Either chemistry or biology (is, are) a prerequisite.
6. Headphones and maps (is, are) provided for the tour.
7. Either French or Japanese food (seem, seems) to suit her taste.

Compound Verbs

Many sentences have two or more verbs that go with the same subject. Be sure to make all such verbs agree with their subjects; it is easy to slip and not notice that one of them, usually the last one, does not agree with the subject. Notice the error in this sentence:

> Derrick always gets up at seven, drives to work, and spend his whole morning at the office.

How many verbs go with the subject *Derrick?* Which one does not agree?

> ## Exercise 1

Compound Verbs

Circle the incorrect verbs in these sentences and write the correct forms in the blanks. If a sentence is correct, write C.

_____ 1. Sociology, as an academic discipline, is fairly modern and have a less ancient tradition than history or philosophy.

_____ 2. Although their methods are less rigid than those of chemists or physicists, sociologists apply scientific methods to social problems and uses mathematical analysis.

_____ 3. Their subject of study, human behavior, cannot be put on a microscope slide and are harder to predict than the weather.

_____ 4. The researchers themselves are susceptible to bias but tries to be as objective as biologists or astronomers.

_____ 5. The French sociologist Emile Durkheim is famous for his studies of suicide and are often named as the first to use scientific research methods in sociology.

_____ 6. Talcott Parsons' writings set a high standard of sophistication for American sociology but were difficult to read.

_____ 7. Symbolic interactionism, a sociological approach also created in the United States, identifies symbolic meanings in society and emphasize how people interpret what they see.

Verbs in _Who, Which,_ and _That_ Clauses

Verbs that come after _who, which,_ or _that_ are usually tricky because these relative pronouns can be either singular or plural. You cannot tell whether a clause should read "who is" or "who are" without knowing whether the _who_ is singular or plural. You must identify the **antecedent,** or preceding word that _who_ represents. _Who, which_ and _that_ are **relative pronouns;** that is, they _relate_ to something earlier in the same sentence. The verb depends on the word that _who_ or _which_ represents. For instance, you would use a singular verb in the phrase "a student who _registers_ for Spanish," but a plural verb in the phrase "students who _register_ for Spanish." Use a singular verb in the phrase "a course that _requires_ a term paper," but a plural verb in the phrase "courses that _require_ term papers."

> ## Exercise 1

Verbs in _Who, Which,_ and _That_ Clauses

Underline the antecedent of _who, which,_ or _that_ in each sentence and supply a verb form that agrees with it.

1. A person who _____ a lie detector test is being measured for certain bodily responses.

2. These responses, which _____ pulse rate, breathing, and skin sensitivity, may indicate whether the person is telling the truth.

3. A person suspected of a crime who _____ false information while taking a lie detector test may register sudden changes in heart rate, perspiration, or blood pressure.

4. Persons who _____ very anxious about the situation in which they take the test, however, may register such changes without lying.

5. Furthermore, experts who _____ been able to train themselves to control their reactions have succeeded in passing lie detector tests even when they were lying.

6. A defendant who _____ to strengthen his case in court may sometimes take a lie detector test to help prove his innocence.

7. Attorneys who _____ ways to include results of lie detector tests in their defense cannot rely mainly on such evidence.

Review Exercise I

Subject-Verb Agreement

Underline the subject or subjects and circle the correct form of the verb in each sentence.

1. Half of the grant money (has, have) already been spent.
2. Most of the assistants in the program (is, are) graduate students.
3. Surfing the World Wide Web and eating pistachio nuts (is, are) two of Monica's favorite pastimes.
4. Inside the entrance to the business school (hang, hangs) pictures of two former deans.
5. Trying to solve computer problems without help (lead, leads) to frustration.
6. Alumni who (donate, donates) large amounts of money are invited to attend the honors convocation.
7. Either cable television channels or radio stations always (announce, announces) school closings during snowstorms.

8. Students who (insist, insists) on leaving early may miss part of the home-work assignment.
9. Here (is, are) the first batch of applications we have received.
10. (Do, Does) all of the papers have to be double-spaced?

Review Exercise II

Subject-Verb Agreement

Underline the subject or subjects and write in a correct verb form in each sentence.

1. Parapsychology, which studies mental experiences outside the normal range of human perception, _____ controversy.

2. Supporters, who claim that it is a legitimate science, _____ that it will reveal exciting truths.

3. Opponents, who deride it as a pseudoscience, _____ it to be harmful because it encourages irrational thinking.

4. Among some of the parapsychological subjects _____ *telekinesis* (movement of objects with the power of thought alone) and *telepathy* (mind reading).

5. A belief in precognition, or the ability to tell the future, _____ widespread in many societies.

6. Extrasensory powers such as *clairvoyance* (the ability to perceive events and objects beyond the reach of the senses) _____ been claimed by some people and exhibited to the public.

7. Psychics called in for assistance by the police _____ sometimes been helpful in solving crimes.

Review Exercise III

Subject-Verb Agreement

Rewrite the following paragraph, converting it from plural to singular. Remember to include *s* endings on singular verbs. Instead of beginning the paragraph with Ellen and Janet, begin with just Ellen. Use *she* instead of *they*.

Ellen and Janet have teenage daughters who insist on dressing and behaving in ways that antagonize their mothers. They disapprove of their daughters' hairstyles, which usually are spiked and have shades of purple. They often get angry over their choice of clothes as well. Their daughters often wear their jeans with holes in the knees and wear dresses and skirts that are so short that their mothers think they look like prostitutes. Their daughters resent what they consider their mothers' bossiness and intolerance, especially when it comes to choice of friends. They think they should be able to choose their own friends, but their mothers believe they always cling to the wildest and most antisocial individuals among their peers. Both mothers are afraid that their daughters are going to become drug addicts or get killed in a car accident caused by a drunken driver. They are also afraid that their daughters will drop out of school and become pregnant. They have tried to involve their daughters in family counseling, but the results have been only temporarily successful. Ellen and Janet both hope they can survive their daughters' adolescence without any major catastrophes.

S ENDINGS: A REVIEW

Many writers have trouble with *s* endings. This happens because *s* endings can be added to words for different reasons. Some words, of course, already end in *s,* like *kiss* or *class.* There are four *s* endings that we *add* to words:

Adding *S* Endings

1. Add *s* or *es* to verbs in the third person singular, present tense: The dancer move**s.**
2. Add *s* or *es* to plural nouns: The dancer**s** move.
3. Add *'s* to singular possessives: a dancer**'s** movements.
4. Add *s'* to most plural possessives: four dancer**s'** movements.

(Exception: Add *'s* to plural possessives when the plural does not already end in *s:* women**'s** opinions.)

> **EXERCISE 1**

S Endings

Identify which of the *s* endings listed in the box above is underlined in each sentence and write the number from the box (1, 2, 3, or 4)

Example:

_____1_____   The jury wants more evidence.

_____   1. Most citizens know their constitutional rights.
_____   2. The public needs to be informed about the Constitution.
_____   3. Most states' constitutions have similar features.
_____   4. Changes in constitutions take the form of amendments.
_____   5. The first ten amendments to the Constitution of the United
                 States are called the Bill of Rights.
_____   6. Passing an amendment requires a three-fourths majority of the
                 states.
_____   7. Amendments can also be repealed.
_____   8. The prohibition amendment's unpopularity caused it to be
                 repealed in the early 1930s.
_____   9. The most recent amendment to approach a three-fourths vote
                 was the Equal Rights Amendment.
_____   10. The National Organization for Women still supports this
                 amendment.

Exercise II

S Endings

Proofread the paragraph that follows. Circle the _ten_ errors in the use of _s_ endings—
either incorrect or missing endings. Write the correct endings above the errors.

Stacy's Pet Peeves

Stacy made a list of her pet peeves. She decided that the list would include only

things that could be called annoyance, not serious dangers or threats. The first one

that occurred to her was what she calls "fall-outs." These are the subscription cards

that fall out every time she pick up a magazine to read. Another one is the ball-

point pen that is supposed to clip into her shirt or blouse pocket but falls on

the floor every time she bend down. Outside Stacy building there are some more

irritation. She particularly dislikes the scaffolds that are erected to renovate

storefronts because they makes it impossible for two people to walk side by side.

Many restaurant's noise levels also add to the nuisances in Stacy's life. She finds it hard to talk to friend over the hubbub of voices and pots and pans. Like many people she also object to people smoking in buses, airplanes, and other closed-in places. And she hates to go on very hot days to movie theaters, restaurants, or supermarket where the air-conditioning is so cold that she has to wear a sweater to keep from shivering.

Special Problems with Verb Tenses

Verb tenses present many special problems. We will consider the following nine.

- Recognizing past, present, and future tenses
- *d* endings in the past—regular verbs
- When not to use *d* endings
- The past tense of irregular verbs
- Forming past participles
- Past participles with helping verbs
- Past participles as adjectives
- Past participles of irregular verbs
- Avoiding shifts in verb tense

RECOGNIZING TENSES

To use correct verb tenses and avoid awkward shifts in tense, you must know the verb tenses and what they mean. There are three basic verb tenses:

Present:	Phyllis *enjoys* racquetball.
Past:	Phyllis *enjoyed* racquetball.
Future:	Phyllis *will enjoy* racquetball.

Present Tense

In the **present tense,** all verbs take **s endings** (singular, third person) or **no endings** (plural and first and second person singular).

	Singular	*Plural*
First person:	I succeed	We succeed
Second person:	You succeed	You succeed
Third person:	He, she, it succeeds	They succeed

Past Tense

In the **past tense,** verbs fall into two categories: **regular verbs,** which take *d* endings, and **irregular verbs,** which change their spelling and do not take *d* endings.

Past Tense for Regular Verbs	*Past Tense for Irregular Verbs*
succeed<u>ed</u>	became
walk<u>ed</u>	bought
kiss<u>ed</u>	saw
stamped<u>ed</u>	drank
murder<u>ed</u>	sang
worshipp<u>ed</u>	took
doubt<u>ed</u>	drove
discuss<u>ed</u>	broke
wander<u>ed</u>	spent

Future Tense

All verbs form the **future tense** by adding the helping verb *will* to the main verb *with no ending.*

will succeed	will study
will deliver	will purchase
will work	will spend
will register	will jog

D ENDINGS IN THE PAST TENSE

One of the most common writing errors is dropping or forgetting to add *d* endings on regular verbs. Be careful to edit for *d* endings when writing in the past tense.

Exercise I

D Endings in the Past Tense

Circle incorrect verb forms and write the correct forms in the blanks. Some sentences may have more than one error.

_____ 1. Many natural disasters have occur in the twentieth century.

_____ 2. Avalanches, floods, earthquakes, hurricanes, and mudslides have happen all over the world.

_____ 3. The San Francisco earthquake in 1906 cause terrible fires and demolish hundreds of beautiful buildings.

_____ 4. The worst flood in modern times occur when the Hwang-Ho River overflow in 1931, killing millions of people.

_____ 5. In 1959 Typhoon Vera nearly destroy Nagoya, Japan's third largest city.

_____ 6. The most lethal earthquake in recent years was the one in Armenia in 1988, in which over 55,000 people perish.

_____ 7. Hurricane Andrew pass through southern Florida in 1992 and cause billions of dollars' worth of property damage.

Exercise II

D Endings in the Past Tense

Rewrite the following paragraph in the past tense. Be sure to include all necessary _d_ endings.

Richard visits Tijuana, Mexico, with his girlfriend Pauline. They discover that the gasoline costs very little in that country, so they fill the tank. While browsing in the tourist shops, they hear other shoppers bargaining with storeowners and realize that the prices seem to be negotiable for most items. Soon they enjoy haggling about the cost of sombreros, jewelry, and dresses. They consider going to a bullfight but decide that they prefer to continue shopping and exploring. Richard stops at a body shop and asks about the cost of repairing the rear fender of his Mercury Sable. He learns to his satisfaction that the repair work appears excellent and the prices seem reasonable. Pauline buys several onyx jewelry boxes and a chess set as presents for relatives. She and Richard agree that it is getting late, but they expect to return the following week for more shopping.

WHEN _NOT_ TO USE _D_ ENDINGS

If you tend to omit _d_ endings in the past tense, remember that there are a few places where _d_ endings should _not_ be used. No _d_ endings:

1. **After the helping word _did_.** _Did_ is already in the past tense and does not need another past tense form to go with it:

   Did you _discuss_ (not _discussed_) the salary?
   It really _did happen_ (not _happened_) that way.

2. **After other helping verbs (except _be_ and _have_):** _may, might, can, could, will, would, must,_ and _should:_

   We _will walk_ (not _walked_) there together.
   He _could learn_ (not _learned_) a lot from you.

3. **After the word _to_.** A verb with the word _to_ in front of it is called an **infinitive;** it is not in the past tense and does not take a _d_ ending:

   We used _to live_ (not _to lived_) in Cincinnati.
   They tried _to reach_ (not _to reached_) the turnoff.

Exercise III

D Endings

Write the correct form of each verb in the blank. Remember that regular verbs in the past tense need *d* endings and that verbs following helping verbs (other than *have* and *be*) do not.

1. Epics are long stories or poems about heroic actions that _____ (happen) long ago.

2. The names of the writers who _____ (compose) the earliest folk epics are often unknown.

3. Folk epics _____ (appear) in many countries—for instance, the *Mahabharata* in India, the *Sundiata* in Mali, the *Iliad* in Greece, and *Beowulf* in England.

4. The heroes of these stories usually _____ (possess) superhuman strength or magical powers.

5. Epics also often _____ (contain) lessons and moral advice that the listeners were supposed to _____ (follow) in their own lives.

6. Stories of this kind _____ (carry) down religious traditions from century to century and were thought to _____ (preserve) historical truths.

7. Sophisticated writers in later times, such as Vergil and Dante, _____ (copy) the epic form to _____ (create) more polished and artificial poems, sometimes called art epics.

8. In modern times some poets have _____ (attempt) to _____ (compose) long autobiographical works in this tradition called *personal* epics.

9. Walt Whitman's "Song of Myself," the best known example of this type, _____ (influence) many other American poets to try this form.

10. Ezra Pound's *Cantos,* William Carlos Williams' *Paterson,* and Derek Walcott's *Omeros* _____ (pass) on this tradition and did _____

(attract) the attention of poets even though the general public does not

_____ (enjoy) these works as often as they should.

THE PAST TENSE OF IRREGULAR VERBS

Irregular verbs never take *d* endings. Instead, they change in different ways—*go* changes to *went, think* to *thought,* and so on. Most of these verbs you know by usage, but some do cause frequent mistakes. Look over this list to see if you recognize the past tenses.

Present	Past	Present	Past
be (am, is, are)	was, were	make	made
become	became	meet	met
begin	began	pay	paid
bring	brought	put	put
buy	bought	quit	quit
choose	chose	rise	rose
cost	cost	seek	sought
do	did	sell	sold
cut	cut	send	sent
feel	felt	shine	shone
fly	flew	sing	sang
get	got	spend	spent
give	gave	stand	stood
go	went	steal	stole
have	had	swim	swam
hear	heard	take	took
keep	kept	teach	taught
know	knew	tear	tore
lay	laid	think	thought
lead	led	throw	threw
lie	lay	write	wrote
lose	lost		

▶ Exercise 1

Past Tense of Irregular Verbs

Without looking at the preceding chart, fill in the past tense of the following verbs. After checking your answers, be sure to memorize any that you found you did not know already.

Present	Past	Present	Past
1. I spend	I _____	3. I go	I _____
2. I send	I _____	4. I meet	I _____

5. I feel	I _____	21. I seek	I _____
6. I keep	I _____	22. I teach	I _____
7. I lead	I _____	23. I hear	I _____
8. I write	I _____	24. I stand	I _____
9. I steal	I _____	25. I lay	I _____
10. I choose	I _____	26. I do	I _____
11. I rise	I _____	27. I begin	I _____
12. I sell	I _____	28. I sing	I _____
13. I become	I _____	29. I swim	I _____
14. I give	I _____	30. I know	I _____
15. I lie	I _____	31. I fly	I _____
16. I make	I _____	32. I throw	I _____
17. I pay	I _____	33. I quit	I _____
18. I think	I _____	34. I put	I _____
19. I buy	I _____	35. I cut	I _____
20. I bring	I _____		

Exercise II

Past Tense of Irregular Verbs

Circle any incorrect past verb form and write the correct form in the blank.

_____ 1. The meal and hors d'oeuvres probably costed them over two hundred dollars.

_____ 2. Mona send an express letter to you last night.

_____ 3. The book laid on the library table for three days.

_____ 4. The sun shine brightly as we left for the islands.

_____ 5. The company spend more than a million dollars in its advertising campaign last year.

_____ 6. Television programs lead her to think that her life would be like a soap opera.

_____ 7. My son brought a video camera at Macy's last week.

_____ 8. Burglars stold the radio and battery from the car.

_____ 9. I told them that I had payd the bill over three weeks ago.

_____ 10. The school choose members of the honor society already.

Exercise III

Past Tense of Irregular Verbs

Supply the correct past tense forms for the verbs in parentheses.

Abraham Maslow has done much to change our views of human nature. He (1)_____ (begin) as an experimenter who (2)_____ (spend) most of his time studying emotional illness. He (3)_____ (write) a book on abnormal psychology but then (4)_____ (become) dissatisfied with approaches that (5)_____ (seek) only to understand the disturbed person. Instead, he (6)_____ (choose) to examine the characteristics of the unusually healthy person. He (7)_____ (make) many original contributions to modern psychology and (8)_____ (bring) a new emphasis on health and potential rather than sickness. He (9)_____ (know) that many mysteries still (10)_____ (lie) unsolved in the psychology of the healthy personality. He (11)_____ (teach) for many years and (12)_____ (be) so popular he was called the Frank Sinatra of Brooklyn College. He later (13)_____ (go) to Brandeis University and finally to California. His many articles and influential books (14)_____ (do) much to win fame for him and his theories. Certain of his concepts, such as self-actualization and the hierarchy of needs, (15)_____ (take) their place among the leading ideas of modern psychology.

PAST PARTICIPLES

Past participles are used with forms of *be* and *have* for special purposes. Past participles of regular verbs are formed by adding *d* endings. Past participles of irregular verbs often differ from the past tense.

Regular Verbs

Present	*Past*	*Past Participle*
I believe	I believed	I have believed
I dance	I danced	I have danced
I study	I studied	I have studied

Irregular Verbs

Present	*Past*	*Past Participle*
I go	I went	I have gone
I sing	I sang	I have sung
I send	I sent	I have sent

Past participles cause some of the same problems in writing as the past tense does. You should avoid dropping *d* endings on participles formed from regular verbs, and you should learn the correct participle forms of irregular verbs from memory.

Past Participles with Helping Verbs

Past participles are used with helping verbs in two ways.

1. With *have, has,* and *had* to form the perfect tenses:

Past perfect: I *had* already *given* a brilliant performance.
                        I *had* previously *entered* the competition.

Present Perfect: I *have* always *done* my taxes by myself.
                        I *have* never *cheated* on an examination.

Future Perfect: I *will have begun* by the time you arrive.
                        I *will have reached* Charleston by noon.

2. With forms of *be* (*is, are, was, were*) to form the passive voice. The passive voice is not a tense; it is an arrangement of words in which the subject receives the action.★ In the active voice, the way we usually make statements, the subject does the action.

Active voice: Sharon *admired* Hector.
Passive voice: Hector *was admired* by Sharon.

In the active voice, the subject, Sharon, does the admiring; in the passive voice, the subject, Hector, receives the admiration. Form the passive voice with forms of *be* and the past participle:

★See Using the Active Voice for Strength in Unit 4.

Active voice:	Sidney *threw* a party.
Passive voice:	A party *was thrown* by Sidney.

Past Participles as Adjectives

Past participles are sometimes used as adjectives, either before or after the nouns they describe:

Participle before noun:	I sent a *registered* letter.
Participle after noun:	I sent a letter *registered* on March 5th.
Participle before noun:	A *frozen* daiquiri is tasty.
Participle after noun:	A daiquiri *frozen* properly is tasty.

Exercise I

Past Participles

In the following sentences, circle past participles with missing *d* endings. Remember that past participles may appear after *have, has,* or *had;* after *is, are, was,* and *were;* and before and after nouns.

1. A close friend of mine name Henry just won the lottery.
2. Rachel was dress well for the interview.
3. The students were confuse by the examination questions.
4. Old people should not be force to retire.
5. It could have happen to you if you had been there.
6. If the real assailant had not confess, he might have been convicted.
7. The mayor was ask to preside over the ceremony.
8. The manager was face with a crucial decision.
9. Julia was divorce three years ago.
10. A young woman marry to an older man has to make adjustments.

Exercise II

Past Participles

Write sentences using the following phrases. Don't forget the *d* endings!

1. got married	2. was named	3. were forced to	4. has happened
5. is finished	6. are convinced	7. is concerned	8. have faced
9. has promised	10. was reached		

Past Participles of Irregular Verbs

The past participles of irregular verbs are usually different from the past tense. Do not use the past tense in place of the participle with *have* or *be.*

Not:	I *have drank* all the tea you gave me.	
Correct:	I *have drunk* all the tea you gave me.	
Not:	The bicycle *was stole* while I was shopping.	
Correct:	The bicycle *was stolen* while I was shopping.	

Here is a list of irregular past participles that often cause mistakes:

Present	*Past*	*Past Participle*
become	became	become
begin	began	begun
bring	brought	brought
choose	chose	chosen
come	came	come
cost	cost	cost
do	did	done
drink	drank	drunk
drive	drove	driven
eat	ate	eaten
fall	fell	fallen
forget	forgot	forgotten
get	got	gotten
give	gave	given
go	went	gone
have	had	had
hide	hid	hidden
hurt	hurt	hurt
keep	kept	kept
know	knew	known
lay	laid	laid
lead	led	led
lie	lay	lain
meet	met	met
pay	paid	paid
quit	quit	quit
ride	rode	ridden
rise	rose	risen
run	ran	run
see	saw	seen
send	sent	sent
shake	shook	shaken
shine	shone	shone
sing	sang	sung
speak	spoke	spoken
spend	spent	spent

steal	stole	stolen
take	took	taken
throw	threw	thrown
write	wrote	written

Exercise III

Past Participles

Write the correct past participles in the blanks.

1. Has she ever _____ (go) to Guatemala?

2. I have _____ (send) you a wonderful present.

3. The company has _____ (throw) many parties for clients.

4. The bill was _____ (pay) by the manager.

5. The photograph was _____ (take) with fast film.

6. The team could have _____ (ride) in a limousine.

7. The flood waters have_____ (rise) two feet already.

Exercise IV

Past Participles

Use the correct form, either the past tense or the past participle, in each sentence.

1. Marie has _____ (spend) half her week's salary on her books.

2. Three kinds of beverages were _____ (drink) at the reception.

3. The district attorney has _____ (bring) charges against the suspect.

4. The hot sun _____ (shine) brightly on the landscape.

5. Donald has _____ (run) three small businesses.

6. Vincent _____ (lead) the team in shooting percentage.

7. The cafeteria has _____ (begin) to serve bagels.

Review Exercise I

Past Tense and Past Participles

Write the correct form of the verb in the blank.

1. Many kinds of special words and phrases, which are _____ (call) figures of speech, are _____ (use) to express ideas vividly.

2. Poets have _____ (invent) thousands of metaphors; Shakespeare, for instance, _____ (write) that "All the world's a stage."

3. Through such imaginative comparisons, writers have _____ (give) us means of perceiving our lives in new ways.

4. Similes, comparisons using *like* or *as,* have also _____ (appear) frequently in literature. When Christina Rossetti wrote, "My heart is like a singing bird," she _____ (choose) a simile to express joy.

5. Synecdoche, referring to something by naming part of it, has also _____ (take) its place in literature.

6. You have probably _____ (hear) someone ask, "Do you have wheels?" He or she really wants to know if a car is available.

7. Metonymy, naming something by referring to an idea or fact associated with it, has also _____ (play) its part in writing.

8. For instance, you may have _____ (notice) the term "grandfather clause" in labor agreements. It refers to rules that apply to people who have _____ (work) for the company a long time, associating time with the age of grandfathers.

9. A euphemism, a mild term that takes the place of a blunter one, may be _____ (use) to avoid offending readers, but some writers have always _____ (consider) it better to be direct.

10. Prostitutes, for instance, _____ (use) to be _____ (call) "ladies of the evening."

AVOIDING SHIFTS IN VERB TENSE

Once you can recognize verb tenses and use the correct verb forms, learn to write without shifting awkwardly between tenses. What's wrong with this passage?

When I *got* up this morning, I *felt* excited. I *know* I *have* an exam at eleven o'clock, but I *was* ready for it because I *study* hard the night before.

If you are writing in the past, *stay in the past tense:*

When I *got* up this morning, I *felt* excited. I *knew* I *had* an exam at eleven o'clock, but I *was* ready for it because I *had studied* hard the night before.

What's wrong with this description of a story?

This story *is* about two girls who *lived* in the South. Although they *are* sisters, one of them *was* bright while the other *is* slow and simple. The mother *tries* to be a good parent to both, but she *couldn't* treat them the same way.

When discussing a story, *stay in the present tense:*

This story *is* about two girls who *live* in the South. Although they *are* sisters, one of them *is* bright while the other *is* slow and simple. The mother *tries* to be a good parent to both, but she *can't* treat them the same way.

Verb Tenses in Writing: Some Guidelines

- **Stay in the same tense as long as the time you are writing about does not change.**
- **If the time changes, the verb tense *should* change, even in the same paragraph or sentence:** I once *believed* that money *makes* people happy, but now I *realize* that happiness *depends* on your inner self and your relationships.
- **Tell about the plot of a play, novel, or story in the present tense:** *Moo* is a novel that *satirizes* the way faculty and students *behave* at a Midwestern university.
- **Statements about eternal truths may be in the present even when you are telling about past events:** The child *learned* quickly that not all people in this world *can be trusted*.
- **If you are writing about experiences that you remember, statements like "I recall" or "I remember" are in the present.** The events happened in the past, but you are recalling them now: I *remember* (not *remembered*) how cold the winters used to be in Wisconsin when I was a child.
- **Use helping words correctly:** *may, can,* and *will* in present and future tenses and *might, could,* and *would* in the past.

Exercise I

Shifts in Verb Tense

Rewrite the following paragraph so that it stays entirely in the past tense. Underline the verbs you have changed from present to past.

David Bowie was born in Brixton, a lower-middle-class section of London, on January 8, 1947. His father did odd jobs, and his mother is an usherette at a movie theater. As a teenager, he began playing saxophone in a band. In his late teens he becomes a singer, and, after a number of not-so-successful records and a change of managers, he produced *Space Oddity,* his first successful album. He makes a few more albums in both England and America; then he posed as "Ziggy Stardust" in elaborate stage performances. In 1973 he decides to retire, but he reappeared a year later with another character known as "Aladinsane." In 1976 he retires again as "The Thin White Duke." About this time he made his film debut as a space visitor in *The Man Who Fell to Earth*. After spending several years in Berlin being rehabilitated from a serious drug problem, he reemerges as an actor in the 1980s. He played the Elephant Man on Broadway and a series of bizarre film roles, including the Goblin King in the puppet epic *Labyrinth,* a vampire in *The Hunger,* and Pontius Pilate in *The Last Temptation of Christ*. Although not all his films are box office successes, he was possibly the best actor of all the rock stars who performed in films. By the early 1990s, having discontinued his heavy drug use and bisexuality of the seventies, he turns his ambitions toward writing and directing films. He also won worldwide attention on April 24, 1992, by his marriage to the famous model Iman from Somalia. In 1996 he is inducted into the Rock and Roll Hall of Fame in Cleveland, Ohio, along with Pink Floyd, the Velvet Underground, and other long-time recording groups. He also played the role of Andy Warhol in the 1996 film *Basquiat*.

Exercise II

Shifts in Verb Tense

Rewrite the following paragraph so that it remains entirely in the present tense, with no shifts to the past. Underline the verbs you changed from past to present.

Shirley Jackson's short story, "The Lottery," shows real human behavior in a fantasy setting. The story takes place in an imaginary village that resembled a New England or Midwestern town in modern times. Although the villagers were just like real small town people, with their gossip and chatter about tractors and taxes, the town has an annual custom that was not at all like everyday life. Every June the people held a lottery in which the "winner" was stoned to death by friends, neighbors, and even family members. The lottery itself is a fantasy, but the way people behaved toward it was realistic. They conformed to a tradition without questioning its harmful effect. No one protests even though they knew they were being cruel to someone they loved. "The Lottery" taught a valuable lesson about how people were able to hang onto worn-out customs and conform to the behavior of their peers even when they should have known better.

Group Project

Shifts in Verb Tense

Have each of the members of your writing group compose a paragraph describing an activity that person does often. Write all paragraphs in the present tense; have each person tell what he or she does on a job or in some other activity such as a sport or hobby. Exchange paragraphs and rewrite each other's paragraphs in the past tense. Read them aloud and listen for any shifts of tenses that may need to be corrected. Check the verb forms carefully for *D* endings.

If English Is Not Your First Language (Progressive Tenses)

Verb tenses often present difficulties for anyone learning to speak and write English as a second language. In addition to mastering the basic verb tenses, which are not far different from those of many languages (except that some Asian languages do not use verb tenses), one must learn to use the *progressive forms*. These are the tense forms using verbs with *-ing* endings and helping verbs. **Very few languages use progressive forms as frequently as English does.**

What is the difference between these two statements?

A. My little brother *listens* to rock music on the radio.
B. My little brother *is listening* to rock music on the radio.

The simple present tense (sentence A) makes a general statement:

My brother *listens* to rock music for two hours every evening.

The present progressive tense (sentence B) describes action going on at a particular moment:

My brother *is listening* to rock music this very minute.

Progressive forms are also used in the past and the future to describe action in the moment.

Use the simple past for general statements or to describe actions already completed:

> My brother *liked* radio programs when he was a child.
> My brother *repaired* the radio last week.

Use the past progressive for action happening at a particular moment but not completed at that moment:

> My brother *was listening* to the radio last night when I called.

Use the simple future to make general statements or to describe an event that will be completed in the future:

> She *will* always *arrive* on time
> He *will win* the election.

Use the future progressive to describe actions that will be happening at a particular moment in the future:

> I *will be waiting* when you arrive.

Some common mistakes:

Do not use the progressive form to denote a single act already completed:

Wrong: He *was hitting* the ball and *was running* to first base.
Correct: He *hit* the ball and *ran* to first base.

Do not use the simple form to describe action going on at a particular moment:

Wrong: At the time he bought the stock, prices *rose*.
Correct: At the time he bought the stock, prices *were rising*.

Do not shift between the simple form and the progressive in the same statement:

Wrong: Manuel *was watching* television and *studied* at the same time.
Correct: Manuel *was watching* television and *studying* at the same time.

> ## Exercise 1

Progressive Tenses (For ESL Writers)

If the sentence is correct, write C in the blank. If the verb form is wrong, under-line the incorrect form and write the correct form in the blank.

_____   1.   Jessica walked over to the teller and was asking for information.
_____   2.   After the driver was putting on the brakes, the truck stopped.
_____   3.   Because it rained, Aaron brought along an umbrella.
_____   4.   Although many Democrats were voting for the bill, it did not pass.
_____   5.   Because Rachel was expecting to win, she looked happy.
_____   6.   Stanley watched the news on television when the telephone rang.
_____   7.   Lester is knowing the names of every country in Asia.
_____   8.   Pamela was taking out her passport and showed it to the agent.
_____   9.   The athletes were putting on their uniforms and joked with each other.
_____ 10.   A stranger approached and was slipping a flyer under the door.

Adjectives and Adverbs

People often confuse adjectives with adverbs, and vice versa.

TELLING THE DIFFERENCE BETWEEN ADJECTIVES AND ADVERBS

The most common mistake people make with adjectives and adverbs is to write *good* when they mean *well*.

Not: This car runs *good*.
But: This car runs *well*.

Good is an adjective; *well* is an adverb. What is the difference?

Adjectives tell *which, what kind of,* or *how many;* they modify nouns or pronouns:

a *violent* storm   a *busy* street
the *first* exit   *five* drinks

Adverbs tell *how, when,* and *where;* they modify verbs, adjectives, and other adverbs:

She talks *brilliantly.*
an *extremely* tall man
We are parked *nearby.*

He will write *soon*
They played *very* skillfully.

Another common mistake is to omit the *-ly* ending on adverbs. Many adjectives can be converted into adverbs by adding *-ly.*

Adjective	**Adverb**
a *quick* meal	We ate the meal *quickly*
a *real* diamond	*really* fine diamond
a *bad* feeling	They arranged it *badly.*
The answer was *correct.*	They answered *correctly.*

Remember to use adjectives after forms of *be* (*is, are, was, were*); these adjectives modify the subject. Also use adjectives after verbs of the senses such as *feel, smell, sound,* and *taste.*

1. The novel sounds *exciting.* (*Exciting* modifies *novel.*)
2. The quiche smells *delicious.* (*Delicious* modifies *quiche.*)
3. I feel *good* this morning. (*Good* modifies *I.*)
4. The fish tastes *stale.* (*Stale* modifies *fish.*)

Do not confuse these adjectives (called predicate adjectives because they come after the verb, not before the noun) with adverbs that come after verbs.

1. The novel reads *smoothly.* (*Smoothly* modifies *reads.*)
2. The chef makes quiche *expertly.* (*Expertly* modifies *makes.*)
3. I dress *quickly* in the morning. (*Quickly* modifies *dress.*)
4. She catches fish *frequently.* (*Frequently* modifies *catches.*)

Do not confuse *well,* the adverb, with *well,* the adjective:

1. You certainly can swim *well.* (*Well* [adv.] modifies *swim.*)
2. You look *well* now that you've recovered. (*Well,* meaning healthy, is an adjective modifying *you.*)
3. You look *good* in that skirt. (*Good* is an adjective modifying *you.*)

Some Tricky Adverbs

Certain adverbs are often confused with adjectives. Be on the lookout for:

Adjective	**Adverb**
most people	*almost* always
She feels *bad.*	She sings *badly.*

an *easy* job	He does it *easily.*
an *everyday* task	He swims *every day.*
a *smooth* landing	We landed *smoothly.*
a *slow* pace	Drive *slowly.* (*Slow* is also accepted as an adverb.)

Exercise I

Adjectives and Adverbs

Circle the correct form in each sentence.

1. Television newscasters have to be (real, really) articulate.
2. Educational programs help children learn (easy, easily).
3. Some people feel (bad, badly) after watching too much television.
4. Soap operas have become an (everyday, every day) activity for many people.
5. Commercials are (most, almost, mostly) always louder than the programs.
6. Some children behave (violent, violently) after watching (violent, violence, violently) programs.
7. To choose programs (careful, carefully), you should read reviews of the programs first.

Exercise II

Adjectives and Adverbs

Supply the missing forms.

Adjective	*Adverb*
She is *stylish*.	***She dresses*** stylishly.
1. The response was *quick.*	They responded _____.
2. The problem was *easy.*	She solved the problem _____.
3. The ending was _____.	The film ended *happily.*
4. They gave it *careful* consideration.	They considered it _____.
5. They felt _____ about the job.	They worked *badly* together.
6. They created a *good* plan.	They planned _____.
7. The manager was *efficient.*	The manager worked _____.

Exercise III

Adjectives and Adverbs

Compose sentences using the following words and phrases.

1. feels good
   feels well
2. especially
   special
3. bad
   badly
4. probable
   probably
5. everyday
   every day
6. careful
   carefully
7. real
   really

Special Practice with *Good* and *Well*

Write the adjective *good* or the adverb *well* in each blank; remember that *well* may be an adjective meaning "healthy."

1. The pilot flew jet planes _____.

2. She had _____ training and understood aircraft _____.

3. After an illness, she had gotten _____ again; she was waiting for a _____ day to resume her flying.

4. It felt _____ to be in the air once again.

5. She remembered all the instruments on the panel _____.

6. As the engines roared, they sounded _____ to her.

7. This was a _____ career, and it paid _____.

ADJECTIVES IN COMPARISONS

Besides their simple forms, adjectives have two forms that are used in comparisons. The comparative form is used to compare two unequal things, and the superlative form is used to set one thing off from all the others.

Simple Form	Comparative Form	Superlative Form
good	better	best
young	younger	youngest
strange	stranger	strangest
gentle	gentler	gentlest
happy	happier	happiest

Adjectives with three or more syllables always take *more* and *most* rather than the *er* and *est* endings.

beautiful	more beautiful	most beautiful
exciting	more exciting	most exciting

Your dictionary will show that some two-syllable words take *er* and *est* while others take *more* and *most*.

heavy	heavier	heaviest
friendly	friendlier	friendliest
subtle	subtler	subtlest
cheerful	more cheerful	most cheerful
precise	more precise	most precise

Use the comparative form when comparing two things or people:

> She is *wealthier* than her cousin.
> She is the *wealthier* of the two cousins.

(Remember to use *than*, not *then*, in making comparisons.)
Use the superlative form to set off one from a whole group:

> She is the *wealthiest* woman in the group.
> She is the *wealthiest* of the three cousins.

ADVERBS IN COMPARISONS

Adverbs also have comparative and superlative forms. Nearly all adverbs take *more* and *most*. The only exceptions are the few that serve as both adjectives and adverbs—*early, late, hard, fast, low,* and *straight*. These take *er* and *est: earlier, earliest*.

Simple Form	*Comparative Form*	*Superlative Form*
easily	more easily	most easily
violently	more violently	most violently
recently	more recently	most recently
happily	more happily	most happily

We also make negative comparisons, using adjectives and adverbs in combination with *less* or *least*.

expensive	less expensive	least expensive
difficult	less difficult	least difficult
safely	less safely	least safely
forcefully	less forcefully	least forcefully

Do not use both the *er* or *est* ending and the helping words *more, most, less,* or *least.*

Wrong: You are *more better* than the last shortstop.
                                         They are *less healthier* than they should be.

Right: You are *better* than the last shortstop.
                                         They are *less healthy* than they should be.

Wrong: This was the *most saddest* film I have seen.
                                         This was the *least richest* pastry on the menu.

Right: This was the *saddest* film I have seen.
                                         This was the *least rich* pastry on the menu.

Exercise I

Adjectives in Comparisons

Write the correct form of the adjective or adverb in the blank.

1. Most people enjoy films that are _____ (long) than ordinary ones.

2. Being longer, of course, does not make a film _____ (good).

3. Still, audiences often expect a longer film to provide a _____ (rich) experience than a short one.

4. One of the _____ (great) efforts of all time in filmmaking was the Russian version of *War and Peace,* which ran eight hours and twenty-seven minutes.

5. A Japanese film company made a still _____ (ambitious) film called *The Human Condition,* which lasted nine hours and twenty-nine minutes.

6. Much _____ (early), in 1925, a seven-hour, fifty-eight-minute silent film called *Sparks of the Flame* was made in the Soviet Union.

7. Two years _____ (late) a French filmmaker, Abel Gance, created a six-hour, eighteen-minute epic on Napoleon.

Writing Assignment

Adjectives and Adverbs in Comparisons

To practice using comparative forms in your writing, compose a short essay comparing yourself with a sibling, a close relative, or close friend. First do some brainstorming to collect as many similarities and differences as possible. Next write a rough draft, first writing about what you have in common, then writing about how you differ. Look over your draft and underline every comparative form you have used. Correct any adjectives or adverbs that are incorrect. Make any other revisions needed. Write a final draft.

Exercise II

Comparative and Superlative Forms

Write a sentence converting each adjective or adverb from comparative to superlative form.

Example:

Comparative: Mike is *taller* than the other team's center.
Superlative: *Mike is the **tallest** center in the league.*

Comparative: This film is *less interesting* than *Pulp Fiction*
Superlative: *This film is the **least interesting** one available on video.*

1. This car runs *better* than the one you rented last time.

   _____

2. The weather is *worse* this January than it was last year.

   _____

3. Karen is *smarter* than most of her teachers.

   _____

4. Grammar is *more interesting* than bungee jumping.

   _____

5. Sleeping in class is *more pleasant* than studying.

   _____

6. Robert moves *more quickly* than his opponent.

   _____

7. He is *richer* than the other candidates.

   _____

MISPLACED AND DANGLING MODIFIERS

Modifiers are adjectives, adverbs, or phrases that function as adjectives or adverbs. Modifiers describe or change the meaning of other words in the sentence, so they should be close to the words that they modify. If they are too far away from the words they modify and cause confusion, we call them **misplaced modifiers.** If the words they modify are not really in the sentence, we call them **dangling modifiers.**

Misplaced Modifiers

> *As a child,* my grandmother took me to see a bullfight.
> *Standing on a curb,* a bicyclist whizzed by and almost knocked Joyce over.

The italicized phrases in both sentences are out of place. If we take them to be describing the words next to them, the meaning is confused. It sounds as if the grandmother were a child, and the bicyclist were standing on the curb. Rearrange sentences like these to say what you mean. Better:

> *When I was a child,* my grandmother took me to see a bullfight.
> *While Joyce was standing on the curb,* a bicyclist whizzed by and almost knocked her over.

Another way:

> *As a child,* I went to see a bullfight with my grandmother.
> *Standing on the curb,* Joyce was almost knocked over by a bicyclist.

Dangling Modifiers

> *While drying her hair,* the clock radio suddenly began blasting.
> *As a teenager,* school became boring and homework was a drag.

These dangling modifiers are not much different from misplaced modifiers, except that in these sentences there is no word at all that the modifiers describe. Who was drying her hair? Who was a teenager? The reader has to guess. Add the necessary words. Better:

> *While Karen was drying her hair,* the clock radio suddenly began blasting.
> *As a teenager, I* found school boring and homework a drag.

Identifying Misplaced and Dangling Modifiers

If you write misplaced and dangling modifiers, the meaning may seem clear to you but may not be to your reader. Misplaced and dangling modifiers are often introductory phrases, so watch for them at the beginning of your sentences. However, they can occur in the middle or at the end of sentences:

Sergio reached for the drawer *filled with anger and resentment.*
A hurricane was moving slowly up the coast *while at Cape Cod.*

In the first sentence, the italicized phrase is misplaced: It should describe Sergio, but appears to describe the drawer. Better:

Filled with anger and resentment, Sergio reached for the drawer.

In the second sentence, the modifying phrase would be dangling no matter where we put it; the sentence must say *who* was at Cape Cod. Better:

A hurricane was moving slowly up the coast *while we were at Cape Cod.*

Exercise I

Misplaced and Dangling Modifiers

Underline the misplaced word or phrase and rewrite the sentence correctly.

Example: He will pick up the car that was wrecked <u>tomorrow morning.</u>

Tomorrow morning he will pick up the wrecked car.

1. She will have to repair the radio that was damaged with a screwdriver.

   _____

   _____

2. Sitting on the top shelf I discovered a copy of *The Catcher in the Rye.*

   _____

   _____

3. She wanted an apartment that would be large enough for two children with plenty of light.

   _____

   _____

4. Nearly starved, the helicopter pilot spotted the hikers shivering in the snow.

   _____

   _____

5. Decorated with rhinestones, the salesman placed the sweater back in the display case.

_____

_____

6. Puffed up with air, the scientist placed the bag over the flame.

_____

_____

7. Several people in Arizona reported seeing flying saucers in the newspapers.

_____

_____

Exercise II

Misplaced and Dangling Modifiers

Rewrite each sentence, placing the italicized phrase where it logically belongs.

Example: _with its headlights on_
The crowd watched the limousine roll silently onto the ferryboat.

The crowd watched the limousine, with its headlights on, roll silently onto the
ferryboat.

1. _with a view of the river_
They were looking for a colonial house big enough for a growing family.

_____

_____

2. _hoarse from shouting_
Two minutes after the game the coach congratulated the whole team.

_____

_____

3. _in V formation_
We watched the jets flying overhead.

_____

_____

4. *purring with contentment*
The children found the kitten in the back seat of the car.

_____

_____

5. *that included word processing*
She finally found a course at a community college nearby.

_____

_____

6. *that was too salty*
Several customers sent the lamb stew back to the chef.

_____

_____

7. *listed in the telephone directory*
Sally gave the names of three dentists to Tom's cousin.

_____

_____

▶ Exercise III

Misplaced and Dangling Modifiers

Rewrite these sentences, adding or changing words so that the modifying phrases are not misplaced or dangling.

Example: Proud of America's new importance in the world, the 1920s were entered by the younger generation with enthusiasm.

Proud of America's new importance in the world, the younger generation entered the 1920s with enthusiasm.

1. Often called the Jazz Age, many people now think of the 1920s as a period of wealth, entertainment, and reckless high living.

_____

_____

© 1998 by Addison-Wesley Educational Publishers Inc.

2. Aware of the complexities of that decade, however, many social problems such as poverty and racism are evident to historians of the period.

_____

_____

3. Government officials launched an irrational attack on unions, political outsiders, and members of minority groups, afraid of the government being overthrown by "Reds."

_____

_____

4. A period of sudden blossoming by black writers, musicians, and artists, historians often refer to the 1920s as the Harlem Renaissance.

_____

_____

5. Afraid of a threat to traditional values, immigration was restricted by a series of laws in the 1920s.

_____

_____

6. The 1920s began with the prohibition of alcohol, after passing the Volstead Act and the 18th Amendment in 1919.

_____

_____

7. This exciting decade was brought to an end by the stock market crash of October 12, 1929, remembered fondly by some as the Roaring Twenties.

_____

_____

▶ Review Exercise

Misplaced and Dangling Modifiers

Correct any misplaced or dangling modifiers in these sentences by rewriting the sentences. Write C if the sentence is correct.

1. Susan gave Ted a poster for his room in the dormitory that looked like a spring landscape.

    _____

    _____

2. After buying three tickets, on the way home it became apparent that they would need four.

    _____

    _____

3. Henry had to drive his old Ford to get to the party on time without a spare tire.

    _____

    _____

4. Learning how to use the home computer, a surprising number of tasks suddenly became easier.

    _____

    _____

5. Checked three times by the examiners, his answers nevertheless proved all correct.

    _____

    _____

6. While using the hair dryer, the doorbell was inaudible.

    _____

    _____

7. The people usually vote for a candidate they see on television with charm and poise.

    _____

    _____

 ## If English Is Not Your First Language

English relies on word order and phrasing more than some other languages because it is less *inflected,* i.e., verbs and nouns, except for *D* and *S* endings, do not have many forms. If you are learning to speak English, you may expect to have some difficulty with the positioning and arrangement of words. This is not what most people mean by *grammar* because phrasing cannot be summed up in a few rules. You must learn it primarily by getting plenty of practice speaking English.

However, you can learn to spot certain patterns that will speed up your mastery of English. One rule that may help you avoid a common ESL error is the following:

Never put a modifier between a verb and the object of the verb.
Many verbs, called *transitive verbs,* take *objects:*

                    s   v   Direct Object
        Jeremy tore the <u>poster</u> from the wall.

It is not correct to put a modifier between the verb *tore* and the object *poster.*

Incorrect: Jeremy tore <u>angrily</u> the poster from the wall.

Put the modifier *angrily* either before the verb or at the end of the sentence:

Correct: Jeremy <u>angrily</u> tore the poster from the wall.
Correct: Jeremy tore the poster from the wall <u>angrily</u>.

▶ Exercise I

Placing Modifiers (for ESL Writers)

In each sentence, circle the misplaced modifier and draw an arrow to a spot in the sentence where it belongs. If the sentence is correct, circle the modifier and write C in the blank.

Example:

_____   I like (a lot) this story. ↖
___C___   The mayor (quickly) answered the questions.

_____ 1. Esther read carefully the biology assignment.
_____ 2. Helen proceeded to play expertly the concerto.
_____ 3. The branch manager gave hurriedly instructions to the new employees.
_____ 4. Alex picked up suddenly his jacket and left the room.
_____ 5. Polling experts make once in a while inaccurate predictions.
_____ 6. Eating disorders usually create vitamin deficiencies.
_____ 7. Making her way step by step, she reached eventually the top of the cliff.

Pronouns

Pronouns cause several kinds of writing difficulties. Learn the correct pronoun forms.

Types of Pronouns

Personal Pronouns Used as Subjects	*Reflexive Pronouns*
I	myself
you	yourself
she	yourselves
he	herself
it	himself
we	itself
they	ourselves
	themselves

Personal Pronouns Used as Objects of Verbs and Prepositions	*Impersonal Pronouns*
me	one
you	each
her	either
him	anyone, anybody
it	everyone, everybody
us	someone, somebody
them	none
	no one
	nobody

Pronoun Case

Probably the most frequent difficulty people have with pronouns lies in choosing the correct case for personal pronouns. This means knowing whether to use *I* or *me, we* or *us, she* or *her,* and *he* or *him.* When one of these pronouns occurs by itself, we can usually pick the correct form by the sound. However, when there are two pronouns or when a pronoun is joined with a noun, choosing may be more difficult.

Which is correct?

> Between you and *me,* the boss plans to promote Carol.
> Between you and *I,* the boss plans to promote Carol.

Are you surprised to find out that the *first* one is correct? Both *you* and *me* are the objects of *between.*

Which is correct?

> My brother and *I* tried out for a professional soccer team.
> *Me* and my brother tried out for a professional soccer team.

The *first* one is correct again, because both *I* and *brother* are the subjects of the verb *tried*.

How can you tell which is right? The easiest way is not to analyze the grammar but to take out the other word, whether noun or pronoun, and read the sentence without it:

> *I* tried out for a professional soccer team.

Exercise I

Pronoun Case

Circle the correct pronoun(s) in each sentence. (Read the sentence in your mind without the other word.)

1. Send applications to (she and I, her and me).
2. Wait until the neighbors hear about you and (I, me).
3. (Me and my sister, My sister and I) live a block from each other.
4. The proceeds will go to Bob and (he, him).
5. After (she and I, me and her) save enough money we will visit Cuba.
6. (We, Us) students should organize a bridge team.
7. Ted and (I, me) are learning to operate a small business.

Exercise II

Pronoun Case

Write sentences using the following combinations correctly. Remember to read your sentences with each pronoun by itself to be sure they are correct.

Example: her and me

They gave voice lessons to her and me.
_____

1. you and I

_____

2. me and my friends

_____

3. she and her brother

_____

4. we three applicants

_____

5. him and his sister

_____

6. her and me

_____

7. us Americans

_____

▶ Exercise III

Pronoun Case

Circle the correct forms in parentheses.

For many of (we, us) young movie fans nowadays, Jim Carrey has become the funniest comic actor of them all. His crazy behavior and facial expressions make (my friends and I, me and my friends) laugh harder than any other performer. My mother says that Carrey didn't appeal to either (she, her) or my father at first, but after a while they got to like him. His wacky television roles in *In Living Color* reminded them of comics like Jerry Lewis in (his or her, their) day. Just between (you and I, you and me), Carrey is a lot better than the old comedians. His roles are more varied; (it, they) include action–fantasy in *The Mask,* a scary character in *The Cable Guy,* and even a female bodybuilder named Vera De Milo in *In Living Color.* Maybe (we, us) younger fans like Jim Carrey because he began his career as a class clown in his elementary school in Ontario, Canada, and he knows how to entertain the young and appeal to (his or her, their) sense of humor. His many hit roles on television and in films since the early 1980s, however, have allowed him to develop (his, their) adult comic talent as well. In *Liar, Liar* (it, they) was very much in evidence.

PRONOUN CASE: USING *WHO* AND *WHOM*

Using *who* and *whom* correctly is a tricky business. Few speakers get the distinction right every time in conversation, and only the most careful grammarians always use the correct form in writing. In conversation, you can get away with using *who* when you aren't sure, but in college writing, you are expected to know when to use *whom*.

Remember that *who* is the form to use as a subject, and *whom* is the form to use as the object of a verb or preposition. To most people, it sounds right to say "to whom," "for whom," and "with whom." In more complicated phrases, however, you have to begin by identifying the main clause in the sentence and separating it in your mind from the relative clause (the *who* or *whom* clause). The relative clause determines whether you should write *who* or *whom*: write *who* if it is the subject of the verb; write *whom* if it is the object of the verb or of a preposition:

1. Allison is the student <u>who</u> sits in the front row. (*who* as subject of verb)

2. Allison is the student <u>whom</u> the teacher likes. (*whom* as object of verb in relative clause)

3. Allison is the student with <u>whom</u> the tutor is speaking. (*whom* as object of preposition)

In conversation, we might phrase sentence 3 differently: "Allison is the student *whom* the tutor is speaking with." Strict grammarians may tell you not to end a sentence with a preposition this way, but even if you do, *whom* is still the object of *with* in the sentence.

Exercise 1

Using *Who* and *Whom*

In each of these sentences, circle the entire relative clause; then write *who* or *whom* in the blank. Explain how the pronoun functions, as subject or object, in the relative clause.

Example: Raoul named the person who he thought was harassing him.

1. Bill Gates is a young man _____ built a fortune on computer software.

2. He and his partners _____ created Microsoft Corporation became billionaires within a decade.

3. People with _____ he has worked find him to be an obsessive worker.

4. Users of personal computers, at _____ the advertising campaign to promote Windows 95 was directed, recognize the face of Bill Gates.

5. Starting as a computer hacker _____ grew up in Seattle and dropped out of Harvard, Gates began creating computer software in the 1970s.

6. Gates, _____ IBM helped enormously in the early 1980s by contracting with Microsoft to provide basic operating software for IBM's personal computers, became the richest man in America.

7. Gates is seen as a visionary genius by those _____ he helped make rich.

8. He is seen as ruthless by those _____ he has defeated in the competition for control of the software market.

9. Gates was the child of a lawyer and a teacher _____ were both active in civic affairs.

10. He will continue to be a corporate figure about _____ there will be controversy.

Exercise II

Using *Who* and *Whom*

Compose sentences modeled on the form of the following sentences.

Example: The couple *whom* you met last night are moving to Delaware.

Your sentence: *The students whom you saw in the bookstore are sophomores.*

1. The player who scores the most points will return next week.

Your sentence: _____

_____

2. The article referred to three people who tested positive for HIV.

Your sentence: _____

_____

3. The voters preferred the candidate who they thought would create jobs.

Your sentence: _____

_____

4. The children whom the article described all grew up in other countries.

Your sentence: _____

_____

5. The personnel officer by whom you will be interviewed is a psychologist.

Your sentence: _____

_____

6. From whom were the packages sent?

Your sentence: _____

_____

7. Whom would she prefer to see marry her son?

Your sentence: _____

_____

PRONOUNS AND ANTECEDENTS

Since pronouns are words that take the place of nouns, they always have nouns called **antecedents,** usually in the same sentence or the one just before it, to which they refer. Pronouns must agree with their antecedents in number, person, and gender.

Example:

1. **Pronouns and Antecedents Agree in Number**

> The *book* lost *its* cover. (*Book* and *its* are both singular.)
> Most *people* enjoy *their* birthdays. (*People* and *their* are both plural.)

2. **Pronouns and Antecedents Agree in Person**

> The *company* changed *its* name. (*Company* and *its* are both in the third person.)
> *You* must wear *your* tuxedo. (*You* and *your* are both in the second person.)

3. **Pronouns and Antecedents Agree in Gender**

> *Inez* had *her* diploma framed. (*Inez* and *her* are feminine.)
> *James* found *his* diskette. (*James* and *his* are masculine.)

Most mistakes in agreement of pronouns and antecedents have to do with number. Do not shift from a singular noun to a plural pronoun, or vice versa.

Awkward shifts:

> The *college* changed *their* financial aid rules this year. (*College* is singular; *their* is plural.)
>
> People who use *drugs* often underestimate how harmful *it* is. (*Drugs* is plural; *it* is singular.)

Better:

> The *college* changed *its* financial aid rules this year.
>
> People who use *drugs* often underestimate how harmful *they are*.

Note: Indefinite pronouns like *everyone, everybody, anyone, someone,* and *nobody* are singular. Use singular forms like *he* or *she* to agree with them:

> *Anyone* who does that is putting *his or her* life at stake.

Exercise I

Pronouns and Antecedents

Circle the correct pronoun in each sentence.

1. Every woman in the audience knows this is true for (them, her, she).
2. All of the people who voted in the last election expressed (his, her, their) preferences.
3. A law that is not enforced loses (their, his, its) validity.
4. Steps are being taken to prevent looting because (they, it) causes enormous damage.
5. The standard of living has risen slightly, but (they, he, it) may rise faster in the next year.
6. Mothers and fathers have recently pooled (her, his, their) knowledge in writing this book.
7. A firefighter who stays on the force for twenty years receives (his, her, his or her, their) retirement benefits.
8. Students of astronomy find that (he, she, they) need mathematics.
9. A father of small children often finds (their, his, its) time taken up with domestic responsibilities.
10. Songs are often presented to the public in video clips that express (its, his, their) feeling visually.

Exercise II

Pronouns and Antecedents

Rewrite the first five sentences by changing the pronouns and antecedents from singular to plural. In the last five, change them from plural to singular. Be sure that all verbs agree with their subjects.

Example: An ambitious entertainer usually has an agent to look after his or her interests.

Plural: *Ambitious entertainers usually have agents to look after their interests.*

1. Singular: An undergraduate who hopes to pursue a graduate degree has to earn high grades in his or her major subject.

   Plural: Undergraduates who _____

   _____

2. Singular: The last job at which I worked offered too few rewards for its difficulties.

   Plural: The last two jobs _____

   _____

3. Singular: A child who writes poetry often develops his or her imagination and language skills at the same time.

   Plural: Children who _____

   _____

4. Singular: A man who wants to become a professional chef can pursue his career at a college of culinary arts.

   Plural: Men who _____

   _____

5. Singular: A company that uses computers effectively can increase its efficiency and maximize its profits.

   Plural: Companies that _____

   _____

6. Plural: Women who run for public office often make their way against opposition from their peers.

Singular: A woman who _____

_____

7. Plural: Pedestrians who refuse to obey the lights are risking their lives.

Singular: A pedestrian who _____

_____

8. Plural: Men who attend colleges that were once for women only sometimes find themselves in a minority group.

Singular: A man who _____

_____

9. Plural: Newspapers that sensationalize the news they print and use simple language are called tabloids.

Singular: A newspaper that _____

_____

10. Plural: Children who skip grades in school have to adjust to finding themselves in more mature social groups.

Singular: A child who _____

_____

Shifts of Person

When you write a paragraph or essay, you may write it in the first, second, or third person.

First Person
The **first person** refers to the writer or speaker (I) or to the group including the writer or speaker (we). Stories and essays are often written in the first person, meaning that the writer or narrator (an imaginary speaker) refers throughout the story to himself or herself by using *I, me, my,* and *mine.* Editorials in newspapers and company reports sometimes use the first person plural, the "editorial we." Such editorials and reports sound as if they are expressing the opinions of a whole group.

Second Person
The **second person** means the reader or listener (*you*). Whole essays are seldom written entirely in the second person. Procedural writing, which contains a series of instructions to the reader, often is. Personal letters usually contain many

statements in the second person because the writer is addressing a specific reader whom he or she knows.

Third Person
The **third person** means any person or thing written about. Most college writing is in the third person because most of it is about topics studied in college courses, not about the personal life of the writer or reader. A statement that someone does something ("James writes country music") is in the third person. It may be singular (*she, he, it*) or plural (*they*).

Shifts of Person
Do not shift awkwardly from one person to another in your writing. Watch especially for the temptation to slip *you* into an essay that is supposed to be in the third person:

> A *person* who wants to learn how to sing well has to think about several elements at once. *He* or *she* has to learn to open and relax the throat. *You* also have to use the diaphragm to support *your* breathing.

This sort of shift from *he* or *she* to *you* is awkward and confusing. Either write the whole set of instructions in the second person, using *you* throughout, or keep it in the third person, using either *he* (or *she*) or *one*. (Note: You may shift between *one* and *he* or *she*, since you are remaining in the third person.)

Writers also sometimes make the mistake of shifting into the first person (*I*) when it is not appropriate:

> Before *you* go out to run or participate in a vigorous sport, *you* should warm up with some stretching exercises. Before jogging, *I* always do leg stretching exercises and touch *my* toes several times.

This whole passage should remain in the second person, *you should* instead of *I*. Remember that when you give commands or instructions, the word *you* is often understood and does not have to be repeated frequently: "Always do leg stretching exercises" is shorter than "You should always do leg stretching exercises."

Exercise I

Shifts of Person

Underline the words containing shifts of person and write the correct words above them.

Example: When you look at the statistics, <u>one</u> *(you)* might think twice about getting married.

1. Most people realize that college has changed a lot since since your parents' time.

2. Our parents did not feel as much pressure to get a college degree as I do.

3. Women often thought it was their destiny to get married and settle down; now she usually wants to go to college and start a career.

4. A typical student in the 1950s went straight through college in four years or dropped out, but now they usually take longer and often attend part time.

5. This means that students today begin their careers at a later age than he did in his parents' time.

6. One often has to take on huge debts before they graduate nowadays.

7. Students used to take all of their courses in the classroom, but now he or she is likely to take some of them online.

Exercise II

Shifts of Person

Complete each sentence using a form of the pronoun that is used at the beginning. If the sentence has a noun rather than a pronoun, use a third person pronoun (*one, he, she,* or *they*) to complete the sentence. Do not shift persons in completing the sentence.

Example: If you want to become a doctor, *you should excel in your science courses.*

1. If a woman wants to become a movie director, _____
   _____

2. When teenagers go to a shopping mall, _____
   _____

3. After you have read the article,_____
   _____

4. While I am waiting in the dentist's office, _____
   _____

5. If we see a coffee shop on the way, _____

_____

6. Although a man may be born in poverty, _____

_____

7. If a parent is too permissive,_____

_____

Exercise III

Shifts of Person

The following paragraph should be in the second person throughout. Some-times, however, it awkwardly shifts to the first or third person. Underline all the pronouns that erroneously appear in the first or third person, and write the correct pronouns above them.

To write an effective essay, you have to consider at least three elements: content, organization, and correctness. He or she has to have a clear main idea and develop it. Your content includes your main thought as well as the specific material you use to support it. I should have plenty of examples to illustrate my main idea. Sometimes it helps to jot down more examples than you will ever use. Organization is important too. One should not just state facts in any order without thinking of how I am going to arrange them. Your first example should be a powerful one; your last should be the most important of all. And we should not forget to make transitions between examples. Finally, I should always proofread my essay to find mistakes in grammar or phrasing. Never assume that the first draft needs no corrections or revisions. Always be ready to make any small

corrections or improvements the essay needs. As the last step, you should give
your essay an interesting title. Good titles will often occur to me when I am composing an essay, not beforehand. The title should suggest the topic and arouse
interest but not necessarily declare the main point. Often the conclusion of his
or her essay will echo a word or phrase used in the title. Our first impression and
our last should be closely connected by this means.

Parallelism

Parallelism in sentences means that certain parts fit together smoothly—nouns
matched with nouns, adjectives with adjectives, prepositional phrases with
prepositional phrases, and so on. Parallelism is necessary when two parts of a
sentence are joined by *and* or when three or more parts are listed in a series with
commas separating them.

Examples of Parallel Combination

       noun   *noun*   *noun*

1. We found a Sony Walkman, a skateboard, and a basketball in the schoolyard.

                prep. phrase   *prep. phrase*

2. The marathon went along the avenue, over the suspension bridge, and
prep. phrase
into the park.

       adj. *adj.*   *adj.*

3. The party was noisy, wild, and hilarious.

Examples of Combinations that Are Not Parallel

    noun *noun*   *noun*   *verb phrase*

1. We discovered a battery, a radio, a generator, and looked for a hubcap.

        adj. *verb phrase*   *adj.*

2. Both women were attractive, worked in publishing houses, ambitious, and
   adj.
talented.

                noun   *noun*   *whole clause*

3. The schools need newer equipment, smaller classes, and the dropout rate
needs to be lowered.

Parallel and Nonparallel Sentences Compared

Nonparallel

1. She is tall, athletic, and has skill.
2. They wanted to advance in their jobs, earn a lot of money, as well as enjoying their work.
3. The visit to Eastern Europe left her better informed, more tolerant, and an optimist.
4. Jason studied before school, after work, and he read assignments during lunch break.
5. I got a headache from too little sleep and because I was anxious about the examination.

Parallel

1. She is tall, athletic, and skillful.
2. They wanted to advance in their jobs, earn a lot of money, and enjoy their work.
3. The visit to Eastern Europe left her better informed, more tolerant, and more optimistic.
4. Jason studied before school, after work, and during lunch break.
5. I got a headache from too little sleep and anxiety over the examination.

Exercise I

Parallelism

It helps to think of parallel elements as lists. When you number the parts, you can see more easily which one may not fit. In the following lists, circle the part that does not fit. Then rewrite it in the blank in a form that is parallel with the others.

Example:

1. well-coordinated
2. quick
3. (has a lot of accuracy)
4. strong   *accurate*

1. knows several languages
2. sings country music
3. acquainted with foreign countries
4. understands computers

1. famous
2. wealthy
3. unusually talented
4. good voice   _____

1. over the bridge
2. the highway
3. under the viaduct
4. around the museum   _____

1. knee bends
2. doing push-ups
3. lifting weights
4. jumping rope   _____

1. willingly
2. rapidly
3. efficiency
4. calmly   _____

1. who lived many years
2. working for the post office
3. who belonged to a union
4. who founded a political party   _____

1. to participate in sports
2. to build electronic gadgets
3. how to draw blueprints
4. to develop photographs   _____

1. afternoon
2. in the evening
3. before lunch
4. at bedtime   _____

Exercise II

Parallelism

Circle the nonparallel part in each sentence and rewrite the sentence so that all parts are parallel.

Example: She was young, ambitious, and (had a lot of talent.)

She was young, ambitious, and talented.

1. He is articulate, sociable, and has a lot of poise.

   _____

   _____

2. We searched on the sidewalk, in the vestibule, and even looked in the theater.

   _____

   _____

3. Shirley knows how to make films, choreograph musicals, and can even play the viola.

   _____

   _____

4. When you are shopping for a home computer, be sure to compare prices, talk with friends who own computers, find out about built-in software, and asking advice of people who work with computers.

   _____

   _____

5. As a child, Melanie was extroverted, liked to take charge, and organized.

   _____

   _____

6. The vehicle started, stopped suddenly, and was going in reverse.

   _____

   _____

7. Casually, confident, and purposefully, she began her presentation.

   _____

   _____

Parallelism

Have the members of your writing group interview one another, collecting facts about one another's education, hobbies, and personal traits. Write three parallel sentences about the other person, the first telling about three facts of the person's schooling, the second identifying three ways the person spends his or her spare time, and the third mentioning at least three traits that the person says he or she possesses. Read all of the sentences aloud, and examine them for parallel construction. If any seem faulty, the group should discuss how to improve them.

Mixed Sentences

Some writers have problems putting the words of their sentences together. They may leave out necessary words, phrase ideas awkwardly, put words in the wrong order, or use words in the wrong form—as nouns instead of adjectives, for example. Such problems either make the sentences hard to understand or make them read awkwardly. What is wrong with these sentences?

1. In trying to swim with her clothes on was difficult.
2. I wondered was she the right girl for me.
3. Tim was a quarterback belonged on a professional team.
4. Our society is too militarism.

Each of these sentences contains a familiar kind of mistake.

Sentence 1 contains a phrase that does not match the rest of the sentence: "In trying to swim" cannot be the subject of "was difficult." The sentence should read:

> Trying to swim with her clothes on was difficult.

Or

> In trying to swim with her clothes on, she had difficulty.

Sentence 2 contains words in the wrong order. The sentence begins as a statement, then switches to a question. The sentence should read:

> I wondered if she was the right girl for me.

Or

> Was she the right girl for me?

Sentence 3 has a word missing. The sentence should read:

Tim was a quarterback *who* belonged on a professional team.

Sentence 4 contains a word used in the wrong form. *Militarism* is a noun when the word needed is an adjective. The sentence should read:

Our society is too *militaristic*.

Exercise I

Mixed Sentences

Each of the following sentences contains a phrase that does not fit. Rewrite the sentence so that all parts fit together.

1. By agreeing to their demands was a sure way to get the hostages killed.

   _____

   _____

2. In studying the review sheets helped him do well on the test.

   _____

   _____

3. While listening to the radio announcement caused him to forget the number.

   _____

   _____

4. After growing up in San Francisco was why she liked art and culture.

   _____

   _____

5. By leaving their charge cards at home kept them from spending too much.

   _____

   _____

Sentences 6 and 7 contain mixed-up word order. Rewrite the sentences with the phrasing straightened out.

6. She wondered should she get a master's degree in business.

_____

_____

7. Tony wanted to know did they believe everything they heard on television.

_____

_____

Exercise II

Mixed Sentences

Each of the following sentences has a word or set of words missing. Indicate where the word is missing with a caret (^) and write the missing word or words above the line.

Example: She was a worker ^ never shunned a difficult task.
who

1. A college degree is an investment never loses its value.

2. After the argument were too tired to keep on talking.

3. Because of low hourly pay isn't easy for many families maintain a good standard of living.

4. A heavy drinker can't control his habit may need psychiatric help.

5. There too many politicians who care more about winning than about helping their country.

6. Although it was too late to order breakfast, was too early for lunch.

7. Tom and Sandy be in Chicago when you visit in July.

Exercise III

Mixed Sentences

In the following sentences, a word appears in the wrong form. Cross out the word and write the correct form above it.

interesting
Example: The lyrics were not very ~~interested.~~

1. Some people insist that America is still a sexism society.

2. *Santa Evita* is a very interested novel.

3. How you dress for a job interview is very importance.

4. The assailant was not presence when the police arrived.

5. The traffic on the beltway was worst today than it was yesterday.

6. Working with children takes a lot of patients.

7. In his day there were few education opportunities.

 ## If English Is Not Your First Language

Students who learn English as a second language may have difficulties using **articles** (*the, a,* and *an*). Some languages do not use articles at all, and others use them differently than English does. There are even slight differences between how Americans use them and how the British use them (we say "in *the* hospital"; the British say "in hospital"). Mastering the use of articles takes time and experience speaking English, but it will help to notice a few patterns.

- Use *a* and *an* before nouns that can be counted: *a* college, *an* airplane, *a* gold album
- Do not use *a* and *an* before abstract or general noncount nouns: happiness, not *a* happiness; excitement, not *an* excitement; inflation, not *an* inflation
- Use *the* before a noun referring to a specific thing, place, or person: *the* car, *the* airplane, *the* album, *the* teacher, *the* United States

Exercise IV

Mixed Sentences and Use of Articles (for ESL Students)

If the sentence is correct, mark C in the blank. If an article is missing, mark an X over the place where it should be, and write the correct article in the blank. If the sentence contains an article that does not belong, circle the incorrect article.

Example:

_the___   X
                We came to United States four years ago.

_____ 1. We knew that she felt a gratitude for the help we had given her.

_____ 2. He was worried because he had exam the next morning.

_____ 3. She was busying studying the American history.

_____ 4. The company gave him an extra day off.

_____ 5. The class discussed topic of drug addiction.

_____ 6. Freshman are invited to workshop on the purpose of a liberal arts degree.

_____ 7. George found the economics to be an interesting subject.

_____ 8. Sherri and Eric were looking for apartment near the campus.

_____ 9. The books assigned for the course are available in the bookstore.

_____ 10. Congress may make changes in policies toward the immigration.

Punctuation

The major elements of punctuation are commas, apostrophes, end of sentence marks, semicolons, and colons.

COMMAS

Know the rules for commas, and use commas only according to the rules. Putting in too many commas does more harm than leaving some out. Use commas:

1. in dates and place names
2. in a series and between several adjectives in a row
3. after introductory phrases and clauses
4. before and after interrupters
5. before and after nonrestrictive who and which clauses
6. before and after appositives
7. before short conjunctions in compound sentences
8. before and after persons spoken to
9. before and after contrasting parts
10. before and after direct quotations
11. in correspondence
12. to prevent confusion

Commas in Dates and Place Names

Put commas between the day of the week, the date, and the year. Most writers use a comma after the year as well:

He was born on Wednesday, January 6, 1910, and grew up in Ohio.

Many writers do not put a comma between the month and year:

The Chicago fire occurred in October 1871.

Separate a street address from the city and the city from the state or country, but do not put a comma before the zip code:

He worked at 199 Chambers Street, New York, New York 10007.

Exercise
Commas in Dates and Place Names

Insert commas where they are needed.

1. Jackie Robinson was born in Cairo Georgia on January 31 1919.
2. President Kennedy was assassinated on November 22 1963 in Dallas Texas.
3. Richard Nixon left the White House on August 8 1974.
4. Astronauts landed on the moon in July 1969.
5. The address is 1600 Broadway New York New York 10019.
6. She was born on Wednesday October 10 1968.
7. On May 6 1974 they were married in Cincinnati Ohio.

Commas in a Series and Between Several Adjectives in a Row

Place a comma after each element in a series except the last one; the comma before *and* is considered necessary in college writing, though newspapers often leave it out.

Preferred: They ate sandwiches, potato salad, and pie for lunch.
Informal and
News Style: They ate sandwiches, potato salad and pie for lunch.

A series can contain any kind of words or phrases.

Nouns: Books, records, and magazines lay on the table.
Verbs: We ate, drank, sang, and danced at the party.
Pronouns: I think that you, we, and they all look alike.
Adjectives: The letters were terse, hard–hitting, and factual.
Adverbs: The Jets played aggressively, efficiently, and shrewdly.
Prepositions: The detective looked in, around, over, and under the safe.
Phrases: The company preferred sales managers who were cordial with employees, knew the business, and demonstrated loyalty to the organization.

Exercise I
Commas in Series

Put commas where they belong in these series. One sentence does not need commas.

1. We toured China Japan and the Philippines.
2. The invitations were sent the presents were bought and the house was decorated for the party.
3. The child ran and ran and finally caught up with the dog.
4. Slowly delicately thoughtfully and thoroughly she explained the problem.
5. Separation from home from parents from a spouse or from friends produces anxiety.
6. Pay attention to the rhythm the notes and the dynamics at the same time.
7. Make your essays concise fluent and cohesive.

Exercise II

Commas in Series

Write four sentences using commas to separate items in a series.

1. _____

2. _____

3. _____

4. _____

Commas Separating Coordinate Adjectives

Several adjectives in a row modifying the same noun are called **coordinate adjectives.** They should be separated by commas if you could put *and* between the adjectives in place of the comma: a large, comfortable room (compare with a large *and* comfortable room). Do not put a comma between the last adjective and the noun.

> an intimidating, overpowering defense
> an enchanting, imaginative, subtle performance
> a squat, talkative official
> a large, hairy, playful sheepdog

In these examples you could put *and* between the adjectives: a large *and* hairy *and* playful sheepdog. When you cannot put *and* between the adjectives, do not use commas:

> a fine old chair (not a fine *and* old chair)
> a navy blue beach towel (not a navy *and* blue *and* beach towel)

Exercise I

Commas Between Coordinate Adjectives

Put commas where they are needed. Remember to test each series of adjectives by putting *and* between them.

1. She always wrote prompt courteous lively notes.
2. An ambitious young woman joined the faculty.
3. The counselor was prepared for a quarrelsome rebellious student.
4. A well-polished 1980 Corvette was parked next to a tired-looking over-loaded Ford pickup.
5. Talkative entertaining vital people attended the meeting.

Exercise II

Commas Between Coordinate Adjectives

Write four sentences using commas correctly between coordinate adjectives.

1. _____

2. _____

3. _____

4. _____

Commas After Introductory Phrases and Clauses

Put commas after most introductory words, phrases, and clauses:

> Well, you can never be sure.
> No, that is not a good idea.
> Otherwise, the plan will work.
> A few hours later, she began to cry.
> When you have finished reading the article, may I borrow the magazine?

Interjections (single words at the beginning like *well, yes, oh,* and *ah*) are followed by commas. **Interrupting words** like *however, otherwise, meanwhile, first, nevertheless,* and *consequently,* when they begin a sentence, should be followed by a comma. **Interrupting phrases** (also called **parenthetical phrases**) like *of course, by the way, after all,* and *in a sense* normally take commas as well when they begin a sentence. Short **descriptive phrases** like *in a minute, after the game, next to the produce, along the railing,* and *during the performance* are usually followed by commas.

Sometimes, however, they fit smoothly into the sentence and do not need them. Compare these two examples:

> After a thirty-minute wait, she saw the doctor.
> In the fifth problem there was a typographical error.

In the first sentence, the introductory phrase has a pause after it and should be followed by a comma. In the second sentence, the introductory phrase is necessary to the statement and reads better without a comma after it.

Whole clauses (word groups containing subject-verb combinations) normally are followed by commas when they begin sentences:

> Although the pay was good, the job was unsatisfactory.
> When he thought about the past year, he felt pleased.
> Since you joined the faculty, the students have been ecstatic.
> Because the message was translated, we could understand it.

Exercise I

Commas After Introductory Parts

Put commas where they are needed after introductory parts in these sentences. If the sentence is correct without a comma, write C after it.

1. Yes this segment of *The Young and the Restless* is certainly absorbing.★
2. Having read the letter Stan sent before he died of AIDS-related complications Keesha is devastated to realize she could be infected.
3. Instead of going to her regular doctor Keesha visits another physician.
4. When the results come back positive the new doctor gives the results to her primary care physician.
5. Taking her baby along Phyllis joins Peter on a business trip to Orlando without telling her husband where she is going.
6. When Danny finds out where she is staying he shows up at their hotel.
7. Unhappily for Phyllis he has not come with the intent to reunite with her.
8. Pretending to be a doctor Matt sneaks into Amy's room at Fairview Sanitarium.
9. As they begin making love Amy remembers that Matt raped her.
10. After Amy gives a statement to Nick's lawyers and Sharon informs him of his impending release Nick is overjoyed.

★Adaptation of "The Young and the Restless," *Soap Opera Digest* 17, (January 30, 1996): 134–135. Reprinted by permission of K-III Magazine Corporation.

> **Exercise II**

Commas After Introductory Parts

Compose sentences using commas after the introductory parts suggested.

1. Write a sentence beginning with a one-word interjection like *yes, no, oh,* or *well.*

    _____

    _____

2. Write a sentence that begins with an interrupting word like *otherwise, meanwhile, consequently, however,* or *nevertheless.*

    _____

    _____

3. Write a sentence that begins with a dependent clause in which the first word is *although, because, since, if,* or *when.*

    _____

    _____

4. Write a sentence beginning with a prepositional phrase like *after a few minutes, during the semester,* or *in the beginning.*

    _____

    _____

Commas Before and After Interrupters★

Sentence interrupters, or **parenthetical expressions** (think of *parentheses* before and after a phrase), are separated from the rest of the sentence by commas. When they appear in the middle of a sentence, put commas before and after them. Of course, when they come at the beginning, you can't put a comma before them; when they come at the end, you put a period after them.

Here are some of the common interrupters:

however	of course	as a matter of fact
consequently	by the way	for example
nevertheless	in a sense	in fact
to be sure	in my opinion	in the first place

These interrupters are usually set off by *pairs* of commas:

> She knew, *by the way,* that the television set didn't work.

★See Free Modifiers in Unit 4.

The subway, *in my opinion,* is too noisy.
The check, *however,* will not be honored at this bank.

Descriptive phrases containing past participles and present participles (*-ing* verb forms) after a noun often serve as interrupters as well:

The captain, *puzzled by the strange blips on the radar screen,* cut the speed of the craft.
An immigrant stonemason, *hoping for steady work,* appeared in the office.

Adjective phrases that come after nouns are also set off by pairs of commas.

The instructions, *dense and hard to read,* gave them little aid.
Two fathers, *anxious about their sons' grades,* called the principal.

Exercise I

Commas Around Interrupters

Put commas *before* and *after* the interrupting phrases in these sentences.

1. The income tax laws complicated and confusing take up volumes.
2. The causes of alcoholism in my opinion are both psychological and physiological.
3. Students without courses in chemistry will however have to fulfill their science requirements later.
4. Professional sports according to many fans have changed from a religion to show business.
5. Some people as a matter of fact still believe in exorcism.
6. Investors cautious about the latest changes in the prime rate did little trading on Thursday.
7. Some new cars for example have too much fiberglass.

Exercise II

Commas Around Interrupters

Write sentences modeled after the ones below, using commas before and after interrupters.

1. Write a sentence using a one-word interrupter like *consequently* or *however.*

Model sentence: The money, *however,* had all been spent for groceries.

Your sentence: _____

_____

2. Write a sentence using an interrupting phrase like *in my opinion, by the way,* or *as a matter of fact.*

Model sentence: This book, *by the way,* belongs to the library.

    Your sentence: _____

    _____

3. Write a sentence using a participial phrase after the subject.

Model sentence: The commercial, *designed to heighten public interest in health foods,* ran for two months.

    Your sentence: _____

    _____

4. Write a sentence using an adjective phrase after a noun.

Model Sentence: The lion, *hungry and weary from the pursuit,* charged at the hunters.

    Your sentence: _____

    _____

Commas Before and After Relative Clauses

Descriptive clauses beginning with *who, which,* or *that* are called **relative clauses.** Relative clauses beginning with *who* or *which* are sometimes set off by commas. Here are the rules:

> *Do not* set off restrictive clauses with commas.
> *Do* set off nonrestrictive clauses with commas.

What are **restrictive clauses?** Restrictive clauses contain information necessary to the meaning of the sentence and therefore should not be separated from the rest of the sentence by any marks of punctuation.

> *Example 1:* Students who receive A grades may skip the second course.

The clause *who receive A grades* should not be separated by commas because without it the sentence "Students . . . may skip the second course" means something completely different.

> *Example 2:* The essay that won the prize was about illiteracy.

The clause *that won the prize* is restrictive; without it, the sentence does not specify which essay was about illiteracy.

> *Example 3:* The town in which the research took place was in California.

The clause *in which the research took place* is restrictive because the sentence has no specific meaning without it.

What are **nonrestrictive clauses?** Nonrestrictive clauses are relative clauses beginning with *who* or *which* (clauses beginning with *that* are always restrictive). Nonrestrictive clauses add extra details to the sentence but are not crucial to the meaning.

Example 1: Electronic mail, which sends messages instantaneously, is beginning to replace "snail mail," as some call the postal service.

The clause *which sends messages instantaneously* is nonrestrictive because it merely adds information but is not crucial to the meaning of the sentence.

Example 2: Philip Johnson, who designed some of America's most interesting buildings, failed the New York State licensing examination.

The clause *who designed some of America's most interesting buildings* is nonrestrictive because it adds information but is not necessary to identify the subject, Philip Johnson, whose name is already given.

Exercise I

Commas with Relative Clauses

Put commas before and after the relative clauses in these sentences if the clauses add descriptions of subjects that are already specific. Do not add commas if the subjects are vague and need the clause to identify them. (Note: A relative clause at the end of a sentence, of course, ends with a period.)

1. Dorothy Day who was a famous journalist and creative writer supported the cause of American socialism.
2. A person who lives in luxury may have a misunderstanding of poverty and unemployment.
3. Acronyms which are short words formed by the initials of other words have become widely used.
4. CREEP which stood for Committee to Reelect the President was an acronym used during the Nixon administration.
5. An acronym that is familiar to most people is SNAFU, a combination that stands for "situation normal; all fouled up."
6. CINCUS which meant Commander in Chief, U.S. Fleet was an acronym that had to be abandoned after Pearl Harbor.
7. A person who specializes in pediatrics needs patience and humor.
8. Alfred Kinsey who was a pioneer in sex research was known in high school as the boy who never had a girlfriend.

9. Elvis Presley who was to become the most famous popular singer in his era failed his first audition for the Arthur Godfrey show.

10. The population of the world which is now almost 6 billion is increasing rapidly.

Exercise II

Commas with Relative Clauses

Write sentences using *who, which,* and *that* clauses as follows:

1. Write a sentence using a *which* clause that contains extra information; use commas to set off the clause.

Model sentence: My Ford Mustang, *which has stayed in the garage for six months,* needs a new battery.

Your sentence:_____

_____

2. Write a sentence with a *that* clause that identifies the subject and is not set off by commas.

Model sentence: A car *that has been left unattended* may be stolen.

Your sentence:_____

_____

3. Write a *who* clause that contains extra information; use commas to set off the clause.

Model sentence: My brother Edward, *who attends the University of Illinois,* is an economics major.

Your sentence:_____

_____

4. Write a *who* clause that identifies the subject and is not set off by commas.

Model sentence: A student *who majors in economics* must also take courses in statistics and sociology.

Your sentence:_____

_____

Commas Before and After Appositives

Appositives are phrases that come after nouns or pronouns and describe or identify them. They are usually set off by pairs of commas:

Arno, *the great cartoonist,* was voted America's best–dressed man in 1941.

Neil Armstrong, *the first man to step on the moon,* earned his pilot's license when he was 16.

Some very short appositives are not separated by commas:

The *Emperor Nero* was a psychopath.

My sister Karen will join us.

Exercise

Commas with Appositives

Put commas before and after the appositives in these sentences unless they are very short and read without a pause.

1. Samuel Taylor Coleridge a romantic poet of the nineteenth century was a heavy user of opium.
2. My uncle Ted used to be an opera singer.
3. Sandra the youngest member of the board voted for the proposal.
4. Dr. Benjamin Spock the author of the famous book on baby care joined the peace movement in the 1960s.
5. Malcolm X the Black Muslim political leader studied languages and history in prison.
6. Jason the smartest student in his biology class explained how to dissect a frog.
7. A. Philip Randolph the great labor leader organized a union of Pullman car workers.

Commas Before Short Conjunctions in Compound Sentences

Use a comma plus a short conjunction to link independent clauses in compound sentences. The short conjunctions are *and, but, or, for, nor,* and *so.* Remember to put commas *before* them but not *after.*

Independent clause	*Independent clause*

1. The location was desirable, *and* the price was reasonable.
2. Efforts were made by the police, *but* no suspects were found.
3. You may pay by check today, *or* you may have the store bill you later.
4. The first group stayed in the city, *for* they came from urban environments themselves.
5. The passengers were not injured, *nor* was the boat seriously damaged.
6. Sally had visited Puerto Rico before, *so* she knew where to eat in San Juan.

Remember that these short connectives are used in other ways and often do not have commas before them when they connect shorter parts such as words or phrases:

Ted *and* Mary took a walk along the shore. (*And* joins two subjects.)

The prizes went to Sam *and* Alice, *and* the awards for leadership went to Beverly. (First *and* connects two nouns; the second joins two independent clauses.)

The engine *but* not the suspension system was rebuilt. (*But* joins two subjects.)

I suggest the veal *or* the shrimp. (*Or* joins two nouns.)

Neither the acting *nor* the script was exceptional. (*Nor* joins two subjects.)

The beach was *so* beautiful that they went swimming as soon as they arrived. (*So* used with *that* is an adverb—no comma.)

Exercise I

Commas Before Conjunctions

Put commas before short conjunctions that join independent clauses in these sentences. Do not put commas before them if they join shorter elements.

1. I like to study with the radio on but this music makes me nervous.
2. Buying lottery tickets gives me a sense of adventure and I always expect to win a million dollars next time.
3. You can turn left at the next light or you can follow the main highway for three blocks.
4. The history of World War II and the history of socialism are both special interests of Professor Jones.
5. My cat is ill so I plan to take her to the veterinarian.
6. The college has room for 900 freshmen but 1500 high school seniors have applied for admission.
7. The view was so breathtaking that they stared at it for hours.

Exercise II

Commas Before Conjunctions

Compose your own compound sentences using the following short connectives. Put commas before the connectives: 1. *and* 2. *but* 3. *or* 4. *for* 5. *so* 6. *nor*

Commas Before and After Persons Spoken to (Direct Address)

When you speak directly to a person, using his or her name in a sentence, separate the name from the rest of the sentence. Use commas in pairs unless the name comes at the beginning or end of the sentence:

I remember, *Martha,* how you looked in high school.
Martha, I remember how you looked in high school.
I remember how you looked in high school, *Martha.*

Omitting these commas may change the meaning: "I remember Martha" is not the same as "I remember, Martha."

Exercise I

Commas with Direct Address

Put commas in these sentences to separate the names of persons spoken to from the rest of the sentence.

1. You know Steve that the rest of us agree with you.
2. Barbara will you please give me some advice.
3. These are the photos that you took in Arizona Richard.
4. You may find Gladys that you like the other therapist better.
5. Herman can we send you a brochure about life insurance?
6. Here is good news cardholders for those of you planning to travel.
7. Tony please describe the area.

Exercise II

Commas with Direct Address

Write three sentences of your own using commas to separate the name of a person spoken to from the rest of the sentence.

1. Sentence with the name at the beginning:

_____

2. Sentence with the name in the middle (two commas):

_____

3. Sentence with the name at the end:

_____

Commas Before and After Contrasting Parts

Use commas before and after contrasting phrases beginning with *not:*

The Yankees, *not the Dodgers,* won that series.
The weather was cooler, *not warmer,* than predicted.
The capital of Pennsylvania is Harrisburg, *not Philadelphia.*

Exercise I

Commas with Contrasting Elements

Put commas in these sentences to separate contrasting elements.

1. The women not the men supported the action.
2. Arkansas not Tennessee was the first state to open a branch.
3. Lessons are available in karate not kung fu.
4. The clocks should be set forward not back.
5. Drive through the intersection not onto the service road.
6. Ham and cheese not liverwurst is what I ordered.
7. These sweaters come in blue not green.

Exercise II

Commas with Contrasting Elements

Write three sentences of your own using contrasting elements—one with the contrasting parts at the beginning, one with them in the middle, and one with them at the end.

Commas Before and After Direct Quotations

Before quoting a whole statement, put a comma after the introductory word (*said, stated, asked,* and so on):

He *said,* "This is the road to Seattle."
She *asked,* "Will this book explain how to sell real estate?"
The catalog *stated,* "This course includes intermediate algebra."

Put commas after quotations when the quotations come at the beginning of sentences. Commas belong inside quotation marks:

"*After dinner, let's play Scrabble,*" Sue suggested.
"*Don't leave any questions blank,*" the instructor said.

Short quoted phrases often fit smoothly into the sentence and should not be set off by commas:

Trevor called his brother a *"universal genius."*
Joanne was often called the *"Whitney Houston look-alike."*
Shakespeare called music the *"food of love."*

Exercise I

Commas with Quotations

Use commas to separate the following quotations. Do not use commas when a short quoted phrase fits smoothly into the sentence.

1. Sheila said "You have the same opinion I do."
2. "Let's meet in the cafeteria for lunch" Harry suggested.
3. They termed the procedure "a computerized approach to gambling on sports."
4. "I admire your determination" the manager said. "However, there are some errors in the reports."
5. The author stated "Few crime statistics reveal the source of the problem."
6. "The first day may be difficult" she explained.
7. Sandra asked "Why should we wait for them to call us?"

Exercise II

Commas with Quotations

Write three sentences of your own. In the first, put the *he said* or *she said* before the quotation; in the second, put the quotation first. In the third, fit a short quoted phrase into your sentence without a comma.

Commas in Correspondence

In business letters and personal letters, the closing is always followed by a comma:

Business Letters	*Personal Letters and Notes*
Sincerely yours,	Yours truly,
Yours very truly,	Yours,
Yours truly,	As always,
Cordially yours,	Best wishes,
	Love,
	Yours,

In personal letters, put commas after the greeting:

Dear Janet,	Dear Mom,
Dear Tom,	Dear Grandpa,

Commas to Prevent Confusion

Occasionally, you may need a comma to separate words that might appear to belong together when the meaning requires that they be separated. Watch especially for prepositions (*in, around, over, through,* etc.) that appear to go with the words after them when they do not:

> *Inside,* the room looked bright and airy. (*Inside the room* is not a phrase to be read together.)
> *Not long after,* the candidates gave speeches. (*After the candidates gave speeches* is not meant to be a clause.)
> *All around,* the landscape looked lush and mysterious. (*Around the landscape* should not be read as a phrase.)

Exercise

Commas to Prevent Confusion

Put commas in these sentences to prevent confusion.

1. Far and near the house and the whole property were snowbound.
2. I knew that when he thought it over the top figure would not seem very high.
3. The board decided that if the company ever went under the margin of profit among the competitors would increase.
4. It appeared that when the auditors were through the office would be more relaxed.
5. People who can usually buy cars on credit.
6. Those who should always win early promotions.
7. Joe thought that since he had enough to get by the funds that remained in the trust were not necessary to him.

APOSTROPHES

Apostrophes are used for two purposes.

Uses of Apostrophes

1. Use apostrophes in contractions, where letters have been left out:

   do not = don't
   should not = shouldn't

2. Use apostrophes to indicate possession:

   's for singular possessives: Karen's dress
   s' for plural possessives: four students' grades

Exception: plurals that do not take *s,* such as *men* or *children,* take *'s* in the possessive:

   men's hats
   children's games

Some Common Mistakes

- Carelessly leaving apostrophes out of contractions: *dont,* instead of *don't; shes,* instead of *she's; wouldnt,* instead of *wouldn't*
- Writing possessives without apostrophes: *Karens* dress, instead of *Karen's* dress; *womens* opinions, instead of *women's* opinions
- Putting apostrophes in the wrong place: my *mothers'* attitudes, instead of my *mother's* attitudes; *its'* cold, instead of *it's* cold
- Using apostrophes with personal pronouns: write *hers,* not *her's; yours,* not *your's* (Impersonal pronouns do take apostrophes: *everyone's* opinions; *somebody's* car.)

Exercise I

Apostrophes

Circle the correct form in parentheses.

1. The English language (doesn't, dosen't, doesnt) go back as far in history as Latin and Greek.
2. According to most (experts, expert's, experts') opinions, Old English, or Anglo-Saxon, (didnt, did'nt, didn't) exist in the time of the ancient Greeks.
3. Old English, in any case (couldn't, could'nt, couldnt) really be called English as we speak it.
4. Many influences altered the way English was spoken over the centuries, but English (hasnt, has'nt, hasn't) lost its basic structure.
5. After the Norman Conquest in A.D. 1066, the biggest change in English came from the French (aristocrats', aristocrat's, aristocrats) speech.
6. Consequently, most languages (cant, can't, cann't) compete with English for richness of vocabulary.
7. Still, people in (Shakespeare, Shakespeares', Shakespeare's) time (would'nt, wouldnt, wouldn't) have guessed how widespread their language would become.

Exercise II

Apostrophes

Write the correct contractions or possessives for each of the phrases given.

Examples:

have not   *haven't*

The coat belonging to Sam   *Sam's coat*

1. the car belonging to Lucy

2. are not

3. the opinions of students

4. will not

5. was not

6. the staff of the mayor

7. they are

8. stories for children

9. were not

10. rights of citizens

END PUNCTUATION: PERIODS, QUESTION MARKS, AND EXCLAMATION POINTS

Use periods to end statements and indirect questions:

Statement: The store had a sale on January 2.
Indirect question: Sam asked whether the store was having a sale.

Use question marks after direct questions:

> Is this book overdue?
> When will you be back?
> Why, if no one objects to the proposal, are we waiting until March to begin?

Don't forget to put the question mark at the end of long, complicated questions like the last one.

Use periods, not question marks, after requests:

> Would you please send me an application form.
> Would you please let me know if you are interested.

Use exclamation points after sentences that express excitement or strong feeling:

> Get out of my sight!
> Watch out for that elephant!
> That was a fabulous performance!

Use exclamation points after single words or phrases that express astonishment or strong emotion:

> Help!
> Stop!
> No more war!

Exercise

End Punctuation

Put the correct end punctuation after these sentences.

1. The instructor asked whether the class had read the assignment
2. If you want help, why don't you ask one of us for it
3. Get out of that van It's going to explode
4. Would you please send me travel literature and maps of Florida
5. Will you be spending your vacation in Greece
6. Ask for the color and size that you want
7. If the restaurant is open, shall I make a reservation

SEMICOLONS

Use **semicolons** to separate independent clauses in compound sentences when there are no short connectives.

> Children of illegal aliens often attend public schools; some states have asked the federal government to pay for the cost of their education.
> Buying on credit has disadvantages; one may overestimate one's ability to pay.

Semicolons, not commas, should also be used to separate independent clauses when there is a long connective word (a conjunctive adverb) like *however, therefore, meanwhile, nevertheless, consequently,* or *moreover* between the clauses. Use a comma <u>after</u> the connecting word:

> Separate conference rooms are available for the two meetings; *however,* you may convene together afterward if you like.
> We have already sent you a brochure; *meanwhile,* we are awaiting your request.

Use semicolons to separate independent clauses with the word *then* between them. *Then* is not a short connecting word like *and;* do not put a comma before it:

© 1998 by Addison-Wesley Educational Publishers Inc.

Not: We always swim at four o'clock, then we do aerobics.

But: We always swim at four o'clock; then we do aerobics.

Use semicolons to separate parts of a series when the individual parts have commas within them:

She had lived in Dallas, Texas; San Mateo, California; and Stamford, Connecticut.

You will have to pass three examinations: a reading test, in multiple-choice format; a writing test, in the form of a one-hour essay; and a mathematics test, given on a computer.

Exercise I

Semicolons

Put a C next to the correctly punctuated sentence in each pair.

_____ 1. The road was bumpy; it caused many blowouts and accidents.
_____   The road was bumpy, it caused many blowouts and accidents.

_____ 2. A medical checkup every few years may not seem necessary, however, it could save your life.
_____   A medical checkup every few years may not seem necessary; however, it could save your life.

_____ 3. Exploring the planets strikes some people as a waste of money; but we never know what benefits may come from it.
_____   Exploring the planets strikes some people as a waste of money, but we never know what benefits may come from it.

_____ 4. The cast will include Rosalinda, playing a therapist, Victor, playing a jazz musician, and Wanda, playing a screenwriter.
_____   The cast will include Rosalinda, playing a therapist; Victor, playing a jazz musician; and Wanda, playing a screenwriter.

_____ 5. We used to go surfing on Saturday afternoons, then we would bake clams on the beach.
_____   We used to go surfing on Saturday afternoons; then we would bake clams on the beach.

_____ 6. The police had not enforced the law against selling marijuana; therefore, the two men were surprised to be arrested.
_____   The police had not enforced the law against selling marijuana, therefore the two men were surprised to be arrested.

_____ 7. Three special dates in Nicole's life are January 15, 1982; May 24, 1985; and October 10, 1991.

_____ Three special dates in Nicole's life are January 15, 1982, May 24, 1985, and October 10, 1991.

Exercise II

Semicolons

Write sentences of your own using semicolons.

1. Write a sentence using a semicolon with no connecting word.

Model sentence: The course is too easy; you should take a more advanced one.

Your sentence:_____

_____

3. Write a sentence using a semicolon before _however._

Model sentence: We appreciate your concern; however, the bill cannot be reduced.

Your sentence:_____

_____

4. Write a sentence using a semicolon before _meanwhile._

Model sentence: The student government will vote on the issue next Monday; meanwhile, students are signing a petition.

Your sentence:_____

_____

5. Write a sentence using a semicolon before _then._

Model sentence: Lay the wooden pieces on the diagram; then glue them together at the corners.

Your sentence:_____

_____

COLONS

The **colon**(:) is used to introduce something. Use colons after _as follows_ or _the following_ to introduce lists:

She called out the following names: Roberta, Carl, Tracy, Janice, and Lamont.

Open the bottle as follows: press down on the lid, align the arrows, and turn lid to the left.

Use colons when you introduce a list formally:

The ceremony will proceed in this order: first the procession into the auditorium, next the speeches, and finally the presentation of degrees.

A reader can enjoy the book except for a few shortcomings: its unrealistic plot, its difficult style, and its improbable ending.

Use colons to separate main clauses in compound sentences when the second clause explains the first:

Joan approached the interview with only one thought in mind: She intended to show them that she understood the job.

Do not use colons after informal introductory expressions (*like, such as, including,* or the abbreviation *e.g.*):

| Not: | We ordered five books including: *Like Water for Chocolate.* |
| Better: | We ordered five books, including *Like Water for Chocolate.* |

| Not: | You need three liberal arts electives, such as: sociology, history, and literature. |
| Better: | You need three liberal arts electives, such as sociology, history, and literature. |

| Not: | You need to eat more nutritious food, e.g.: oat bran and citrus fruit. |
| Better: | You need to eat more nutritious food, e.g., oat bran and citrus fruit. |

EXERCISE 1

Colons

Insert colons in any of the following sentences where they belong.

1. In the spring of 1997, scientists made an important announcement a sheep had been successfully cloned.
2. Before that, cloning had been successful only on simpler forms of life such as plants and amphibians.
3. Later it was announced that a still more dramatic step had been taken the cloning of two monkeys.

4. These exciting breakthroughs raised speculations in the following areas of study biology, physics, philosophy, psychology, and law.

5. President Clinton soon took a stand on the ethical issue he discouraged any attempts to clone human beings.

6. Some religious leaders disapproved of human cloning in the following ways calling for laws banning the cloning of human beings, preaching against human cloning, and expressing moral outrage in television interviews and debates.

7. Some scientists, however, explained some possible benefits of animal cloning including medical research, improvement of livestock, and understanding of growth process.

8. Laws against cloning human beings will not prevent the practice for one chief reason U.S. laws do not control what scientists do in other countries.

9. There is one question people are asking each other everywhere who is the person you would most like to see cloned?

10. In all these discussions we should bear one fact in mind the clone of a person would be genetically the same as that person but different in other ways such as experience and education.

Exercise II

Colons

Write sentences using colons.

1. Write a sentence using *as follows* to introduce a list.

Model sentence: Do the procedure as follows: remove the lid, loosen the blue and green wires from their terminals, and attach them to the terminals on the left side.

Your sentence:_____

_____

2. Write a sentence using *the following* to introduce a list.

Model sentence: The course included the following topics: geriatric nursing, nursing the handicapped, and surgical nursing.

Your sentence:_____

_____

3. Write a sentence introducing a list with a formal statement.

Model sentence: The new model possesses these features: a tinted windshield, a cassette tapedeck, rear speakers, and a rear window.

    Your sentence:_____

_____

4. Write a sentence in which the second independent clause explains or completes the first.

Model sentence: Sam knew exactly what he would do next: He would forget Susan and ask Pauline for a date.

    Your sentence:_____

_____

5. Write a sentence using *such as* to introduce a list; do not use a colon.

Model sentence: There are many forms of entertainment in a big city, such as discos, theater, night clubs, opera, and trade fairs.

    Your sentence:_____

_____

Capitalization

Learn the rules for using capital letters.

What You Should Capitalize

- The first word of every sentence and the first word of every quoted sentence: He said, "The tape is missing."
- The word *I* and the proper name of every person: Mr. Smith, Demi Moore, Jerry Seinfeld.
- The name of every city, state, country, and other specific place name: San Juan, Puerto Rico; Yankee Stadium, Golden Gate Park.
- The name of every day of the week, month, and holiday: Monday, October, Thanksgiving Day (but *not* spring, summer, fall, and winter).
- The title of every book, play, magazine, short story, film, song, or television show: "The Oprah Winfrey Show," *Time Magazine, A Raisin*

---

in the Sun, Gone with the Wind. (Note: Little words like *of, the* and *a* are not capitalized unless they begin a title.)

- The name of a company, organization, religion, school, or college: The Ford Motor Company, Livingston High School, Carleton College, St. Luke's Church. (Note: Do not capitalize words like *church, high school, company,* or *college* if they are not part of a specific name.

- The name of a specific product: Coca Cola, Wheaties, Rolls-Royce. (Note: Do not capitalize the word for the category of product: A Mack truck, Smirnoff vodka, English toffee.)

- A person's nationality: a French woman, a Japanese student, a Canadian hockey player, a Native American.

- The title of a specific course: Sociology 101, Mathematics 104, American History 110. (Note: Do not capitalize subjects like sociology or mathematics when not used to name specific courses.)

Exercise I

Capital Letters

Proofread the following passage and circle the *ten* errors in capitalization.

Janet's Favorite Films

Although Janet likes most kinds of films, her favorites are about historical events and famous persons. The first film about American History she ever saw was *Gone with The Wind.* She loved it so much that she went to Video shack, bought the video of it and watched it again and again. Another old film she loved was *Spartacus,* which was about the roman Empire. She even likes old hollywood epics about the bible, like *The Ten Commandments.* More recent films portraying major events in The United States, like *Glory, Mississippi Burning,* and *The last of the Mohicans,* interest her very much. Most of all, she loves movies that tell about the lives of famous people, both good and bad, like *Gandhi, Bonnie And Clyde, Freud, Malcolm X,* and *Patton.* Janet says, "films about history and biography I always like best. One I didn't like was a silent film called *The Birth of a Nation* because it was so racist."

Exercise II

Capital Letters

Write the following, using correct capitalization:

1. The name of your college   _____

2. The name of a store where you shop   _____

3. The name of a product you use   _____

4. The name of a public official
   (with title)   _____

5. The title of a course you are taking   _____

6. The city and state in which you
   were born   _____

7. Today's date (including day of
   the week)   _____

Spelling

To become a better speller, attack the problem from several directions at once. And don't expect to improve rapidly without really concentrating and memorizing. Only a few rare people can spell correctly without effort; the rest of us need a many-sided strategy, along with old-fashioned study and repetition.

What should you do to improve your spelling?

- **Learn the patterns and rules.** Although English spelling is irregular, with most rules having exceptions, you will do well to learn the rules.
- **Master the look–alikes/sound–alikes.** A large percentage of misspellings come from words being confused with others that look or sound almost like them.
- **Drill on frequently misspelled words.** Study tricky words, or spelling "demons," especially those in your area of work or study. A corporate employee should never misspell *business* nor should a nurse misspell *medicine*.
- **Take personal responsibility for your spelling.** Don't expect any book, course, computer spelling check or teacher to work magic for you. It's up to you; make lists of your own most often misspelled words and study them.

SPELLING RULES

The first step toward spelling competence is to learn the few main patterns—even though they may have exceptions.

Rule 1: Position of *i* and *e*

You probably have heard, and may know, the old rule:

> *i* before *e*
> except after *c*
> or when sounded like *a*
> as in *neighbor* or *weigh*.

Learn the jingle if you do not already know it. But be prepared to run into many exceptions. Study the patterns.

1. *i* before *e*: Bel*ie*ve. Most words with an *e* sound do follow the rule when there is no *c* before the combination:

    ach*ie*ve (*ch,* but not *c*)
    fr*ie*nd (even though pronounced *eh*)
    f*ie*nd
    gr*ie*ve
    l*ie*n
    n*ie*ce (the *c* comes *after ie*).
    p*ie*ce
    p*ie*rce
    pr*ie*st
    rel*ie*ve
    repr*ie*ve
    retr*ie*ve
    shr*ie*k
    th*ie*f

2. Except after *c*: Rec*ei*ve. Despite exceptions, this pattern usually holds true, too:

    *ce*iling
    con*ce*ited
    con*ce*ive
    de*ce*ive
    per*ce*ive
    re*ce*ipt

3. Or when sounded like *a:* W*ei*gh. Combinations that are sounded like *a* or *i* are usually *ei:*

   *ei*ght
   fr*ei*ght
   h*ei*ght
   n*ei*ghbor
   v*ei*n
   w*ei*ght

4. Some exceptions to the rule: A few words take *ie* even though it comes after *c:*

   finan*cie*r
   so*cie*ty
   spe*cie*s

   A few *ei* words with the *e* sound and no *c* before them can fool you, too:

   *ei*ther
   l*ei*sure
   n*ei*ther
   s*ei*ze
   w*ei*rd

Rule 2: Keeping or Dropping the Final *e*

When adding an ending to a word with a final *e*, keep the *e* if the ending starts with a consonant:

   arrange + ment = arrang*e*ment
   hope + ful = hop*e*ful
   nine + ty = nin*e*ty
   sincere + ly = sincer*e*ly
   face + less = fac*e*less
   manage + ment = manag*e*ment

Drop the *e* if the ending starts with a vowel:

   give + ing = giving
   have + ing = having
   erase + ure = erasure
   locate + ion = location
   guide + ance = guidance

Exceptions: To keep a *g* or *c* soft before a vowel, we sometimes keep the *e:*

>   age + ing = ageing *or* aging
>   manage + able = manageable
>   service + able = serviceable

The word *judgment* does not keep the *e* except in British spelling. *Dyeing* keeps the *e* to prevent confusion with *dying.*

Rule 3: Doubling Final Consonants

This rule is somewhat complicated, but it does not have many exceptions and it includes many common words. Learn the pattern.

The rule applies to words like *begin, control,* and *occur.* When you add an *ed, ing,* or *er* ending to these words, do you double the final consonant? Yes: beg*inn*ing, contr*oll*ed, and occu*rr*ed.

What do these words have in common? The rule says that they **end with a single consonant** (not *ck* as in shock, or *st* as in post) **preceded by a single vowel** (not a double vowel, as in br*ea*k or m*ee*t). And the accent must be on the last syllable (not earlier, as in *travel,* where the *l* does not have to be doubled, or *pivot,* where the *t* is not doubled).

To sum up: These words contain

- A single final consonant: begi*n*
- A single vowel preceding the final consonant: beg*i*n
- An accent on the last syllable: be*gin*

Many common words follow this pattern. When you become familiar with it, the rule is extremely useful. Here are only some of the examples:

begi*nn*ing	exce*ll*ing	omi*tt*ed
commi*tt*ed	forge*tt*ing	prefe*rr*ing
contro*ll*ing	occu*rr*ing	refe*rr*ed

(The rule applies to one-syllable words as well: be*tt*ing, sto*pp*ed, so*bb*ing, etc.)

Exercise I

Spelling Rules

Some of the following words are correct, and some are misspelled. Write C next to the correct ones, and spell the others correctly in the blanks. Review the rules first; try not to guess.

1. belief	_____	11. stately	_____
2. occurance	_____	12. noticeable	_____
3. placing	_____	13. hopful	_____
4. arrangment	_____	14. movement	_____
5. weight	_____	15. chief	_____
6. percieve	_____	16. refering	_____
7. writeing	_____	17. replacment	_____
8. definitly	_____	18. removing	_____
9. achieve	_____	19. permiting	_____
10. commited	_____	20. strokeing	_____

Notice any words you did not spell correctly in the first set. Review the rules to see why the misspellings occurred; then do these twenty the same way.

1. neighbor	_____	11. niece	_____
2. loseing	_____	12. advisment	_____
3. sincerly	_____	13. controlled	_____
4. ninty	_____	14. blameless	_____
5. feirce	_____	15. exciteing	_____
6. deterring	_____	16. shamful	_____
7. combating	_____	17. forgeting	_____
8. spiteful	_____	18. height	_____
9. leaveing	_____	19. deceive	_____
10. conceited	_____	20. begining	_____

> Exercise II

Spelling Rules

Review the rules one more time, and do this exercise perfectly. Circle the correctly spelled word in each pair.

1. soceity   society
2. chaseing   chasing
3. friend   freind
4. movement   movment
5. patroling   patrolling
6. believing   beleiving
7. saving   saveing
8. practicing   practiceing
9. lovely   lovly
10. ceiling   cieling
11. placment   placement

12. thief   theif
13. priceless   pricless
14. peacful   peaceful
15. alloting   allotting

COMMON MIX-UPS

The following words are often misspelled because they contain combinations that are easily confused with those in similar words. Study the groups carefully, looking for the trouble spots.

1. ability
   responsibility
   possibility

   (The last two do *not* contain *ability*.)

2. accumulate
   accommodate
   recommend

   (Study the *c*'s and *m*'s in these common words.)

3. across
   address

   (Both are often misspelled; notice the single *c* and double *d*.)

4. alone
   along

   (Two simple words but often carelessly mixed up)

5. amount
   among

   (Be careful not to write *amoung*, even though it rhymes with *young*.)

6. arithmetic
   athletics
   mathematics

   (Not atheletics or athelete, and don't forget the *e* in *mathematics*.)

7. believe
   receive

   (These two most common *ie/ei* words do follow the rule.)

8. committee
   committing
   commitment

   (Note the single *t* in *commitment*.)

9. definitely
   immediately

   (Don't confuse *-itely* with *-ately* words.)

10. develop
    developed
    envelope

    (There is no such word as *develope*.)

11. divide
    decide

    (Not d*e*vide)

12. familiar   (The extra *i* in *familiar* gives it an extra syllable.)
    similar

13. fulfill   (Don't spell it *for*fill or *fore*fill.)
    foretell

14. necessary   (Only one *c* in *necessary,* one *s* in *occasionally,*
    occasionally   and one *f* in *professional*)
    professional

15. pastime   (Don't double that *t* in *pastime.*)
    part-time

16. accidentally   (Not public*a*lly)
    publicly

17. relevant   (Two difficult words; notice the *e*'s and *a*'s
    prevalent   and the *l*'s and *v*'s.)

18. separate   (Not sep*e*rate)
    desperate

19. surprise   (Do not write *sup*rise or *sur*pose.)
    suppose

20. strictly   (Not stric*k* or stric*k*ly)
    stick
    quickly

21. till   (Not unti*ll*)
    until

Exercise 1

Spelling Mix-ups

The following paragraph contains fifteen misspelled words. Underline them and write the correct spellings in the margin.

Writing well is definately a marketable skill that you should develope. In business, law, and medicine, effective writing is neccessary. Students who do not beleive this is true are often supprised to discover too late that they lack this important proffesional requirement. Not untill they learn the hard way—by recieving criticism of their work—do many employees realize how prevelant the demand for good writing is. Amoung executives it is understood that the committment to writing goes alone with the strickly technical aspects of a job. Colleges accross the country are publically declaring their dedication to effective career writing.

Exercise II

Spelling Mix-ups

Each of the following groups contains one misspelled word. Circle it and write the word correctly in the blank.

1. accumulate
   athletics
   seperate   _____

2. relavent
   suppose
   part–time   _____

3. decide
   similiar
   strictly   _____

4. adress
   necessary
   till   _____

5. accomodate
   publicly
   fulfill   _____

6. prevalent
   receive
   surpose   _____

7. desperate
   pastime
   devide   _____

8. occassionally
   familiar
   across   _____

9. responsability
   professional
   recommend   _____

10. definitely
    possibility
    amoung   _____

> ## Exercise III

Spelling Mix-ups

Write these misspelled words correctly.

1. accidently _____

2. immediatly _____

3. past-time _____

4. comittment _____

5. develope _____

6. athelete _____

7. beleive _____

8. reccomend _____

9. occassionally _____

10. seperate _____

PRONOUN MIX-UPS

Forms of the common pronouns—*I, you, he, she, they,* and *we*—are often confused with other words. Study the groups below; these are simple words you should know perfectly.

He, his, he's	*His* means belonging to him; *he's* is short for *he is. He's* looking for *his* wallet.
Its, it's, its'	*Its* shows possession; *it's* is short for *it is* or *it has.* The jury made *its* decision. *It's* a cool day for July. *It's* (it has) been an entertaining evening. There is no such word as *its'.*
Mine, mind, mines	Don't confuse *mine* (belonging to me) with *mind* (a smart *mind*). Although *mines* is widely spoken in dialect, there is no such pronoun in standard written English. (That pen is *mine,* not *mines.*)
Our, are, or	*Our* is possessive—belonging to us: *our* schedules. Don't confuse it with the verb *are:* Sally

and Timothy *are* married. *Or* is a connective word: Either Tom *or* Randy will wait for you.

They, their, they're there, there's, theirs	The word *they* is used as a subject, referring to a number of people or things: *They* belong to the gang. *Their* means belonging to them: *Their* ideas are right. *They're* is short for *they are*: *They're* going to be rich. *There* means at that place, or it may be just a structure word: *There* is a new hair style this year. *There's* is short for *there is* or *there has*: *There's* a noisy party upstairs. *Theirs* means belonging to them: *Theirs* is the best pizza in town.
We're, were, where, wear, ware	*We're* is short for *we are*: *We're* the first people here. *Were* is a verb: *Were* those books expensive? *Where* asks about the place something happens: *Where* did you go last night? Don't mix up *where* and *were*. They look similar but don't sound alike. *Wear,* as a verb, means to clothe: *Wear* your designer jeans. The noun *wear* also refers to clothing: Men's *wear* is sold here. *Ware* refers to equipment and utensils: hard*ware*, soft*ware*, silver*ware*. Don't confuse this with formal *wear* or evening *wear,* the noun, referring to clothing.
Who's, whose	*Who's* is short for *who is* or *who has*: *Who's* the manager of the store? *Who's* been making long distance calls? *Whose* asks about ownership: *Whose* book is this?
You're, your, yours,	*You're* is short for *you are*: *You're* never home when I call. *Your* shows possession: *Your* contract is in the mail. Use *yours,* not *yours'*: That idea was *yours*.

▶ Exercise I

Pronoun Mix-ups

The following paragraph contains fifteen misspellings. Underline them and write the correctly spelled pronouns above them.

If your having trouble remembering names and facts, its very likely that you can benefit from using memory tricks called mnemonic devices. Their the little gimmicks, like rhymes, that help people remember names, words, numbers, and spellings. Theirs a familiar device for recalling names, for instance, that is often used at parties. Each person tries to remember all the names of the people their by joining there names with crazy adjectives—Ferocious Fran, Studious Stu, and so on. Most of us find that are memories work better when we associate new names or facts this way with familiar words or traits. Suppose you meet a new acquaintance who's name is Richard, and suppose that his expensively dressed. You're easiest way to remember his name is to think of him as "rich." Its also easier to remember spelling words by using tricks. Notice were the problem letters are, and exaggerate the pronunciation: say Feb *roo* ary, for instance. Unless you're memory is sharper than mines, your going to need such mnemonic devices now and then.

▶ Exercise II

Pronoun Mix-ups

In each pair of sentences, one sentence is correct (write C in the blank) and the other contains a misspelled word. Write the corrected word in the blank.

1. They're going to join the society
next week.
The teacher is reading there scores.   _____

2. Its been a wonderful visit.   _____
The tree lost all of its bark.   _____

3. Theirs a riot going on in the suburbs.   _____
There's a new way to solve those
equations.   _____

4. We rented are house to a young couple.   _____
Our vacation this year was exciting.   _____

5. Whose been making those crank calls?   _____
Do you know whose sneakers these are?   _____

6. Where have all the customers gone?   _____
Some of them where at the parade.   _____

7. Would you mind giving me a hand?   _____
That idea was mind, not yours.   _____

Exercise III

Pronoun Mix-ups

Circle the correct words in these sentences.

1. A player (who's, whose) planning to retire usually looks for a college (were, where) a coaching job is available.
2. The trouble with (you're, your) handwriting is that I can't read it when (you're, your) writing rapidly.
3. (Are, our, or) town has cable television, and (were, where, we're) planning to make it available to rural customers.
4. (They, there, their) are seven fast food outlets between here and (there, their, they're).
5. (It, it's) been delightful meeting (your, you're) family.
6. Campers along the shore (were, where, we're) alarmed because they had been swimming (where, were, we're) the undertow was strongest.
7. The Nets won first place in (their, there, they're) division by concentrating on (their, there, they're) defense.

LOOK-ALIKES/SOUND-ALIKES

This list contains words that are often confused with each other because they look or sound alike. Say each word aloud in its example in order to hear the differences. Since these are common words, you should master all of them.

a, an, and, any	Use *a* before consonants, *an* before vowels: *a* computer, but *an* old computer. Use *an* before words beginning with silent *h:* an honest worker. Use *a* before *u* words that start with a *y* sound: *a* union leader. Use *a* before *one* because of the *w* sound: *a* one-cylinder motor. The rule is to use *a* before consonant sounds and *an* before vowel sounds. *And* is the connective word: Sam *and* his wife. *Any* refers to an amount or unit: We do not have *any* new employees.
advice, advise	Pronounce them correctly, and you will spell them correctly; *Advice* contains the word *ice:* You give *advice* (a noun). *Advise* rhymes with *wise* and is a verb: You *advise* someone.
affect, effect	*Affect* is the verb: This *affects* all of us. *Effect* is the noun: What is the *effect* of crime? (Exception—*effect* can sometimes be a verb, which means to bring about or create: Let's *effect* an improvement in communications.)
a lot, alot	Always write this as two words: We need *a lot* of financial backing. There is no such word as *alot*.
already, all ready	*Already* means now; *all ready* means prepared: It is *already* two o'clock; we are *all ready* to leave.
always, away	These do not sound alike, but because they look similar, many writers mistakenly write *alway*. Don't drop the *s*.
bought, brought	Be sure to write these as they sound; *bought* is the past tense of *buy:* We *bought* a surfboard. *Brought* is the past tense of *bring:* I *brought* it to the beach.
breath, breathe	Pronounce them. *Breath* is the noun, rhyming with *death:* I took a deep *breath*. *Breathe* is the verb, rhyming with *seethe:* Try to *breathe* through your nose.
buy, by	To *buy* is to purchase: We *buy* merchandise. *By* is usually a preposition: We pass *by* the museum.

choose, chose	The present form is *choose*—rhymes with *news:* I *choose* a different program each week. *Chose* is the past tense—rhymes with *rose:* Last month we *chose* the spot for our vacation.
conscience, conscious	Your *conscience* (pronounce it: kon shuntz) is your sense of right and wrong: Let your *conscience* be your guide. To be *conscious* (kon shuss) is to be aware: She was *conscious* of someone approaching.
convenience, convince	Listen to the sound: *convenience* (kun veenyuntz). I'll do it at your *convenience*. I'll *convince* (kun vintz) you to buy it.
does, dose	Notice the spelling and the sound; *does*—sounds like *duzz:* She *does* everything. *Dose* rhymes with *close:* a *dose* of medicine. Notice the spelling of *doesn't* (not *dosen't*).
fine, find, fined	*Fine* means excellent: She was a *fine* dancer. To *find* means to locate: *Find* a date for your cousin. *Fined* (pronounced the same as *find*) means to be ordered to pay a *fine:* She was *fined* for double parking.
have, of	Don't write, I would *of* enjoyed that. It should be, I would *have* enjoyed that. Watch all those combinations—should *have,* might *have,* must *have,* could *have. Have* sounds like *of* in some phrases: she *should've* been here—short for should *have.*
know, no, now	*Know* and *no* sound alike and are often confused. Remember the word *knowledge*—that which you *know.* Don't write, I *no* how to swim. *Now* (rhymes with *cow*) means at present: We are *now* in the fourth act.
lead, led	*Lead* (or *leads*)—rhymes with *need*—is present tense: I usually *lead* the trumpet section. *Led* is the past tense: She *led* (rhymes with *red*) the parade last year. However, the metal *lead,* as in a *lead* pipe, is pronounced the same as *led.*

loose, lose, loss, lost	Pronunciation is the key again. *Loose,* meaning not tight, rhymes with *moose:* The nails had come *loose.* *Lose* is the verb, rhyming with *fuse:* Don't *lose* your temper. *Loss* is a noun: One *loss* won't affect your league standings. (*Loss* rhymes with *boss.*) *Lost* (rhymes with *cost*) means gone: They were *lost* in the forest.
pass, passed, past	The verb is *pass* (present tense) and *passed* (past tense): I *pass* the store every day; I *passed* all my courses last semester. Use *past* as the noun or the preposition: She lives in the *past;* We drove *past* her house.
personal, personnel	*Personal* means private: a *personal* letter. *Personnel* (accent on the last syllable, rhymes with *shell*—and notice the double *n*) means employees: a *personnel* manager.
principal, principle	*Principal* means important: the *principal* of the school, the *principal* part in a play. Remember that *principle* (it has *le* like *rule*) means a rule or law: the *principle* of gravity.
quiet, quit, quite	Notice the extra syllable in *quiet,* meaning silent: The room was *quiet.* (*Quiet* rhymes with *diet.*) To *quit* (rhymes with *hit*) means to stop: He *quit* his job. *Quite* (rhymes with *white*) means *very:* She is *quite* talented.
rise, raise	Both are verbs, but only *raise* takes an object: The sun will *rise* by itself; You *raise* the blinds. (Past tense: The sun *rose;* You *raised* the blinds.)
since, sense	*Since* is the connecting word: It has been lonely *since* you left. *Sense* means understanding: She has good business *sense.*
sit, set	*Sit* means to take a seat: She always *sits* in the front row. (Past tense: She always *sat* there.) *Set* means to place something: He *sets* the cans on the shelf. (Past tense: He *set* the cans there.)

sort, sought	*Sort* can be a noun or a verb: A *sort* of all around athlete; They *sort* the pastries in rows. *Sought* is the past tense of *seek:* They *sought* everywhere for an apartment. Don't write, "It was *sought* of cold today."
suppose, supposed	Remember the *d* ending in statements like "You are *supposed* to attend." Use *suppose* without the *d* only as a verb in the present tense: "I *suppose* you agree with her."
taught, thorough, though, thought, threw, through, throughout, tough	Master this difficult group by pronouncing each word carefully. *Taught* (rhymes with *fought*) is the past tense of *teach:* She *taught* calculus. *Thorough* (rhymes with *borough*) means complete: a *thorough* investigation. *Though* (rhymes with *go*) is a connective word: *Though* he was nervous, he performed well. *Thought* (rhymes with *bought*) is the past tense of *think:* We *thought* it was a good restaurant. *Threw* (rhymes with *new*) is the past tense of *throw:* We *threw* a big party. Don't mix up *threw* and *through;* they sound the same. *Through* (sounds the same as *threw*) means finished (when they were *through* eating) or inside (*through* the tunnel). *Throughout* (pronounced throo owt) means everywhere within an area: *throughout* the whole state of Ohio. *Tough* (rhymes with *puff*) as in "rough and *tough*" means hard or difficult.
than, then	Use *than* for comparisons—funnier *than* Eddie Murphy. Use *then* for time: *Then* we started dancing.
to, too, two	*Two,* the number, is usually spelled right: There were *two* cars in the garage. The trick is to know when to use *too.* Remember that *too,* with *more* than one *o,* means *more* than enough: There is *too* much noise here. It also means in addition: You come *too.* All the other meanings take *to:* travel *to* Cuba; *to* win at poker.

use, used

Remember the *d* ending in statements like "We *used* to live in Arkansas" or "She is *used* to working late." *Use* without the *d* ending is a verb in the present tense: "I *use* my microwave oven frequently."

worse, worst

Both are forms of bad: bad, *worse, worst.* Use *worse* to compare two things, persons, or situations: Her illness became *worse;* This film is *worse* than the other one.

Worst is the superlative form; it describes one thing that stands out from the rest: the *worst* dinner I ever ate; the *worst* car in the lot.

▶ Exercise I

Look-alikes/Sound-alikes

Choose the correct word in each sentence and circle it.

1. Many people give (advice, advise) without being asked.
2. The (principles, principals) of economics are complex.
3. Do you (no, know) how to check a patient's vital signs?
4. This proposal has too many (loose, lose) ends.
5. Students who have (past, passed) the test will take English 2.
6. Have you ever (taught, thought, through) about buying a condominium?
7. Banks nowadays have (too, to, two) many kinds of checking accounts.

▶ Exercise II

Look-alikes/Sound-alikes

Underline the incorrect word in each sentence and write it correctly in the blank.

1. Marie considered musical comedies a sought of lowbrow form of entertainment.

   _____

2. Changes in society have not effected the popularity of marriage: There are more weddings every year.

   _____

3. The filmmakers should of studied teenage vigilante groups like the Guardian Angels before shooting the film.

   _____

4. From her shy and quite appearance,
   no one would guess that Eleanor had
   been an Air Force officer.   _____

5. Tournaments that include to many
   basketball teams are likely to lose
   public interest.   _____

6. Motorcycle racing in the desert
   demands more stamina and expertise
   then driving a racing car.   _____

7. Mario had to get use to driving in
   high temperatures.   _____

Exercise III

Look-alikes/Sound-alikes

Circle the correct phrase in each group.

1. alot of money
   a lot of money
2. alway prepared
   away prepared
   always prepared
3. a loss treasure
   a lost treasure
   a lose treasure
4. two much attention
   to much attention
   too much attention
5. worse than a tornado
   worst then a tornado
6. an original taught
   an original thought
   an original though
7. the total affect
   the total effect
8. sensible advise
   sensible advice
9. and hour later
   an hour later
   a hour later
10. should have remembered
    should of remembered

11. hotter then the Sahara
    hotter than the Sahara
12. quit intelligent
    quite intelligent
    quiet intelligent
13. the personnel office
    the personal office
14. brought at Macy's
    bought at Macy's
15. She past the test
    She pass the test.
    She passed the test
16. sit the table
    set the table
17. plenty of common sense
    plenty of common since
18. raise the flag
    rise the flag
19. a find performance
    a fine performance
20. a clear conscious
    a clear conscience

Review Test

Name _____

This test may help confirm that you have learned the grammatical rules presented in Unit 5. If you find after taking this test that there remain areas of grammar or spelling on which you need further work, return to those sections of Unit 5 that will help you overcome your remaining problems.

Part One: Sentence Divisions

In each group of sentences, only one is correct—a, b, or c. Write the letter of the correct one in the blank.

1._____
    a. Daniel's grades fell slightly in the fall semester. Because he tried to take eighteen credits and continue working in the bookstore.
    b. Daniel's grades fell slightly in the fall semester, he tried to take eighteen credits and continue working in the bookstore.
    c. Daniel's grades fell slightly in the fall semester because he tried to take eighteen credits and continue working in the bookstore.

2._____
    a. After Margaret got her driver's license. She began taking long scenic drives along the Pacific coast.
    b. After Margaret got her driver's license, she began taking long scenic drives along the Pacific coast.
    c. After Margaret got her driver's license; she began taking long scenic drives along the Pacific coast.

3._____
    a. First the lecturer explained the principles of modern music; then she played several selections to illustrate her points.
    b. First the lecturer explained the principles of modern music. After which she played several selections to illustrate her points.
    c. After explaining the principles of modern music. The lecturer played several selections to illustrate her points.

4._____
    a. Athletes must maintain at least a 2.5 average; otherwise, they may lose eligibility for varsity sports.
    b. Athletes must maintain at least a 2.5 average otherwise they may lose eligibility for varsity sports.
    c. Athletes must maintain at least a 2.5 average. Or lose eligibility for varsity sports.

5._____
    a. Newspapers must be separated from other waste materials they will be picked up on Thursdays.

    b. Newspapers must be separated from other waste materials. Because they will be picked up on Thursdays.

    c. Newspapers, which must be separated from other waste materials, will be picked up on Thursdays.

6. _____

    a. The theater began presenting plays in many languages, soon audiences from diverse ethnic backgrounds were coming to see them.

    b. The theater began presenting plays in many languages. Soon audiences from diverse ethnic backgrounds coming to see them.

    c. The theater began presenting plays in many languages; soon audiences from diverse ethnic backgrounds were coming to see them.

7. _____

    a. Tamara read a book called *Internet for Idiots.* Hoping to find out how to shop and do her banking on her computer.

    b. Tamara read a book called *Internet for Idiots* to find out how to shop and do her banking on her computer.

    c. Tamara read a book called *Internet for Idiots;* hoping to find out how to shop and do her banking on her computer.

8. _____

    a. Bungee jumping did not appeal to Kevin because he had a fear of heights.

    b. Bungee jumping did not appeal to Kevin. Because he had a fear of heights.

    c. Bungee jumping did not appeal to Kevin, he had a fear of heights.

9. _____

    a. Certain dishes have made the restaurant popular. Especially the rack of lamb, the spare ribs, and the salmon soufflé.

    b. Certain dishes have made the restaurant popular, especially the rack of lamb, the spare ribs, and the salmon soufflé.

    c. Certain dishes have made the restaurant popular customers especially like the rack of lamb, the spare ribs, and the salmon soufflé.

10. _____

    a. World War II had two major results: It destroyed totalitarianism, and it set the stage for the Cold War.

    b. World War II had two major results, it destroyed totalitarianism, and it set the stage for the Cold War.

    c. World War II had two major results. Which were that it destroyed totalitarianism, and it set the stage for the Cold War.

Part Two: Verb Forms, Endings, and Agreement

Write the correct forms in the blanks at the left.

_____ 11. The manager looked over the reports and (place, placed, places) them on the table.

_____ 12. Some of the events reported in the television news stories never (happen, happens, happened).

_____ 13. Anne plans to (spend, spends, spent) more than three thousand dollars decorating her apartment.

_____ 14. Licensing for emergency medical workers (use, used, uses) to involve training and work experience.

_____ 15. The United Nations has (send, sent, sends) peacekeeping forces to many troubled areas in the world.

_____ 16. A responsible parent always (insist, insists) on discussing serious decisions and problems with teenagers.

_____ 17. One of the best dancers in that company (is, are) my cousin Lydia.

_____ 18. Earning her bachelor's degree and raising her son (is, are, was) extremely important to Vivian.

_____ 19. Students who (persist, persists) in their studies usually succeed.

_____ 20. Either breakfast or lunch (is, are) optional on the plan.

Part Three: Spelling

If the word or phrase is correct, write C in the blank; if not, write the correctly spelled form of the misspelled word in the blank.

_____ 21. occasionally

_____ 22. commiting

_____ 23. in there opinion

_____ 24. received

_____ 25. She past the exam.

_____ 26. deeper then the ocean

_____ 27. It had no affect.

_____ 28. begining

_____ 29. Its the truth.

_____ 30. Is that handbag yours'?

_____ 31. a new adress

_____ 32. a familiar face

_____ 33. Whose jacket is that?

_____ 34. a jewelry store

_____ 35. a desparate attempt

Part Four: Punctuation

If the sentence is punctuated correctly, write C in the blank. If not, circle the spot where a punctuation mark is missing and write the correct mark in the blank. No sentence has more than one punctuation error.

_____ 36. The package contained letters, ten dollar bills audiotapes, and photographs.

_____ 37. Excited by the opportunity to see the First Lady the riders rushed to the front of the bus.

_____ 38. Oliver made the following New Year's resolutions he would begin listening to his girlfriend's advice, he would pass his mathematics requirement, and he would stop smoking.

_____ 39. A tape of speech was shown on local television in Grand Rapids Michigan on October 15, 1996.

_____ 40. Mark Twain wrote "Reports of my death are grossly exaggerated."

_____ 41. Denise tried a variety of jobs, which included acting, coaching, film directing, and choral conducting.

_____ 42. The class wanted to watch a film about the Civil War but the professor assigned a chapter in the textbook instead.

_____ 43. Steve Martin, already well known as a comic actor in films has also written several stage plays.

_____ 44. Changes in the economy have made it difficult for college graduates to find jobs however, some young people with specialized skills are succeeding.

_____ 45. One of the games was close down to the last seconds the other was a complete rout.

Part Five: Pronouns, Parallelism, and Modifiers

If the sentence is correct, write C in the blank. If a word or phrase is incorrect, circle it and write the correct word or phrase in the blank.

_____ 46. If you read the assignment real fast, you may finish it before class.

_____ 47. Janet is imaginative, creative, and has a lot of intelligence.

_____ 48. Cheryl and me look exactly like each other.

_____ 49. While being interviewed, the television audience could see that the mayor was becoming irritated.

_____ 50. One mother must have left their child's prescription in the doctor's office.

_____ 51. Douglas decided to treat hisself to a vacation in the Caribbean.

_____ 52. By showing that he understood their viewpoint helped him persuade them.

_____ 53. The therapist asked did they want to have sessions on Wednes-days.

_____ 54. While writing in her journal, Rita had a brilliant idea for a term paper.

_____ 55. Except for she and her brother, no one else knows the password.

_____ 56. The number of people using the Internet grows more bigger every year.

_____ 57. The jeep climbed the hill, paused at the top, and rolling down the other side.

_____ 58. If the alumni don't contribute no more money, the college will have to reduce its operating budget.

_____ 59. By remaining calm during the emergency, Patricia was able to help others escape from the airplane.

_____ 60. Many people think is better to lease a car than buy one

Possible Score: _____ 60   Your Score:_____

Reminders About Proofreading Your Writing

◆ **Proofread** your next-to-last draft carefully to correct errors in grammar, punctuation, phrasing, and spelling. Read your work aloud slowly and listen for missing endings; notice where your voice drops at the ends of sentences. If necessary, point to each word to notice careless mistakes.

◆ Learn to identify **subjects and verbs** in order to understand sentence structure. Remember that the subject is usually near the beginning of a sentence, and the verb usually follows it, but there are many exceptions. Watch for sentences that have more than one subject or verb.

◆ Learn to identify and correct different kinds of **sentence fragments.** If you find that fragments continue to appear in your writing, watch particularly the beginnings of your sentences for the danger words (subordinate conjunctions), and identify the types of fragments you tend to write. Reading aloud will help you catch some fragments.

◆ Identify the **three basic sentence types: simple, compound, and complex.** Knowing these sentence types will make it possible for you to identify basic sentence faults. Practice writing a simple sentence, adding a clause to make it compound, and then changing it to a complex sentence.

◆ Find and correct **run-together sentences** and **comma splices.** If you find yourself leaving these two sentence faults, read your revised drafts aloud, listening for the places where your voice drops. Watch for the words that begin new sentences, and remember not to use commas as periods. Use semicolons to divide clauses in compound sentences only if you are confident that you will use them correctly.

◆ Use correct **subject-verb agreement:** match singular verbs with singular subjects, plural verbs with plural subjects. Remember that plural <u>nouns</u> have *s* endings, but singular <u>verbs</u> have *s* endings.

◆ Use the correct **verb tenses,** with *d* endings where needed and past tense forms for irregular verbs; don't shift tenses awkwardly. Memorize the irregular verb forms you are not familiar with, and use the progressive forms and perfect tenses correctly. If English is not your first language, practice converting sentences and paragraphs from one tense to another.

◆ Use correct forms of **adjectives** and **adverbs.** Correct misplaced and dangling modifiers. Watch especially the beginnings of your sentences for danglers.

◆ Use **pronouns** correctly. Use correct pronoun case and make pronouns agree with their antecedents. Use plural subjects when making general statements to avoid repeating him/her awkwardly in the singular.

◆ Avoid **awkward shifts** between first, second, and third person. Use the first person sparingly in essays that are not about your own experiences.

◆ Use **parallelism** to match words or phrases in a series. Watch especially the last element in a series, which is often the one that goes wrong. Remember that parallelism is about the <u>form</u> of each element in the series (i.e., its part of speech), not the content.

◆ Correct awkward elements in **mixed sentences.** If English is not your first language, you may have some difficulties with mixed sentences. Read your work aloud slowly to catch awkward combinations. Keep a journal of sentences that your instructor has corrected to see if your errors follow recognizable patterns. Practice speaking English frequently.

◆ Learn the rules for correct use of **commas.** Remember that few commas are absolutely mandatory, so when in doubt, leave them out. Writers more often cause problems for themselves by cluttering up their writing with unnecessary commas than by omitting important ones.

◆ Use **apostrophes** correctly with possessives and contractions. To make it easier for yourself, try avoiding contractions altogether: You can always write *do not* rather than *don't, it is* rather than *it's.*

◆ Punctuate the ends of your sentences correctly with **periods, question marks,** or **exclamation points.** Most errors in end punctuation come from carelessness rather than lack of knowledge—forgetting to put a question mark after a long question, for example.

◆ Use **semicolons** and **colons** correctly. Remember that colons come only after formal introductions, using phrases like *as follows* or *the following,* not after *such as.* If you have doubts about semicolons, don't use them. You can write perfectly good English without them.

◆ Learn the rules for **capitalization** of words. Above all, don't make mistakes with the simple rules, such as capitalizing names of countries, nationalities, and so on. Remember to capitalize the beginning of a quoted sentence.

◆ Improve your **spelling** by mastering the spelling rules, common spelling mix-ups, and look alikes/sound alikes. Use your computer spell check for careless misspellings, but don't expect it to catch the look-alikes/sound-alikes. These you must review; make lists of any you are not sure about. Always take responsibility for your spelling; you will be judged by it.

INDEX

A, an, and, any, 343–344, 381
A lot, 381
Accounting, 20
Acronyms, 352
Active voice, 185–189, 202–204
Addiction, 81–82
Addresses, commas in, 344–345
Adjectives, 220, 240, 310–323, 340–341, 392
    coordinate adjectives, 346–347
    in comparisons, 313–316
    predicate adjectives, 311–316
Adverbs, 241, 310–316, 392
    in comparisons, 314–316
Agreement
    pronoun-antecedent, 392–393
    subject-verb, 237, 275–294
AIDS, 139, 174
Already, all ready, 381
And, use of, 241, 268, 354–355, 381
Angelou, Maya, 60, 195
Animal rights, 107–108
Anorexia nervosa, 76–77
Antecedents, 329–332
Anxiety disorders, 201
Apostrophes, 359–361, 393
Appositives, 211–212, 353–354
Argumentation, *see* Persuasive Writing
Articles, 343–344
Ashe, Arthur, 238
Atomic bomb, 56–57
Audience, 19–22
Autobiographical essay, 153–159
Automatic writing, *see* Freewriting
Auxiliaries, *see* Helping verbs

Bad, badly, 311–312
Basketball, 23
Be, forms of, 240, 247, 249, 280–382, 301–302, 311
Bellow, Saul, 258
Bibliography, 128
Bilingual education, 156–158, 176–177
Body paragraphs, 99–101, 116–119, 127, 132, 134, 150,
    152–153, 156, 160, 163
Bolivar, Simon, 270
Bowie, Davie, 307

Brainstorming, 7–9, 15, 29, 31, 33, 38, 53, 55, 70,
    74–75, 83, 111–113, 119, 128,134, 138, 153, 169,
    197, 251
Bungee jumping, 214
Business writing, 20, 87, 106–110, 375
But, use of, 241, 268, 354–355

Canada, Geoffrey, 160
Capital punishment, 164–171
Capitalization, 367–369, 393
Careers, 20, 47–48, 105, 149, 154–155, 185–189
Caribbean Islands, 130–132
Carrey, Jim, 326
Case of pronouns, 324–329
Categories, dividing into, 9–11, 31, 62, 81–83
Cause and effect paragraphs, 83–87
Civil rights, 135, 139
Clarity, 19, 23, 36, 45, 48, 76–8, 81, 84, 96–97,
    190–191, 340
Classification paragraphs, 81–83
Clauses, main, 225, 252–253, 257, 264–272, 354–355
Clauses, relative, 351–353
Clauses, restrictive and nonrestrictive, 351–353
Clauses, subordinate, 225–229, 272–274
Climactic sequence, 53–55
Cloning, 365–366
Clustering, 11–15, 31, 33, 38, 85–86, 123, 130, 179
Coherence, of Paragraphs, 48–55, 93
Collective nouns, *see* Group nouns
College, writing about, 10, 22, 26, 37, 47–49, 50,
    54–55, 78, 87, 94–95, 105, 108, 111–119, 139, 150,
    154–155, 162, 185–186
Colons, 364–367
Combining sentences, 216–229, 231
Comma Splice, 268–274
Commands, 245–247
Commas, 344–359, 393
    rules for, 344
    in dates, 344–345
    in addresses, 344–345
    in a series, 345–346
    with coordinate adjectives, 346–347
    after introductory clauses and phrases, 347–349
    around interrupters, 349–351
    around relative clauses, 351–353

Commas (con't):
   around appositives, 353–354
   before coordinating conjunctions, 354–355
   with direct address, 355–356
   around contrasting parts, 356–357
   with quotations, 357–358
   in correspondence, 358–359
   to prevent confusion, 359
Common spelling mix-ups, 374–377
Comparative degree, 313–316
Comparison/contrast, 72–75, 313–316
Complex sentences, 264–265
Compound sentences, 264–265
Compound subjects, 287–8
Compound verbs, 260, 288–289
Computer viruses, 255–256
Computers and writing, 29–32, 95–96, 106–110, 179–180, 182, 203, 229–230
Concluding paragraphs, 99, 109–110, 119, 127, 134, 153, 162, 172, 180
Conjunctions, coordinating, 241, 268, 354–355
Conjunctions, correlative, 241
Conjunctions, subordinating, 241
Conjunctive adverbs, 362–364
Connotation, 191–194, 230
Conscience/conscious, 382
Consistency of number, *see* Pronouns
Consistency of person, 332–336, 392
Consistency of tenses, 305–308
Constitution of the United States, 293
Coordination, 268–269
Correspondence,
   commas in, 358–359
Credit cards, 44, 246–248
Crime, writing about, 22, 85, 151–152, 207
Critical thinking, 26–27, 32, 65, 70–1, 84–85, 88–91, 97, 116, 129–130, 144, 148–150, 163–164, 175
Curfews, 160–162

D endings, 233, 237, 295–298, 322
Dangling modifiers, 317–323
Dates, commas with, 344–345
Death penalty, 164–171
Definition paragraphs, 78–81
Denotation, 191
Dependent clauses, *see* Subordinate clauses
Descriptive essays, 129–138, 181
Descriptive paragraphs, 66–71
Details, 66–71, 129
Development,
   of paragraphs, 60–63, 93
   of essays, 99–182
Diagnostic test, 235–239
Dialogue method of development, 163–175
Diction, 190–208, 229

Dictionary, 78, 192–193, 206
Diets, 23
Dinosaurs, 274
Direct address, 355–356
Direct objects, 323
Direct quotation, 357–358
Disasters, natural, 295–296
Diversity, 131–132
Divorce, 9, 87, 265
Do, forms of, 280–282, 296
Douglass, Frederick, 58–59
Drafts, first and second, *see* Revision
Drugs, 22, 35–36, 81, 85, 171–174

Economics, terms of, 283
Education, 141–142, 156–159, 175
Effect/affect, 381
Ei/ie spelling, 370–371
Either/or, 287–288
Electoral system, 254
Ellison, Ralph, 258
Embedding, 216, 219–223
End punctuation, 361–362, 393
English, history of, 360
Enumerating examples, 140–143
Enumerating reasons, 160–163
Epics, 297–298
ER (television show), 215–216
Er/est with adjectives, 313–316
ESL (English as a Second Language), 3, 233, 243, 278 308–310, 322–323, 343–344
Essays, 98–182, 335–336
   recognizing, 99
   building out of paragraphs, 99
   narrative mode, 111–128
   descriptive mode, 129–138
   expository, 139–159
   persuasive, 160–175, 182
   Euphemism, 305
Euthanasia, 263
Examinations, 50, 76
Exclamation point, 361, 393
Expository essays, 139–159

Family, American, 265
Faulty parallelism, 336–340, 392
Feedback from listeners, 18–19, 134, 153, 159, 179
Figures of speech, 305
Films, 315, 368
Find/fine/fined, 382
First and second drafts, *see* Revision
First person, 64–65, 111, 119–120, 332
Fitzgerald, F. Scott, 222, 258
Fixed-form helpers (modal auxiliaries), 249–250
Fluency, 2–6, 15, 197

Focused writing, 5–6, 15, 18–19, 22, 31, 33, 38, 55, 59, 65, 86, 162, 164, 179
Format of essay, 99
Fragments, 233, 243, 246–264
   subordinate clause fragments, 253–255
   added-clause fragments, 255–256, 259–260
   added-phrase fragments, 256–260
   added-verb fragments, 260–262
   methods of correcting, 257–264
Free modifiers, 219–223
Freewriting, 2–4, 22, 31
Fromm, Erich, 78–79
Future perfect tense, 301
Future shock, 106, 110
Future tense, 295

Gates, Bill, 70, 327–328
Gender of pronouns, 329–332
Gerunds, 250
Ginott, Haim G., 205
Goals for Paragraph and Essay Writing, 27
Good/well, 310–313
Grades, 46, 78
Group nouns, 286
Group projects, 6, 9, 19, 21, 27, 42, 50, 59, 61, 75, 77, 83, 91, 104, 108, 110, 128, 132, 143, 147, 149, 164, 172, 175, 188, 194, 197, 205, 251, 259, 264, 284, 308, 340
Grouping, 9–11

Harlem Renaissance, 321
Have, forms of, 249–250, 280–285, 301–302
Have/of, 382
Helping verbs, 249–250
Hemingway, Ernest, 258
Here*, sentences beginning with*, 283
Holidays, 281
Homer, Winslow, "The New Novel," (watercolor), 71
Hopper, Edward, "Office at Night," (oil on canvas), 133; "Nighthawks," (oil on canvas), 198
Houston, Whitney, 357
Howard University, 67
How-to paragraphs, 76–78
Hurston, Zora Neale, 258

Idiomatic usage, 206–208, 231
Immigration, 43, 87, 175, 194, 234, 362
Independent clauses, *see* Main clauses
Indenting paragraphs, 34
Indirect questions, 340, 361–362
Infinitives, 250
Interjections, 241
Internet, the, 100–101, 174
Interrupters, commas with, 349–351
Introductory paragraphs, 76, 99, 105–108, 116, 127, 134, 153, 162, 172, 180

Introductory phrases and clauses, 210–212
Investing, 279
Invisible writing, 30
IQ tests, 38–9
Its/it's/its', 377

Jackson, Shirley, "The Lottery," 201, 307–308
James, Henry, 258
Jazz Age, 320
Jobs, writing about, 78, 15–16, 20, 22, 35–36, 44, 63, 73–74, 78, 145–146, 189, 251, 285
Johnson, Magic, 238
Journal writing, 7, 31, 33

Kahlo, Frieda, 133
Kernel sentences, 216–217, 223
Key words, 40–45
Kiss, 61
Know/no/now, 382
Koch, Edward I., 164–169

Lasers, 266–7
Latin America, 270–271
Laws, scientific, 272
Lead-in, 105, 107
Learning log, 17
Less/least, 314–316
Letters, 17, 358–359
List making, 163–164, 171
Look-alikes/sound-alikes, 29, 369, 380–386
Loose/lose/loss/lost, 383
Love, 79

Main clauses, 225, 252–253, 257, 264–272, 354–355
Main idea, *see* Thesis
Marriage trends, 22–23, 174
Martin, Steve, 390
Maslow, Abraham, 300
McVeigh, Timothy, 121–126
Metaphors, 305
Metonymy, 305
Mexico, 296
Mind/mine/mines, 377
Misplaced modifiers, 317–323
Mixed sentences, 340–343, 392
Mnemonic devices, 379
Modal auxiliaries, 249–350
Modes, rhetorical
   in paragraphs, 63–91
   in essays, 111–175
Modifiers, dangling and misplaced, 317–323
Money, 283
Monsters, 253–354
More/most, 313–316

Multiple illustration, 140–143
Music and art courses, 185–188

Narrative mode,
    in paragraphs, 64–66, 96–97
        in essays, 111–128, 181
No/know/now, 387
Nonrestrictive clauses, 351–353
Nouns,
    as subjects, 240, 275–277,
    group nouns, 286
Novels, American, 258
Nutrition, 188

Oklahoma bombing, 120–127
Organization, 9–17
    of paragraphs, 45–55, 63–91
    of essays, 99–175
Outlining, 15–17, 29, 150, 153
Outside/inside pattern, 51

Paragraphs, *see* Unit Two, 33–97
    recognizing, 34
    signaling, 34
    length, 34
    topic sentences, 36–43, 65, 88, 92, 96, 102
    key words, 40–5
    unity, 45–48, 93, 97
    coherence, 48–55, 93
    transitions, 55–60, 64, 96–97
    development, 60–63, 93
    types of, 63–91
    narrative, 64–66, 96–97
    descriptive, 66–71, 96–97
    expository, 72–87, 96–97
     comparative, 72–75
     how-to, 76–78
     definition, 78–81
     classification, 81–83
     cause/effect, 83–87
    persuasive, 87–91, 96–97
Parallelism, 336–340, 392
Parapsychology, 291
Parenthetical expressions, 349–351
Participles, 211–212, 250, 300–305
Parts of Speech, 239–241
Passive voice, 185–189, 202–204
Past tense, 294–309
Past/passed/pass, 383
Perfect tenses, 303
Periods use of, 361–362, 393
Person, consistency of, 64, 332–336, 392
Person, portraying a, 134–138
Persuasive writing,
    in paragraphs, 87–91, 96–97

    in essays, 160–175, 182
Phillips, John A., 56–57
Phobias, 201
Phrases,
    introductory, 211–212
    prepositional, 257, 286–287
Physician assistants, 47
Plea bargaining, 207
Plural nouns, 275–278
Poe, Edgar Allan, 222
Point, making a, 23–24, 32
Polygraph tests, 289–290
Pornography, 23, 173–174
Precision, 187, 190–191
Prepositional phrases, 257, 286–287
Prepositions, 241, 286
Present tense, 294–309
Prewriting techniques, 1–32, 38, 51, 53, 55, 70, 74–75,
    83, 85–86, 111–113, 119, 123, 128, 130, 134,138,
    150, 153, 162, 164, 169, 179, 197, 251
Principal/principle, 383
Problem/solution essays, 143–153
Process analysis and procedural writing, 76–78
Progressive tenses, 308–310
Pronouns, use of, 56, 240, 324–332, 392
    to achieve variety, 209–210, 231
    agreement with antecedents, 329–332
    as subjects, 242–243, 275–278, 324–326
    spelling of, 377–380
    impersonal, 240, 360
    reflexive, 324
    case of, 324–329
    possessive, 360
Proofreading, 232–325, 391–393
Punctuation, 238–239, 344–367, 393
    apostrophes, 359–361
    colons, 364–367, 393
    commas, 344–359, 393
    end, 361–362, 393
    exclamation points, 361–362, 393
    periods, 361–362, 393
    question marks, 361–362, 393
    quotation marks, 357–358
    semicolons, 266–267, 362–364, 393
Purpose, main, see Thesis

Questions, 17, 340, 361–362
Question marks, 361–362, 393
Quiet/quit/quite, 383
Quotations, 357–358

Readers' opinions, 21, 88
Reading aloud, 17–18, 27, 31, 233
Reading vs. media, 28
Redundancies, 188, 199

Regular verbs, 233, 237, 295–297
Relative clauses, 223–225, 289
    agreement in, 289–290
Repetition, avoiding, 188, 199, 209–210
Restrictive clauses, 351–353
Review test, 387–391
Revision
    of paragraphs, 64, 75, 85, 92–5
    of essays, 115–116, 153, 175–179
    for style, 184–231
Resume, writing a, 189–190
Rhetorical modes,
    in paragraphs, 63–91
    in essays, 111–175
Ripken, Cal, Jr., 60
Rock music, 61, 141, 202
Rodriguez, Richard, 156–158
Roget's Thesaurus, 192
Rowan, Carl T., 135–138
Run-together sentences, 233, 265–268
    ways of correcting, 266–268
Rushdie, Salman, 238

S endings with verbs, 233, 237, 292–294, 322
Salinger, J.D., 258
Science, laws of, 272
Second person, 332–333
-Self pronouns, 324
Semicolons, 266–267, 269, 362–364
Senses, using the five, 17, 67–68
Sentence combining, 216–229, 231
Sentence fragments, 235–7, 246–264, 391
Sentences,
    beginnings, 210–213
    combining, 216–229, 231
    kernel, 216–217, 223
    variety, 185–189, 213–216
    effectiveness, 208–216
    fragments, 235–237, 246–264, 391
    mixed, 340–343, 392
    run-together, 235–237, 392
    comma spliced, 235–237, 392
    parallel structure in, 336–240
Series, commas in, 345–346
Sexism, 9, 243
Shakespeare, William, 357, 360
Shifts in tense, 305–308
Shifts of person, 332–336
Shopping malls, 89–90
Similes, 305
Simple sentences, 264–265
Singular and plural subjects, 275–277
Slang, 20
Sociology, 289
Software, computer, 30

Space exploration, 260–261, 282
Spatial sequence, 51–53, 68–70, 129, 132
Specific words, 67–68, 74, 96, 194–197, 230
Spelling, 29, 230, 232–233, 237–238, 369–386, 393
    rules, 369–374
        common mix-ups, 374–377
        pronoun mix-ups, 377–380
        look-alikes/sound-alikes, 380–386
Spock, Benjamin, 80, 354
Sports, 24, 38, 139
Steinbeck, John, 258
Straw man technique, 163
Style, Unit 4, 183–231
Subjects, 241–252, 391
    identifying, 242–247
    multiple, 244–245
    hard-to-find, 245
    agreement with verbs, 275–294
Subordinate clauses, 252–256
Subordinating conjunctions, 225–226, 252–253, 273
Subordination, 225–229, 252–256, 272–274
Substance abuse, 9
Subways, 5
Superlative degree, 313–316
Supporting a point, 25–26, 28, 88–90, 172–175
Swimming, 38
Synonyms, 21

Taught/thorough/though/thought/threw/through, 384
Taxonomic classification, 82
Technical language, 20–21, 76, 190
Television, 23, 25, 40, 234
Tenses, verb, 280, 294–300, 392
    progressive, 308–310
Than/then, 384,
The, use of, 343–344
Their/there/they're, 29
There, sentences beginning with, 283
Thesaurus, 192, 231
Thesis, 102–105, 117, 125, 127, 148, 152, 156, 159, 162, 172
Thesis statements, 102–105, 117, 129, 152, 159–160, 162, 172–174, 175, 181
Third person, 333
Third person narrative, 120–128
Third person singular, 64, 66
Time sequence, 49–51, 59, 64, 111, 120
Toffler, Alvin, 106
To/too/two, 384
Topic, exploring a, *see* Prewriting
Topic sentences, 36–43, 65, 88, 92, 102
Topics, limiting, 67
Transitional expressions, 36, 55–60, 64, 120
Tucker, Preston, 65
Twain, Mark, 238, 258, 390

UFO's, 215
Unemployment, 285
Unity in paragraphs, 45–48, 93, 97

Vague words, 67–68, 74, 96, 194–197, 230
Variety, sentence, 185–189, 213–216
Verbals, 245, 250
Verbs, 240–242, 391
    agreement with subjects, 275–294
    compound, 248–249, 260, 288–289
    identifying, 247–249
    of action and being, 247
    helping, 249–250
    regular, 233, 237, 295–297
    irregular, 298–300
    tenses, 280, 294–300, 392
    transitive, 323
    use of strong, vivid, 204–206, 231
Videotapes, 284
Virtual reality, 214
Vocabulary, 20–21, 76, 185
Voice, active and passive, 185–189, 202–204
Voice, finding the right, 20

Walker, Alice, "Everyday Use," 200
War of the Worlds, 57–58

Was/were, 280–285
Well/good, 310–313
Welles Orson, 57–58
We're/were/where/wear/ware, 378
Which, that, and *who* clauses, see Relative clauses
Who/whom, 327–329
Who's/whose, 378
Winner, Ellen, 141
Women's issues, writing about, 11–16, 139, 162, 173, 175, 177–178, 243, 292
Wharton, Edith, 258
Word (Microsoft), 30
Word choice, 190–208, 229–330
WordPerfect, 30
Word processing, 29–31, 203, 229–231
Wordiness, 197, 229–31
World Wide Web, 100–101, 204, 290
Worse/worst, 385
Writing Assignments, 26, 44, 51, 53, 55, 59, 62, 63, 65, 66, 68, 70, 75, 78, 81, 83, 86–87, 119, 128, 134, 138, 153, 159, 162, 171, 174, 244, 247, 316

Yet as conjunction, 241, 268, 354–355
Young and the Restless, The, 348
You're/you/yours/yours', 378